A Slave's Place, a Master's World

THE BLACK ATLANTIC

General Editor: Polly Rewt, The Open University and University of Stirling

Series Advisers: Caryl Phillips, novelist; David Dabydeen, Centre for Caribbean Studies, University of Warwick; Vincent Carretta, Professor of English, University of Maryland; Angus Calder, writer

The cultural and theoretical parameters of the Black Atlantic world are explored and treated critically in this timely series. It offers students, scholars and general readers essential texts which focus on the international black experience. The broad scope of the series is innovative and ambitious, treating literary, historical, biographical, musical and visual arts subjects from an interdisciplinary and cross-cultural perspective.

The books address current debates on what constitutes the Black Atlantic, both geographically and theoretically. They include anthologized primary material and collections of seminal critical value to courses on the African diaspora and related subjects. They will also appeal more widely to a readership interested in biographical and other material that presents scholarship accessibly.

Also published in the series:

Alasdair Pettinger (editor), *Always Elsewhere: Travels of the Black Atlantic*
James Walvin, *An African's Life: The Life and Times of Olaudah Equiano, 1745–1797*
Paul E. Lovejoy (editor), *Identity in the Shadow of Slavery*
James Walvin, *Making the Black Atlantic: Britain and the African Diaspora*

A SLAVE'S PLACE, A MASTER'S WORLD

Fashioning Dependency in Rural Brazil

NANCY PRISCILLA NARO

CONTINUUM
London and New York

Continuum
The Tower Building, 11 York Road, London SE1 7NX
370 Lexington Avenue, New York, NY 10017–6503

First published 2000

British Library Cataloguing-in-Publication Data

A catalogue record for this book is available from the British
Library.

ISBN 0–8264–5295–7

Library of Congress Cataloguing-in-Publication Data

Naro, Nancy.
    A slave's place, a master's world: fashioning dependency in
rural Brazil/Nancy Priscilla Naro.
        p. cm. — (The Black Atlantic)
    Includes bibliographical references (p.   ) and index.
    ISBN 0–0–8264–5295–7 (hc.)
    1. Slavery—Brazil—Psychological aspects. 2. Power (Social
sciences)—Brazil—History. 3. Brazil—Rural conditions.
    4. Agriculture—Economic aspects—Brazil—History.
    5. Agricultural laborers—Brazil—History. I. Series.
    HT1126.N37   1999
    306.3'62'0981—dc21   99–43275
                                                              CIP

Typeset by YHT Ltd, London
Printed and bound in Great Britain by The Cromwell Press,
Trowbridge, Wiltshire

Contents

List of Figures

List of Tables

Acknowledgements

Many persons and organizations in Brazil, the United States and the United Kingdom have contributed their time and knowledge to further this study along to completion. Without the cheerful support and encouragement of the Lewis, Naro, Maciel, Sampson and, latterly, the Watts families, the challenges of a study that involved research in a number of different locations would have been much more difficult.

I am grateful to the staffs of various archives and libraries, including the Biblioteca Nacional, the Instituto Histórico e Geográfico Brasileiro, the Arquivo Nacional, the Arquivo Público do Estado do Rio de Janeiro, the Library Company in Philadelphia, the libraries of the University of Pennsylvania, Columbia University and Johns Hopkins University. I am particularly indebted to Sr Mário Luz of the Biblioteca Nacional and to Sr Eliseo of the Arquivo Nacional, who were not only generous with their time and extremely helpful in locating materials but were equally forthcoming in their assistance to the many students who accompanied me on research visits. Equally deserving of an enormous vote of thanks are D. Mercedes Simões, owner of the Cartório Público do Primeiro Ofício de Notas of Rio Bonito, and Professor Sônia Mota of the Faculdade Severino Sombra, who organized the Ordem dos Advogados documentation centre in the Forum of Vassouras. Both women generously provided working spaces for me and the students Ana Cristina de Souza Bouças, Flávio Giglio Barbosa, Margarete Pereira da Silva and Myriam Bessa, whose reading and evaluation of legal documents was facilitated by the neatly arranged and carefully classified postmortem inventories and court records.

Maria Yedda Linhares has provided intellectual guidance for many years, both as a colleague at the Universidade Federal Fluminense and as a friend, and I dedicate this study to her in recognition of her contributions to historical research. Through Dona Yedda, I met and collaborated for many years with Ciro Flamarion Santana Cardoso, Robert Wayne Slenes, Francisco Carlos Teixeira da Silva, Ismênia de Lima Martins, Eulália Lahmeyer Lobo and the confident and inspired students and colleagues who participated in the seminars and conferences organized by the História Social de Agricultura of the Departamento de História of the Universidade Federal Fluminense. To them, and to João Luís Ribeiro Fragoso, Hebe Maria Mattos de Castro, Sheila de Castro Faria, Sidney

Chalhoub, Gladys Sabino Ribeiro, Martha Esteves and Manolo Garcia Florentino, I am indebted for stimulating discussions of data, theoretical interpretations and historiographical trends. The revisions to the historiography of Brazil, and most particularly of Rio de Janeiro, are the fruits of their earnest efforts, creative insights and dedicated research. I am thankful also to the late Warren Dean, to Franklin Knight, Robert Conrad, Steven Topik and Mary Karasch, who read early versions of the first two chapters, and to David Watts, whose careful reading led to revisions in the first draft of the entire manuscript. Mary Karasch worked through the materials with a fine-tooth comb and the final manuscript reflects her insightful suggestions and judicious comments. Finally, my thanks go to supportive colleagues at King's College and the Institute of Latin American Studies of the University of London; to James Walvin for directing my attention to this series; to Polly Rewt, the series editor; and to Philippa Hudson, Sandra Margolies and Janet Joyce at Continuum for seeing it through to completion.

In memory of Warren Dean

1

The Persistence of Africa in Post-emancipation Brazil

The marketplace was abustle: the large 'Minas' negresses, with their headdress in the shape of a muslin turban, with their faces full of scars and seams, having a chemise and a skirt with ruffles as their clothing, are squatted on mats, near their fruits and vegetables; at their sides are their boys and girls, in complete nudity . . . Children were fastened at the mother's breast with a large piece of striped cloth, passed two or three times around the bodies, after having placed the child on their hips, feet and arms straddled.[1]

At first reading, this description fitted the São Pedro market in Luanda, Angola, where I lived from 1971 to 1973. Yet, the book I was reading was not about African market-places and the writer was not travelling anywhere in Angola or visiting any market in Central West Africa. Adèle Toussaint-Samson, a French traveller to Brazil, was recalling her visit in the 1870s to the downtown market-place of Praça XV, located on the Bay of Guanabara in urban Rio de Janeiro.[2] Her observations offer today's historians important insights into the social fabric and street culture of the city of Rio de Janeiro in the decade prior to the official abolition of Brazilian chattel slavery on 13 May 1888. Toussaint-Samson documents the persistence of African facial markings, the specific forms of headwear worn by the 'Minas' women, the hand-woven mats used for the display of foodstuffs and wares and the babies who were supported on their mother's hips by multiple layers of cloth wound around her body, allowing for the unimpeded movement of arms and hands. Most significantly there were young boys and girls – children and infants – a family that may or may not have included a partner or husband, father or other kin.

Toussaint-Samson's description of the market-place was a testimony to the fact that more than three centuries after the initial landings of enslaved Africans in Brazil, their presence was still visible. The bearers of traditions that their forebears carried in the ships' holds, the descendants of forced migrants, they had outlived what historian Stuart Schwartz has termed a 'deadly demography'. This was a natural rate of decline fostered by the reliance on the Atlantic slave trade to replenish slave labour forces and to expand slave-based agriculture.[3] From Maranhão to the coastal northeast, from the shores and hinterlands of Rio de Janeiro and São Paulo to the far south, and to the mining districts of Minas Gerais and Goiás, slaves and chattel slavery were the labour mainstays of a system of unequal social relations that, under the plantation complex, harked back to the country's settlement and development.[4]

Individuals, clergy and government officials, bearing the sanctions of their respective patrons, religious orders and governments, privately appropriated large land-holdings and subjected captive labour to toil. According to David Eltis and David Richardson, between 1660 and 1867, 10.1 million captive African people, carried in British, Portuguese and French ships, left Africa to face lives of slavery in America.[5] Forty per cent, mainly from West Central Africa, were transported across the Atlantic Ocean to their final destinations in Brazil by regular shiploads that averaged 300 slaves each until the transatlantic slave trade was abolished in 1850.[6]

Rio de Janeiro in the southeast and Salvador, Bahia, in the northeast were Brazil's major ports of destination for ships in the African trade. This trade expanded after 1808 when Brazilian ports were opened to international trade following the transfer of the Portuguese royal family and approximately 15,000 court members to Rio de Janeiro. The colonial port city became the centre of empire and, in Luiz Felipe de Alencastro's terms, 'the civilizing pole of the nation'.[7] The population of the urban core of the city expanded from 43,000 in 1799 to 79,000 in 1821; the slaves represented 35 and 46 per cent of these totals, respectively.[8] At mid-century when the transatlantic slave trade was abolished, slaves accounted for over one-third (38 per cent) of the city's population of 79,000.[9] Two decades later, Brazil's first national census of 1872 registered the decline of the slave population in the city of Rio de Janeiro to 18 per cent or 48,939 of a total population of 274,972.[10] In proportional terms, the court and the coffee-producing regions of southeast Brazil – Rio de Janeiro, Minas Gerais, São Paulo and Espírito Santo with 32.3, 18, 18.7 and 27.5 per cent, respectively – effectively concentrated Brazil's slave population, outdistancing the traditional sugar-producing regions of the northeast where export production had been concentrated since the early colonial period.[11]

The origins of the respective captives sent to Salvador and Rio de Janeiro was also different. Sixty per cent of the emigrants from the Bight of Benin went to Bahia, an entrepôt for slaves who were then distributed to the city of Salvador and the Bahian hinterland, the provinces of Minas Gerais to the south and Pernambuco and Amazonas to the north and northwest. Slaves introduced to the port of Rio de Janeiro, where distribution was undertaken to supply slave markets in Minas Gerais, São Paulo and areas further south, were mostly drawn from ports in West Central Africa, although one-fifth to one-quarter came from East Africa.[12]

Human merchandise

In all of Brazil's coastal ports recently arrived slaves shared a similar condition. In addition to the irreparable emotional scars of separation from loved ones, the horrors of captivity also inflicted survivors of the crossing with emaciation, the *mal de Luanda* (scurvy) and loathsome itchy skin eruptions on the legs, feet and ankles.[13] In contrast to the assimilated and Brazilian-born slaves (*ladinos*) who passed them in the streets hawking wares, displaying ornate headgear and exchanging shouts and greetings in the markets, newly arrived survivors of the transatlantic crossing moved slowly through the streets or were carried from the beaches where they had landed.[14] Malnourished, traumatized and disoriented, they were scantily clad, bereft of personal possessions and alienated from familiar surroundings, shelter and food. The purveyors of African languages, customs, cures, beliefs, farming skills, trading, warring and culinary practices, and display-ing diverse hairstyles and facial markings, they represented cultural traits that persist in Brazilian culture to this day. But during slavery their chanted longings and grievings for their 'homelands' were audible as they were taken through downtown streets to slave depots to await their fate at the 'crossroads', Mary Karasch's term for the urban slave markets in Brazil's coastal ports.[15]

Even after suspension of the transatlantic slave trade, the demand for slaves continued unabated. Human *peças* ('pieces', also 'fragments') were subjected to the merchandising of deft and devious vendors who were experts in the arts of camouflage and cosmetics. Maladies were disguised, and physical defects that were exposed during minute examination at public auction were played down.[16] Prices fluctuated with the supply and demand of local markets, and the negotia-tions between vendor and purchaser involved intense haggling over what each perceived to be the physical appearance, medical state, submissiveness and mental astuteness of each slave in question. A process of examination, inspec-tion, questioning, bargaining and price fixing juxtaposed prospective purchaser and vendor in a verbal dual that would usually determine a slave's destiny to brutal exploitation in the plantations, to service in the great houses of rural and urban areas, to navigation, skilled artisanry, trade and manual labour in the streets and port.[17]

The demands of Rio de Janeiro's urban labour market were competitive and selective. Newspaper advertisements for slaves emphasized skills, appearance and character – 'a wetnurse with abundant milk', 'a skilful shoemaker, with a very good body, about twenty years of age, with no vices or bad habits', or 'one who irons and does laundry, another a baker and laundress, and the third also a laundress, all with very good bodies and able to perform every kind of household work'.[18] Fear of collective mobilization by slaves from the same area led some prospective buyers to select slaves from different parts of Africa, but the over-riding consideration was obedience and the ability of slaves to execute menial, manual and sexual tasks as ordered.[19]

The persistence of Africa

Three centuries of uninterrupted transatlantic trade to re-supply the plantations with bodies and spirits also replenished Africans and their offspring with customs, religious practices, devotion to African deities, festivities, farming practices, martial arts, diet and linguistic ties that connected them to Africa through the water-borne journey.[20] The persistence in fragmentary form or in their entirety of ancestral customs – lineage, kingship, and descent – attested to the continuity of a long-standing correspondence that Africans brought to Portuguese and Brazilian lifestyles.

For Robert Wayne Slenes, slaves forged identities during captivity in Africa, in the holds of slavers and on plantations. In his analysis of the diverse meanings of the word *malungu*, the collective association of slaves with the shipboard experience of the transatlantic crossing, he finds the genesis for slave bonding in the New World context.[21] Philip Morgan advances a different argument. For him, the varied origins of ethnic identities contributed to strategies and survival tactics that enabled slaves to confront the issues and problems of their own enslaved status: 'The cultures of slave-based communities were essentially new and owed more to the conditions that Africans encountered in America than to their upbringing in Africa.'[22] Joseph Miller's view of fluid and permeable ethnic identities also endorses the adaptation, modification and invention that contributed to the emergence of hybrid societies where 'culture jostled and converged in combinations and permutations of dizzying complexity'.[23]

Slavery in the capital and court city of Rio de Janeiro, the port and hinterland of Salvador and, to a lesser degree, São Luís de Maranhão, Recife and the hinterlands, the mining and agricultural belts of Minas Gerais and the rural *fazendas* (farming estates) of São Paulo vibrated to an African, albeit not uniform, pulse – Africa's nations in America conveyed themselves through the facial markings, head coverings, hairstyles and arrangements of dress and beads that slaves displayed openly in the streets, markets, homes and public gardens and fountains.[24] Rio de Janeiro was the favourite urban setting for foreign artists like Thomas Ewbank, Jean Baptiste Debret and Johann Moritz Rugendas, who recorded movement, flair and diversity in the dress of ambulant street and market vendors, in the outfits of slaves who accompanied elite families to church, in slave ornamentation, music and dance, and slave punishments in the public and private spaces of the city.[25] Depictions of scraggly, deformed and dishevelled semi-naked slaves engaged in vile and debasing menial tasks that included the carrying of water and the dumping of barrels of night-soil contrasted sharply with elegantly attired and sensual street vendors (*quitandeiras*), prostitutes and domestic slaves, whose images entertained the fashionable in European drawing rooms.[26] Descriptions of slave women and their daily lives in the service of a master or a mistress were also colourful entries in the diaries of travelling foreigners, whose readers would share their astonishment and horror at slave life.

African facial markings, dialects, dress and ornaments were external manifestations of deeper customs, traditions and spiritual beliefs that defied the imposed exile and family fragmentation wrought by the institution of slavery. According to Mary Karasch, tribal rituals, beliefs, tributes to African deities, farming ceremonies, the practice of *capoeira* and other martial arts, and the whole or partial maintenance of dietary habits enforced identification with Africa.[27] The hairstyles, colourful beads, amulets, ribbons, shapes and uses of cloth, scars and bodily ornamentation testified to the local and tribal identities of slave *quitandeiras*, domestic servants and freed Africans, who were colourful figures on the public thoroughfares of the bustling port cities. European ladies and aspirants to their social status shunned the use of such accoutrements and frowned upon slave concubines whose lovers dressed them in European-style clothing, including shoes, French and English stays and gowns, and gold jewellery that violated official, but rarely enforced, dress prohibitions for slaves.[28]

Culinary and healing practices made use of African, indigenous Brazilian and European knowledge of herbs, such as cloves, cinnamon, nutmeg, rue, rosemary and bay leaf, and their medicinal and dietary use. Indigenous Brazilian tribes who made a drink from fermented sweet manioc root, called *cauim*, for ritual purposes, found a counterpart in the African variant, *aluá*.[29] Cabalistic brews were concocted into painkillers, poisons, abortion potions and stimulants. African slaves added ginger, palm oil, malagueta peppers, coconut milk, or bacon fat to mandioca mush and to maize dishes, introducing variety to the Brazilian dietary staples of manioc, maize, beans, sugar and, by the end of the eighteenth century, rice and coffee.[30]

Centuries of contact and religious indoctrination did little to endear master and slave to one another. Nor did they blur distinctions between African spiritual beliefs and European religious practices. Roman Catholicism was the official state religion, and Portuguese colonizers and the Church fathers carried it to the missions and settlements of Brazil, Portuguese Africa and Asia. The Catholic Church regarded masters and slaves as equals in the sight of God but did not officially condemn the enslavement of Africans. Captives were regarded as human beings with souls that were worthy of salvation and were given a rapid Christian baptism prior to their embarkation or, under colonial laws that were in effect until the 1840s, at a Catholic church where they were divided into groups according to the name they were to receive.[31] Masters were expected to acquaint newly imported slaves with the fundamentals of Christian doctrine, baptism, regular attendance at Mass on Sundays and holy days, and rest from labour on those days, a task that was often assigned to virtuous or long-standing slaves, who acted as godfathers to new slaves.[32] Under canon law, slaves were to be married in the Church and a married couple was not to be separated by their master. The moral authority of the Church was, however, compromised by monasteries, brotherhoods, charities, orphanages and clergymen who were members of the slave-holding classes, beneficiaries of the plantation complex, defenders of slavery and the slave trade, and themselves practitioners of the brutality inherent in the institution. Church officials enjoyed the same benefits from slave-holding as laymen and purchased and sold slaves for personal as well as institutional service. Church and Church brotherhoods, such as the Benedictine Order, were committed to the protection of slaves but the establishment by slaves of black religious brotherhoods was indicative of social separation. The patroness of many of them, Our Lady of the Rosary, was a black invocation of the Virgin Mary and was among the most revered by brotherhood members.[33]

In some instances, masters and slaves attended Mass together and plantation masters stood as godparents at the baptism and marriage of their slaves. One of the rare descriptions of a slave wedding suggests, however, considerable leeway between priests' formal adherence to Christian rituals and their actual treatment of black brothers of the faith. Described by a foreign visitor, the black bride in a white muslin dress and coarse white lace veil and the husband in a white linen suit were harshly treated by a Portuguese priest, who ordered them to kneel at the altar in a tone that 'was more suggestive of cursing than praying'. Having uttered his blessing he 'hurled an amen at them, slammed the prayer-book down on the altar, whiffed out the candles, and turned the bride and bridegroom out of the chapel with as little ceremony as one would have kicked out a dog'.[34]

The encouragement of slaves and ex-slaves to partake in the Catholic rituals of baptism, marriage and burial may have tied in with aims of parish priests to weaken dissimilar religious and cultural traditions by bringing slaves into the Church through high-spirited festivals. The following description of slave celebrations that appropriated a Catholic feast day suggests that, collectively and individually, slave participants sidelined any of its religious aims or components. As described by Maximilian I, who attended the festival of the Church of Our Lady of Bomfim in Salvador, Bahia, in 1860, the participants who were plied with *cachaça* (sugarcane whisky) celebrated in a theatrical manner, paying little heed to the solemn spiritual and religious nature of the festivity:

> To a good Catholic the whole of this proceeding could not but appear most blasphemous; for at this festival the blacks mingled heathen notions to a most improper extent with their ideas of pilgrimage ... All moved hither and thither in a confused mass. Here, were two acquaintances greeting and kissing each other; there, two negro slaves from distant parts of the town were shaking hands; here a matron shouted 'Good day', over the heads of those around her, to an approaching Amazon; there groups of people had collected and were chattering merrily over the events and love-adventures of this happy day. Mirth and unrestrained happiness reigned everywhere: one could see that it was a long-looked-for festival, at which the negroes felt quite at home ... The yellow-complexioned priest was going through the ceremony of the mass (I cannot call it celebrating mass), as though he were giving an oration at this public festival. I could no longer doubt; we were in the church; the large, mirthful dancing-hall was a Brazilian temple of God, the chattering negroes were baptized Christians, were supposed to be Catholics, and were attending mass.[35]

The dismayed visitor, accustomed to the solemnity and ritual of a European Catholic Mass, viewed the scene as an unsettling mayhem. Yet his description attested to the transformation of a Catholic celebration into a festive social occasion. An early twentieth-century Angolan intellectual, António de Assis Júnior, argued in his novel, *O segredo da morta*, set in Dondo, Angola, in 1900, that Africans remained true to their own traditional religious values and bent Catholic values to them.[36]

African-derived ceremonies were led by African priests and priestesses but embraced celebrants for whom the rituals sometimes complemented and at other times compromised traditional Catholic beliefs. Despite Catholic clerics' association of the spirits that informed slave celebrations with pagan beliefs and diabolic practices, slaves held to cosmic identities that originated over the ocean. Yemanjá, a Yoruba deity who reigned over the seas, Yansã, Oxossi, Oxalá and Ogum formed a pantheon of spirits for descendants of West Africans and West Central Africans who continue to this day to invoke spirits from different homelands in Africa.[37] Karasch has argued on the basis of data for the city of Rio de Janeiro that in that multi-ethnic and multi-religious environment, slave religions were essentially African and especially Central African.[38]

The enslavement of Africans from many different regions brought to the plantations of the Americas local beliefs and devotions that were fused into shared linguistic codes, fictive kinship, gestures, languages, signs, rituals and practices, some of which had counterparts among indigenous societies. The Bantu, mainly Kimbundu words, *calunga, camondongo, quilombo, quitandeira, quitute, inhame, calundú* and *mucama* are but samplings of the hundreds of African terms that continued to inform the Brazilian Portuguese vernacular in the aftermath of emancipation.[39]

Cultural dismissal

Slaves brought the many peoples of Africa to Brazil and, as Mary Karasch, Eduardo da Silva and Carlos Eugênio Líbano Soares have shown, the street celebrations, daily activities, language and use of ornamentation – beads, ribbons, hairstyles and banners, which function as identifiers of rival groups, religious celebrants or individual taste – attested to cultural, social and labour practices that marked the city of Rio de Janeiro with a signature of survival born out of captivity.[40] Whereas elderly slaves carried on religious traditions and offered instruction to slave children that sometimes reflected the beliefs of parents but might also reflect practices that evolved in Brazil, Brazilian slave-owners were ignorant of the many peoples and cultures of Africa. Nor was any kingdom of Africa a focus or concern of nineteenth-century Brazilian theatrical, literary and printed musical works.[41] Apart from Queen Ana Nzinga Mbandi Ngola of Matamba, who ruled in the seventeenth century and whose triumphant battles were still recalled by slaves of Brazil in the nineteenth century, those great conquests, battles, religious celebrations and rituals that had enriched the chronicles of early European travellers, and African-based pidgin tongues that had amused spectators at the popular theatre of sixteenth-century Lisbon aroused little curiosity among slave-holding Brazilians.[42]

In contrast to idealized portrayals of Brazilian Indians in Dias Gomes's opera, *O Guarani* (1857), José de Alencar's novel, *Iracema*, (1865), the unfinished

Gonçalves Dias work, *Os Timbiras* (1857) and the romantic paintings of 'noble savages' that embellished public buildings and the salons of prominent statesmen, the African heritage was underplayed or ignored. Brazilian Indians gained a reputation for courage, valour and nobleness that their African slave counterparts were denied. 'African' was synonymous with 'slave', although Brazilian-born creoles and Indians had also been subjected to slavery.[43] David Brookshaw has observed that in José de Alencar's novel, *Til* (1872), all slaves were depicted as so submissive by nature that they dampened the independent spirit in the Indian, João Fera.[44]

Non-white and white Brazilian writers and playwrights perpetuated the social myth of slave servility, docility and submissiveness, ignoring decisive battles, resplendent kingships, technical advancements in metalwork, the tales, traditions and music of Africa. In the Brazilian plays of Martins Pena from the 1830s and 1840s, the social hierarchy as perceived by the master class highlighted the worlds of authority and wealth that prevailed over the poor freemen, freedmen and slaves. Slaves were given no names and were listed last on the playbill, reflecting a perception of them as brutish, ignorant and gullible beings.[45]

Yet there were exceptions, as revealed in the timely novel *O tronco do Ipê*, set in Vassouras and published by José de Alencar in 1871. The portrayal of the elderly slave as a bearer of cultural traditions and practices centred on Pai (Father) Benedito, described as a forlorn African slave whose long-time companion addresses him as *calunga*, in reference to the shared experience of the sea journey from Africa. A mystique surrounded Pai Benedito, who lived in a cabin set apart from the slave quarters on a promontory overlooking the Paraíba River. It was said that he held a pact with the Devil and every night the souls of the underworld who frequented his cabin were invited to accompany the drumming and 'dance the night long a furious samba under the aged Ipê tree'. In an immense cavern in the tree trunk, littered with crosses, a figure of the Virgin Mary, a small image of Saint Benedict, charms made of sticks, amulets, dried rue branches, human bones, rattlesnake rattles and teeth, Pai Benedito communicated with spirits.[46] A trusted slave of long-standing service to the *fazenda*, he guarded a secret regarding his master and the descent to ruin of the once-prominent Fazenda of Nossa Senhora do Boqueirão. This secret was vital to elevating the social standing of Mário, a young man who lived on the *fazenda* with his widowed mother. Pai Benedito, a minority among Brazil's thousands of captives, became empowered by knowledge of the people and events surrounding the *fazenda*. Like the ancient tree, he was held in regard and awe by other slaves and by his master's family for his healing powers.

Alencar's novel not only highlighted the importance of slaves in long-standing service to the wellbeing of a rural estate's operation but also focused upon the interrelationships that complemented the slave–master relationship on the great *fazendas* belonging to the senhorial class. The novel revealed that underlying the rigid vertical social hierarchy of planter-class society were multiple codes of social interaction in the rural milieu that attested to a 'hierarchy of complementarity' within the society as a whole. I have taken anthropologist Roberto da Matta's use of this term in his analysis of relations in the house and in the street, as one that enables one 'to "read" the extensive system of rituals as evidence of a society in debate over differentiated visions of itself'.[47] In differentiating between the identities and strategies of slave-owners and slaves, property-owners and land-less farmers, skilled and unskilled labourers and their lifestyles, I seek reflections of different social values and codes that suggest complementary and inter-related social relations instead of unilateral strategies or exclusive forms of dominance.

This book aims to chart the process of transition from slave to free labour in rural Brazil, highlighting the ways in which slave-owners, slaves and growing numbers of ex-slaves accompanied the gradual creolization of rural society as they sought incorporation into the rural labour landscape of the plantation complex. I have taken the concept of landscape from the late Carl Sauer who understood it to be a 'continuous process of development or of dissolution and replacement'.[48] Sauer held that the works of man expressed themselves in the cultural landscape, which was in turn derived from the natural landscape.

The way in which man expressed his place in nature as a distinct agent of modification is evaluated through the physical and population changes that the intensive production of coffee brought to the province of Rio de Janeiro.[49] The settlement and development of two rural towns and their surrounding areas (municípios) in the hinterlands of the province of Rio de Janeiro illustrate the different strategies that the planter class, slaves and free farmers employed in the formation of rural society. Vassouras, a magnet for historical research since the pioneering study of the município by Stanley Stein in 1957, is located in the western part of the highlands chain of hills, known as the Paraíba Valley that extends along the Paraíba do Sul River from São Paulo to the Atlantic coast. Vassouras was a coffee município, where coffee production for the international market was in its heyday from the 1840s to the 1870s.[50] Returns from the sales of high-grade coffee favoured the development of a local economy that benefited merchant-planter elites with close ties to the international coffee markets and extensive connections in the corridors of the imperial court of Rio de Janeiro. Public land in the most desirable areas near to rivers and their tributaries was no longer available by the 1840s and planters who held large holdings of cultivated and forested land on their *fazendas* had, by the 1870s, either sold or divided their lands among family members. Planters in Vassouras also resisted alternatives to slavery, as indicated by the increase in demand for slaves over ten years of age in the highland slave markets throughout the 1870s and into the 1880s, despite the growing and locally plentiful free and freed non-white population.[51] Vassouras was among the Paraíba Valley towns to suffer reversals at the outset of the 1880s as the coffee economy was engulfed in chronic crises, aggravated by the impact of the abolition campaigns on the slave population and the 1888 abolition of chattel slavery.

The second *município*, Rio Bonito, previously unstudied, is located in the lowlands 60 kilometres northeast of Niterói. Studies of transition from slave to free labour in Rio Bonito, São Gonçalo, Araruama and Capivary are recent and have drawn attention to food-producing *municípios* and their importance to local and regional production and trade. The towns in the Restinga region were given over to coffee, sugar and food production, supplying local needs and the trading networks that served Guanabara Bay, the provincial capital of Niterói and the imperial court of Rio de Janeiro.[52] In the Restinga region, the slave population over the age of ten steadily declined, replaced by an equally steady influx of free and freed non-white migrants in search of available farming land.[53] Rio Bonito's small elite enjoyed limited ties to the international markets and to the political centres of power in the court. In contrast to Vassouras, an open social milieu developed that incorporated rather than excluded local labour. The diversification of agricultural crops and production for local and regional markets offset the impact of the crises that affected the highlands coffee economies in the 1880s. In contrast with Vassouras, the *município* of Rio Bonito represents a different transition process and one that was more in keeping with the rest of Brazil.

Both *municípios* were rural but I have approached them less as territorial categories of social space than as illustrative cases of the process of rurality. I have taken rurality, in Sarah Whatmore's terminology, to be centred on social and political struggles and the ways in which they impacted on rural identity and environment.[54] The process of transition is thus evaluated with a view to the political and social struggles that involved the employment of different strategies and tactics by the planter class, slaves, free cultivators and others in providing an infrastructure for, and shaping, a free labour market.

Neither Vassouras nor Rio Bonito existed at the end of the eighteenth century but, as discussed in Chapter 2, by 1840 both towns were undergoing a rapid process of development as claims and settlement displaced indigenous societies and ushered in a change to the landscape that drew on slave labour for planters, traders, merchants and small-scale cultivators, involved in disputes over rights to land.

Chapter 3 highlights the coffee *fazenda* and its emergence at the hub of the nineteenth-century rural hinterland society in southeast Brazil. The *fazenda* was a rural estate, the nineteenth-century equivalent of the northeastern sugar-producing mill or *engenho* that has provided a basis for monographs and studies of slavery, slave revolts and transition to free labour in that region.[55] I relate the development of the *fazenda* to the acquisition of land and the ownership of involuntary slave labour. *De jure* claims by landowners and slave-owners to property are juxtaposed with *de facto* claims based on customary rights to land and produce by slaves, ex-slaves, landless farmers and planters. The dynamics of hierarchical complementarity are also explored as racial and gender empowerment, often secretly acquired and displayed in informal, coded and disguised ways in the great house. The organization of labour, the impact of gender and the bearing of colour and social standing are discussed with reference to Vassouras, where the prominent and prosperous rural estates of the Paraíba Valley were distinguished from their smaller and more modest counterparts. Vassouras is, in turn, compared with Rio Bonito in terms of the spatial dimensions of its great houses, grounds, fields and forests and the social uses and areas of negotiation that challenged the rigid social hierarchy of the *fazenda* and brought to bear the presence of the public sphere on the private world of the rural estate.[56]

Chapter 4 focuses on domestic and field slaves, drawing on manumission data and court cases to highlight the difficult paths that slaves on the *fazendas* and smaller production units pursued to freedom. The findings suggest that African slaves of long-standing service and their offspring held privileged positions on the large estates. Privileges and favours were negotiated directly between slaves and their masters and mistresses or through mediators of the master class and, in addition to freedom, were related to customary rights. Whereas traditional customary privileges and expectations concerning access to land had been met by landowners to attract the labour of free non-white and ex-slave farmers, the granting to slaves of plots for food production and the raising of small farmyard animals was a privilege that they had to earn. As Sidney Mintz pointed out from examples in the Caribbean areas, and as Ciro Flamarion Santana Cardoso and, later, Eduardo Silva identified in Brazil, this practice gradually developed during the transition process into a customary right. I argue that the passage from earned privilege to the customary right to land use was an important stage in the formation of a proto-peasantry and a major feature of the refashioning of the labour landscape.[57]

The expectation that slaves and ex-slaves would have use of land brought no long-term guarantees of land use or the transfer of such rights to family members if freedom was achieved. Similar practices in both towns suggest that the passage to freedom marginalized slaves from the ownership of property and from the inheritance of possessions in land from their masters. The daily contact between slaves and the growing free non-white and ex-slave population in all areas of work and leisure that obscured the boundaries between bondage and freedom and became centred on the thorny issues of *de facto* versus *de jure* claims to land ownership and usage continued unresolved in post-emancipation society.

Chapter 5 deals with individual and collective mobilization against slavery and the various ways in which slaves were drawn into the abolition process in the two towns. I argue that slaves in Vassouras, where planters resisted alternatives to slave labour until the 1880s, fashioned freedom in a confrontational way that involved African slave leadership, adopting strategies that reflected the intensifying struggles of the abolitionist campaigns. Court-appointed public defenders who were assigned to handle criminal charges against slaves were by the 1870s denouncing victimization by overseers, masters and mistresses as they pressed the courts to approve slave claims to freedom. In Rio Bonito, slaves also engaged the public sphere of the courts in struggles that increasingly focused public attention on the injustices of slavery. In this town, however, the creolization of the population coincided with the formation of the free labour market that attracted an influx of non-white freed and free farmers in search of farming lands. The struggle for emancipation in Rio Bonito provided an infrastructure for rurality in post-emancipation society that was based on incorporation rather than exclusion through family-based farming, trade, food production and marketing networks.

Chapter 6 raises the issues of post-emancipation citizenship and national identity. Freedom from bondage in 1888 transformed all slaves from being somebody else's property to being citizens of the Brazilian national state. Few Africans or Brazilian-born slaves would return to their homelands. Although Brazilian-born slaves had learned about African customs and practices in the slave quarters, few would seek a life of freedom in Africa, choosing instead to contribute to the fashioning of an Afro-Brazilian post-emancipation 'patria'. Ex-slaves who remained in freedom in rural Brazil drew on customary ties to land

and kin as they shaped rurality through the formation of an identity with familiar places of work and residence.

Emancipation officially changed the status of slaves from 'non-citizen' to 'citizen', although literacy requirements, prosecution for vagrancy and begging, government repression of Afro-Brazilian spiritual centres and meagre government and private incentives to advance education, small farming, technical training and artisanry excluded ex-slaves from any collective exercise of political and social citizenship. Post-emancipation society provided for the incorporation of ex-slaves into the ranks of the rural labour force through tenantry, sharecropping, day labour and domestic labour but limited any upward mobility through dependency ties between the landless and the landed, between the poor and the prosperous. Appealed eviction cases and land records from both towns suggest that legal constraints, like literacy, posed restrictions on the exercise of citizenship through electoral participation. The data suggest that citizenship was reached the wrong way round, or in Portuguese *às avessas*, as a response to diverse modernizing agendas involving issues of land occupation that are still unresolved today.

Notes

1. Adèle Toussaint-Samson, *A Parisian in Brazil* (Boston: James H. Earle, 1891), pp. 40–1.
2. The market-place was in front of the imperial palace that is today's Praça XV.
3. Stuart B. Schwartz, *Slaves, Peasants, and Rebels* (Urbana: University of Illinois Press, 1992), p. 72.
4. Philip D. Curtin defines the plantation complex as 'the economic and political order centring on slave plantations in the New World tropics' (*The Rise and Fall of the Plantation Complex: Essays in Atlantic History* (Cambridge: Cambridge University Press, 1990), p. ix).
5. David Eltis and David Richardson, *Routes to Slavery: Direction, Ethnicity, and Mortality in the Atlantic Slave Trade* (London: Frank Cass, 1997), p. 2. See also Paul E. Lovejoy (ed.), *Africans in Bondage: Studies in Slavery and the Slave Trade. Essays in Honor of Philip D. Curtin* (Madison: University of Wisconsin Press, 1986), and with Nicolas Rogers (eds), *Unfree Labour in the Development of the Atlantic World*, special edition of *Slavery and Abolition* (1994).
6. Eltis and Richardson, *Routes*, p. 6. The average number of slaves per ship is taken from Herbert S. Klein and Stanley Engerman, 'Long-term trends in African mortality in the transatlantic slave trade', in Eltis and Richardson, *Routes*, p. 36.
7. Luiz Felipe de Alencastro, 'Vida privada e ordem publica no Império', in Luiz Felipe de Alencastro (ed.), *Império: a corte e a modernidade nacional*, vol. 2 of Fernando A. Novais (ed.), *História da vida privada no Brasil*, 4 vols (São Paulo: Companhia das Letras, 1998), p. 13.
8. *Ibid.*, pp. 13–14.
9. *Ibid.*, p. 13.
10. The 1872 data were revised by the Laboratório de Especialização de Dados – Centro Brasileiro de Análise e Planejamento (CEBRAP), São Paulo, 1997. See Alencastro (ed.), 'Vida privada e ordem publica no Império', Tables 8 and 10.
11. The percentages of slaves in the northeastern provinces were: 12.1 per cent in Bahia; 10.4 per cent in Pernambuco; 12.8 per cent in Sergipe; 10.2 per cent in Alagoas; 4.4 per cent in Ceará; 5.7 per cent in Paraíba; and 5.5 per cent in Rio Grande do Norte. See Alencastro (ed.), *Império*, Table 10, p. 479.
12. Eltis and Richardson, *Routes*, p. 7.
13. James Henderson, *A History of the Brazil; Comprising Its Geography, Commerce, Colonization, Aboriginal Inhabitants, etc.* (London: Longman, Hurst, Rees, Orme and Brown, 1821) p. 75. One cure was a nightly wash in warm water and cane whisky (*cachaça*). *Sarna*, or scabies as it is commonly called today, was one such itchy and contagious skin disease.

14. On *ladinos*, see Alencastro, 'Vida privada e ordem publica no Império', in Alencastro (ed.), *Império*, p. 92.
15. Mary Karasch, *Slave Life in Rio de Janeiro, 1808–1850* (Princeton: Princeton University Press, 1987), pp. 29–30.
16. *Ibid.*, pp. 40–8; Robert E. Conrad, *Children of God's Fire* (Princeton: Princeton University Press, 1983), document 1.9, pp. 48–52.
17. Karasch, *Slave Life*, Ch. 2.
18. Conrad, *Children*, document 3.1, pp. 111–15.
19. Manolo García Florentino has highlighted the pervasiveness of slavery among the poor free population due to the inexpensiveness and abundance of available slave labour. See *Em costas negras: uma história do tráfico atlântico de escravos entre a Africa e o Rio de Janeiro (séculos XVIII e XIX)* (Rio de Janeiro: Arquivo Nacional, 1995).
20. John Thornton, *Africa and Africans in the Making of the Atlantic World, 1400–1680* (Cambridge: Cambridge University Press, 1992), Part 2, Chs 7, 8 and 10.
21. Robert W. Slenes, ' "Malungu, ngoma vem!": Africa encoberta e descoberta no Brasil', *Cadernos Museu Escravatura* (Luanda: Ministério da Cultura, 1995).
22. Philip Morgan, 'The cultural implications of the Atlantic slave trade: African regional origins, American destinations and New World developments', in Eltis and Richardson, *Routes*, p. 13.
23. Eltis and Richardson, *Routes*, pp. 13, 136, 142.
24. Karasch, *Slave Life*, Table 3.3, p. 62.
25. Jean Baptiste Debret, *Viagem pitoresca e histórica ao Brasil*. Translated and edited by Sérgio Millet (São Paulo: Martins, 1954); João Mauricio [Johann Moritz] Rugendas, *Viagem pitoresca através do Brasil* (São Paulo: Martins, [1940], 1967); Thomas Ewbank, *Life in Brazil* (New York: Harper & Brothers, 1856), pp. 94, 101, 111, 114, 116, 117, 223, 277.
26. Robert M. Levine, 'The Faces of Slavery' video (Florida: University of Miami, 1994).
27. Karasch, *Slave Life*, Ch. 8; Thornton, *Africa and Africans*, Part 2, Chs 7, 8 and 10.
28. A. J. R. Russell-Wood, *The Black Man in Slavery and Freedom in Colonial Brazil* (London: Macmillan, 1982); Karasch, *Slave Life*, p. 223.
29. Luís de Câmara Cascudo, *Antologia da alimentação no Brasil* (Rio de Janeiro: Livros Técnicos e Ciêntíficos, 1977), p. 85.
30. Palm oil, or *dendê* oil, was used by household slaves as a condiment to season food. See Toussaint-Samson, *A Parisian*, p. 41.
31. Karasch, *Slave Life*, p. 254.
32. *Ibid.*, p. 256.
33. *Ibid.*, Table 3.3, p. 272; Russell-Wood, *The Black Man*, pp. 38, 135 and Ch. 8 for details of brotherhoods.
34. Professor and Mrs Louis de Agassiz, *A Journey in Brazil* (Boston: Ticknor and Fields, 1868), p. 130.
35. Maximilian I, 'Recollections of my life' (1868), in Conrad, *Children*, pp. 195–7.
36. Alfredo Margarido, *Estudos sobre literaturas das nações africanas de língua portuguesa* (Lisbon: A Regra do Jogo, 1980), p. 394.
37. Karasch, *Slave Life*, p. 59, for spirits of the water.
38. *Ibid.*, p. 261.
39. See John T. Schneider, *Dictionary of African Borrowings in Brazilian Portuguese* (Hamburg: Helmut Buske Verlag, 1991).
40. Karasch, *Slave Life*, Chs 1, 8 and 9; Eduardo Silva, *The Prince of the People* (London: Verso, 1992); Carlos Eugênio Líbano Soares, *A negregada instituição: os capoeiras no Rio de Janeiro* (Rio de Janeiro: Prefeitura da Cidade do Rio de Janeiro, Secretária Municipal de Cultura, Departamento Geral da Documentação e Informação, Divisão de Editoração, 1994), Introduction.
41. David Brookshaw, *Raça e Côr na Literatura Brasileira* (Pôrto Alegre: Mercado Aberto, 1983), p. 26.
42. Luís da Câmara Cascudo, *Made in Africa: pesquisas e notas* (Rio de Janeiro; 1965), cited in Karasch, *Slave Life*, fn. 103, p. 248.

43. Luiz Carlos Martins Pena, *Obras*. Playbills that emphasize the subservient and submissive roles of slaves include *O cigano* and *O juiz de paz na roça*.

44. Brookshaw, *Raça e Côr*, p. 27.

45. See Martins Pena's plays, *O cigano*, *O juiz de paz na roça* and *O dour ou o maquinista inglês*.

46. José de Alencar, *O tronco do Ipê* (Rio de Janeiro: Garnier, 1871) (reprinted edition, Rio de Janeiro: Ediouro, Coleção Prestígio, n.d.), Ch. 1, 'O feiticeiro', p. 12.

47. On hierarchical complementarity, see Roberto da Matta, *A casa e a rua* (Rio de Janeiro: Editora Guanabara, 1987), p. 67. For a full explanation of complementarity, see pp. 31–71, especially p. 52; also by da Matta, *Carnivais, malandros e heróis* (Rio de Janeiro: Zahar, 1978), pp. 74–8.

48. Carl Sauer, *Land and Life: A Selection from the Writings of Carl Ortwin Sauer*, edited by John Leighly (Berkeley: University of California Press, 1963), p. 333.

49. *Ibid.*, pp. 333 and 342.

50. By the 1870s, the 'first phase' was showing signs of economic reversal but the 'second phase' of the constantly evolving coffee economy was flourishing in the Eastern Paraíba Valley, and was expanding in the northeastern and western regions of São Paulo and in the *zona da mata* (forest zone) of Minas Gerais. By the end of the century, Minas Gerais and Espírito Santo were developing new areas for coffee production, as was São Paulo, which had edged out Rio de Janeiro and its final frontier for coffee in the northeastern extremity of the state.

51. Robert W. Slenes, 'Grandeza ou decadência? O mercado de escravos e a economia cafeeira da província do Rio de Janeiro, 1850–1888', in Iraci del Nero da Costa (ed.), *Brasil: história econômica e demográfica* (São Paulo: Instituto de Pesquisas Econômicas, 1986), pp. 105–6; Graph 1, p. 112.

52. A listing of these studies can be found in Nancy Priscilla S. Naro, 'Rio studies Rio: ongoing studies of Rio de Janeiro, Brazil', *The Americas*, vol. 43, no. 4 (April, 1987), pp. 429–40.

53. Slenes, 'Grandeza ou decadência', Graph 1, p. 110; Table 2, p. 115.

54. Sarah Whatmore, *Farming Women: Gender, Work and Family Enterprise* (London: Macmillan, 1991).

55. For Bahia, see Pierre Verger, *Flux et refluxe* (Paris: Martin, 1968); Stuart B. Schwartz, *Sugar Plantations in the Formation of Brazilian Society: Bahia, 1550–1835* (Cambridge: Cambridge University Press, 1985); Katia Queirós Mattoso, *Ser escravo no Brasil* (São Paulo: Brasiliense, 1988); Bert Barickman, *A Bahian Counterpoint: Sugar, Tobacco, Cassava and Slavery in the Reconcavo, 1780–1860* (Stanford: Stanford University Press, 1998). For Pernambuco, see Peter L. Eisenberg, *The Sugar Industry of Pernambuco, 1840–1910: Modernization without Change* (Berkeley: University of California Press, 1974). Jaime Réis, 'From *banguê* to *usina*: social aspects of growth and modernization in the sugar industry of Pernambuco, Brazil, 1850–1920', pp. 369–97. João José Réis, *Rebelião escrava no Brasil: a História do levante dos Malês 1835* (São Paulo: Brasiliense, 1986), pp. 369–97.

56. I initially used appeals cases from the *município* of Rio Bonito to the Corte da Relação in Rio de Janeiro in 1988 to evaluate the types of local court decisions that one or both parties in a lawsuit found unacceptable and appealed to the highest court of jurisdiction. See Naro, 'Limites do comportamento aceitável e mecanismos de dominação social no meio rural brasileiro, 1850–1890', *Estudos Afro-Asiáticos*, no. 15 (1988), pp. 34–42.

57. Ciro F.S. Cardoso, *Agricultura, escravidão e capitalismo* (Petrópolis: Vozes, 1979); *Escravo ou camponês? O protocampesinato negro nas Américas* (São Paulo: Brasiliense, 1987). Eduardo Silva and João José Réis, *Negociação e conflito: a resistência negra no Brasil escravista* (São Paulo: Companhia das Letras, 1989), Ch. 2.

2

Ordering the Wilderness

Four years after the 1763 transfer of Brazil's colonial capital from Salvador, Bahia, in the sugar-producing northeast to the central southern port of Rio de Janeiro on Guanabara Bay, the governor-general of the captaincy of Rio de Janeiro was presented with a topographical map of the area. Identified were major inland rivers, their tributaries, canals and mountain ranges, providing colonial authorities with a guide to the hinterland landscapes that lay beyond the colonial capital. The map traced the well-travelled Caminho Novo road that led north from the port capital of Rio de Janeiro to the mining towns and regional markets of the neighbouring captaincy of Minas Gerais. Vast stretches of hinterland highland terrain to the west of the road remained in Crown hands to discourage contraband of gold and precious stones. As the mining economy waned after 1760, the potential of this area for mineral extraction and plantation agriculture led to royal land grants or *sesmarias* with the aim of effectively transforming the sparsely settled wilderness areas of the public domain.[1] In 1782, in recognition of the trade routes he had opened from the mountainous hinterlands of the captaincy of Rio de Janeiro to the lowlands and the port city of Rio, Francisco Rodrigues Alves was awarded a vast forested land grant in the highland areas that covered almost one-third of the present-day Paraíba Valley. A second grant, called Rio Bonito (no relation to the lowland area of the same name), was awarded in the same year to Luís Homem de Azevedo.[2]

Settlers, squatters, traders and their slaves rushed into the area. In less than a generation, bustling hamlets spread along the river valleys between the Serra da Mantiqueira and the Serra do Mar mountain ranges. Traversed by the broad and navigable Paraíba River and its tributaries, the Paraíba Valley formed a rolling interconnected chain of dome-shaped hills that ranged from 15 to 80 metres high, spreading from southwest to northeast between the captaincies of São Paulo, Rio de Janeiro and Minas Gerais. Fertile soil, plentiful water and coffee, the nineteenth-century equivalent of gold and diamonds, catapulted the southeast to economic prominence and provided the economic mainstay of nineteenth-century post-independence Brazil. The Paraíba Valley would become the 'valley of slavery and huge coffee *fazendas*'.[3] At the hub of the grandeur associated with this area was Vassouras.

A common juncture for trade between the highlands and the port city of Rio de Janeiro were the Guanabara Bay ports that lay to the east of the capital on the expansive Bay of Guanabara. The river and bay ports dated from the seventeenth century and thrived from local dynamic private and Church-owned sugarcane plantations that co-existed with small semi-subsistence food-producing holdings, supplying Rio de Janeiro and the Atlantic coast economy. One such port was on the Iguaçu River where propertied elites, clergy and wealthy Portuguese administered a population, half of which was enslaved. Sugarcane was the dominant export staple, followed by a bustling trade in wood and foodstuffs. Official recognition of the prosperous colonial merchants and small-scale traders who plied their trade through the river networks and Bay ports contrasted with the condemnation and repression of parallel contraband and illegal networks, operated by fugitive slaves, ex-slaves and traders, which sold and exchanged foodstuffs, game, wood and pilfered goods to local outlets. Since colonial times, armed encampments of slaves had sprung up throughout the Americas in forests and in remote and usually hilly places that served as refuges for fugitives. The Brazilian variant of such hideaways, known as *quilombos*, were 'fortified clusters of huts for defence against apprehension', and included any grouping of six or more slaves.[4] Distinguished from *ranchos*, temporary shelters for travellers and pack animals, the *quilombos* were located in inhospitable forested, mountainous and swampy terrain.[5] The Bantu term *ki-lombo* was the name of a male initiation society or circumcision camp where young men were prepared for adult warrior status. The term was linked to the Imbangala or 'Jaga' warriors who swept into what is present-day Angola in the sixteenth century. The Imbangala lived in a permanent state of warfare and, although they were reported to kill the babies born to their women, they adopted and integrated other children into their ranks, forming a multi-ethnic force united by a military structure.[6] The substitution of kinship by warfare as a unifying feature for some slaves thus preceded their arrival on American shores, but it also provided a unifying mechanism for Africans whose kinship ties were destroyed under slavery.[7] Stuart Schwartz has highlighted several features of Imbangala organization that provide a basis for the structure of Brazil's most studied and enduring *quilombo*, a seventeenth-century hideaway called Palmares. Palmares attracted thousands of runaway slaves and their free supporters, who occupied a palm-shaded remote area in the interior of the present state of Alagoas in northeastern Brazil. Although most inhabitants were runaway African slaves, the *quilombos* also harboured freedmen, deserters and middlemen linked to informants, tavern owners and traders.[8]

Palmares was razed in 1695, a year after its acclaimed leader and chief, Zumbi, perished. Yet slavery continued to inform the Brazilian plantation complex. The population of slaves in 1798 was 1,582,000, approximating but not surpassing the free population of 1,666,000. By 1817, however, the reverse was true: the slave population exceeded the free population, 1,930,000 to 1,887,900.[9] Armed encampments of runaways also continued to be a feature of colonial society. A police count taken in 1826 reported 426 *quilombolas* (fugitive slaves who sought refuge in a *quilombo*) in the hilly topography of the port city and capital of Rio de Janeiro.[10] An additional 469 were scattered throughout the hinterland of the province. Most of these were centred in the Bay port areas of long-standing settlement but a few dotted the Atlantic coast between Cabo Frio and Paratí and stretched into the highlands.[11] Colonial officials and private landowners who were threatened either personally or economically by the fugitive hideaways hounded and raided the retreats, but the raids by the fugitives on settled areas continued. The booty from these raids was traded clandestinely with tavern keepers, roving traders and slave go-betweens, who protected the hideaways as long as they profited from the informal commercial networks.[12] *Quilombos* also competed with landowners, merchants and religious estates to supply staples, foodstuffs and wood to regional markets and to the city of Rio de Janeiro. The juxtaposition of the informal slave economies with the formal economy characterized the interdependent, complementary, yet often competing, set of relationships that accompanied the *de jure* and *de facto* occupation of land, roads and waterways and the interplay among slaves and free people who defined society in the hinterlands during the nineteenth century.[13]

Whereas the Guanabara Bay port of Iguaçu handled and trans-shipped products from the sparsely populated highland and lowland agricultural peripheries that fed into the colonial capital, the Bay port of Porto das Caixas served an area to the east that stretched through lowland forested areas, interconnected rivers, tributaries and canals to the coastal sugar-producing region of Campos. Hinterland hamlets, named after the Catholic saints who were honoured in their rustic chapels, dotted the rivers, attesting to the advantages of water over land travel for exploration, commerce and internal communication at this time.

To the northeast of Porto das Caixas, the Casseribú River wound along the bases of the Taquara and Sambê mountain ranges to the Rio Bonito River and from there to the d'Ouro River. In 1682, a Crown land grant to Pedro de Souza Pereira covered the 'land between the Casseribú and Tanguá Rivers'. In 1760, five years after the arrival of the first settlers, the chapel of Madre de Deus, at the site where the two rivers converged, marked the settlement that would give birth to the parish of Rio Bonito in 1768, named a *vila* (town) less than a century later in 1846, and a city in 1890.[14] Set against a backdrop of the Serra do Mar mountain range, the territory was uncharted and the limitations facing exploration and settlement were summed up by the following description: 'backlands occupied by wild Indians'.[15]

Riverside hamlets, shrines and chapels also dotted the rivers that flowed at the bases of low-lying hilly ranges to the south of Porto das Caixas, gateways to the estates of Crown land grantees. A Crown land grant issued in 1751 to Paulo da Mota Duque Estrada destined the rolling hillsides of the Sambê and Catimbau for settlement. By 1767, there was a handful of privately owned sugarcane estates – Engenho Pacheco, Engenho Monte Velho and Engenho do Lagarto – that processed cane and produced a whisky known as *paratí* or *cachaça*. The mills attested to the limited, albeit prevalent, extension of unequal social relations that involved masters and slaves in colonial production for the plantation complex (see Figure 1).

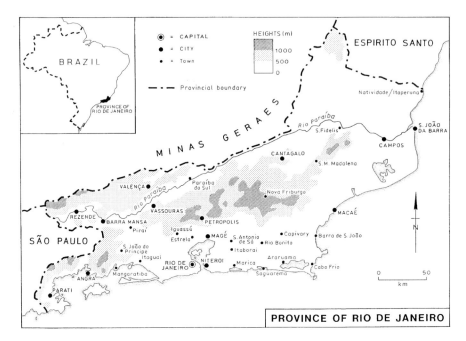

Figure 1 Settlement map of the province of Rio de Janeiro, 1868.
Source: Cândido Mendes de Almeida, Atlas do Império do Brazil, 1868. Redrawn by Keith Scurr, Geography Department, University of Hull.

Two towns

In the cool hilly areas above the valleys where sugarcane had provided Brazil with a colonial mainstay, the introduction of coffee production caused widespread deforestation in the wake of the intensive cultivation of land, and led to the use of involuntary labour by the powerful who made legal claims to the plantation complex, the small-scale producers of Brazil's dietary mainstays of manioc, maize, beans and coffee who farmed the land and the freedmen and slaves whose labour and farming shaped it.

Rio Bonito, which lies in the lowland Restinga micro-region[16] across Guanabara Bay, 60 miles to the east of the Bay port of Niterói, and Vassouras, which is situated 137 miles northwest of Rio de Janeiro in the highlands of the Western Paraíba Valley, were each approximately a day's journey from Rio. Neither *município* existed in the late eighteenth century, although sparsely populated parishes of traders, food producers and an occasional sugar estate dotted both areas.[17] The Brazilian geographer, Alberto Ribeiro Lamêgo, described Vassouras as a 'miracle of a geographical error', a city that emerged outside of the convergence of trade routes, developed without official support and presented no geographical reasons to warrant its development.[18] From the derelict mining areas of neighbouring Minas Gerais and from the court city of Rio de Janeiro, land grantees and their slaves, prompted by the potential profits to be made from Brazilian highland coffee in international markets, migrated into the highlands.

Table 2.1 Brazilian sugar and coffee exports, 1821–40

Years	Sugar			Coffee		
	Annual weight in tons	Average value in pounds (£)[a]	Percentage of total export value	Annual weight in tons	Average value in pounds (£)[a]	Percentage of total export value
1821–5	41,174	983,600	23.2	12,480	739,600	17.6
1826–30	54,796	1,369,600	37.8	25,680	698,200	19.7
1831–5	66,716	1,091,500	23.5	46,980	2,001,500	40.7
1836–40	79,010	1,320,800	24.3	69,900	2,428,000	46.0

[a] Nominal value unadjusted for inflation
Source: Adapted from Peter L. Eisenberg, *Modernização sem mudança* (São Paulo: UNICAMP/Paz e Terra, 1977), Table 2, p. 34.

They subsequently displaced the Coroado Indians, cleared forests and planted coffee, drawing on the Paraíba River and its tributaries for irrigation, shipment and trade.[19] Private appropriation of land and the demand for captive labour to farm it formed an integral part of that migration and the societies that emerged from it.

As Rio de Janeiro was transformed from a colonial outpost to a cosmopolitan seat of government after the arrival of the Portuguese court in 1808, the construction of the Commercio, Rodeio and Polícia roads extended communications between the capital and the hinterland in support of the coffee economy. By 1840, paths and overland routes connected lowland areas to river and Guanabara Bay ports, forging links to the highland villages, towns and districts of the Paraíba Valley. Established planters whose extensive holdings of land derived from *sesmaria* grants turned from sugarcane to coffee production as newcomers swept into the area. The export market for sugarcane remained dynamic in the northeast but in southeast Brazil the reliance on sugar production for the international market was eclipsed by the international demand for coffee. Whereas sugar exports represented 23 per cent of total exports compared to coffee's 17 per cent between 1821 and 1825, international demand reversed those figures, and coffee exports reached 40 per cent of the total value of exports in the early 1830s in contrast to almost unchanging figures for sugar (23 per cent) (Table 2.1).

The five prominent sugarcane and *aguardente* (sugarcane spirit) producers, Antonio Félix de Oliveira Braga, Camillo José Pereira de Faro, the heirs of José Clemente Pereira, Lauriano Corrêa e Castro and José Gomes Ribeiro de Avellar were among the esteemed coffee-producing oligarchies as the Paraíba Valley, with Vassouras at its hub, became the world's largest area of coffee production between 1850 and 1900.[20] Fortunes made from the coffee-export market provided comfortable lifestyles for these and numerous newcomers, who became known as the 'coffee barons', a plantocracy of merchant-planter elites whose reputations for wealth, vast holdings of slaves and land preceded them in the corridors of power in the imperial court of Rio de Janeiro. For most of the nineteenth century, their wealth lay in land and in the African and Brazilian slaves who laboured under the arduous plantation regime that was galvanized to meet international demand. For the latter, fortune was equated with survival and eventual freedom.[21]

Rio Bonito, on the other hand, was an outlying parish in the county of Itaboraí, a major colonial producer of sugarcane that lay inland from the provincial capital of Niterói. From inauspicious beginnings, Rio Bonito developed into a regional market town where sugarcane and the cross-cropping of coffee with foodstuffs supported a local elite of planters and traders with powerful regional links and tenuous ties to the export markets of the imperial court. As will be seen, although the coffee economy was important to Rio Bonito, the smaller scale of land-holdings, the diversity of production and the alternatives to slave labour made coffee cultivation less vital to the wellbeing of the *município* than was the case for Vassouras.

Distant origins of a bitter bean

Coffee was not native to Brazil. The most common of the diverse origins attributed to the *rubiacea* bean are the mountain forests of Ethiopia. A folkloric tale attributes the first use of coffee to the superior of a convent of friars on Mount Sinai, who offered an infusion of coffee to sleepy choristers after observing the excessive vivaciousness of goats that had consumed the plants. Another version singles out the Turks for the spread of coffee consumption throughout Islam.[22] A hot black beverage was known by the Egyptians as *elcave*, by the Persians as *cahveh*, by the Arabians as *cachua, caoua* and *cahouah*, and from these words originated the terms commonly known in Europe: *caphé, café, coffi, coffee* and *coffea*.[23] A 1591 description of a pleasant ink-coloured drink called *chaube* that was good for illness, chiefly of the stomach, was given by Prosper Alpinus, a physician to the Venetian consul, who remained in Egypt from 1580 to 1593. Known in England by 1650, and the object of considerable attention in the first coffee-house that opened in 1652, the medicinal properties and benefits of coffee lay at the heart of controversies over stomach and nervous disorders. These were associated as much with excessive consumption of the brew as with the questionable morals of the fashionable European urban coffee-houses that became the forums of thinkers, plotters and connoisseurs.[24] The addictive properties of the bitter-tasting mixture prompted Johann Sebastian Bach to compose the amusing seventeenth-century 'Coffee Cantata' about the fraught and afflicted maiden, Liesgen, whose intransigent father threatened to abandon his search for a suitor if she did not desist from her consumption of coffee.[25] Controversies raged over the etymology of the bitter black beverage that some associated with nausea, others with appetite stimulus, and still others with vigour and stamina.[26] Among coffee's virtues were its invigorating qualities, stimulating effect on the circulation, acceleration of digestion, treatment of colic and curbing of flatulence.[27] It was said to stimulate the onset of menses, was used with some success in cures of dropsy, and was effective in the treatment of parasites, headache, vertigo, lethargy, catarrh, ticklish coughs and apoplexy. Coffee was an antidote to the hypnotic or sleepy effects of opium, and those 'comatose, anasarcous, and such other diseases as arise from unwholesome food, want of exercise, weak fibres, and obstructed perspiration'.[28]

The coffee seeds that were introduced into the New World by European colonial powers were derived from two Yemeni varieties, *tipica* and *bourbon*.[29] The Dutch transported coffee plantings to the Caribbean in the early 1700s, and by 1718 coffee bushes were reported in Dutch Surinam. Gabriel des Clieux took plants to the French Caribbean in 1728, although there were reports of coffee in 1721 in French Cayenne and in 1727 in Martinique. English Jamaica was producing coffee in 1728, and in Spanish America coffee was growing in Puerto Rico in 1736, in Cuba in 1738 and in Guatemala between 1750 and 1760.[30] A popular Brazilian brand of coffee called *Palheta* traces its name to Francisco de Melo Palheta, a Brazilian army officer who is credited with bringing coffee seeds from French Cayenne to Belém, Pará, around 1727. The cultivation of the seeds generated little interest in Brazil until the promulgation of a decree on 4 May 1761 that exempted the product from custom-house duties.[31] During the governorships of the Conde de Bobadella and the Marquis of Lavradio, small-scale coffee production intensified and by 1790 approximately one ton of coffee was circulating in local markets.[32] The popularity of coffee in the urban centres of Europe was not shared by Portuguese consumers, who preferred tea and hot chocolate, but the growing demand for it may have prompted the enlightened Portuguese friar, José Mariano da Conceição Velloso, to include coffee among the staples he recommended for intensive cultivation in his multi-volume *O fazendeiro no Brasil*, published in 1798 in Lisbon.[33]

The exact date of coffee's first appearance in the Captaincy of Rio de Janeiro is unknown, although it is likely that the Society of Jesus, known in the Portuguese empire for crop experimentation, was involved in its early cultivation. An article in the *Tea and Coffee Trade Journal* in 1917 attributed the propagation of coffee in Rio to the Capuchins and the Bishop of Rio. Catholic institutions were among the principal suppliers of coffee seeds. Bushes were reported in the gardens of the Santo Antônio Convent in 1754 and among the plantings of the Barbadinho friars on the Rua Evaristo da Veiga around 1760, the Santa Teresa Convent, the Capião do Bispo estate and in the gardens of Padre Antônio de Couto da Fonseca in Campo Grande around 1780.[34] The latter's crop experimentation post in Campo Grande was said to supply mule trains with shipments of seed for the ascent into the highlands.[35] The artist, Jean Baptiste Debret, dated coffee planting from the 1770s.[36]

The transition of coffee production from domestic household use to extensive cultivation probably coincided with the intensification of international demand for Brazilian 'green gold' *cofea arabica linneus* (*pentandria monogynia*) that followed the revolution in Saint Domingue. According to Gilberto Ferrez, a prominent nineteenth-century photographer, the units of under 20,000 trees that dotted the hillsides of Rio de Janeiro, the Tijuca rainforest and the parishes of Andaraí and Jacarepaguá were not sufficient to satisfy North American and Western European buyers. Ferrez claimed that intensive production of upwards of 50,000 trees only took place after 1816 when the Haitian refugee, Louis François Lecesne, arrived in Rio de Janeiro.[37] Claimants to land migrated with slaves from the port city west

Table 2.2 Production, export and price of coffee, province of Rio de Janeiro, 1840–60

Year	Exported from port of Rio (*arrobas*)	Production in province of Rio (*arrobas*)	Price per *arroba*
1840–1	4,982,221	–	3$519
1845–6	7,720,221	–	3$028
1849–50	5,706,833	–	3$866
1851–2	9,673,842	7,535,844	3$396
1852–3	8,312,561	6,535,113	3$764
1853–4	10,128,908	7,988,551	3$896
1854–5	12,024,063	9,369,107	3$890
1855–6	10,918,148	8,602,658	4$301
1856–7	10,426,449	8,097,879	4$627
1857–8	9,415,843	7,593,200	4$167
1858–9	10,286,504	8,082,953	5$199
1859–60	10,606,394	8,746,361	5$829

Source: Adapted from Stein, *Vassouras*, Table 4, p. 53. Until 1942, Brazilian currency was based on réis, mil-réis and contos. 1000 réis = 1 mil-réis; 1000 réis = 1 conto. For example, 1:300$519 reads 1 conto 300 mil-réis, 519 réis.

to Itaguaí and from there into the forested highlands of the Paraíba Valley, where they formed the nucleus of intensive coffee cultivation.[38] On the opposite side of the bay from Rio de Janeiro, coffee production expanded from São Gonçalo, through lowland areas like Rio Bonito, into the foothills of Magé, and from there, more gradually than in the western areas, to the highlands of the Eastern Paraíba Valley. Cross-cropped with corn and beans, and vying with manioc and sugar as a mainstay of the Brazilian diet, coffee's rapid advance took place within four decades from the outset of production, redesigning Rio de Janeiro's physical landscape and turning slave labour into a feature of the hinterland labour landscape.

The reign of coffee

Coffee production intensified with international demand. During the 1840s, for example, coffee exports, valued at £22,655, accounted for 47 per cent of total Brazilian exports. During the following decade, the value of coffee exports more than doubled to £49,741, as the figure increased to 54 per cent of total exports.[39] Rising coffee prices, which had fluctuated between 3$300 and 3$900 per *arroba* (15 kilograms) in the first half of the 1850s, increased to 4$627 in 1856–7 and, despite poorer harvests in 1857–8, prices reached a high of 5$829 in 1859–60[40] (Table 2.2).

Coffee prices fell abruptly in the world purchasing centres in 1857 and 1858, declining from 11 to 10.4 cents per pound in New York, and generated a run on the banks in the capital as coffee factors attempted to cover their clients' orders for foodstuffs and imported goods.[41] The recovery of international markets at the end of the decade set in motion the cycle of intensive coffee production that responded to steadily increasing prices per sack, reaching a high in 1863, declining during the rest of the decade and regaining a generally upward trend in the 1870s.[42] Food shortages continued to plague the highlands and, in 1861, as provincial officials protested the outlandish prices of foodstuffs, coffee planters decried their dependency on external suppliers.[43] That year marked the death of Baron Lacerda Werneck, a planter-merchant whose fortune had not endowed him with the sagacity to foresee that the uncontrolled ravaging of the region's natural resources would create irreversible imbalances. Swiss consul, Johann Jakob von Tschudi, who published his travel observations in 1862, perceived the irony of a situation where the mainstays of corn, rice and beans were imported from the United States and from Europe, paid for by the increased state and government income derived from coffee.[44] Vassouras planters who were caught in the paradox took their market cues from foreign markets. Whether they were aware of it or not, the international returns from the sale of coffee were underwriting the costs of importing food, including salted beef from Argentina, to feed the slave and free labour forces that were producing it in the first place!

The French traveller, Charles de Ribeyrolles, exhorted Brazilians to preserve the sources of their nutrition and not be bound by the immediate gains offered by coffee:

> Brazilians, do not disparage the pig, or anil or the silkworm, or the bee or the banana. Plants, fruits, animals may be secondary but they are nourishing; one only drinks coffee at dessert . . . But, coffee sells so handsomely![45]

The regional drift of the Rio de Janeiro provincial population, *c.* 1840

The 1840 census of the province of Rio de Janeiro provides a detailed register of the composition and distribution of the *fluminense* population during coffee's heyday and acts as a point of departure for comparisons with later census data. The census attests to the virtual extinction of the Indian nations that figured so prominently in the 1767 map, eclipsed from the human topography through disease, enslavement, warfare and miscegenation. The category of 'Indians' no longer existed, and had been replaced by the term *caboclos*. *Caboclos* were distinguished from *bugres* (uncivilized people and a generic term for Indians), equated by some historians with a mixed-breed peasantry.[46] The low numbers are typical of mission figures, although the term *aldeiados* (village dwellers) does not appear in the census.[47] *Caboclos* accounted for little more than 1 per cent of the total provincial population, in a census total of 407,241 that I have revised to 404,705. The largest concentrations were clustered in tiny settlements on the peripheries of the frontier in Barra Mansa, Itaguaí, Campos and Cabo Frio (Table 2.3).

En route to one of the last Puri Indian encampments in the Eastern Paraíba Valley on the borders of Rio de Janeiro and Minas Gerais in the 1840s, the

Table 2.3 *Caboclo* population of Rio de Janeiro province, by county, 1840

County	Males	Females	County total	% provincial population
Rezende	851	859	1710	0.42
Vassouras	390	357	747	0.18
Cantagalo	17	16	33	0.008
Niterói	108	110	218	0.05
Itaboraí	57	38	95	0.02
Campos	314	349	663	0.16
Cabo Frio	531	563	1094	0.27
Angra dos Réis	528	517	1045	0.25
Grand total	2798	2817	5615	1.38

No census data was forthcoming from Nossa Senhora da Conceição do Paquequer in the district of Cantagalo; Jacotiaga, Pilar, Inhomerim in the district of Niterói; Tamby, Santíssima Trindade in the district of Itaboraí; Desterro de Quissamã, Curato do Carapebús, Curato do Barreto in the district of Cabo Frio. See Appendix One for breakdown by *município*.
Source: BN, *Quadro Estatístico da Província de Rio de Janeiro, segundo condições, sexo e côres, 1840.*

Austrian traveller, Ida Pfeiffer, happened upon a settlement of *caboclos* at a place that she described as the 'last settlement of the whites' (see Figure 2):

> Twelve miles inland from the Pomba River stood a largish wooden house surrounded by a few miserable huts 'as that of the slaves'. Each of four rooms was occupied by a white family and was furnished with a few hammocks and straw mats. The detached kitchen resembled a very large barn with openings in it; upon a hearth that took up nearly the entire length of the barn, several fires were burning, over which hung small kettles, and at each side were fastened wooden spits. On these were fixed several pieces of meat, some of which were being roasted by the fire and some cured by the smoke. The kitchen was full of people; whites, Puri Indians, and negroes, children whose parents were whites and Puris, or Puris and negroes – in a word, the place was like a book of specimens containing the most varied ramifications of the three principal races of the country.[48]

Ida Pfeiffer's description attested to the coming together of the poor and dispossessed on the peripheries of settled areas. The indigenous lifestyle of the Puri Indians was assimilating with other races and ethnicities and adopting a semi-sedentary way of life as *caboclos*. The fruits of the forest and basic and meagre hand-fashioned domestic possessions provided a means for some indigenous ways to survive; but most aspects of tribal and linguistic identity were replaced by the Portuguese language and ethnic inter-mixture.

Figure 2 Indigenous encampment. *Source:* Jean Baptist Debret, *Viagem Pitoresca e Histórica do Brasil*, 1834. Photo taken between 1816 and 1831.

Of greater numerical significance was the free population, hovering in the 40 per cent range in most counties and subdivided between white, *pardo* (mulatto) and *preto* (black) men and women. The white population was the largest, and white males slightly outnumbered white females. *Pardos* outnumbered free blacks by more than three to one; *pardo* females slightly outnumbered *pardo* males. At this time, the non-white free population of approximately 64,000 people was sizeable and probably included *mestiços* (mixed-race) and assimilated Indians, but was below the numbers of masters and, as will be seen, slaves (Table 2.4). (See Appendix 2 for a breakdown by county.)

In the county of Vassouras, where the production of coffee for the export economy was concentrated, free males outnumbered females in all three categories. The same was true in Resende and Cantagalo but not in lowland areas where, among whites, males outnumbered females in Niterói, Cabo Frio and Angra dos Réis. Among the non-white population in the lowlands free women outnumbered free men, indicating the co-existence or even the advance of female-headed family units of production engaged in the expanding advance of cross-cropped coffee and foodstuffs in areas that were formerly dominated by sugarcane.

Slaves represented the third and largest category of the 1840 provincial census, accounting for 55 per cent of the provincial population. Slaves were divided into two subcategories: *pardo* and *preto*. Slaves listed as *preto* accounted for 94 per cent (210, 320 of the total slave population of 223,568), and of these 62 per cent were males. With the exception of Vassouras, slave and free numbers were about equal in each county. Slaves were involved in unskilled and skilled tasks that ranged from domestic service and weaving to animal care, field and

Table 2.4 Free population of Rio de Janeiro province, by county, 1840

County	White		Pardo		Black		Total
	Male	Female	Male	Female	Male	Female	
Resende	6956	6361	2363	2145	460	396	18,679
Vassouras	8226	6620	3963	3469	930	847	24,055
Cantagalo	2030	1755	733	669	170	133	5490
Niterói	6871	6124	3523	4287	1393	1854	24,052
Itaboraí	8626	8721	4758	5396	979	1209	29,689
Campos	9272	9398	3253	3732	946	1147	27,748
Cabo Frio	6362	6110	3049	3516	504	655	20,196
Angra dos Réis	9137	8361	3027	3293	813	978	25,609
Sum total	57,482	53,450	24,669	26,507	6195	7219	175,522*
Sum total by category	110,932		51,176		13,414		
Percentage of total	63.20		29.16		7.64		

* I have revised the additions in the census and have a total of 175,522.
No census data was forthcoming from Nossa Senhora Conceição do Paquequer in the district of Cantagalo; Jacotiaga, Pilar, Inhomerim in the district of Niterói; Tamby, Santíssima Trindade in the district of Itaboraí; Desterro de Quissamã, Curato do Carapebús, Curato do Barreto in the district of Cabo Frio.
Source: BN, *Quadro Estatístico da Província de Rio de Janeiro, Segundo condições, Sexo e côres, 1840.*

garden farming, itinerant trading, construction, road and fence building, labour in manufactories, foundries, artisan workshops, transportation and personal services; in short, almost every kind of manual labour.

Slave numbers were high in areas of long-standing settlement – the lowland port and provincial capital of Niterói overlooking Guanabara Bay, the Atlantic fishing village of Cabo Frio and the sugarcane-producing lowland areas of Campos, Itaboraí and Angra dos Réis – but these were giving way to the labour demands of the emerging nuclei of coffee production in the highland counties exemplified by Vassouras.[49] Whereas the ratio of males to females was 165:100 in the province, not very different from the figure of 156:100 in traditional areas of colonial sugar-production like Campos, the sex ratio in the highland coffee areas was well over 200:100, confirming the existence of a dynamic plantation society where predominantly African male slaves were in the highest demand (Table 2.5).[50]

The distribution of male and female slaves sheds light on local land allocation and usage. By 1840, the intensive production of sugarcane for the export market that had concentrated slave labour on lowland estates during colonial times was now engaged in production for regional sugarcane markets. At the time of his travels in the 1820s, the English traveller, James Henderson, heralded 'the Campos sugars [as] the best in Brazil' but added that they 'were only consumed

Table 2.5 Slave population of Rio de Janeiro province, by county and by colour, 1840

County	Number of slaves	As percentage of county population (free and slave)	As percentage of province total of slaves	Pardo		Preto		Sex ratio
				M	F	M	F	
Resende	22,199	52	10	440	407	14,753	6,599	223
Vassouras	46,871	65	21	658	563	32,026	14,624	218
Cantagalo	5412	49	2	16	81	3,506	1,709	205
Niterói	30,172	55	13	917	805	17,179	11,271	152
Itaboraí	31,084	51	14	1818	1155	16,151	12,590	128
Campos	37,318	55	17	1488	1468	20,966	13,396	156
Cabo Frio	22,506	53	10	2011	758	11,291	8,446	133
Angra dos Réis	28,006	52	13	1135	1058	15,215	10,598	143
Total	223,568	100	100	8583	6295	131,087	79,233	165
Total by category					14,878		210,320	

Source: BN, *Quadro Estatístico da Província de Rio de Janeiro, Segundo condições, Sexo e côres, 1840.*

domestically'.[51] With the downward spiral in sugar prices and the contraction of the foreign export market for sugarcane, a shift from large-scale intensive production of sugarcane to small-scale food production occurred in these areas. Henderson wryly noted on his journey to Paratí, Ilha Grande and Angra dos Réis in the early 1820s that sugar estates and distilleries were giving way to small farms where figs, wine, rice, beans and maize were grown, and some cattle and poultry raising took place.[52] He described the area as being in 'a state of mediocrity'. For semi-subsistence producers, an expanding coastal trade that not only provisioned passing ships but also supplied foodstuffs to the expanding local markets in Rio de Janeiro provided a modest but viable alternative to plantation labour. The existence of *quilombos* in nearby Mangaratiba and Paratí, as well as a proliferation of taverns in the area, linked a coastal network of boatmen into an informal economy that operated in tandem, and sometimes surpassed, the registered and licensed channels of production and commerce in the Iguaçu and Bay port areas already mentioned.[53]

Slaves and slave ownership

Ownership of slaves was indicative of wealth and was directly related to one's socio-economic standing in Brazil's agrarian society. The larger and younger the holdings of human property, the greater the public association with wealth, prosperity and social standing of their owners. As mainstays of the rural economy and the plantation complex, cheap and abundant land and labour were in demand and represented a source of speculation for investors.[54] In 1850, however, legislation was introduced to regulate access to public lands and the Eusébio de Queirós Law (No. 581 of 4 September) curtailed the supplies of transatlantic labour, setting in motion the process of transition to a free labour market. The Eusébio de Queirós Law marked the culmination of negotiations that had begun in 1826 when Brazil signed a diplomatic agreement with England to halt the traffic in captive Africans. Both Brazilian and foreign ships in Brazilian territorial waters that carried, or were outfitted to carry, slaves, whose importation was prohibited by the law of 7 November 1831 were to be apprehended and judged under acts of piracy. Slaves on apprehended vessels would be returned to their ports of embarkation or other foreign ports, where they would be held under the tutelage of the government for service until re-exported.[55] The law was not enforced, however, and the transatlantic trade between Africa and Brazil continued unhindered for another decade until British pressure proved an effective deterrent: under the Aberdeen Bill of 1845, the British navy was empowered to board slave ships within Brazilian territorial waters. Although confiscation of ships and slave cargo followed, at least 371,615 African slaves were smuggled into Brazil between 1840 and 1851. Intense government debate and the irate reaction of Brazilian slave-owners confirmed not only the dynamic Brazilian market for imported captive African labour but attested to a generalized resistance to consider or seek alternatives to slavery.[56]

The passage of the Eusébio de Queirós Law officially ended the transatlantic slave trade to Brazil. It also laid the foundations for the establishment over the following four decades of a free labour market for Brazil's two to two and a half million mulatto and black slaves.[57] Yet the demise of the transatlantic trade did not deter slave traders from seeking alternatives to supplying the lucrative slave markets of the southeast. Through an inter-provincial slave trade, traders bought and transferred slaves from the northern and northeastern provinces of the country to Rio de Janeiro and intensified the internal provincial market as well, profiting from the increasing prices for slave labour until curtailed by the passage, in 1880, of a provincial law that imposed a tax on the registration of imported slaves. In the 1850s, for example, the average nominal slave price was 787$; in the 1860s, the average price increased to 914$; in the 1870s it rose modestly to 973$, but then declined sharply in the 1880s to 727$ (Table 2.6).

Since regulation of the inter-provincial trade was precarious, the precise numbers of slaves involved are difficult to calculate. According to historian Leslie Bethell, 34,688 slaves were imported by sea from the northern provinces into the capital between January 1852 and July 1862.[58] For the province of Rio de Janeiro, Stanley Stein claimed that in a two-year period (1852–4), 26,622 slaves were imported.[59]

The highest proportion of slaves in the province were held in Vassouras's three parishes, where slaves accounted for 55 to 75 per cent of the population in 1850. Slave-holdings and land were both concentrated in the parishes of Nossa Senhora da Conceição and Paty do Alferes. Paty do Alferes, site of an eighteenth-century sugar mill, had a long-standing reputation as a producer and supplier of

Table 2.6 Average nominal slave prices, by year, 1850–87

Year	Average price in mil-réis	Year	Average price in mil-réis	Year	Average price in mil-réis
1850	320$	1863	900$	1876	1:026$
1851	449$	1864	1:032$	1877	1:094$
1852	694$	1865	897$	1878	932$
1853	806$	1866	797$	1879	1:035$
1854	669$	1867	768$	1880	893$
1855	811$	1868	860$	1881	918$
1856	874$	1869	932$	1882	608$
1857	1:006$	1870	1:008$	1883	550$
1858	1:152$	1871	816$	1884	584$
1859	1:090$	1872	859$	1885	767$
1860	1:016$	1873	976$	1886	325$
1861	938$	1874	958$	1887	450$
1862	1:007$	1875	1:028$	1888	–

Source: Adapted from Joseph E. Sweigart, 'Financing and Marketing Brazilian Export Agriculture: The Coffee Factors of Rio de Janeiro, 1850–1888,' unpublished PhD dissertation, Department of History, University of Texas, 1980, p. 303. Published in 1987 as *Coffee Factorage and the Emergence of a Brazilian Capital Market, 1850–1888 (New York: Garland.*

foodstuffs and farm animals to Rio de Janeiro. On its peripheries, six *quilombolas* were reported in 1826, suggesting once more that formal and informal economies, and the lifestyles that profited from them, formed the bases for *de jure* and *de facto* claims to the land and labour.[60] In the parish of Sacra Família do Tinguá, 3966 slaves accounted for over half (56 per cent) of the local population and were mainly held by the Fazenda São Marcos. In the same area there was a sizeable freed population (17 per cent), who probably had kinship ties to slaves on the estate and links to the three *quilombos* that had existed there in 1826. The proximity of freed and fugitive slaves suggests not only viable lifestyles to slavery in the area but alternatives to formal channels of production, *de jure* holdings and trade. In 1850, small-scale family-based cultivators predominated and no *quilombos* had been reported in the area (Table 2.7).[61]

In general, the free non-white population of the three parishes of Vassouras was smaller than the provincial average and reflected a rigid social hierarchy of prosperous and less prosperous slave-owners and the slaves they owned. Unlike their counterparts in Cuba, Brazilian slaves were not all occupied with one monotonous elementary activity and the range of unskilled and skilled, albeit captive, labour displaced skilled free labour.[62] Under such an arrangement, it would be expected that the free non-white population would move elsewhere and even disappear over time. Yet, in the same areas where land ownership was concentrated and slave labour predominated, the census recorded a growing

Table 2.7 Population of Vassouras, 1850

Parish	Total population	Total non-white*	Free** No.	Free** %	Slave No.	Slave %	Free non-white No.	Free non-white %
N.S. da Conceição	10,086	8,033	3,291	33.0	6,795	67.0	1,238	12.0
Paty do Alferes	11,489	10,097	3,040	25.0	8,449	75.0	1,648	14.0
S.F. do Tinguá	7,063	5,144	3,097	44.0	3,966	56.0	1,178	17.0
Total	28,638	23,274	11,428		19,210		4,064	
Rio de Janeiro province	454,499	293,554	160,945***	35.0	196,925	65.0	96,629	21.0

* Refers to *pardos* and blacks (*pretos*) but not Indians.
** Refers to whites, *pardos* and blacks but not Indians.
*** Refers to whites only.
Sources: BN, *Relatório do Presidente da Província do Rio de Janeiro*, 1850. Herbert S. Klein, 'Nineteenth-century Brazil', in David W. Cohen and Jack P. Greene, (eds), *Neither Slave nor Free: The Freedom of African Descent in the Slave Societies of the New World* (Baltimore: Johns Hopkins University Press, 1972), p. 313.

population of free skilled and semi-skilled inhabitants – retail merchants, artisans, tradesmen and producers – and vagrants and brigands, who shaped their lifestyles around and within the plantation, carving out a living in a predominantly slave regime.[63]

Harnessing the wilderness: refashioning the land and the landscape

Claims to public land fell into two major categories. Private appropriation of land was formalized by *sesmarias*, land grants bestowed by the Crown on successful individual petitioners in the seventeenth, eighteenth and early nineteenth centuries. *Sesmarias* were also granted to deserving subjects in recognition of patriotic acts, such as defence of the Crown, and public services, such as road improvements and maintenance, construction of hospitals or other beneficent institutions, and provision of foodstuffs or goods during local shortages.[64] Despite numerous abuses that included the sale and exchange of grants, many Crown lands granted in *sesmaria* were effectively occupied and cultivated. One notable example of a long-standing concern was the highland *engenho* of Pau Grande in the parish of Paty do Alferes that developed from a *sesmaria* granted to Antonio Ribeiro Avellar in the 1700s. Pau Grande represented a diversified production unit from which sugarcane, cane whisky, pork, foodstuffs, and fruit were shipped down the Iguaçu River to its lowland port and from there to Rio de Janeiro.[66] The strategic location of Paty do Alferes as a gateway to the highlands was recognized by its elevation to the status of *vila* of Nossa Senhora da Conceição do Paty do Alferes and the extension of its jurisdiction over the parishes of Nossa Senhora da Conceição e Apóstolos São Pedro e São Paulo da Paraíba Nova and Sacra Família do Caminho Novo do Tinguá, later to form part of the *município* of Vassouras.[66]

Sesmaria grants were suspended on 17 July 1823, in the aftermath of Brazil's independence. Public lands were henceforth poorly regulated and the *de facto* private appropriation of land preceded the bureaucracy that was meant to regulate it. Private holdings were attainable by purchase or by donation but were distributed on the sole basis of a probable location on a map.[67] Where maps and surveys did not exist, claimants staked out the *terras devolutas* (unoccupied national lands), marking out their claims with the natural boundaries of rivers, waterfalls, stone markers, hillsides and forests.[68] Estimates and exaggeration prevailed over scientific accuracy, as local potentates recorded the width of their claims but estimated the depth to be 'as far as the eye can see', or more commonly *com quem de direito for* ('up to the lands of a neighbour'). Small holders also endorsed this practice, claiming their lands extended to the boundaries of a prominent neighbour or relative who was often the claimant's benefactor.

Another form of claim was by effective occupation of the land or *posse*. Squatters effectively occupied land, but the empire did not recognize squatter claims and few became officially registered landowners. Land use in this category varied according to the intention of the occupant and included mineral extraction, the cultivation of dyes and spices, forestry, farming, grazing, the establishment of *quilombos* and *ranchos* that housed semi-nomadic freemen, and Indian villages.

The *ranchos* were as precarious as the lifestyles of the people who built them and were a feature of the landscape along roadsides and in forest clearings. The Englishman, John Luccock, advancing northward on horseback from the hamlet of São Pedro in the Eastern Paraíba Valley into dense, pristine forest, came upon cleared land with a few huts that

> were said to be the dwellings of a low race of people, who hid themselves from notice in order to escape taxes and the military service; cultivated a little corn for their own use, and cut dyeing wood sufficient to procure them tobacco and a few other trifling luxuries.[69]

The informal economy survived from cutting and selling timber, game, other forest products and food crops. Despite public associations with villainy and crime, encampments of semi-nomadic wanderers, slave runaways and semi-subsistence farmers provided vital services to local markets. Landowners made use of itinerant labourers, and granted squatters permission to cultivate foodstuffs and graze barnyard animals on small plots of land in exchange for a modest fee or quitrent (*foro*) and protection from poachers and rival claimants to the land.[70] The free and freed tenant farmers (*foreiros*) who thus served as human buffers might be described as a 'fictive peasantry', tenants with no leases, holders of some capital and tenuous family units whose semi-migrant lifestyles placed them somewhere between land grantees and landless squatters.[71]

The French naturalist, Auguste de Saint-Hilaire, claimed that the roadside corn vendors he passed in the vicinity of Vassouras faced the levelling of their modest shelters (*choupanas*) and eviction from the uncultivated stretches of land if they displeased or failed to comply with the wishes and orders of the land-owner.[72] His observation confirms an unequal power relationship that rested, in the final analysis, on the dependency of landless people on the favour or otherwise of title-holders to land and on local officials, army recruiters, tax collectors and thugs.[73]

John Luccock divided the *foreiros* into two groups. He named one group *moradores*, Brazilians of European descent with families and a few slaves who, although part of the local population, did not remain in residence for very long. Ignorant, violent and lazy, these wanderers were fiercely independent with no fixed abode and moved on after harvesting their crops and settling their obligations. The second group of *foreiros* more closely resembled *lavradores* (farm labourers) and possessed or acquired a small amount of capital to purchase cattle and slaves and farmed for cash or the exchange of foodstuffs and items of daily use. If the tenant planted cane, the landowner received a share of the crop, usually half, and also processed or distilled the tenant's share.[74] For Luccock, the small quitrent farms (*sítios*) benefited landowners by increasing crop yields and contributing directly or indirectly to operating capital, without challenging property ownership.

The occupation and use of land in this way established an unwritten customary practice under which landless and small-scale family-based producers established a hold on the rural milieu. Quitrent farms with garden plots, cabins and livestock changed hands among landless farmers without prior consultation of the landlord.[75] Newcomers took on plots that were already cultivated and passed capital to departing tenants without altering the service to the landowner. Unprotected by law or by contract, the tenure of tenants was subject to the goodwill of landowners, who could muster local support to expel them and appropriate all improvements. Structural improvements such as fences, houses, barns and irrigation networks were rare among this group and investments were restricted to movable property: slaves, cooking utensils, bedding and domestic animals.

On 18 September 1850, the Brazilian Land Law organized the distribution and future occupation of public lands (*terras baldías*). Initially aimed at making unoccupied public lands available for European colonization, the law legitimized all extant *sesmarias* and, by so doing, perpetuated the long-standing practice of concentrating land-holdings in private hands.[76] The law also recognized claims to title based on effective occupation of land, and if this was proved, the claims were registered in parish land offices. Smallholders with long-standing claims to cultivated land were protected by the law, but holdings of a temporary nature – plots, slash-and-burn holdings, *ranchos* and provision grounds – did not qualify, nor was there any cover for claims to occupied land by *quilombos*.[77] In addition to limiting the opportunities for squatters and slaves to claim the land they farmed on the basis of customary usage, the law stipulated that deed of purchase would henceforth become the only valid means of registering claims to public lands. In this way, the law restricted the transfer of public lands to moneyed and propertied interests and left squatters and other effective occupants, slave or otherwise, without legal recourse to claims or protection by local authorities on the land they farmed.[78] Owing to a lack of the human resources required to implement the registration and measurement of lands, a weak central bureaucracy at local level, resistance on the part of local landowners and non-compliance by squatters and effective occupants, the law did not change the agrarian structure of the country, nor did it result in large-scale colonization.[79]

Claims that were registered in 1854 in Vassouras and Rio Bonito reveal differences in the rural land structure of the two places and enable one to classify production units into three broad categories of increasingly complex size and organization. Illustrating the poorer end of a broad spectrum of land-holdings was the small subsistence holding: typically a free-standing family farm of less than 40 hectares (96 acres), which was divided into distinct farming and pasture areas and located within or at the periphery of a *fazenda*. When she died, Joanna Maria de Jesus, married and mother of six children aged twelve to twenty-three, was not the owner of her land. She left to her surviving husband and two unmarried children a modest cabin on a derelict field and a corral. Her household possessions were meagre – a teapot, 40 bottles, 2 cots, 2 hand-operated grinders and 42 one-pound weights of unspecified use. Field implements included an axe, a hoe and a sickle used on a small planting of poorly tended coffee bushes. A few barnyard animals – two pigs and two goats – completed her unpretentious estate, valued at approximately US$300.[80]

In contrast, the second category of unit comprised vast aggregates of contiguous holdings that spanned an entire parish. The estate of Rio Bonito coffee planter Alexandre Pereira dos Santos, which was typical of a privately owned production unit under 2000 hectares, held from 25 to 150 slaves, and was characterized by coffee and some production of foodstuffs. In this broad category of landowner, property was held in land and slaves, with the exception of a few farmers and planters who invested in partnerships, businesses, and banks near to their dwellings.[81] Processing units on the estate included drying and roasting ovens for coffee, manioc presses and ovens and a brick factory for the manufacture of roof tiles for the great house and outbuildings. Sheds, barns, stables, storage silos and slave quarters completed the building layout. Pereira dos Santos owned four separate properties in an equal number of local parishes, but only on his main *fazenda* was there a great house near to the works and a *venda*, or country store, the predecessor of today's *barracão* or *tienda de raya*. The *venda* was a commercial outlet known for conducting dubious dealings in suspect goods. It bought or exchanged foodstuffs produced by slaves and smallholders and cornered rural trade and the extension of credit on purchases by slaves and free farmers of salt, kerosene, candles and other basic items.

Smallholders were dispersed throughout the *fazenda* grounds under arrangements that varied from unauthorized occupation to payment of rent and exchange of labour for a farming plot. The long-term nature of the occupancy of some of the small farms was suggested by the installation of processing facilities for corn, beans, coffee, sugar and manioc and the holdings of slaves to handle these and related tasks.

The third and most complex category included numerous free-standing properties and a number of holdings within *fazendas* that belonged to other landowners. These *fazendas* were upwards of 2000 hectares and contained diverse production and processing units, such as mills and brick factories, extended marketing networks that included general stores and depots near to the Bay of Guanabara, and mule trains, canoes and oxcarts for transportation. Holdings in slaves numbered in the thousands but were not the sole source of investment. Urban real estate, business partnerships, joint stock companies, stocks, bonds and letters of credit extended investments from local to regional networks, and included stocks and bonds in private and family-owned financial institutions in Rio de Janeiro. Planters who invested in the financial markets were listed as capitalists: the commercial-cum-political directory, the *Almanak Laemmert*, contains a noticeably full entry in the pages that describe the coffee-exporting towns of the Paraíba Valley, while the entry for a regional market town like Rio Bonito is practically non-existent. In 1865, for example, as the coffee boom was peaking, the *Almanak* listed seventeen capitalists in Vassouras to Rio Bonito's one. Two decades later, during a widespread crisis in the coffee sector, Vassouras's fifteen capitalists were listed but for Rio Bonito the category no longer existed.[82]

Displacement or incorporation in Vassouras: slaves, foodstuffs and coffee

As long as unclaimed public lands and forests were abundant, the landscape supported the uneasy co-existence of *de jure* land claimants, *de facto* cultivators and *quilombo* encampments. According to Stanley Stein, landless farmers in Vassouras 'continued to exist from 1830 to 1850 and afterwards, [but] their position grew increasingly subordinate as the wealth of the *município* became synonymous with the coffee production of the large *fazenda*'. Vassouras historian Inácio Raposo associated the decline in anil-dye cultivation and in pig-rearing (a common investment for poor people's capital and a rich source of protein) with the expansion of coffee production in the 1840s.[83]

Coffee, like sugar before it, transformed modest commercial outposts into showcases of hinterland greatness. The golden age of Vassouras, which lasted from 1850 to 1875, boasted a flourishing urban centre and an outlying area that contained almost one-third of the province's entire population during the heyday of the coffee boom.[84] According to the *Almanak Laemmert* of 1851, Vassouras, with its 246 *fazendeiros* and *lavradores de café* and 68 businessmen, was second only to its highland neighbour, Resende, in prominence. The addition of the parish of Santa Cruz dos Mendes, created by provincial law No. 808 on 29 December 1855, added 36 *fazendas* and 9 commercial houses to the *município*, whose population reached 28,638 in 1857. For geographer, Alberto Lamêgo, Vassouras represented an inexplicable association of countryside and city, a 'phenomenon of urban sociability' created by generations of tireless aristocrat farmers who had devoted themselves to the embellishment and transformation of their *vila* into a flourishing urban-rural culture.[85]

Land registers of the town parishes reveal the variety of land-holdings that existed at mid-century. Among the approximately 450 claimants to land in Vassouras in 1854, smallholders shared the registers with capitalists whose contiguous holdings overlapped parish boundaries. Most of the original *sesmaria* grantees were deceased by 1850, but the offspring and heirs of intermarried clans and families like the Correia e Castros, Clemente Pereiras, Avellar e Almeidas, Pereiras, Teixeiras and Wernecks expanded family land-holdings in the centre and peripheries of Vassouras, enhancing their local social, political and economic standing as well as their family prestige in the imperial court. In the central urban parish of Nossa Senhora da Conceição and in the outlying rural parish of Paty do Alferes, long-standing landowners vied with newcomers who were establishing a hold on the coffee economy and the profitable markets in the exchange, sale or appropriation of land and labour.[86] Despite subdivisions among heirs of original *sesmarias* that had increased the total of singly-owned land claimants, the planter elites guarded their claims to family properties. In some cases, original boundaries were altered or expanded by purchase, exchange and inheritance to maintain merchant-planter control over the agrarian structure. Whereas the frontier conditions in Vassouras had initially provoked intense speculation over land and attracted a massive influx of outsiders, the unavailability of public lands in the area and the movement east of the coffee frontier were attracting speculators elsewhere. In the parishes of Vassouras, wealthy merchant-planter families were initiating a process of concentration of local property that, by the end of the 1880s, would find 20 per cent of the landowners in Conceição and Sacra Família owning over 70 per cent of the area of those parishes.[87] In Paty do Alferes, 22 per cent of the plots measuring more than 400 hectares, roughly equivalent to a medium-sized land-holding by Paraíba Valley standards, covered 43,978 hectares or 79 per cent of the legally owned lands. But the vast majority of plots measured less than 400 hectares, yet encompassed only 11,613 hectares or 21 per cent of the claimed land.

Spread over the uneven contours of the Serra do Mar coastal range, the third parish, Sacra Família do Tinguá, was economically less prosperous than the other two, but contained the most concentrated pattern of land-holding due to the Fazenda São Marcos, a 17,500 hectare estate belonging to the Marquess of São João Marcos, Pedro Dias Paes Leme, that covered most of the parish.[88] The single holding represented almost 65 per cent of the plots over 400 hectares, skewing the average holding to more than 2000 hectares. Without the *fazenda*, this average dropped to 822.[89]

The parish land registers also reveal a significant population of free small-scale cultivators whose claims to incorporation in the rural society of Vassouras cannot be ignored (Table 2.8). Freed slaves who operated smallholdings in the area and *quilombos* that were scattered throughout the region were involved in food production, the raising of domestic animals and informal trade relations with itinerant traders and the tavern-keepers of the *vendas* that were located at the peripheries of large estates and along well-travelled trade routes. Coffee production accommodated large and small legal claimants and *de facto* cultivators, aggravating already extant tensions over access to land, purchasers and markets.

Table 2.8 Land distribution in four Vassouras parishes, 1854–6

Size of plots (hectares)	Number of landowners	Percentage of total	Total number of hectares	Percentage of total	Average size of plots (hectares)
		N.S. da Conceição			
Over 400	26	17	33,046	75	1271
Under 400	127	83	10,919	25	86
Total	153	100	43,965	100	287
Incomplete	15	9			
		Paty do Alferes			
Over 400	28	25	43,978	79	1571
Under 400	82	75	11,613	21	142
Total	110	100	55,591	100	505
Incomplete	24	18			
		Sacra Família do Tinguá (with São Marcos)			
Over 400[a]	13	18	27,367	78	2105
Under 400	60	82	7669	22	128
Total	73	100	35,036	100	480
		Sacra Família do Tinguá (less São Marcos)			
Over 400[b]	12	17	9867	56	822
Under 400	60	83	7669	44	128
Total	72	100	17,536	100	244
Incomplete	14	16			
		Mendes			
Over 400	1	2	575	10	575
Under 400	44	94	4978	90	113
Total	45	96	5553	100	123
Incomplete	2	4			
		Totals			
Over 400	68[a]		194,966		1550
	67[b]		87,466		1346
Under 400	313		35,179		112
Total	381[a]		140,145		368
	380[b]		122,645		323

[a] With the Fazenda São Marcos measuring 17,500 hectares.
[b] Less the Fazenda São Marcos. By deducting it and its area, the average area of properties over 400 hectares is reduced to 1346 hectares.
Source: APERJ, Niterói: Registros Paroquiais de Terra, Vassouras, 1854–5, 4 volumes. Adapted from Nancy Priscilla Naro, 'Customary rightholders and legal claimants to land in Rio de Janeiro, Brazil, 1870–1890', *The Americas*, vol. 48, no. 4 (1992), Table 1, p. 494.

Alternative agendas: Rio Bonito

Like Vassouras, the Eastern Paraíba Valley highlands and the lowland area that included the town of Rio Bonito had been sparsely populated in the eighteenth century, traversed by roaming indigenous populations, a scattering of large estates and their slave labour forces and subsistence producers whose modest farms emerged from dense forested surroundings. The land rush occurred later, was less intense and more widespread than its Western Paraíba counterpart. Whereas the displacement of small-scale farmers was in full swing from 1830 to 1850 in Vassouras, this process was just beginning at mid-century in the Eastern Paraíba town of Cantagalo. Ida Pfeiffer noted occasional well-tended sugar and coffee plantations that were surrounded by dense forest, which provided a livelihood for cultivators who were being displaced from their holdings:

> The valleys were generally narrow, and the uniform appearance of the woods was often broken by plantations [plantings]. The latter, however, did not always look very promising, most of them being so choked up with weeds that it was frequently impossible to perceive the plant itself, especially when it was young and small.[90]

Squatters, runaway slaves and passers-through who left cultivated plots in the forest did not threaten the forest cover or its wildlife reserves. The 'not very promising' appearance of the plantings confirmed the ability of the forest to recover from pervasive and short-term clearing, before the firebrands and broad-axes heralded the advance of the coffee frontier.

In the lowland areas to the east and west of Rio de Janeiro the expansion of the coffee economy was less intense than in the Western Paraíba Valley. The Itaboraí parish that was elevated to the *vila* of Nossa Senhora da Conceição do Rio Bonito in 1846, was a modest trading post of twenty businessmen (*negociantes*) with a farming population in the surrounding area of 86 *lavradores* and *fazendeiros*.[91] In contrast to Vassouras, a coveted hinterland pearl in the crown of court society during its golden age, Rio Bonito was a modest market town that handled inter-regional trade between Guanabara Bay and the far-flung agricultural belt of Campos, Macaé, São João da Barra, and Araruama to the east.

From the sparsely populated river hamlet that merited only a dot on the 1767 map, Rio Bonito drew migrants and their slaves from the Guanabara Bay port of Porto das Caixas, from derelict sugar estates of Itaboraí and from Capivary, Maricá and Saquarema. In 1850, the total slave and free populations were more or less equally distributed, with a slightly greater proportion of slaves in the parish of Nossa Senhora da Conceição do Rio Bonito. The proportion of free non-whites was almost double that of Vassouras and was significantly higher than that of the province, making up about one-third of each parish (Table 2.9).

A traveller from the highlands would have noticed immediately that the largest land-holdings did not exceed a modest 2000 to 3000 acres in contrast to the highlands where John Luccock had described estates that measured 10, 20, even 30 miles long by 3 miles wide.[92] Although Rio Bonito boasted few *sesmarias*,

Table 2.9 Population of Rio Bonito, 1850

Parish	Total population	Total non-white*	Free**		Slave		Free non-white	
			No.	%	No.	%	No.	%
N.S. da Conceição do Rio Bonito	15,600	11,947	7244	46.0	8356	54.0	3591	30.0
N.S. da Boa Esperança	7150	4941	3736	52.0	3414	48.0	1527	31.0

* Non-white refers to the total population minus the white population.
** Includes *pardos* and blacks (*pretos*) but not *caboclos*.
Source: Rio de Janeiro, *Relatório do Presidente da Província do Rio de Janeiro*, 1850.

these private bastions of prominent Crown favourites and their descendants provided the main reference points for the municipal boundaries that passed along rivers and mountain ranges, named by indigenous founders, when the parish of Nossa Senhora da Conceição do Rio Bonito was elevated to a *vila*. On 14 May 1849, Article 1 of the local statues stipulated that the *vila*

> begins at the bridge of the Casseribú River, at the fazenda of Captain Bazilio, leading from there along the Tanguá River to the top of the Tinguy mountain range, and from there along the Catimbão road to the fazenda of Captain-Major Marinho; from where, crossing the fields of that fazenda, the line will follow the road that passes the house of Fróes, on the road that leads to Campos . . .[93]

In contrast to Vassouras, where the rapid privatization of public lands was completed by the mid-1840s, public lands in Rio Bonito remained available for purchase into the 1880s. Northwest of the town centre of Nossa Senhora da Conceição, sugarcane cultivation was yielding to mixed production, a feature that was also prevalent further east as an occasional *venda* appeared in a landscape of small-scale family farms where coffee was grown together with foodstuffs. To the south, sugar estates in the prosperous parish of Nossa Senhora da Boa Esperança diversified production into foodstuffs and coffee as farmers registered holdings that extended into the hilly forested areas that a century earlier had been named the Peak of the Quilombo after the slaves who escaped there. From this strategic location in what the map labelled the Serra do Amor e Querer (the Mountain of Love and Desire), runaway slaves could raid local settlements and, reinforced by other escaped slaves from the nearby coastal port of Saquarema, could trade with local traders and the markets that were expanding in the area.[94]

In 1854, the land claims by 409 residents that represented roughly 21,000 hectares of the total area of 560 square kilometres had stretched the municipal boundaries to the peripheral area of Quilombo. Only one-third of the registers

Table 2.10 Land concentration in lowland and highland *municípios*, 1854–6

Município	Size of plots (hectares)	Number of plots	Percentage of total	Occupied area (hectares)	Percentage of total area	Average area (hectares)
			Lowlands Restinga			
Rio	Over 400	6	2.0	7,237	35.0	1206
Bonito	Under 400	276	98.0	13,611	65.0	49
	Total	282	100.0	20,848		
Capivary	Over 400	19	6.4	24,568	57.0	1293
	Under 400	182	60.9	18,330	43.0	100
	Incomplete	98	32.7			
	Total	299	100.0	43,928		
Araruama	Over 400	25	5.0	27,671	50.0	1106
	Under 400	456	93.0	27,328	50.0	59
	Incomplete	8	1.6			
	Total	489	100.0	54,999		
			Highlands Western Paraíba Valley			
Vassouras	Over 400	73	16.0	99,441	72.0	1362
	Under 400	397	84.0	39,482	28.0	99
	Total	470	100.0	138,923		

Sources: For Rio Bonito and Vassouras: APERJ, Niterói Registro Paroquial de Terras, 1854. For Capivary: Hebe Maria Mattos de Castro, *Ao sul da história* (São Paulo: Brasiliense, 1986). For Araruama: Maria Paula Graner, *A estrutura fundiária do município de Araruama: 1850–1920. Um estudo de distribuiçao de terras: continuidades e transformações,* unpublished MA dissertation (Departamento de História, Universidade Federal Fluminense, 1985).

contained complete specifications of the length, width and depth of the claimed land. Sixty-five per cent of the registered plots were less than 400 hectares and, although land ownership was concentrated, the data confirm a larger population of smallholders in Rio Bonito than in the neighbouring lowland towns of Capivary and Araruama where the statistics were 43 and 50 per cent respectively (Table 2.10).[95]

In fact, the agrarian structure of Rio Bonito was similar to the more remote Vassouras parishes of Mendes and Sacra Família do Tinguá. The pattern of land-holdings revealed a society where the Marinhos, Paivas and Bazilios were among a handful of planter elites who held positions of local authority. Local production was held in numerous properties and smallholdings by planters and producers who relied initially on slave labour but increasingly sought alternative arrangements that included seasonal employment, tenancy, sharecropping, property rentals and squatting.

Rio Bonito's coffee economy could not compete with that of Vassouras and most of the highlands. The coffee was low grade in quality and had an unpleasing, even repugnant, taste that was shunned by international buyers and was classified as 'Rio' coffee.[96] Its inferior grade and lower yields may have been related to the sea air, poor lowland soil, humidity and primitive cultivation methods, but quality was also adversely affected by the inferior technology used to process the beans. On the large progressive *fazendas* of the highlands, the drying process was preceded by the mechanical separation of the pulp from the bean and the subsequent washing of the beans, which qualified them for the higher-priced category of 'washed coffee'. On Rio Bonito's and most other lowland estates, there was little or no mechanization of production units. Coffee beans were dried in the sun until hardened and then the pulp removed by pounding with sticks or grinding in stone mills. One foreigner remarked that coffee beans processed in this primitive manner appealed to consumers of 'undiscerning taste' but sold well in local markets.[97]

Despite official exclusion from the export markets, inferior, mainly lowland, coffee was bought by Rio de Janeiro traders and merchant houses. As the disparity between coffee prices and those of sugar and foodcrops increased, farmers shifted production to coffee. In times of lower coffee prices, food and sugar production predominated. Lowland estates were more modest and producers were freer to shift crop priorities than highland planter-merchants, who had borrowed on the following year's harvests to purchase mechanized processing equipment and were held to annual production quotas by their creditors. Rio Bonito producers also had a wider choice of outlets that included the coastal trade, regional markets and the imperial court, an advantage they held over highland planters, who were bound to a specific coffee broker and a pre-established price in the court markets. Rio Bonito contributed only marginally to Brazil's status as the world's greatest coffee producer but played a pivotal role in the foodstuffs supply chain to Rio de Janeiro.[98]

Coffee in abundance: food in short supply

Before the middle of the nineteenth century, there was a tenuous but workable balance between coffee production and foodstuffs supplies in Rio de Janeiro. In the 1850s, however, reports of shortages of basic foodstuffs in Rio Bonito and Vassouras directed official attention to the agricultural sector. Intensive plantation production of coffee was not thriving in Rio Bonito at this time, and there was widespread small-scale cross-cropping of coffee with foodstuffs. Administrators directed their measures towards the regulation of sales of basic foodstuffs to middlemen in the Guanabara Bay trade, whose terms of purchase and large orders were aimed at supplying the bustling markets of Rio de Janeiro.

In Vassouras, the thriving plantations were stifling the growth of local market towns. Officials were quick to point out that the growing disparity between coffee prices and those of other crops, in addition to steady demand for the *rubiacea* bean, were the main reasons for the clearance of forests for new fields and the purchase of more labour by major planters, a practice that was also followed by small and medium producers. Johann Jakob von Tschudi, alarmed at the transfer of land and labour to coffee production in light of his calculation that the slave population was declining annually by 2 per cent, warned that the supplies of rice, corn, beans and manioc, the dietary mainstays (with pork and salted beef) for the free and slave population would be adversely affected:

> When coffee reached a high price quotation in 1852, the *fazendeiros* found it more advantageous to concentrate all efforts there in detriment to other products ... The number of producers of foodstuffs decreased annually whereas the number of consumers increased with the population each year. The results were not long in coming. The dietary mainstays increased in price, and after a few years, the increase reached 100 to 200 per cent. Brazil cultivated a lot of coffee but few foodstuffs.[99]

Intensified coffee production not only affected the supply of foodstuffs to local residents in Vassouras but also heaped more hours onto the work regime of slave field labourers, leaving less free time to devote to provision grounds. The crops from provision grounds provided a source of capital for slaves, who sold excess produce, pigs and chickens to taverns and local markets. In one area where there was a reported increase in the numbers of slave runaways, slave-owners forbade slaves from attending markets in the town. The cause of the increase in runaways is not stated and may have been a clear indication of slave protest against the expansion of coffee production. The prohibition resulted in a near rebellion and a devastating scarcity of local foodstuffs.[100]

The prominent coffee planter, Francisco Peixoto de Lacerda Werneck, Baron of Paty do Alferes, owner of seven fully operating *fazendas* with almost 1000 slaves and extensive holdings of land and rest-stops or inns (*pousos*) along the Estrada do Comércio thoroughfare to the lowlands, advocated crop diversification. His ideal was a self-sustaining estate capable of combining the provision of basic foodstuffs – corn, manioc, beans, fruits, coffee and sugar – with pig, chicken and livestock farming, cotton production and the cultivation of tea.[101] He was not alone. In her memoirs, the daughter of a Portuguese planter in coastal Campos remembered her father's insistence on growing manioc, corn, beans, coffee, rice, squash, potatoes, melons and bananas, despite the fact that this would reduce his sugar yields by hundreds of cases. He held that the welfare of the estate depended on its ability to meet its own food needs, a practice he shared with his slaves who planted new seedlings after each manioc harvest.[102]

The advice contained in Lacerda Werneck's planter manual, however, fell on deaf ears, as priorities for coffee cultivation reduced production of foodstuffs. The Baron blamed poor weather for the meagre harvests of beans and corn on several of his properties but found little solace in purchasing foodstuffs from local producers, whose high prices reflected not only the scarcity and costliness of slave labour but also the greater pressures placed on family labour. Lacerda Werneck paid his coffee factor in Rio de Janeiro what he termed 'exorbitant' transport costs to supply beans from the lowlands, probably from Rio Bonito and other regional suppliers to the court. He then requested further advances to cover the purchase of 25 animals to collect beans from local highland suppliers despite their unusually high price for each sack. The newly acquired animals increased his need for the maize required to feed them, sending him further into arrears with his coffee factor.[103]

The prominent Vassouras merchant, Caetano Furquim de Almeida, publicly addressed the gravity of food shortages in his report to the provincial legislature in 1857:

> Whoever resides in the interior or travels throughout our province can observe that basic food items are expensive and are in short supply everywhere. At times one purchases foodstuffs in small interior villages at prices that exceed those of the huge markets of the Court. Planters face shortages of foodstuffs and are often forced to buy them from the Court since nobody nearby has any to sell.[104]

Measures to rectify the shortages included the construction in 1858 of a local warehouse to stock foodstuffs. In addition, the town council approved a reduction to 5 per cent of a 15 per cent tax on the marketing of salted cod, *peixe pau* (*callianymus lyra*), wheat flour, manioc, maize and salt. Aimed at attracting local and regional suppliers of items of popular consumption, this also benefited interprovincial wheat-flour merchants.[105] The measures proved ineffective and generalized food shortages reached crisis proportions in 1859. The municipal council instituted a Sunday market to distribute manioc flour, beans, corn, vegetables, fruit, sugar, coffee, oil, fowl, eggs and fish. A council edict prohibited the sale of scarce items outside the *município* but, as in Rio Bonito, the edict proved no more successful than earlier efforts to deter local food producers from selling produce at a higher profit to external buyers who supplied the court.[106]

Food prices also soared in the court. Wholesale prices for an *alqueire* (13.5 litres) of beans increased from 2$300 in 1850–1 to 3$980 in 1854–5, and to 4$980 in 1858–9. In the same period prices for an *alqueire* of corn increased from 1$150 to 1$530 between 1850 and 1855, but more than doubled to 3$750 in 1858–9. Highland planters paid even more. Bills from local retail suppliers to Vassouras planters for an *alqueire* of corn ranged from 1$600 in 1850–1 to 2$500 in 1855–6 and in 1860–1 reached an unprecedented 8$000.[107]

In the face of chronic shortages of foodstuffs, officials blamed large estates for concentrating slave labour but it is not clear whether this meant the concentration of slave labour in coffee production or the purchase by large landowners of slaves who had been involved in food production on small-scale farms. Additionally, renewed campaigns against *quilombos* to recover runaway slaves disrupted food production and distribution.

A broader range of factors also contributed to food shortages. First, there was the reduction in African slave labour after the 1850 suspension of the transatlantic slave trade. Second, the expansion of Rio de Janeiro increased the pressure on peripheral and hinterland areas, where precarious overland routes and waterway transportation contributed to increased costs. Local and regional markets raised tariffs on the sale of foodstuffs, credit for small producers was limited, due in part to high interest on loans, and there were monopolies over trade.[108] Middlemen within the province and those engaged in the inter-provincial trade in manioc, maize, and salted beef reputedly manipulated the laws of supply and demand to their own advantages, creating food shortages in Rio de Janeiro. For example, manioc shipments from the southern province of Rio Grande do Sul in 1852 and 1853 forced up prices in Rio markets. These contrasted with the large shipments and low prices of southern maize that supplied the markets between 1853 and 1855. In 1857, the situation was reversed, as high maize prices in the Rio markets reflected shortages that year in the south. Another reason for high prices in the Rio markets in 1852 was related to a decline in supplies of pork, sugar, poultry and brown sugar from the neighbouring province of Minas Gerais, a trend that continued in 1859 and 1860 and coincided with the intensification of coffee production in the southern *zona da mata* of that province.[109]

From wilderness to occupation: *fazendas*, slaves and coffee

In Vassouras and Rio Bonito, the sparsely settled wilderness clusters that were mapped out in 1767 underwent a process of appropriation that, by formal and informal means, took less than a century to complete. For Elizabeth Helsinger, appropriation was 'an idea of order continually working on local disorder, where general structures emerged in an encounter with the messily articular or the unrecognizable wilderness'.[110] Vassouras and Rio Bonito represent different approaches to appropriation of the wilderness but, in both cases, the onset of coffee production was crucial to the eclipse of forested lands and the concentration of African slave labour in production.

In Vassouras, the ordering of the wilderness was initiated rapidly through Crown mediation in the distribution of public lands. Planters were encouraged to re-shape a pristine landscape with rows of bushes that bore ripe red coffee berries, cultivated by intensive slave labour and destined for European and North American buyers.

In 1859, the photographer, Victor Frond, captured a 'virgin forest with its mystery, solemnity, and brilliant colour'. Frond's photograph was a cloudy mass of shapes and images. A century later, in 1949, Stanley Stein photographed the same terrain and noted that the gradual contours and 'slope of the land from the Serra do Mar to the Parahyba River, interrupted by tenuous, elongated basins, and a shallow valley flanked by hills' remained unchanged from the previous century.[111] The forested areas that had figured in Frond's photograph were, however, no longer a part of the landscape. Instead, the terrain comprised fenced-in grassland punctuated by an occasional tree and set against a deforested mountain range that had been transformed by slash-and-burn techniques to create a landscape dominated by coffee. This rural milieu contained coffee producers, holders of extensive *fazendas* and concentrations of slave labour, *quilombos*, squatters, slave provision grounds and semi-subsistence producers. Tensions involving land and labour pervaded all aspects of farming and trade and the formal and informal productions of coffee and foodstuffs.

In Rio Bonito, the process of land appropriation and settlement was gradual. Large numbers of small-scale producers and fugitive cultivators co-existed with a few large landowners in a regional economy that evolved with the settlement of areas inland from Guanabara Bay, the court city of Rio de Janeiro, the provincial capital of Niterói and the eastern coastal areas. Coffee cultivation was pervasive in the regional economy but, despite yearly price and crop fluctuations, did not marginalize food production or the local producers, who were less attuned to international responses than the highland coffee-export *municípios*.

In both towns and their surrounding areas, on large and small estates, coffee production impacted on land and labour, estate layouts, the configuration of the rural landscape and the kin ties of the labour force that shaped it. The organization of the rural estate and the corresponding social uses of space in the great houses, slave quarters, fields and forests formed a post-independence microcosm of rural society. Yet the landscape that it shaped and that shaped it, mediated through the unequal social relations of the conflicting agendas of planters, poor farmers and slaves, etched into Brazilian identity the framework of the free labour market that emerged after 1850. These issues will be considered further in the next chapter.

Notes

1. Enacted in 1375 by King Dom Fernando I, the Lei das Sesmarias aimed at redistributing grants of land that were not effectively occupied or adequately cultivated by their owners. Charles Ralph Boxer, *The Golden Age of Brazil, 1695–1750* (Berkeley: University of California Press, 1962), p. 227.
2. Affonso de Escragnolle Taunay, *Pequena história do café no Brasil (1727–1937)* (Rio de Janeiro: Departamento Nacional do Café, 1945), p. 39; and Inácio Raposo, *História de Vassouras* (Niterói: SEEC, 1978), 2nd edn, p. 25.
3. Louis Couty, *O Brasil em 1884: esboços sociológicos*, (Brasília: Senado Federal, 1984), cited in Eduardo Silva, 'A função ideológica da "Brecha Camponesa"', *Revista da Sociedade Brasileira de Pesquisa Histórica*, Anais da IV Reunião, 1985, p. 192.
4. 'Acordão de 4 de setembro de 1757', in Sílvia Lara, *Campos de violência* (Rio de Janeiro: Paz e Terra, 1986), p. 301.
5. Flávio dos Santos Gomes, 'Quilombos do Rio de Janeiro no século XIX', in João José Réis and Flávio dos Santos Gomes (eds), *Liberdade por um fio: história dos quilombos no Brasil* (São Paulo: Companhia das Letras, 1996). See p. 264 for map of the *quilombos* in the Guanabara Bay area.
6. Stuart B. Schwartz, *Slaves, Peasants and Rebels* (Champagne: University of Illinois, 1992), p. 126.
7. Joseph C. Miller, *Way of Death: Merchant Capitalism and the Angolan Slave Trade, 1730–1830* (Madison: University of Wisconsin, 1988), pp. 28–9, 32.
8. Schwartz, *Slaves*, pp. 126–7; Kátia de Queirós Mattoso, *Ser escravo no Brasil* (São Paulo: Brasiliense, 1988), Ch. 4; Robert Nelson Anderson, 'The *quilombo* of Palmares: a new overview of a maroon state in seventeenth century Brazil', *Journal of Latin American Studies*, vol. 28, no. 3 (1996), pp. 545–66.
9. Robert E. Conrad, *The Destruction of Brazilian Slavery, 1850–1888* (Berkeley: University of California Press, 1972), Table 1, p. 283.
10. Mary C. Karasch, *Slave Life in Rio de Janeiro, 1808–1850* (Princeton: Princeton University Press, 1987), Table 10.4, pp. 309, 314, 315. On *quilombolas*, see Cândido de Figueiredo, *Novo dicionário da língua portuguesa*, 4th edn (Lisbon: Sociedade Editora Arthur Brandão e Cia. [1925]).

11. Karasch, *Slave Life*, Table 10.4, pp. 309, 314, 315.

12. *Ibid.*, p. 311; dos Santos Gomes, 'Quilombos do Rio de Janeiro', pp. 263–90.

13. I have used 'informal slave economy' instead of 'internal economy' or 'peasant breach' to distinguish slave activities in production and marketing from the domestic or internal markets. See Betty Woods, *Women's Work, Men's Work: The Informal Slave Economies of Lowcountry Georgia* (Athens: University of Georgia Press, 1995).

14. Alfredo Moreira Pinto, *Dicionário geográfico do Brasil* (Rio de Janeiro: Imprensa Nacional, 1899); *Enciclopédia dos municípios*, Sinopse Estatística do Município do Rio Bonito (Instituto Brasileiro de Geografia e Estatística, 1948).

15. BNRJ, *Carta topográfica da capitania do Rio de Janeiro. Feita por ordem do Côde de Cunha, Capitão General e Vice Rey do Estado do Brazil, por Manoel Vieyra Leão, Sargento Mor e Governador do Castelo de São Sebastião da Cidade do Rio de Janeiro em o anno de 1767*.

16. The Restinga is the micro-region that extends from São Gonçalo outside of Niterói east to Macaé in the state of Rio de Janeiro.

17. Food-crop and sugar production also preceded coffee cultivation in Rio Claro, São Paulo. See Warren Dean, *Rio Claro: Um sistema brasileiro de grande lavoura, 1820–1920* (Rio de Janeiro: Paz e Terra, 1977).

18. Alberto Ribeiro Lamêgo, *O homem e a serra* (Rio de Janeiro: Serviço Gráfico do Instituto Brasileiro de Geografia e Estatística, 1930), p. 107.

19. Von Spix and von Martius claimed that Indians were generally known as *coroados* due to a crown of hair about the temples on otherwise shaven heads. See J.B. von Spix and C.F.P. von Martius, *Reise in Brasilien auf Befehl Sr Majestät Maximilian Joseph I* (Rio de Janeiro: Imprensa Nacional [1823], 1938), p. 183.

20. *Almanak administrativo, mercantil e industrial da corte e província do Rio de Janeiro (Almanak Laemmert)*, 1855, Município de Vassouras, pp. 135–41.

21. On slave visions of freedom, see Sidney Chalhoub, *Visões de liberdade: uma história das últimas décadas da escravidão na corte* (São Paulo: Companhia das Letras, 1990); and Hebe Maria Mattos de Castro, *Das côres do silêncio: Os significados da liberdade no sudeste escravista, Brasil, século XIX* (Rio de Janeiro: Arquivo Nacional, 1995).

22. Carlos Augusto Taunay, *Manual do agricultor brasileiro. Obra indispensável a todo o senhor de engenho, fazendeiro e lavrador, por apresentar huma idéa geral e philosophica da agricultura aplicada ao Brasil, e ao seu especial modo de producção, bem como noções exactas sôbre todos os gêneros de cultura em uso, ou cuja adopção fôr proficua, e tambem hum resumo de horticultura, seguido de hum epitome dos principios de botanica e hum tratado das principaes doenças que atacão os pretos* (Rio de Janeiro: Typographia Imperial, 1839), p. 34.

23. Benjamin Moseley, MD, *A Treatise Concerning the Properties and Effects of Coffee* (London: J. Sewell, 1792), p. 3.

24. *Ibid.*, p. 31, on Charles II's proclamation of December 1675, which closed the coffee-houses. James Walvin has used the colourful London coffee-houses of the eighteenth century as the background for his study of chattel slavery on the coffee and sugar plantations of the Americas. See *Black Ivory: A History of British Slavery* (Fontana Press: 1993), Ch. 1, pp. 3–5.

25. Under the leadership of Bach, the Collegium Musicum met each Friday at the coffee-house of Gottfried Zimmermann, where the cantata was probably first performed in the autumn of 1734 after publication in 1732 as 'Über den Caffe'.

26. Moseley, *A Treatise*, pp. 4–7.

27. *Ibid.*, p. 42.

28. *Ibid.*, pp. 9, 43–5, 57.

29. Warren Dean, *With Broadax and Firebrand* (Berkeley: University of California Press, 1995), p. 179.

30. Moseley. *A Treatise*, p. 34; Taunay, *Pequena história*, p. 24.

31. Nicolau J. Moreira, MD, *Brazilian Coffee* (New York: 'O Novo Mundo' Printing Office, 1876), p. 5. Moreira was a member of the Brazilian Commission to the Philadelphia World Exhibition; Taunay, *Pequena história*, p. 25.

32. See Dauril Alden, *Royal Government in Brazil* (Berkeley: University of California Press, 1968); A.J.R. Russell-Wood, *A World on the Move: The Portuguese in Africa, Asia and America*,

1415–1808 (New York: St Martin's Press, 1992), p. 161. For the identification of two trees in the convent of Ajuda in 1774, see Moreira, *Brazilian Coffee*, p. 5; Francis B. Thurber, *Coffee from Plantation to Cup* (American Grocer Publishing Association, 1881), p. 124; Dean, *Broadax*, p. 179.

33. On the Conde de Bobadella, see James Henderson, *A History of the Brazil; Comprising Its Geography, Commerce, Colonization, Aboriginal Inhabitants, etc.* (London: Longman, Hurst, Rees, Orme and Brown, 1821), p. 44. Steven Topik has provided me with information on the Portuguese preference for tea and hot chocolate.

34. Francisco Freire Alemão, *Revista do Instituto Histórico Geográfico Brasileiro*, vol. 19 (1856), pp. 569–71.

35. The padre was Antonio do Couto Fonseca, whose *fazenda* was in the Campo Grande area. See Stanley Stein, *Vassouras: A Brazilian Coffee County, 1850–1900* (Princeton: Princeton University Press [1957], 1985), p. 4, fn. 3.

36. Jean Baptiste Debret, *Viagem pitoresca e histórica ao Brasil* (São Paulo: 1954).

37. Gilberto Ferrez, *Pioneiros da cultura do café na era da independência* (Rio de Janeiro: Instituto Histórico Geográfico Brasileiro, 1972), p. 16.

38. Dean, *Broadax*, p. 207.

39. Leslie Bethell (ed.), *Brazil: Empire and Republic, 1822–1930* (Cambridge: Cambridge University Press, 1989), Table 1, 'Major exports of Brazil (by decade)', p. 115.

40. Stein, *Vassouras*, p. 52.

41. *Ibid*. For New York quotations, see Joseph E. Sweigart, 'Financing and Marketing Brazilian Export Agriculture. The Coffee Factors of Rio de Janeiro, 1850–1888', unpublished PhD dissertation, Department of History, University of Texas, 1980, Table E.2, 'Indicators of the Rio coffee economy, 1850–1888', p. 302.

42. *Ibid*.

43. 'Posturas da Câmara Municipal de Vassouras', in Francisco Peixoto de Lacerda Werneck, *Memória sobre a fundação de uma fazenda na província do Rio de Janeiro* (Brasília: Senado Federal/ Fundação Casa de Rui Barbosa [1847], 1985); Silva, *Barões e escravidão: três gerações de fazendeiros e a crise da estrutura escravista* (Rio de Janeiro: Nova Fronteira, 1984), pp. 161–7; *Falas do trono*, 1857–1862, for references to high costs of food and the suffering caused to poor people.

44. Johann Jakob von Tschudi, *Viagem às províncias do Rio de Janeiro e São Paulo* (São Paulo: Editora Martins [1862], 1976), p. 49.

45. Charles de Ribeyrolles, *Brasil pitoresco* (São Paulo: Ed. Itatiaia, EDUSP, (Coleção Reconquista do Brasil), vol. 1, no. 29 (1980), pp. 229–30.

46. Von Spix and von Martius, *Reise in Brasilien*, p. 183. According to Alida Metcalf, peasant families in San'tanna de Paraíba, São Paulo, emerged slowly in the seventeenth century from an intermediate group between masters and slaves that included free Indians and poor *mamelucos*, often the 'bastard' children of men of established families. The indigenous population was classified as *pardo*, an indication that the Indians there had become part of the local peasant class. Alida Metcalf, *Family and Frontier in Colonial Brazil* (Berkeley: University of California Press, 1992), pp. 69–70, 83. Basing her later findings on the 1775 São Paulo census, Metcalf identifies nuclear peasant squatter families who, she claims, produced primarily for household consumption but sold excess produce locally. See pp. 82, 132.

47. Mary Karasch, personal communication, 2 May 1999.

48. Ida Pfeiffer, *A Woman's Journey around the World* (London: Office of the National Illustrated Library, 1850), p. 47.

49. No single study of slavery has mapped out over time the location of Brazil's slaves. For colonial Rio de Janeiro city, see Karasch, *Slave Life*, Ch. 1; Manolo G. Florentino, *Em costas negras: um estudo sobre o tráfico atlântico de escravos para o porto do Rio de Janeiro, c. 1790–1830* (Rio de Janeiro: Arquivo Nacional), 1995; Alcir Lenharo, *As tropas da moderação: o abastecimento da Corte na formação política do Brasil, 1808–1842* (São Paulo: Símbolo, 1979), p. 25; João Luís Ribeiro Fragoso, 'A reafirmação do escravismo no Centro-Sul e sua posterior superação', in *História Geral do Brasil* (Rio de Janeiro: Editora Campos, 1996), Part 5, pp. 148–68.

50. Postmortem inventories from the *município* of Vassouras from the 1837–40 period show 81 per cent male slaves and 19 per cent African female slaves. Numbers of Brazilian-born offspring of African slaves (listed as *crioulos*) were low but the ratios of males to females were more balanced: 52 per cent male and 48 per cent female. Flávio dos Santos Gomes, *Histórias de quilombolas: mocambos e comunidades de senzalas no Rio de Janeiro – século XIX* (Rio de Janeiro: Arquivo Nacional, 1993), Chart 2, p. 205.

51. Henderson, *A History of the Brazil*, p. 104.

52. *Ibid.*, p. 45. See also J. B. von Spix and C.F.P. Martius, *Reise in Brasilien auf Befehl Sr Majestät Maximilian Joseph I* (Rio de Janeiro: Imprensa Nacional [1823], 1938), pp. 144–5. John Luccock, *Notas sôbre o Rio de Janeiro e partes meridionais do Brasil* (São Paulo: Editora da Universidade de São Paulo, 1975), pp. 268–83, for travels through Santa Cruz, Mangaratiba, Paratí and Angra dos Réis.

53. Karasch, *Slave Life*, Table 10.4, p. 309, lists two *quilombos* in Paratí and one in Mangaratiba in 1826.

54. According to von Tschudi, the value of rural estates in 1851 doubled due to increases in coffee and slaves, *Viagem*, p. 55.

55. See Paulo Bonavides and Roberto Amaral, *Textos políticos de história do Brasil* (Brasília: Senado Federal, 1996), vol. 2, pp. 170–1.

56. Stein, *Vassouras*, Table 1, 'Slave imports into Brazil, 1840–1851', p. 25. See Conrad, *The Destruction of Brazilian Slavery*; Leslie Bethell, *The Abolition of the Brazilian Slave Trade* (Cambridge: Cambridge University Press, 1970).

57. Bethell (ed.), *Brazil: Empire and Republic*, p. 113.

58. Bethell, *Abolition of the Brazilian Slave Trade*, p. 376.

59. Stein, *Vassouras*, Table 5, 'Estimated slave imports into the province of Rio from other provinces, 1852–1859', p. 65.

60. For *quilombolas*, see Karasch, *Slave Life*, Table 10.4, p. 309.

61. In 1852, Alexandre Joaquim de Siqueira's *Memória histórica do município de Vassouras* (Rio de Janeiro) described the agricultural lands as less numerous and important than those of the other *freguesias* (parishes) into which Vassouras was divided.

62. Manuel Moreno Fraginals (ed.), *Africa in America* (New York: Holmes and Meier, 1984), p. 19.

63. Barickman's *A Bahian Counterpoint* also highlights this point.

64. Stein, *Vassouras*, pp. 10–12.

65. See the description by Monsenhor Pizarro e Araújo, in Raposo, *História de Vassouras*, p. 21.

66. Lamêgo, *O homem e a serra*, p. 108.

67. Luccock, *Notas*, p. 194.

68. *Ibid.* Nancy Priscilla Naro, 'Customary rightholders and legal claimants to land in Rio de Janeiro, Brazil, 1870–1890', *The Americas*, vol. 48, no. 4 (1992), pp. 485–517.

69. John Luccock, 'Notes on Rio de Janeiro and the southern parts of Brazil taken during a residence of ten years in that country from 1808 to 1818', in *The Port Folio*, vol. 12 (July–December 1821), pp. 321–2.

70. Luccock, *Notas*, p. 194.

71. See the comparable description of *lavradores* on the Pernambucan sugar estates by Louis de Tollenare, 'Notas dominicaes', in Robert E. Conrad, *Children of God's Fire* (Princeton: Princeton University Press, 1983), p. 66.

72. Auguste de Saint-Hilaire, *Viagem pelas províncias do Rio de Janeiro, Minas Gerais e São Paulo* (São Paulo: Editora da Universidade de São Paulo, 1975), p. 43.

73. Luccock, 'Notes', pp. 317–18.

74. Luccock, 'Viagens pelo ocidente do Rio de Janeiro', in *Notas*, p. 194.

75. Hebe Maria Mattos de Castro, *Ao sul da história* (São Paulo: Brasiliense, 1987); Naro, 'Customary rightholders'.

76. Law 601 was put into effect by Regulation 1318 on 30 January 1854, *Lei de Terras (disposição sôbre as terras devolutas e as adquiridas por posse ou sesmaria*, in *Império*, vol. 2, Segundo Reinado, pp. 172–6.

77. *Ibid.*, Article 6.

> Não se haverá por princípio de cultura para a revalidação das sesmarias ou outras concessões do Governo, nem para a legitimação de qualquer posse, os simples roçados, deribadas ou queimas de matos ou campos, levantamentos de ranchos ou outros atos de semelhante natureza, não sendo acompanhados da cultura efetiva e morada habitual exigidas no artigo antecedente.

78. In 1854, the Repartição de Terras Públicas was established and empowered parish priests to register lands after local civil servants had located and measured the claims. Police and judges were responsible for informing the government of the existence and location of public lands. See José Murilo de Carvalho, *Teatro das sombras: a política imperial* (Rio de Janeiro: IUPERJ/Vértice, 1988). For discussions of the Land Law, see: Warren Dean, 'Latifundia and land policy in nineteenth-century Brazil', *Hispanic American Historical Review*, no. 51 (1971), pp. 606–25; Jacob Gorender, *O escravismo colonial* (São Paulo: Atica, 1985), pp. 396–402. For Emília Viotti da Costa, the intent of the law may have been to motivate occupation and cultivation of land but the condition of purchase limited access to moneyed interests. See *The Brazilian Empire: Myths and Histories* (Chicago: University of Chicago, 1985), Ch. 4. Mattos de Castro's discussion of the Land Law, with reference to the province of Rio de Janeiro, supports Viotti da Costa. See *Ao sul*.

79. Warren Dean has outlined the flawed attempt of Senator Vergueiro to introduce European immigrants into São Paulo as one example of unsuccessful colonization attempts. See Dean, *Rio Claro*, Ch. 4, pp. 95–115.

80. Cartório Público do Primeiro Ofício do Rio Bonito (hereafter CPORB), Postmortem Inventory: Joanna Maria de Jesus, 1865.

81. *Ibid.*, Alexandre Pereira dos Santos, 1855.

82. *Almanak Laemmert*, Vassouras and Rio Bonito, 1865 and 1885.

83. Raposo, *História de Vassouras*, p. 39. A similar phenomenon occurred in the immediate post-Civil War years in the southern United States, when increased cotton production adversely affected corn production and pig-farming. See Gavin Wright, *Old South, New South* (Baton Rouge: Louisiana State University, 1996), pp. 34–6.

84. Raposo, *História de Vassouras*, Introduction and Ch. 1.

85. Lamêgo, *O homem e a serra*, p. 107.

86. Failure to comply with the 1854 law to register lands in this period is demonstrated by the presence of only 438 deeds for the entire town of Vassouras in the four volumes of Parochial Land Registers for the 1850s. See Arquivo Público do Estado do Rio de Janeiro (hereafter APERJ): Niterói, RJ, *Registro Paroquial de Terras*, Vassouras, 1854–6.

87. Stein, *Vassouras*, p. 225.

88. APERJ Registro Paroquial de Terras, Vassouras.

89. See discussion of land distribution in Naro, 'Customary rightholders', pp. 494–501.

90. Ida Pfeiffer viewed the abandoned corn and manioc patches she encountered along the road from Nova Friburgo to the Paraíba River as plantings by propertyless cultivators. See Pfeiffer, *A Woman's Journey*, p. 40.

91. *Almanak Laemmert*, 1851.

92. Luccock, *Notas*, pp. 195 and 197.

93. Deziderio Jr Municipio de Rio Bonito. Deliberação, 14 May 1849, Article 1, *Legislação sôbre os municípios* (Rio de Janeiro, 1926), p. 354.

94. For a description of *quilombos* and the reference to four in Rio Bonito, see Karasch, *Slave Life*, pp. 311–15, and Table 10.4, p. 309; Gomes, 'Quilombos', pp. 263–90.

95. Average sizes of small and large holdings in the lowlands *município* of Capivary were, for example, similar to those in highlands Vassouras, despite the much greater area of occupied land in the latter.

96. Von Tschudi, *Viagem às províncias*, p. 42.

97. *Ibid.*: 'Mas o pequeno plantador que dispõe de poucos braços e meios reduzidos, usa ainda os processos mais primitivos, encontando mesmo assim bastante compradores no mercado.'

98. On food production in colonial Rio de Janeiro, see Larissa V. Brown, 'Internal commerce in a colonial economy', unpublished PhD dissertation, Department of History, University of Virginia, 1986.

99. Von Tschudi, *Viagem às províncias*, pp. 48–9.

100. Martha Abreu, 'O caso do Bracuhy', in Hebe Maria Mattos de Castro and Eduardo Schnoor (eds), *Resgate: uma janela para o oitocentos* (Rio de Janeiro: Topbooks, 1995), p. 186.

101. Lacerda Werneck, *Memória sôbre a fundação de uma fazenda*, p. 17, 63–75.

102. Maria Eugênia Torres Ribeiro de Castro (1862–1916), *Reminiscências* (Rio de Janeiro: Editora Cátedra, 1893 [1979]), p. 27. Maria Eugênia's recollections of the Fazenda Cachoeira on the banks of the Muriaé River were probably written in the 1840s.

103. Eduardo Silva, Introduction in Lacerda Werneck, *Memória sôbre a fundação de uma fazenda*, p. 39.

104. *Relatório apresentado à Assembléia Legislativa da Província do Rio de Janeiro, na 2a sessão da 11a Legislatura*, 1857, by vice-presidente João Manoel Pereira da Silva, Annexe K, p. 4, in Afonso de Alencastro Graça Filho, 'Os convênios da carestia: crises, organização e investimentos do comércio de subsistência da Corte (1850–1880)', unpublished MA, Departamento de História, Universidade Federal do Rio de Janeiro, 1991, p. 75.

105. Decree 2248 of 13 December 1858, in *Falas do trono* (Brasília: Câmara dos Deputados/INL, 1977), in Alencastro, *Os convênios da carestia*, p. 58.

106. This tendency was identified by Francisco Carlos Teixeira da Silva, who argued that colonial Bahian officials aimed to prevent producers and vendors from dealing outside the *município* to ensure that adequate supplies of food reached the local slave and free populations, who were perceived as the most likely to protest. The measures were unsuccessful in preventing local producers from responding to the liberal market conditions. See 'Morfologia da escassez: crises de subsistência e política econômica no Brasil colonial: Salvador e Rio de Janeiro, (1680–1790)', unpublished PhD dissertation, Departamento de História, Universidade Federal Fluminense, 1990.

107. Stein, *Vassouras*, Table 2, 'Rio wholesale prices, 1850–1859', and Table 3, 'Vassouras retail prices, 1850–1861', p. 49.

108. Alencastro, *Os convênios da carestia*, pp. 70–1.

109. *Ibid.*, p. 97.

110. Elisabeth K. Helsinger, *Rural Scenes and National Representation: Britain, 1815–1850* (Princeton: Princeton University Press, 1997), p. 24.

111. Stein, *Vassouras*, centrepiece photographs.

3

Fazenda Spaces and Social Relations: The Great House, Slave Quarters, Fields and *Sítios*

Coffee *fazendas*

The rural society that developed with the coffee economy in nineteenth-century Brazil was fully operative within half a century, in contrast to the landed planter class, peasant component and slave societies that developed over centuries in the sugar economies of Brazil and the Caribbean. The coffee economy shifted the economic axis of production from the northeast to the southeast, where coffee became Brazil's post-independence economic mainstay. Coffee projected on the hinterland a post-independence plantation ideal that was associated in the southeast with the ordering of the landscape around carefully tended rows of coffee bushes. Branches of coffee framed one side of the imperial seal of the newly established patria, attesting to the interdependence between the plantation complex and the newly formed state, whose links to the world economy bypassed Portugal despite the fact that both states were headed by members of the Portuguese Bragança ruling dynasty.

The organization of the coffee *fazenda* reflected the unequal social relations of a traditional plantation system: rooted in land, and backed by considerable absorption of capital and intensive low-cost, non-wage slave labour, they were under the control of a leisured and in some cases entitled planter class.[1] Whereas the crushing, boiling, distilling and transformation of cane crystals centred sugar-estate activities around the *engenho*, the *fazenda* referred to the entire production unit. Initially employed with reference to cattle ranches, the term became associated in the nineteenth century with slave labour, the coffee economy and the rural estates that spread throughout the hinterlands from the onset of intensive coffee production in the Rio de Janeiro and São Paulo highland areas of the Paraíba Valley.

For the planters, merchants and middlemen who profited from the international prominence of local coffee, the *fazenda* held symbolic importance as the catalyst for the social, political and economic fortune that it brought to the regional economy. On the walls of his dining hall in the urban palatial mansion he built in the 1850s in Rio de Janeiro, now the Catete Palace, a prominent Portuguese merchant-planter commissioned tranquil rural scenes of his extensive land-holdings and coffee-producing fields in Cantagalo.[2] The cultivated landscape, a fitting tribute to the prosperity that he derived from effective occupation of the land, confirmed the rural origins of wealth that Brazil's titled elites enjoyed during the second half of the century. Missing from the walls were the scenes of horror that life under slavery entailed.

Organizing the landscape: *fazenda* layouts

Early *fazendas* were utilitarian in layout and purpose, and resembled the sugar *engenho* that preceded them on Brazil's rural landscape. In a cleared woodland, a one- or two-storey cabin was erected near a source of water with a grazing area and an area for planting crops. Some of the basic units changed little over time and bore a resemblance to the simple cabins erected by squatters and small-scale producers of foodstuffs; others developed into complex and diversified estates. A planter's manual, written in the 1840s by the prominent highlands planter, Francisco Peixoto de Lacerda Werneck, Baron of Paty do Alferes, emphasized the significance of site selection to the layout and development of an ideal estate. Of fundamental importance was proximity to water, even if this required deeper excavation and the construction of hillside retaining walls.[3] The designation of the surrounding lands for buildings, planting and woodland followed, but only after careful scrutiny of the surroundings. Lacerda Werneck advised his son to examine the leaves, branch shapes and the height of specific types of trees in the forest, because they would attest to the potential fertility of the soil. Resources vital to the long-term wellbeing of the estate included lumber, fuel and soil nutrients, not to mention the diverse flora, fauna and wild birds to be found in the forest.[4] He emphasized the importance of the forest and the range of superior hardwoods it could supply, such as *jacarandatã, guarabu, guarapoca* and cedar, to the inferior *ipê* and *muricipau canudo,* since these provided the best indicators of soil fertility and appropriate land usage.[5]

Lacerda Werneck did not share the widespread belief that coffee had to be planted in soil overlain by 'virgin forest', and lamented that too many planters randomly burned down the forests or left wood from cut trees to rot.[6] According to the late historian, Warren Dean, the colonization of areas such as Rio Claro, São Paulo, was preceded by a continual burning of the forests to open clearings for planting. Semi-nomadic in their ways, occupants of the forests dwelt in a precariously built thatched shelter with a dirt floor, a storage place for corn and a mill that served their needs for five or six years until they abandoned the locale and left the forest to regenerate.[7] The practice of a few became the established custom of the rest, and successive generations of colonizers subjected pristine forests to widespread devastation. Dean calculated that if 700 kilograms of coffee represented the average yield per hectare, and if the average grove was productive for a period of twenty years, some 7200 square kilometres of primary forest would have been cleared between 1780 and 1880, an area equal to 18 per cent of the territory of the province of Rio de Janeiro.[8]

By the early 1840s this process was well under way, as *fazendas* of various sizes and complexity dotted the hinterland landscape, attesting to the pre-eminence assumed by the rural estate in the advancement of post-independence Brazil. Lacerda Werneck viewed the *fazenda* as both a private family institution and a commercial enterprise, linked through his ideal model to the development of the interior and the progress of rural society. For the French traveller, Charles Ribeyrolles, the *fazenda* comprised a main dwelling for the owner, slave quarters, cultivated fields and forests.[9] Most *fazendas* included these features, but their layouts varied widely according to the socio-economic disparities of the planters who owned or ran them. Whereas holdings of modest semi-subsistence plots under 40 hectares comprising a one or two-storey cabin that housed a farmer, his family and slaves, along with a handful of barnyard animals, would not be considered in the category of a *fazenda*, estates like the imperial Fazenda de Santa Cruz that belonged to the royal family and held 1500 slaves would qualify.[10] The highland *fazenda* owned by Antonio Clemente Pinto in Cantagalo was part of his fortune (equivalent to US$3.5 million) and included fourteen coffee *fazendas*, a factorage firm and several town houses. Brazil's largest slaveholder José de Souza Breves, who lived in Barra do Piraí, held upwards of 2000 slaves, who were distributed over production units that covered thousands of hectares.[11]

As in the American South, prominent landowners employed one or two estates as showcases, with a spacious great house that overlooked accommodation for administrators and managers, an infirmary and an apothecary. In addition to stables, storerooms, sheds for brick-making, carpentry and masonry, the layout included vast reservoirs that supplied mills, oil presses and processing units for sugar, coffee, maize and manioc. Other production and processing units incorporated transportation facilities for the supply of staples, foodstuffs, cattle and fruit to domestic markets and to the ports for export in the Atlantic trade.

Hierarchical social relations: the great house

The great house was the residence of the landowner, usually the only other white resident besides the overseer who actively supervised the development of the estate and organized the activities of free labourers and domestic and field slaves.[12] During the initial phase of forest clearance and *fazenda* layout, planters resided on their lands and invested capital in the purchase of slave labour for the development of the physical plant – the works, the reservoir and the field – and the seedlings and cuttings that would make the unit a going concern.[13] The owners did not enjoy a luxurious lifestyle and frequently lived with their slaves under one roof in modest, and often precarious, living conditions. A compatriot of the French naturalist, Auguste de Saint-Hilaire, claimed:

> The [money is not spent] constructing solid houses and
> furnishing them. The *fazendeiros* eat rice and beans. Little is
> spent on clothes, and nothing on the education of children who

grow dull with ignorance. Sociability is foreign to them. Coffee brings in their money but coffee cannot be cultivated without slaves. All profits go to purchases of slaves that satisfy their vanity rather than enhance their comfort.[14]

As the physical plan was expanded, slaves were added, and construction would begin on the great house. Acting as the hub of the rural estate, the great house was usually situated in the contours of the hillside or on the crest of a slope, enabling the owner to have a commanding view of his fields and labourers in the surrounding countryside; both the building and the decoration were linked to comfort.

Foremen, administrators and slaves were housed in separate dwellings, forming a transitional space between the domestic sphere of the great house and the 'works'. Stables, processing units, pens for livestock and sources of water extended to cultivated and fallow fields, edged by forested reserves at the extreme of the property.[15]

Into the basic estate layout, Lacerda Werneck introduced a refined and progressive concept of the *fazenda* that was in keeping with its standing as the hub of social life and its function as a commercial undertaking whose every facet of production and marketing provided for the material wellbeing of elite planters, merchants, politicians and liberal professionals. The Lacerda Werneck model represented an ideal of self-sufficiency and was characterized by the following features, most of which were adopted in one form or another in the main houses of the highlands where intensive coffee production was under way. The layout incorporated a great swathe of land at one side of the great house that was divided into three parts. Closest to the great house was an orchard, designed to 'unite the useful with the pleasureable', where herbs, plants and trees were identified for medicinal and edible purposes. The model did not feature the systematic cultivation of ornamental plants for decoration and sale that was an important feature of the great houses of the British Caribbean and American South, which were characterized by geometrically landscaped fruit groves and gardens, modest adaptations of the vast landscaped English and French rural estates. This omission may have been due to the summer heat, inappropriate terrain and the abundance of wild plants, but was probably more indicative of the practical purpose associated with the production unit. With few exceptions, features of aristocratic English-style pleasure gardens, such as axial layouts, grassed and wooded areas traversed by grid patterns, follies, deer parks and gravel walks were not compatible with the utilitarian aims of most rural coffee estates.

Next to the orchard was a vegetable garden stocked with 'sufficient greenery for domestic use', and closely resembling a kitchen garden on an English estate. At its furthest extremes was a pasture. The opposite side of the house was set aside for the 'works', slave quarters, outbuildings and beyond them the 'plantations' or fields and the forests.[16]

Figure 3 Early great house. Private collection of Maria Isabel Perini Muniz.

Eclectic influences

Great-house architecture was a confluence of Iberian, African and Asian concepts that linked those being served to their servants. Expanse, location and refinement were influenced by available capital, the local topography, climate and building materials.[17] Great houses mixed tradition and innovation, expressions of the different cultural associations of patria that found their way from Portugal, Africa and Brazil to the hinterlands of Rio de Janeiro. Many were constructed in the colonial styles that graced Brazilian and African port cities and their hinterlands, resembling the fortress-like Portuguese monasteries, convents and the estates of royalty and nobility that embellished the hills of Sintra, the plains of the Alentejo, the rolling hills to the north of Portugal and the mouths of tributaries in Angola (see Figure 3). Cooled by 2- to 3-foot-thick walls, wooden shuttered windows, or jalousies, and covered verandas that protected dwellers from the intensity of the sun, some had external lateral staircases that were reminiscent of the styles of great houses in Luanda, the colonial sugar estates of the Northeast, and the eastern lowlands of Rio de Janeiro.[18] The unequal social relations that had characterized Portuguese involvement in slave societies since the sixteenth century remained largely unchanged.

Although masters and slaves shared living quarters on early estates, they were socially separated. Settlers moving into the highlands of Rio de Janeiro from Minas Gerais introduced the one-storeyed *fazendola*, a functional structure with a staircase leading from the sheltered ground-level area, which housed the slaves and domestic animals and contained storage areas for produce and machinery, to a separate first-floor common room with peripheral alcoves for the owner and his family.[19] Other slave quarters were constructed around the coffee terrace and figured in a variety of forms in hinterland architecture. Described in the 1860s as 'a singular-looking establishment, low-slung long buildings and very spreading', the largest of them covered quite an extensive area and enclosed an oblong open space or spaces where the coffee was dried.[20]

Neoclassic design, introduced to the court in 1816 by the French architect, Auguste Henri Victor Grandjean de Montigny and members of the French Mission, added formal grandeur that was reminiscent of classical Greek architecture in its simplicity and rational spatial proportions.[21] The Brazilian variant came to be known as the imperial style of Brazilian architecture and was best represented in the *casarão*, a one or two-storeyed courtly mansion that, according to one study, fused the austere eighteenth-century *sobrado* with neoclassic design.[22] Practicality was juxtaposed with a Europeanized order, mediated by the court society of Rio de Janeiro, and was eventually adapted to rural society.[23]

Merchant-planters and prosperous *fazendeiros*, whose wealth from the coffee trade was enhanced by Crown recognition in the form of baronies and other titles of nobility, introduced the imperial style to the interiors of refurbished rural estates around mid-century. The hilly topography favoured houses that were built on two levels. Hidden from the main thoroughfares and accessible by meandering palm-lined *alamedas* (avenues) leading to the grounds and reservoir, the scene resembled a tropical adaptation of Capability Brown's layouts for prominent English country houses. Service roads for ox-carts, mule trains and the movements of *fazenda* slaves and servants led into the estate through separate entrances and branched off to the work areas and the fields.

The *casarão* designs that found favour with rural elites were of three basic forms: L-shaped, U-shaped or quadrilateral buildings with an internal patio that was based on eighteenth-century urban house design.[24] The stark exteriors of colonial houses gained a new façade, verandas, stylized doors, shutters, sashed windows and wrought-iron balconies on the upper storeys. Red, blue and green panes of glass alternated with transparent window-panes, decorative points were added to the edges of sloping roofs, and pastel exteriors diminished the austerity and enhanced the elegance of the rural structures (see Figures 4 and 5). The embellishments reflected a second phase of *fazenda* design that highlighted comfort and wellbeing, the achievements of prominent second-generation land-owners who had inherited the fruits of their forebears' frontier lifestyles and were profiting from the social prestige associated with the life of a prosperous coffee 'baron' during the second half of the century.

In contrast, postmortem inventories taken at five-year intervals from 1845 to 1890 in Rio Bonito confirm that even the wealthiest inhabitants, like Bernardo José de Moraes, owner of 147 slaves, who died in 1860, lived modestly on their lands where they grew sugarcane, cotton and foodstuffs.[25] Most had rudimentary or water-operated *monjolos*, or sugarcane and manioc processing mills, but apart from a few richly furnished two-storey houses, most of the town's residents lived in functional structures devoid of the imperial palms that identified nobility status to the owners.[26]

Figure 4 Former residence of the Barão of Tinguá in Vassouras, Rio de Janeiro, Brazil. Private collection of the author.

Figure 5 Entrance and façade of the front of the great house of the Fazenda Boa Sorte, Vassouras, Rio de Janeiro, Brazil. Private collection of the author.

The spatial dimensions of social complementarity

Past and present were juxtaposed in the interiors of the great houses. John Lukacs has stated that 'the furniture of great houses reflected the interior furniture of minds'; in nineteenth-century Brazil the interior décor and the spatial arrangements reflected not one, but multiple minds that accommodated tradition with innovation and formality with casual informality.[27] Great-house interiors were an eclectic blend of a rustic utilitarian décor, which harked back to the traditional open one-room living spaces that had doubled for social and sleeping room, and a formal and ordered showcase, where rooms were designed for specific purposes and were linked by long corridors instead of doors that opened from one room to another. For the fashionable elite, the imperial style that served as the model for the exterior also contributed bourgeois distinctions to the interior of the great houses, including the separation of social and semi-social spaces from private and family areas. Rooms with sculptured mouldings, imported wallpaper, fashionable European upholstered and gilt furniture, chandeliers and rugs completed the formal, cosmopolitan and European aura of the lifestyles of those who lived 'upstairs'.

In the great houses of prominent families, the drawing rooms, parlours, music room and dining room were social spaces where family members of both sexes mixed with relatives and guests, displaying the latest European fashions and discussing local news and events at court. Female areas in the household included the boudoir and sewing rooms, where free and slave seamstresses fashioned the everyday styles of the family wardrobe, suitable attire for entertaining in the parlour and the clothes worn by slaves in the service areas, including the kitchen and the larder. Male spaces included the administrative offices and sitting rooms, leisure areas for card and billiard tables and adjoining guest rooms for visiting overseers, merchants, factors, planters and guests of corresponding social rank. Children of the household had free run of the house and grounds and slept together in a nursery with a slave nanny-in-waiting. Unmarried sons often shared rooms with each other, as did the daughters, who slept in the interior of the house with no direct access to the outside, surrounded by the rooms of protective parents, brothers and guardians.

Anthropologist Roberto da Matta has described the house interiors as controlled universes where 'everything was in its proper place'.[28] Indeed, the social relations of the great houses were formal, rigidly hierarchical and full of tension, operating multiple forms of dominance and oppression, exemplified by the power of the father over sons, husbands over wives and masters over slaves.[29] Under the patriarchal mantle of nineteenth-century society, the place of all plantation residents – including the planter's wife, sons and daughters, nephews and nieces, dependent relatives, *agregados* (distant kin or residents with some connection to the landowner), overseers and slaves – was defined by the obedience they owed to the senhor. In the household, patriarchalism involved the 'subordination of children and women to the male head of family who held control over the wealth of the family, the sexuality of its women, and the labor power of all its members'.[30]

A set of social relations, rather than the self-sufficiency of a household,

governed patriarchal families. As Dain Borges has argued in his study of elite
Bahian patriarchal families, the effective family was the kin group who lived in
the same household.[31] Under the patriarchal mantle, a married woman of the elite
classes was an adornment, subject to a condition of obedience and submission
that applied equally to housewives, servants, nannies, mistresses and spinsters.
Widows with property and means were an exception and could wield power and
influence over family members. For Shirley Ardener, women in a male-
dominated society were destined to become objects, and to 'perform' as
housewives, servants, nannies, mistresses and spinsters for men.[32] The French
traveller Adèle Toussaint-Samson's impressions of home life on the *fazendas* she
visited in Brazil were consistent with this view:

> When a Brazilian comes home he finds in his house a dutiful
> wife, whom he treats as a spoilt child, bringing her dresses,
> jewels, and ornaments of all kinds; but this woman is not
> associated to him in his business, his preoccupations, or his
> thoughts. She is a doll who he dresses for an occasion, and who,
> in reality, is but the first slave in the house.[33]

A woman who strove to maintain a reputation of decency structured her life
around the domestic sphere and was bound to traditional gender roles that
destined women of means to leave the paternal household only twice – at
marriage and at burial. Elite married women were described by Toussaint-
Samson as the first slaves in the house, but many commanded the slaves they
brought to the marriage as part of the dowry. Property in slaves was a vital
mainstay of their status as well as a source of income.

The social, semi-social and private spaces were for the enjoyment of the
master class, and were cleaned and maintained by slaves and slave children, who
were excluded by rigid social boundaries reminiscent of an 'upstairs/downstairs'
arrangement. Slaves handled all aspects of service, both intimate and impersonal.
A slave midwife was present at birth; a slave wet-nurse (*ama de leite*) suckled her
master's children and lulled them to sleep; in early childhood a young slave might
serve as a playmate; and older slaves entertained household children with tales
and stories. Slaves were the trusted cooks, laundresses and servants to the
females of the household, who played 'all day with the younger [slaves]', a
constant association of elite children with black servants and their children, 'of
whom there are usually a number in every house', that Elizabeth Agassiz held to
be responsible for the general lack of household education in the country.[34]

The slaves's status as property and their limited options for redress made their
bondage very different from that endured by free women under male patriarchal
authority. According to Kátia Mattoso, 'slave servants were required to stand
straight, be silent unless ordered to speak, steadfastly obey, and display a
pleasant disposition, addressing their masters as "senhor", "senhora", and
"dona"'.[35] Women of the household were subject to surveillance by trusted
household slaves, widowed or maiden aunts and siblings, who aimed to safeguard the family from the deception and disgrace of a dishonourable match. In
their roles as servants, female slaves often spent as much time with their

mistresses as close kin or female acquaintances. Slave *mucamas*, valued slaves usually of mixed ancestry (for example, a half-sister, child or concubine of the owner) raised the senhor's children and sometimes served as wet-nurses, prepared the mistress's bath, arranged her clothes, dusted her furniture, shined her shoes, brought her medicines, fetched her embroidery and fitted her garments.[36] Slaves were party to the secrets of household members, acted as bearers of messages, chaperones to lovers and attentive servants-in-waiting at *fazenda* celebrations and ceremonies. For Manuel Querino (1851–1923), an Afro-Brazilian Bahian writer on black culture and history, household slaves were the trusted *mucama*, the trustworthy confidante, the affectionate wet-nurse, the pages, the bodyguards, and the beloved servants.[37]

Within the domestic sphere, mistresses and experienced slaves taught slave and free women the domestic arts of embroidery, sewing and the confection of compotes and other sweets from locally grown fruit and sugar. Under the rigid social hierarchy of the household, slaves executed and were judged on the many tasks they were set by their mistresses. From observing an elder slave and absorbing the teaching of their mistresses, many household slaves perfected the arts of the hostess and became the unofficial female authorities of the households of unmarried men or widows.[38] Slave women whose masters and mistresses upheld a desired image of fashionable subservience dressed them ornately and elaborately. A hierarchy of appearance existed that reflected the status of household servants and was indicated by the quality of the cloth used in clothing, ribbons, bows, pins and European-style adornments, the use of shoes, baptism with the master's family name and presence at the various social events of the household.

Court cases involving slaves focused on their treatment, appearance and authority in relation to the master, his household and other slaves. In one such case, Eufrasina, a twelve-year-old *parda* slave girl, who was raised like a free daughter by her mistress, was sold for 1:000$000 (approximately US$580) in 1856 to a local Rio Bonito solicitor and planter to settle a debt.[39] Leaving her in her mistress's care for a while, probably until she reached puberty, her purchaser, João Correia Benjamin, showered Eufrasina with attention, sending her dresses and taking her with him to 'public sports events and entertainment'. According to her public defender, he then 'cloistered her as his private playmate in his hillside house' miles from the household where he lived with his family and made her his concubine.[40] In 1866, the girl, pregnant and unruly, and whipped for refusing to do field work, was informed by the planter that, despite the letter of freedom she had possessed since 1858, her free status was only conditional. The girl protested that she was free, called him a 'thief, a scoundrel, and a son-of-a bitch', words that she repeated later in the village after fleeing his house. She sought refuge in the home of a nearby coffee planter and refused to return to the service of a man who sent a freed woman to the fields. Correia Benjamin exerted his authority and revoked her conditionally free status, returning her to the position of slave because of her 'ungratefulness to him'.[41]

The incident landed Eufrasina and Correia Benjamin in court. Witnesses testified that Eufrasina was the recognized female authority in the household, a fact that was reflected in her clothing, which was very different from the coarse cotton used by other slaves, and that she wore shoes the planter had provided for the outings they took together in his carriage. Most importantly, during her years of service she attended to only minimal tasks in the household and used the informal form 'Senhor João' when addressing the planter. Passing reference was made to his jealousy and to the previous case of a female slave who had fled his household after a whipping.[42]

The local court held that Eufrasina was not free, only conditionally so until her master's death, and that her departure from his house violated the terms of service to him. The sentence was subsequently upheld by the Tribunal de Relação in Rio de Janeiro in 1868.[43]

Correia Benjamin's sexual demands on Eufrasina were far from unique or unusual. The 'exercise' of human exchange in the slave societies of the Americans disregarded any concept of the slave as a person. Slave women, men and children of both sexes were regarded as sexual objects and were expected to comply with the sexual expectations and demands made on them.[44] Twenty-year-old Adelaide, a creole slave who was sold for 1:200$000 with guarantees that she suffered no diseases or physical defects, became the subject of a court dispute between buyer and seller over her poor performance. The buyer demanded reparation on the grounds that he was sold a false bill of goods. Adelaide was given a medical examination that diagnosed epilepsy, a malady that doctors agreed preceded her sale. When pressed, the seller claimed that Adelaide was prone to attacks of hysteria that he associated with her barren state, a common explanation in those times for women who deviated from the expected norms that associated sexual performance with procreation. Possession of Adelaide's body was an unwritten 'right' in the sales agreement, and discovery of the cause for her inability to work, coupled with her reproductive dysfunction, led the buyer to accuse the seller of fraud, claiming that he sold Adelaide outside the jurisdiction of the *município* where her 'malady' was known and where she would have commanded a lower price. The court upheld his demand for a refund on the grounds that Adelaide's affliction prevented her from fulfilling the expectations of her buyer.[45]

The sexual exploitation of male and female slaves was common. The Brazilian novelist, Erico Veríssimo, writing in the 1890s and reflecting on his own childhood experiences, recalled that female servants, especially the *mulata* (mulatto), exercised a depraved influence on the masters, young and old, and were 'the ruin of our physical and moral manhood':

> As the nurse, the slave girl suckled every Brazilian generation; as
> the personal servant [*mucama*], she lulled them all to sleep; as a
> man, the slave toiled for every generation; as a woman, she
> surrendered herself to all of them.[46]

Veríssimo recalled the adulations of poets who described the *mulata* as a tormenter, a heroine of their verses, idolized for her sensuousness, magic, lust, sorcery and coyness. His most chilling description of intimate relationships was echoed decades later by the sociologist, Gilberto Freyre, who claimed that Brazilian patriarchal society perpetuated the image of the Jezebel or *mulher prostituta* servant women. For Veríssimo, the *mulata* was

> the young mistress's intimate companion and the young master's sweetheart. Thanks mainly to her, at fourteen years of age physical love holds no secrets for the Brazilian, initiated from the tenderest age in the provocative atmosphere that she creates around him, giving him his bath, dressing him, and putting him to bed.[47]

Veríssimo's observations were still in vogue with end-of-century writers who held slavery to be the cause of the moral degeneration of the Brazilian family and household.[48] Proponents of this view did not reflect upon the unequal power relationship implicit in master–slave relations, but their views do confirm that empowerment through intimacy was a tool that enabled slaves to check or mollify patriarchal authority.

The official female titular head of family and household was the decisive authority over household relations, seconded by female relatives and their children, who oversaw service in the great house. The regime of work, the hours and the tasks they assigned to each slave attested to a hierarchy with built-in mechanisms to test skill, trust, ability, and obedience. The tasks given to staff and slaves in the great house were no less demanding than service in the fields or on the road, but were probably less life-threatening. Domestic slaves were said to fare better than field slaves and were depicted as ornamental figures of the great house who were either the master's children or concubines who rivalled for his attentions with the mistress of the household.[49] In the case of Eufrasina, she was set up in a separate house, which she managed in addition to acting as an ornamental figure at her master's side during public outings. Yet her removal from household service by demotion to field labour and the withdrawal of her conditionally freed status were among the worst punishments suffered by domestic slaves, for whom divestment from the kin group of the household was a hefty price for challenges to the moral authority of the master.[50]

Slaves who were especially proficient in a skill were rented or assigned to 'street duty' as *quitandeiras*, pedlars, traders, cooks, prostitutes and seamstresses, earning pocket money for their mistresses. Outside of the household, slaves enjoyed greater autonomy, which enabled them to interpret their subordinate position and to change it. One method was to keep a share of their earnings to pay for the price of their freedom or that of a loved one.

Ambiguous spaces and social boundaries: guest quarters and verandas

Unequal power relations extended beyond the immediate master–slave relationship in the great house to relatives, guests and other visitors. In addition to the landowner, his family, *agregados*, business associates and personal acquaintances, great houses also accommodated wayfarers who requested lodgings. Provisions for guests were a necessity in a developing hinterland, where distances between *fazendas* were great and inns were confined to towns and villages. Travel after nightfall was hazardous due to unlit and often impassable, washed-out roads and the pervasive brigandry of thieves and runaway slaves. An unwritten custom obliged landowners to feed and lodge travellers, although the fear of assassination or violence from poor freemen and slaves, and a distrust of potential male suitors for their daughters, made planters wary of strangers. A customary procedure was followed:

> on reaching a fazenda, any person who desires to stop in the
> middle of the day or the night there, should wait outside and
> ask, through the servant, permission to do so. It is not until his
> application is granted, which is almost always the case, that the
> traveller dismounts from his mule, and enters the building.[51]

Slave pages handled the initial screening of outsiders at the household entrance. After that, introductions and other formalities were followed by a more subtle second screening. Personal appearance and the presentation of a letter of introduction from an official or personal acquaintance of the property owner was mandatory:

> if you have the air of a respectable traveller, you are sure of a
> hearty welcome, shelter and food. The card of a friend or a note
> of introduction assures you all the house can afford for as long as
> you like to stay.[52]

The senhor distinguished socially acceptable equals from less desirable traders and passers-by. The former, including business associates, brokers, politicians, planters and merchants, were received and entertained in the manner that the head of the household would expect for himself in similar circumstances. Less prestigious travellers were offered a meal and a place to sleep. Toussaint-Samson recalled how common it was for servants and slaves to initiate young slaves in sexual practices and to bestow sexual 'favours' on those itinerant merchants who had been reluctantly offered lodging in the guest rooms by the senhor.[53]

Visitors were all attended by the household slaves. Relaxed supervision in the guest quarters allowed for informal personal contact, favours and mediation of the formal social hierarchy. In day-to-day contact in other areas of the great house, formal gestures – subtle nods, furtive smiles and stares, a wink, a quickened pace, a prolonged bow – tested but did not undermine the rigid social hierarchy in the mansion house.

Guest quarters provided a litmus test for the boundaries of social behaviour within the great house, and for this reason I have labelled them 'ambiguous spaces'. Shirley Ardener has observed that the placement of the guests in rooms at the peripheries of the house and overlooking verandas was designed to emphasize the spatial limitations on sociability that the host intended. According to one member of a planter household:

> the rooms comprising the guest quarters were not furnished
> with expensive curtains, carpets, or the thousands of

knick-knacks that were used for decoration in the rest of the house . . . but guests who were lodged there were treated unpretentiously and cordially.[54]

The guest quarters separated outsiders from the private sphere of the *mulher honesta* or *senhora dona da casa*, the female head of the household and her immediate family. The quarters were usually off-limits to female family members, although slaves and servants moved freely about in service to them.[55] Adèle Toussaint-Samson reported that slave-owners designated the most attractive servants and slaves to attend to the bath and care of any prominent family members and intimate friends who were accommodated in guest quarters. She wrote of her personal experience during an overnight visit to a rural *fazenda*, where mulatto women paraded to and fro on the veranda outside the guest quarters as they eyed her husband in the bedroom.[56] Her observations correspond with postmortem inventories in which *parda* slaves held the position of *mucama*.

Mediation and favours

The attention household slaves were expected to offer guests presented them with a rare opportunity to establish intimate and often long-standing ties with regular visitors, allowing slave women to elicit an outsider's interest, sympathy, support or appreciation. Associations with masters, visitors, relatives and friends allowed for informal relationships that, in the ambiguity of the guest quarters, were consistent with subtle forms of complementarity. Manuel Moreno Fraginals stated that 'in urban areas and in solitary mansions, sex was the only device women could use to improve their economic condition'.[57]

Mediation from an outsider, especially a slave's godparent or the father of a slave's child, rarely compromised the outsider's standing or challenged the patriarchal control of the senhor over his household, but might soften the authority of male 'keepers' of the social order. Stanley Stein has argued that slaves skilfully played upon the mix of planter authority and paternalism of masters and other members of the planter class:

> A slave might ward off a lashing by fleeing immediately upon committing an offence to the proprietor of a neighboring plantation. On arrival, the slave would request the planter to 'adopt him' (*tomar padrinho*). If the planter accepted, the slave returned to his master with a note or else the planter personally escorted him back. Then the slave would be admonished not to repeat the offence lest he suffer the consequences.[58]

A number of escaped slaves who voluntarily returned to their masters in the aftermath of a slave rebellion in 1838 (the Manuel Congo movement) were known as *apadrinhados*, slaves who were accompanied by or returned through the intercession of their godparents or other protectors.[59] The case of Ladislau, a favoured Rio Bonito household slave who 'slept in the parlour behind locked doors but under open windows', is an extreme but illustrative example of one slave's expectations of godparenthood. Ladislau, a *mestiço*, impregnated a white girl, who was subsequently welcomed by his mistress into her home. In addition, he was accused of assaulting his mistress's son after the latter had attempted to enlist Ladislau in the army to remove him from the household. Ladislau appealed to his godfather, a local businessman, to intercede with the mistress in the hope that she would agree to his freedom and eventual marriage to the girl. The appeals were unsuccessful. Ladislau was sent to prison for seven years for the assault and the baby was sent away to another town. The proceedings confirm, however, that mediators were influential third parties in the master–slave relationship, even if some slave expectations were unrealistic.[60]

The veranda

A second ambiguous space was the veranda, a crossroads between the private domestic sphere and the world outside. A long-standing external feature of estate architecture on sugar *engenhos*, the veranda was for practical and aesthetic reasons fused with neoclassic styles on the coffee estates. Roberto da Matta has identified the porch or veranda as an ambiguous 'space between the house and the street', where social interaction and behaviour were not rigidly or formally defined.[61]

The veranda was an extension of the social space represented by the parlour that opened on to it and was often used as a play area for frolicking children or as the place of confinement for a misbehaved child. At the close of the day the planter and his household would sip refreshments there as they viewed the setting sun over the countryside and awaited the return of field slaves for the evening's roll call, the *saltar para a reza* (blessing) and dismissal.[62] At night, the veranda served as a place of rest for household slaves, making it their space as well.

The veranda was also a boundary that separated slaves from guests on festive occasions and official holidays. Occasions such as wedding receptions, baptisms, parties in honour of the patron saint of a *fazenda* and its owner and the commemoration of a bountiful harvest provided appropriate opportunities for the social and political elites to conspicuously display comely servants, talented slave musicians, culinary tastes and prevailing European fashions and dress.[63] Festivities physically incorporated masters and slaves in the celebrations, but the socially acceptable limits between their two worlds had a physical counterpart in the veranda. Elizabeth Agassiz described a slave band and slave children who danced for guests in the house while outside 'every door and window was filled with a cloud of dusky faces', testifying to the physical inclusion of everyone in the festivities, despite the social significance of the physical barriers that kept slaves on the veranda.[64]

Trespassing on that space signified defiance of the slave order. The following incident, suggesting the master's fear of slave rebellion, was recorded by Adèle Toussaint-Samson:

> During a saint's day festivity as slaves were performing on the
> coffee terrace, one of the slaves, said to be enebriated by *cachaça*,
> traversed the veranda, entered the main house, and menacingly
> approached his master as he uttered threats. He was immediately
> subdued, the festivities were abruptly terminated, the bonfire
> was extinguished, and the 120 slaves were ordered back to their
> quarters and guests were dispatched as the windows and doors
> of the main house were bolted by a terrified slaveowner.[65]

Disorder and ambiguity in the rigid social hierarchy impacted on the great
house in other terrible and symbolic ways. The American preacher, George
Gardner, recalled a Christmas Day celebration in which the best-behaved male
and female slaves performed on the veranda of the great house. He recalled that
interspersed with their dances was a skit about a young musician who stood
dancing and playing his viola in front of a priest's house. Each slave who was sent
by the increasingly irritated priest to discover the reason for the music was shown
a new dance from Bahia and invited to join in. Eventually, all of the household
slaves were dancing in a circle before the house. The angry priest demanded to
know the cause of the ruckus that was interrupting his dinner. After much
persuasion, he also joined in the dance but at a given moment pulled a whip from
his cloak and flogged all the dancers. The story hardly seems appropriate for a
Christmas Day celebration that marked the occasion when slaves received small
gifts from their masters. However, it effectively demonstrated the consequences for
slaves who dared to affront the authority of the master. The story also reaffirmed
the authority of the planter class over the domestic space of the house and the
public space of the street, and over the human property they contained.[66]

The slave quarters: physical incorporation, social exclusion

In contrast to the British Caribbean and the American South, where slave
quarters and provision grounds remained out of sight of the great house, the
Brazilian *senzalas* (slave quarters) juxtaposed slaves and masters in physically
close but socially separate lifestyles.[67] As we have seen, during the early days of
settlement, masters and slaves were housed under one roof as a defence against
attack from outside, a practice that was common in the kingdom of Angola,
where subjected African *sobas* (chiefs) and their tribes were installed around
Portuguese fortresses as defence buffers and as a source of food and labour.[68]

Although the great house physically incorporated unfree inhabitants into their
masters' worlds, it was in the 'utilitarian-cum-social' spaces of the service areas
of the kitchen, back patio, *quintal* (back yard) and *senzalas* where household slaves
congregated and exchanged information. Service and work areas were assigned to
slaves during the unceasing daily routine of household duties. Night tasks left
most slaves catching brief moments of rest in nurseries and bedrooms, in the
corridors outside the private family quarters, on tables and chairs in the kitchens,
laundry and sewing rooms and on mats on the veranda, sleeping at the beck and
call of family members in spaces that were theirs, if only temporarily.

Figure 6 Slave quarters. *Source:* Johann Moritz Rugendas, *Viagem Pitoresca Através do Brasil*, 1835.

Although some travellers described nurseries for slave babies within the great house, the only areas exclusively designed for slaves were the separate slave quarters.[69] They represented a physical confirmation of the base of a socio-economic pyramid that ascended in wealth, prestige and social importance through the cabins of poor free farmers on the *fazenda* to the great house. Lacerda Werneck's 1840s model *fazenda* envisioned separate slave quarters, sturdy structures that faced east to west and were arranged in rows like fortress barracks and measured 24 palms square. Unmarried slave men and women were to occupy separate quarters, while joint living quarters would be provided for married slaves. Roofed porches were designed to protect slaves from the wind and rain, a provision that was also present in the fields, where *ranchos* were to be located at regular intervals to shield workers from the elements.[70]

The arrangement and design of slave quarters varied according to the slaves' input and planters' attitudes. The African contribution to *senzala* styles was depicted in João Mauricio Rugendas' 1830s drawing of thatched huts grouped around a common area. The proximity of the slave quarters to the great house was also conveyed by Rugendas's portrayal of the mistress surveying the activities in the *senzala* from her balcony (see Figure 6). The African village arrangement continued to serve as a model for slave quarters half a century later, as described at the Fazenda São José in the *município* of Magé, where the slave quarters stood 'before the house and all around it, ranged in a circle ... to the number of seventy about'. The huts, described by Toussaint-Samson as 'gloomy abodes made of clay and mud with dried banana leaves for roofing, no windows, and no chimney', confirm the existence of African arrangements as late as 1880,

Figure 7 Slave quarters. *Source:* Photograph by Victor Frond, *c.* 1857, in Charles Ribeyrolles, *Brasil Pitoresco*, 1859.

but also reveal that slaves relied on locally available materials to construct and arrange their quarters.[71]

The photographs taken by Victor Frond during his travels in the Paraíba Valley in 1859 document a potpourri of *senzalas* that ranged from flimsy, windowless wattle-and-daub huts with thatched roofs, to free-standing wooden cabins, and long rows of barracks. Some of the wattle-and-daub huts had vegetable gardens and an area of beaten earth at the entrances. One photograph depicting a scene of two women in front of a hut is reminiscent of rural villages in Angola (see Figure 7). Clusters of huts between a sugar mill and the great house were also reported on the small sugar-producing estate of Sambayratiba near Porto de Sampaio.[72] An Irish visitor en route to the highlands town of Nova Friburgo in the early 1870s commented on the good condition of slave huts which he termed *cabanas*, a term that usually refers to free-standing huts.[73]

The variety in styles of the slave quarters documented by Frond in the late 1850s attested to slavery's pervasiveness in the hinterlands.[74] The different styles of *senzalas* and disparities in shape, size, materials and space also underscored the different concepts that slaves and masters held of slavery. Free-standing huts suggested a measure of slave autonomy, as did vegetable gardens and possession of carts and farm animals. Barracks-like *senzalas* that opened directly on to the terrace were increasingly common on large coffee and sugarcane estates after 1850. Their construction suggested the regimentation of large numbers of mostly male slaves, purchases from the inter-provincial trade, who were held under close surveillance for fear of their resistance to the unrelenting daily demands of field labour. An American consul described a square 'overlooked from the main dwelling surrounded by the cabins of the slaves', behind which were the mills, shops and brickyard, for the mechanical work of the plantation.[75] The façade of

Figure 8 Interior of the Fazenda do Governo. *Source:* Photograph by Victor Frond, *c.* 1857, in Charles Ribeyrolles, *Brasil Pitoresco*, 1859.

the barracks, its tile roofs and porches, blended in with the physical plan of the great house and terrace, highlighting the physical incorporation of slaves into the production unit. The sentry station in Victor Frond's photograph from the Paraíba Valley highlands documented the lack of corresponding social inclusion (see Figure 8).[76]

Photographs of Rio Bonito and its surroundings have not been located and may not exist, but the descriptions in the postmortem inventories reveal that slave quarters were mostly thatched waddle-and-daub huts with earthen floors. Their location is unclear, but court cases confirm that they were sited next to the main house. Slaves belonging to Carlos Bento Ferreira, for example, informed the court that although they were locked up on the *senzala* for the night, they overheard Bento Ferreira shouting at and beating his ex-slave, a ninety-year-old man, who they claimed had entered his house in search of warmth.[77]

The interiors of slave quarters were sparse. One common style was the *tarimba* (cot) which was up to 3 feet wide and separated from the next by a wooden division about 3 feet high. A wide corridor in the centre was for cooking and a blanket or a mat covered the entry of each cubicle. Ventilation and illumination were provided by barred windows and a 12-foot opening below the roof, which also served as an outlet for the smoke when the permanently lit faggot ignited the firewood for the evening meal.[78]

Figure 9 Fazenda de Santa Anna in Minas Gerais. *Source:* Mr and Mrs Agassiz, *A Journey in Brazil*, 1868.

The terrace

A third socially transitional space was the terrace, or *terreiro*, that connected the domestic sphere of the great house to the work areas and slave quarters. The terrace formed a functional square that was offset on one side by the great house and surrounded with ancillary buildings and slave quarters associated with the 'works' (see Figure 9). Stanley Stein found no mention of terraces in the postmortem inventories prior to 1850 and suggested that since they were initially made out of beaten earth they had no value attached to them and were not included by the estate evaluators.[79] On modest farms, the terrace was little more than a cleared convex-shaped beaten dirt or brick surface, which was occupied by pigs and chickens when harvested coffee was not being spread out for drying. With the profitable returns from coffee, dirt terraces were replaced with brick, cut stone or cemented surfaces that stretched the width of the great house and were enclosed by low stone walls with drain holes to allow excessive rainwater to escape.[80]

On prominent estates, the terrace extended like a proudly crafted quilt on display before the mansion house, a manifestation of the fruits of labour on which rested the bearing and social standing of the senhor. One observer highlighted the utilitarian nature of the *fazenda*, pointing out the spatial proximity between production and leisure just a few yards from the entrance of the great house:

> There were several steps descending very gradually from the
> front door, and below them, a smooth, hard piece of ground,
> swept clean for drying coffee. The prevailing air about the

premises was business, as an example of which, the fowl-yard on one side of the house came up to the veranda.[81]

The terrace was the space where the regimented labour conditions of *fazenda* life were initiated and concluded on a daily basis. The day began with a roll call as field slaves gathered on the terrace to be counted, blessed and assigned daily tasks. Von Tschudi recalled being awoken at dawn by a droning noise outside his guest quarters, as assembled slaves uttered prayers before being dispersed to their daily tasks, an experience that Adèle Toussaint-Samson also witnessed early one morning.[82]

Elderly African *feitores* (foremen) supervised male and female adults and children as they separated branches and leaves from coffee berries that had been washed, selected and spread out to dry in the sun on the terrace. On non-mechanized establishments slaves bearing long poles beat the dry outer shell to separate it, or shook the berries into large stone mortars beneath a wooden scaffolding from which water-powered wooden hammers descended, crushing the husks.[83] The crushed mass was then placed in wooden boxes, fastened in the middle of a long table with small openings at each side, through which both the berry and the husk fell slowly out on to the table or the floor of the mill. Women, children and elderly slaves separated the husks from the berries and then cast the beans into heated shallow copper cauldrons, where they were carefully turned until dried or, alternatively, placed in porous containers for storage in ventilated areas. Considerable care was required during the drying process, as the colour of the coffee depended upon the degree of heat to which it was exposed. If drying occurred too quickly, the bean contracted a yellowish tinge instead of the usual greenish colour.[84] Slave women and children filled cloth sacks with the roasted beans for shipment to merchant houses in Rio de Janeiro. The sacks were then stacked on the terrace for transportation by slaves, ox-driven carts or mule trains to river and overland ports, prior to the onset of the railroads in the 1870s, and on to Guanabara Bay.[85] Jean Baptiste Debret observed in the early part of the century how a slave headman, employing an improvised banner of cloth tied to a stick, established the pace of the bearers through his improvised chants and songs. A foreman, who acted as guide, carried the horns of an ox or a ram as a talisman against misfortune, magic or any infernal influences that might threaten the advance of the group, 'an amulet that heightened his loquaciousness and his authority to play upon the bearers' superstitions'.[86]

After the process of de-pulping and sorting the coffee beans was complete, the coffee terrace reverted to its use as a mixed-gender work space, where slaves equipped with long poles thrashed bean pods, and chickens and barnyard animals scratched for food. At sunset, slaves gathered on the terrace to be counted and, after a short prayer, were dispatched to a communal evening meal that, like the midday break, varied from a thin gruel to boiled beans, bacon, dried meat and manioc flour, supplemented by produce from slave provision gardens when these were permitted.[87]

The terrace was an ambiguous social space because it remained under constant surveillance from the great house and yet also served as an extension of the slave quarters that opened on to it. It was also a social space for slaves who participated in harvest and feast-day celebrations, when, although physically part of the festivities, they were involved in a socially separate but equally emotional dynamic.[88]

Under the peculiar nature of Brazilian slavery, masters did not forcibly repress or eliminate African customs, beliefs or language, and these practices were renewed and strengthened during the African trade. Moreno Fraginals has stated that the dominant class protected and even stimulated the development of the isolated cultural values of the dominated class, as long as these contributed to the reinforcement of the desired structure.[89] Slaves employed a 'hidden language' that was unintelligible to slave masters and overseers, referring to each other by African names and communicating by using words that were derived from Bantu.[90] Rarely mentioned in plantation documentation, African languages, fetishes and wooden figures of Saint Anthony, Saint Benedict and other saints attested to cultural expressions that were distinct from those of the master class, and which linked slaves to each other and to freed and free counterparts.[91] For an outsider, who in 1880 observed the 'strange scene and the savage dancing' on the coffee terrace, communicated in rhythmic responses to beating drums and clapping hands, the gestures and mood were threatening and grotesque. The drumming, chanting, dance movements and body language transmitted shared slave identities that bypassed the rigours and injustices of slavery and imparted hidden meanings that escaped the comprehension of white onlookers.[92]

Slaves took refuge in their culture as a means of identity and survival. Slave-owners generally permitted Saturday night or saint's day one- or two-hour sessions for dancing or performing *capoeira* (a form of sudden violent assault disguised as a rhythmic dance, practised during and after slavery).[93] Stanley Stein has also described slave gestures and activities, involving parody, wit, irony and imitation, that were performed as part of *caxambús* (a slave festival in which drumming, dancing and verse prevail; also a coarse, lively Afro-Brazilian dance), or *batuques*, (generic designation of Afro-Brazilian dances), crosses between religious and secular ceremonies. Slaves recited verses in response to drummers' beats as a king and queen accompanied the drumbeats. The king began the ceremonies, entering the dancing circle and approaching the drums, where he knelt in greeting and sang the two lines of a riddle. Women and men then entered the dancing circle and danced the *jongo* around each other in a counter-clockwise direction, while another *jongueiro* would try to decipher the riddle with two more lines. Word-plays with multiple meanings in African languages made for the best *jongos*, replacing

> persons by trees, birds, and animals of the forest. There was a premium on terseness; the fewer the words, the more obscure the meaning, one not readily deciphered by contesting jongueiros, or one which could be repeated to depict a multitude of situations.[94]

The folklorist, Maria de Lourdes Borges Ribeiro, associated the *jongo* with the *caxambú* and the *catambá* (a popular dance), and although she confirmed that all three were performed in the coffee-producing provinces of the southeast where slaves of Bantu origin predominated, she could not determine whether they were one and the same dance form.[95] Here are some examples of the *jongos* (dance and song of African origin) she collected:

Trevoada tá roncando.	The drum is getting hoarse.
É sinar que é pra chovê.	A sign that it's about to rain.[96]
Debaixo do angu tem carne.	Beneath the mush there is meat.[97]
O mundo tava torto	The world was twisted
São Pedro endireitô	Saint Peter straightened it out
Na sola do seu sapato	On the sole of his shoe
corre água e nasce frô	it rains and a flower grows.[98]

Stanley Stein cited more subtle verses:

Macaco não morre com o chumbo,	Monkey doesn't die by lead,
Morre no laço de bater	He dies in a loop when beaten.

On the jealous anger of D. Maria over her husband's personal relations with a slave woman:

Eu 'tou má com sinhá D. Maria,	I'm in dutch with Dona Maria,
Mais 'tou bem com o senhó Breves	But in the good graces of Senhor Breves.[99]

The *caxambú* took its name from a large drum of African origin used in the dance. Câmara Cascudo traced its use to theatrical presentations called *moçambiques* that slaves from Moçambique performed in the gold-mining regions of Brazil.[100] Dancing and drumming provided a release from the rigours of slavery, and the Saturday-night gatherings enabled slaves to congregate and revitalize rituals that planters attempted to weaken by mixing slaves from different origins and cultures.[101]

A police investigation into the Saturday-night robbery and murder of a tavern keeper on the outskirts of the parish of Paty do Alferes in Vassouras in 1867 revealed that slaves commonly frequented local taverns. The African, Gabriel Benguela, aged thirty-five, single and a mule-train driver and field slave of long-standing service on the estate of Antonio Azevedo Silva in Paraíba do Sul, defended himself from accusations of robbery and murder with the alibi that he was drumming all night on the coffee terrace as slaves from the estate danced the *caxambú*. Another field slave, Jorge Benguela, also thirty-five and single, confirmed Benguela's story, stating that after a day of field labour and before the evening dismissal the overseer gave him, Manoel Moçambique, Baldonio and Bernardo permission to buy tobacco and cane whisky at the local tavern. They soon returned to the estate where they found the other slaves awake and dancing the *caxambú*.[102]

A knife, which authorities suspected was the murder weapon, was discovered in the slave quarters of Jorge Benguela, who claimed it was collateral for a small loan he had made to Gabriel Benguela. The finger of suspicion was redirected to another Angolan, Rodrigo, who worked on the same estate as Gabriel Benguela.

Foodstuffs and other stolen objects, plus a sickle handle used in the murder were found in his slave quarters. Rodrigo confessed that it was his sickle handle that killed the tavern keeper but accused two slaves from a *fazenda* near the tavern of committing the crime. The reaction of the slaves' owner to the accusation provides an insightful commentary on the control, and the limitations of control, exerted by owners over their slaves. Stating two reasons why the accusation was implausible, the owner claimed that first, his slaves were counted and locked up every night and their absence would have been reported. Second, his slaves 'would not have agreed to remain empty handed after a robbery'.

Rodrigo changed his confession, implicating Gabriel Benguela in the killing and robbery, although his own shirt and trousers were covered in bloodstains. Rodrigo claimed that the murdered tavern keeper owed Gabriel money and had refused to pay up. After the murder, as they were dividing the spoils, the police had surrounded the slave quarters and he had hidden the booty in his quarters. Gabriel returned to his room empty-handed. In his defence, Gabriel accused Rodrigo of implicating him in the crime in revenge for rude remarks he'd made about his former girlfriend, the slave Helena, who was now Rodrigo's girlfriend. Helena, a slave from Cabinda, aged thirty-four, who worked as a field slave and laundress, stated that she had been Gabriel's lover but was now the friend of Rodrigo 'whose clothes she washed'. She claimed to know nothing about the robbery and the murder.

Rodrigo finally confessed to murdering the victim single-handedly with a knife that he later disposed of in a river. The motive was 25 mil-réis that the tavern keeper owed him and had refused to pay. Finding only 6 mil-réis in the safe after the murder, Rodrigo grabbed items from the shelves to make up the difference. Rodrigo's confession absolved Gabriel. Rodrigo was sentenced to forced labour and his owner was charged for the court expenses.

Specific references to the use of Bantu or any secret dialects to communicate with one another were not forthcoming in this case. The testimonies confirmed that on the one hand the *caxambú* was an exclusively slave gathering on the *fazendas* in 1860, and a popular Saturday entertainment involving African drumming, dance and chants. The *caxambú* ceremonies were a collective diversion, in which slaves from the Portuguese colonies of Moçambique and from Benguela and Cabinda areas of Angola participated as dancers and drummers.[103] On the other hand, the crossfire of slave accusations against one another also exemplifies the precarious nature of social solidarity among slaves who faced the burden of the white man's justice. Although they shared common places of origin, the relationship between Gabriel and Rodrigo was one of rivalry over the disputed Cabinda slave, Helena.

The testimonies in this case confirm the access that slaves enjoyed to places beyond the *fazenda*. Slaves frequented the social space of the tavern, known as a gathering place for free and freed people, to gamble, drink, cut deals, make loans and trade in contraband or stolen objects and produce. Deals were forged between free, freed and slaves. Rodrigo claimed he was a creditor of the tavern keeper. This fact, along with the loan that Gabriel Benguela made to another slave, confirms that within the bonds of slavery slaves were operating under market conditions, accumulating capital, making loans and demanding collateral for loans. Also, Rodrigo and Gabriel's mobility outside the estate, and the accusations of murder against slaves from another estate, confirms the existence of personal networks that reached beyond the *fazenda*. Rodrigo, Gabriel, Jorge Benguela and Helena were Africans in their mid-thirties in 1868. Helena worked in both domestic and field labour, the slave Gabriel worked as a mule-train driver and as a field slave, and Rodrigo travelled to distant towns like Rio Preto in Minas Gerais but when on the estate he worked in the fields.

The fields: changing gender ratios

The multiple tasks performed by the three slaves in this case also illustrate how planters rationalized their slave labour forces in the fields to guarantee production. As the slave population of 293,554, or 53 per cent of the total provincial population of 556,080 at mid-century, plummeted in succeeding years, wealthy planters purchased slaves from the court city of Rio de Janeiro, from lowland food-producing areas like Rio Bonito and from the inter-provincial slave trade that from the north supplied 90 per cent of the 34,668 slaves who were imported to Rio de Janeiro between 1852 and 1862.[104]

In 1874, slaves represented 39.7 per cent of the provincial population and were unevenly distributed.[105] The highland Paraíba Valley coffee-export areas held 30 per cent of slaves in the Western Paraíba Valley, with the highest concentrations centred on Vassouras, Valença and Piraí. Another 20 per cent of slaves were concentrated in the Eastern Paraíba Valley, where Paraíba do Sul and the coffee *municípios* of Cantagalo and Santa Maria Madalena held the highest numbers. In these areas planter preference for slave labour predominated on rural *fazendas*, but a reserve labour force is suggested by the free non-white population, which, although low in comparison to other areas, accounted for 13 to 20 per cent of the population.

Different circumstances prevailed in lowland areas like Rio Bonito, where coffee and food production was directed to local and regional markets. The decline of slaves to one-third of the *município* population in 1872 was offset by the influx of a free non-white population that reached 26 per cent of the total population in that year, well within the range of 17 to 34 per cent that characterized lowland areas. The availability of public land and the incorporation of free labour into the rural area and the estates of a few important planters provided a labour alternative that was in keeping with small to medium-scale coffee and food production (Table 3.1).

Coffee and food production accommodated adults, children and the elderly in the different stages of planting, weeding, harvesting and drying, and in that respect was distinguished from sugarcane production. On large estates where there was a division of labour, men were assigned to dangerous and physically demanding tasks related to clearing the forest, burning bush, smashing rocks and preparing the land for seed. Weeding, harvesting and general care of the fields was handled by women, as was the removal of burned timber and debris from cleared land and the sowing of seeds onto the exposed earth.[106] After approximately six weeks, slaves would begin to weed the coffee plants, then harvest the

Table 3.1 Analysis of population in selected coffee-export and internal-market *municípios* in Rio de Janeiro province, 1872

	Percentage of total population				
	Slave	Free	Non-white	White	Free non-white*
Western and Eastern Paraíba Valley highland coffee-export *municípios*					
Resende**	33	67	46	54	13
Barra Mansa**	43	57	60	40	17
Vassouras	54	46	73	27	19
Valença	54	46	73	27	19
Paraíba do Sul	48	52	68	32	20
Cantagalo	62.5	37.5	75	25	12.5
S. Maria Madalena**	57	43	70	30	13
Sapucaia	46	54	63	37	17
S. Ant. Padua	34	66			
Itap./Nativ./Itab.			70	30	
Brejo, Restinga and Guanabara mixed-crop regional market *municípios*					
Campos	37	63	64	36	27
Rio Bonito**	28	72	54	46	26
Capivary**	23	77	55	45	32
Araruama**	39	61	60	40	21

* The 1872 census subdivides slaves into *preto* and *pardo*. I have subtracted 'slaves' from the sum of free and slave *pardos* and *pretos* and expressed the free non-white population in percentages.

** *Municípios* where local boundaries were unchanged.

Source: Directoria Geral de Estatística, *Recenseamento da população da Província do Rio de Janeiro, Quadro A. 1872*, 21 vols, Rio de Janeiro, 1873–6. Recompiled by CEDEPLAR. See Appendix 3 for full population values.

mature trees and finally prepare the crop for processing. Weeding separated old men and women from younger, more able, gangs of women and men. Planting, weeding, picking and separating the branches and leaves from the harvested berries were also tasks that small children and the elderly could manage. In addition to duties related to coffee production, women and children also handled weaving, pasturing and the shepherding and care of barnyard animals.

Specialized work that was unrelated to coffee production engaged male slaves and free field labourers on a task-related basis. Gangs of slaves with special training worked alongside freemen felling trees, burning and clearing the forests. Others were engaged in ditch-digging, fence and corral construction and mending, the dispatching of cargo, horse-training, labour supervision, as mule-train drivers, bodyguards for the estate owners and in the landowner's private militia.[107]

Table 3.2 Slave population of Vassouras parishes, by sex, 1850 and 1872

Parish	1850*			1872**		
	Male	Female	Total	Male	Female	Total
N.S. da Conceição	4520	2275	6795	3632	2571	6203
Paty do Alferes	5696	2753	8449	4567	3520	8087
Sacra Família	2324	1642	3966	891	751	1642
Ferreiros	–	–	–	1428	1115	2543
Sum total	12,540	6670	19,210	10,518	7957	18,475

*Município sum total (slaves and free) = 28,538
**Município sum total (slaves and free) = 35,913

Sources: BNRJ, Recenseamento da população da Província do Rio de Janeiro, Quadro A, 1850; Directoria Geral da Estatística, Recenseamento da população da Província do Rio de Janeiro, Quadro A, 1872. Recompiled by CEDEPLAR.

Hoeing, weeding and harvesting activities were shared by men and women and regulated by slaves through an internal organization of gang labour, called corte e beirada. The best hands were spread out in flanks with the cutter and back-up at the end of one flank and two other lead-row men positioned at the other. The four set the work pace for the slower workers, who worked between them as they moved up the rows of coffee, urged on by whip-bearing overseers.[108]

After 1850, ageing male slaves who were no longer able to perform arduous field tasks were gradually replaced by women and children. In 1850 the slave population in Vassouras was predominantly male, and females represented less than half the number of male slaves in the parishes of Nossa Senhora da Conceição and Paty do Alferes, and approximately two-thirds in Sacra Família do Tinguá. In the município as a whole, slave women numbered half of the male slave population (Table 3.2). This relationship had changed two decades later. By 1872, the slave population in the município had declined slightly, but although males still outnumbered females, the proportion of females had increased significantly in Nossa Senhora da Conceição and Paty do Alferes.

There were also changes in the pardo population. In 1872, the slave population of roughly 20,000 was still predominantly preto, despite declining numbers in all parishes, but the pardo population more than doubled in Nossa Senhora da Conceição, increased to five times its 1850 level in Paty do Alferes and tripled in Sacra Família (Table 3.3).

There are several explanations for this. Karasch's data on imported Africans between 1831 and 1840 suggests a strong market preference for male slaves, of whom young boys represented around 43 per cent. Sixty per cent of Africans imported between 1838 and 1852 were between the ages of ten and nineteen.[109] Adult women, whom Africans may have refused to sell to slave traders, were the least likely group to be imported.[110] Yet, a reworking by Karasch of Herbert Klein's 1852 figures for the internal slave trade in Brazil records a greater proportion of older male and female slaves (around 65 per cent), compared with 26 per cent for slaves between the ages of ten and nineteen.[111] By the 1850s, the

Table 3.3 Slave population of Vassouras parishes, by colour, 1850 and 1872

	1850			1872		
	Pardo	*Preto*	Total	*Pardo*	*Preto*	Total
N.S. da Conceição	291	6504	6795	695	5508	6203
Paty do Alferes	283	8166	8449	1698	6389	8087
Sacra Família	157	3809	3966	447	1195	1642
Ferreiros	–	–	–	676	1867	2543
Total	731	18,479	19,210	3516	14,959	18,475

Source: Directoria Geral da Estatística, *Recenseamento da população da Província do Rio de Janeiro, Quadro A, 1872*. Recompiled by CEDEPLAR.

Figure 10 Workers in the field. *Source:* Photograph by Victor Frond, *c.* 1857, in Charles Ribeyrolles, *Brasil Pitoresco*, 1859.

high figures for female slaves in the internal slave trade would appear to confirm Martin Klein's general findings that 'planters showed little or no sexual preferences in labor use and women performed all the basic unskilled manual labor tasks that men worked at'.[112] Although detailed analyses of the ages and sexes of the slaves who were supplied to the inter-provincial slave trade are not available, one might conclude that northeastern slave-owners kept young male and female slaves for the demanding tasks of sugarcane production, while selling older slaves, and possibly more troublesome slaves, in their twenties and thirties, to the coffee fields of the southeast. A photograph taken in the fields of a Vassouras *fazenda* in the late 1850s documents a large proportion of women among the field labourers; children do not appear (see Figure 10).

Table 3.4 Slave population of Rio Bonito parishes, by colour, 1850 and 1872

	1850			1872		
Parish	*Pardo*	*Preto*	Total	*Pardo*	*Preto*	Total
N.S. da Conceição						
do Rio Bonito	1521	6635	8156	1631	2966	4597
N.S. da Boa						
Esperança	237	3177	3414	668	1836	2504
Total	1758	9812	11,570	2299	4802	7101
Population of *município*	1850: 22,750; 1872: 25,872					

Sources: BNRJ, *Recenseamento da população da Província do Rio de Janeiro, Quadro A, 1850;* Directoria Geral da Estatística, *Recenseamento da população da Província do Rio de Janeiro, Quadro A, 1872.* Recompiled by CEDEPLAR.

Whereas there were 200 males for every 100 females in Vassouras in 1840, the sex ratio declined to 186:100 in the 1860–70 period and suffered a further decline to 123:100 in the years 1875 to 1885. In comparison with the free population, where there were 116 free males for every 100 free females, the sexual imbalance among slaves was still great. Small numbers of slave families had always been a feature of rural estates, but the increase in females made slave families viable, even if their formation took several years before making an impact on field labour forces. Women and their children were changing the composition of a slave labour landscape that had been almost exclusively male-dominated, adult and African up to 1850.[113] Stanley Stein's analyses of Vassouras postmortem inventories and testimonies in the 1950s, along with my research from 1987–91, show an increasing percentage of female slaves, rising from 23 per cent in the 1820–9 period to 44 per cent in the final decade of slavery, 1880–8.[114] The data also reveal how the slave population was ageing, as slaves in the fifteen- to forty-year age group, who accounted for 62 per cent of the slave working force in the 1840–9 period, dropped to 35 per cent in the last decade of slavery.[115]

In Rio Bonito, where the slave population was less than half that of Vassouras in 1850, and where the average slave holdings were twenty or fewer, the creolized or *pardo* slave population was larger, averaging one to every five *pretos* (Table 3.4). In 1872, the ratio increased to one *pardo* slave for every two *preto* slaves, making this a more racially diverse population but one in which extensive kinship ties among two or more generations of slaves on the same holding were less identifiable than on the vast coffee estates of Vassouras. After 1850, robust male slaves were sold off to the more profitable coffee markets of the highlands, resulting in a sex ratio of 90.6 males per 100 females in the 1860s and a further decline to 74.6:100 in the 1875–85 period.[116] In the free population, the sex ratio of 94.5 males for every 100 females was more balanced during the 1875–85 period. The fact that Rio Bonito's slave and free population show a nearly equal sex ratio by 1872 suggests that, in contrast to Vassouras, where extensive estates with large holdings of male slaves was common, small-scale production units were the norm. On smallholdings, masters tended to share the workload alongside their slaves,

Table 3.5 Slave population of Rio Bonito parishes, by sex, 1850 and 1872

Parish	1850			1872		
	Male	Female	Total	Male	Female	Total
N.S. da Conceição do Rio Bonito	4287	4069	8356	2283	2314	4597
N.S. da Boa Esperança	1975	1439	3414	1290	1214	2504
Total	6262	5508	11,770	3573	3528	7101
Population of *município*	1850: 22,750; 1872: 25,872					

Sources: BNRJ, *Recenseamento da população da Província do Rio de Janeiro, Quadro A, 1850*; Directoria Geral da Estatística, *Recenseamento da Provincia do Rio de Janeiro, Quadro A, 1872*. Recompiled by CEDEPLAR.

but the high incidence of *pardos* among free and slave males and females may be linked to the influx of non-white free family household units or to the formation over time of households, like that of the Lemos family (discussed in the next chapter), that involved free men and slave women and their offspring.

The nearly equal sex ratio that existed by 1872 further suggests that in this farming community where the holding of small numbers of slaves involved greater health, accident and other risks, the handling of multiple tasks by both men and women was common (Table 3.5).[117]

Between the *senzala* and the great house: *sítios* and small farms

In rural society, the positioning of the huts of free and freed farmers lay between the social extremes represented by the great house and the *senzala*, and clearly signalled a descending, albeit interrelated, social hierarchy. The master class in the great house represented the world of order and government; the freemen and women, skilled and unskilled workers, artisans, farmers and *agregados* and their families represented a hierarchized, dependent world, sometimes linked to crime; and at the base was the world of labour, the world of the slaves.[118]

Distinctions between slave and free labourers in both *municípios* were becoming blurred, not only as free farmers and their families moved on to estates but as the labour arrangements, use of roads and rivers and dealings at the *venda* brought free, freed and slave into constant contact.[119] Portuguese and Brazilian foremen, artisans, traders and farmers, landless Brazilian squatters, dispossessed settlers, smallholders and freed slaves either lived on the boundaries or resided within the confines of *fazendas*, planting fruit and vegetable gardens, tending coffee groves and pasturing small livestock in exchange for a quitrent or service to the landowner. John Luccock had observed a precedent for the incorporation of free farmers into estates in the beginning years of the century. The same precedent would govern the customary rights applied to immigrant families on the emerging coffee fields of São Paulo.[120]

The incorporation of free farmers into the large estates in Rio Bonito coincided with the influx of free labour that was replacing slave labour after 1850. Whereas

Figure 11 Poor family at home. *Source:* Jean Baptiste Debret, *Viagem Pitoresca e Histórica do Brasil*, 1834. Photos taken between 1816 and 1831.

the *fazenda* dominated the landscape of Vassouras, the small farm, *sítio* or *situação* was characteristic of Rio Bonito and other food-producing towns. According to the local language of Rio Bonito and surrounding counties, it described 'an agricultural establishment which included lands and improvements, or only improvements when the land is not owned'.[121] *Sítios* included cabins; on others the holder constructed a hut, usually a modest wattle-and-daub one- or two-room structure with earthen floors, a thatched roof, shutterless windows and wooden doors. The resemblance to slave quarters cannot be overemphasized (see Figure 11). On their travels early in the century, von Spix and von Martius described 'small modest unadorned rural wattle and daub dwellings with earthen floors, trellised or shuttered windows; roofing that was raised a few feet above the walls and on one side of the cabin overhung a veranda'.[122] The description of the American Consul-General Andrews at the end of the century reflected little change:

> Houses, or rather huts of the poor are built of unburned brick
> and are of a brown or earth color, have wooden window-
> shutters, but no glass windows, and usually palm-thatched roofs.
> Generally, near the house is a little patch of ground fenced with
> upright poles of irregular height. Mules, goats and hogs are the
> kinds of livestock most commonly seen.[123]

Furniture, if any, was hand-hewn, rustic and functional. Improved cabins had limestone outer coatings, tile roofs and wooden floors, an indication of investment in the holding that suggested assured tenure on the land. Long-term occupants might receive discarded bedding or a chest from the mansion house to complement the table and stools and sparse household possessions – a few earthenware pots and bowls, a knife and fork and a cup or two. In most cases, however, the meagre possessions of landless farmers – a handful of slaves, animals, manioc presses, earthenware pottery, copper cooking pans, carts and wagons – suggest that dwellers invested in items that could be packed up easily when it was time to move on. Even the sale of *situações* was common among landless free farmers and often transpired without the landlord's knowledge.[124] Capital accumulated in these transactions was invested in the next stopping place, a trend that suggests that physical mobility on the part of semi-nomadic landless farmers paralleled the sale and exchange that exposed most of Brazil's slaves to three or four new environments during their lifetimes.

The provision of a dwelling, garden, pasture for small livestock and plots of land within the confines of the *fazenda* unit was beneficial to landowners, who gained extra labour and established a free population as a buffer zone that might be mobilized for purposes of defence or protection from slave revolts. The arrangement also enabled semi-autonomous farmers to gain access to an infrastructure of transportation, legal recourse, credit and sale of surplus production that was not readily available through squatting.[125] Proximity to a property owner, the use and some participation in the benefits of an operating production unit defined the extent of the arrangement. Ownership of any improvements and tenure on the property were negotiable. Tenure could be seasonal or longer depending on the ability of the plantation structure to accommodate both a sizeable resident free labour force and a predominantly slave labour force.[126] Stuart Schwartz and Jacob Gorender claimed that long-term family dwellers and *agregados* protected the owner and his family. Other free labourers included artisans, contracted workers, vendors, small landowners or renters, who produced foodstuffs for the local market and took up residence within the *fazenda*. Additionally, the labour of women extended from domestic chores and child-raising in the households to carrying meals to their menfolk in the fields and collecting firewood on the return. Women also traded foodstuffs in local markets and from stalls along the roadsides.[127]

Residence on a *fazenda* offered no promise of stability, of ownership of improvements or of tenure on the estate. In the event of the landowner's death, all property was subject to appraisal and the name of the occupant of each *sítio* within the *fazenda* was listed as part of the deceased's estate to be inherited by his heirs. Any agreements that had been made between subsistence farmers and the deceased landowner were subject to renegotiation with the heirs, unless a written contract specifically stipulated a termination date. The continued tenure of free farmers (including ex-slaves) on the estate after the death of the land-owner and compensation for improvements made to the property depended on individual arrangements with the specific heir as to the portion of the property involved. In this way, slave, freed and free farmers faced a common source of tension: the right to improvements made to land, especially food crops.

New fields, new identities: a microcosm for freedom

Early in the century, John Luccock stated that landowners were assigning or renting plots of land to tenants and semi-nomadic farmers. His compatriot, John Mawe, observed the same practice applied to slaves on the imperial Fazenda de

Santa Cruz. Slaves chose small plots to plant crops for their own use and were allotted two days a week and time during major holidays to cultivate them.[128] Provision grounds or small patches that 'each slave was allowed to cultivate for his own use and yielded as much in proportion as the land of the master' were also observed by the English traveller, Maria Graham. J. Friedrich von Weech stated that these grounds enabled slaves to provide for themselves and also kept them occupied.[129]

By the 1840s, the custom of slaves farming their own provisions was commonplace enough to be included in planter Lacerda Werneck's model *fazenda*. A small piece of land was to be assigned for garden plots so that slaves could cultivate coffee, maize, beans, bananas, potatoes, sugarcane, yams and sweet cassava to supplement meagre and deficient diets and to sell the excess produce to their master.[130] The provision ground represented, like the *sítio*, a customary right to one's own economy through usufruct of land that present-day historians have identified with a 'peasant breach' or a proto-peasantry in some slave societies.[131]

Provision grounds figured in the guidelines published by a committee of Vassouras planters in 1854. Following the basic security measures – a balance in the proportion of free persons and slaves, adequate arms for free persons and constant vigilance over slaves – were three additional measures of a cultural nature: permission for slave entertainments; promotion of religious ideas; and the assignment of plots for slave provision grounds. The latter aimed to foster a tie to land that would deter slaves from either fleeing or creating havoc.[132] A report by British traveller Richard Burton in 1867 also attested to these practices in the Morro Velho mine in Minas Gerais. Burton mentioned cultural festivities organized by the administration of the mine that included gambling, 'national dances', drinks and parties. He also observed small slave provision grounds for the production of vegetables, but reported that the prohibition on selling pigs, chickens and foodstuffs figured among the punishments inflicted upon the slaves.[133]

Slaves who produced only a portion of the crops for their own consumption, selling any excess produce to their owner, the nearby local *venda* or tavern or in a local market, were familiar with the dynamics of marketing and credit.[134] At the *venda*, a small tavern-cum-hock shop, where few questions were asked concerning the origins of stolen goods and coffee, produce was valued and exchanged for cane whisky, soap, matches and other items.[135] Records of accounts held by slaves at local *vendas* not only confirm the regular exchange of produce for items of daily use but also attest to purchases made on credit and even to occasional loans from the tavern keeper.[136] One such tavern keeper was Luiz Labriola, an unmarried Italian who died in the parish of Boa Esperança in Rio Bonito in 1877, leaving a will and testament in which he legally recognized his two infant daughters by Presciliana Rosa do Espírito Santo (also unmarried, and to whom he left a token of 300 réis), as the legitimate heirs to his three slaves. He also left goods in his shop that ranged from edibles to articles of mens', women's and children's clothing; oxen and mules to carry goods; and properties in Rio Bonito and Araruama that totalled almost 19 contos.[137] His estate was also left with bills from creditors amounting to 20 contos, more than the total worth of his estate, and with unpaid accounts from customers for almost the same amount. Luiz

Labriola divided his customers into two categories: free and slave. The separate accounts of 371 free customers, all listed by full name except for nine ex-slaves (identified by the name of the former owner), ranged from 248 réis to 437,000 réis, and with sixteen holders of letters of credit totalled 16 contos. Unpaid bills from 99 slaves, whose individual bills ranged from 460 réis to 136,758 réis in outstanding credit, totalled less than 1 conto. Labriola identified slaves by their first name and that of their owner, many of whom were listed in the *Almanak Laemmert* as sugar planters, *fazendeiros* and *lavradores*. Three were officers in the National Guard. Diogo, Joanna, Rita, Gabriel and Leonel owed about 130,000 réis between them and were slaves of Jesuino José de Oliveira; Saturnino, João Moleque, Candido Veríssimo, Darilso Felix, João Rebollo, Geraldo and Alexandre were slaves of Captain José Paulo Figueiredo, the sole owner of a steam-operated sugar and *aguardente* estate; Manoel and Lusia were owned by Antonio Pedro Pacheco, who owned both sugar and coffee estates in the area.[138] It is not known whether the estate of Luiz Labriola ever received the due payments, but after his possessions were auctioned to pay creditors, the fact that the executor of the estate was unable to find family members or wellwishers to take custody of the two daughters suggests that debts were not covered and there was no inheritance left for them.

The nature of purchases made by slaves at the *venda* are not documented but do suggest that favoured slaves enjoyed credit relationships and had been initiated into bargaining, haggling and lending. The loan that the slave Rodrigo made to the murdered tavern keeper is illustrative of the eclipse of one more obstacle on the road to freedom, although in that case the loan exacted a life, some money and a few stolen articles in repayment.

Changing landscapes: conflicting identities

The use of an alternative dialect or hidden language and contacts with freed and free farmers and their families on rural estates, joint undertakings in skilled and unskilled tasks, the adoption of similar farming and gardening practices, the use of the *venda* and the establishment of mixed slave and free households in practice blurred identities that legally and socially maintained distinctions between slave and free. Maria Helena Pereira Toledo Machado has referred to a 'common space', suggesting a 'reciprocity' in the master–slave relationship.

> The perception of slavery as a system of assymetrical relationships established between unequal social groups forged a common space for negotiation and bargaining between masters and slaves, solidified by a paternalistic ideology.[139]

Urban-based abolition movements were taking the struggle for freedom into the rural areas and appealing to slaves, while at the same time the daily work regimes swung the pendulum closer to a free labour market. Despite planter efforts to distance public attention from the arbitrary treatment of slaves on private holdings, magistrates and local officials accompanied the public sphere as courts gingerly penetrated the enclosed confines of the private estate. Cries for freedom went hand in hand with the forging of a free labour market as imperial legislation gradually introduced measures that affected slaves, their families and the growing generations of free-born *ingênuos*.

Freedom, in its various guises and its impact on households, public spaces and the private sphere of the rural estate, was affecting rurality in the 1870s. The following chapters will examine the dynamics of this process and its bearing on land and labour arrangements.

Notes

1. In his extensive writings on capitalism, socialism and serfdom, Evsay D. Domar took Russian society as his point of departure. Ciro Cardoso and Héctor Pérez Brignoli, *História Económica da América Latina* (Rio de Janeiro: Graal Editora, 1983), explored Domar's hypothesis to explain the transition to capitalism. For Domar, the persistence of coercive forms in labour systems was linked to the relative absence of controls by the dominant class over the market for land. With reference to Brazil during slavery and the transition to free labour, Luiz Aranha Corrêa Lago, 'O surgimento da escravidão e a transição livre no Brasil: um modêlo teórico simples e uma visão ao longo prazo', *Revista Brasileira de Economia*, vol. 42, no. 4 (October/December, 1988), pp. 317–69; and Elisa Reis and Eustáquio Reis, 'Elites agrárias e a abolição no Brasil', *Dados*, vol. 31, no. 3 (1988), pp. 309–41, used the Domar hypothesis to compare availability of land and labour in Brazil's northeast, and in early and later areas of coffee expansion in southeastern Brazil.
2. The Catete Palace became the official residence of Brazil's presidents until the transfer of the capital from Rio de Janeiro to Brasília in 1960.
3. J. Friedrich von Weech, *Brasiliens Gegenwärtiger Zustand und Colonialsystem Besonders in Bezug auf Landbau und Handel. Zunächst für Auswanderer* (Hamburg: Hoffmann und Campe, 1828), pp. 132–3. Francisco Peixoto de Lacerda Werneck, *Memória sôbre a fundação de uma fazenda na província do Rio de Janeiro* (Brasília: Senado Federal/Fundação Casa de Rui Barbosa [1847], 1985), p. 57.
4. *Ibid.*, p. 59.
5. *Guarabu* is a leguminous tree; *guarapoca* is a forest tree; *ipê* is in the Bignoniaceous tree family; *muricipau canudo* was not identified. Cândido de Figueiredo, *Novo dicionário da língua portuguesa*, 4th edn (Lisbon: Sociedade Editôra Arthur Brandão e Companhia [1925]).
6. Warren Dean, *With Broadax and Firebrand* (Berkeley: University of California Press), 1995, p. 181.
7. Warren Dean, *Rio Claro: um sistema brasileiro de grande lavoura, 1820–1920* (Rio de Janeiro: Paz e Terra, 1977), p. 25.
8. Dean, *Broadax*, p. 188.
9. Charles de Ribeyrolles, *Brasil pitoresco* (São Paulo: [1859], 1976), vol. 2, p. 31.
10. John Mawe, *Viagens ao interior do Brasil* (São Paulo: Itatiaia and Editora da Universidade de São Paulo [1812], 1978), p. 87.
11. Leslie Bethell (ed), *Brazil: Empire and Republic, 1822–1930* (Cambridge: Cambridge University Press, 1989), Ch. 4, p. 131. Souza Breves was reputed to own 6000 slaves on his vast estates in the Paraíba Valley region.
12. Luccock, *Viagens*, p. 196.
13. John Mawe, *Travels in the Interior of Brazil, Particularly in the Gold and Diamond Districts of that Country* (Philadelphia: M. Carey, 1816), p. 144.
14. Auguste de Saint-Hilaire, *Segunda viagem do Rio de Janeiro a Minas Gerais e São Paulo* (São Paulo: Editora Nacional [1822], 1938), p. 103.
15. *Brasiliens*, Weech, pp. 139–40. Barry W. Higman, *Jamaica Surveyed* (San Francisco: Institute of Jamaica Publications, 1988), p. 198.
16. Lacerda Werneck, *Memória*, p. 58. On the plantation, the instructions were as follows:

A primeira de vossas aberturas deve ser grande, e por tal forma feita que para um lado da fazenda vos fique terreno suficiente, reservado para pastos; no mais ameno e próximo, uma boa quadra para o pomar que é útil e agradável, a um lado do qual, porém debaixo da mesma cerca, deve ficar desocupado terreno suficiente para hortaliça, que deveis ter com variedade para a vossa mesa.

17. Gilberto Freyre, *Brazil: An Interpretation* (New York: Knopf, 1945), p. 32.
18. One extant colonial great house is O Capião do Bispo in the suburb of Piedade in the city of Rio de Janeiro.
19. Richard Burton, *Viagens aos planaltos do Brasil*, vol. 2 [1868], Brasiliana Collection no. 375, p. 7.
20. Mr and Mrs Louis Agassiz, *A Journey in Brazil* (Boston: Ticknor and Fields, 1868), p. 55.
21. Grandjean de Montigny accompanied the French artistic mission to Rio de Janeiro, where he designed the Academy of Fine Arts on the model of the Paris Academy. See Jean Baptiste Debret, *Brasil império* (São Paulo: Difusão Nacional do Livro), p. 32. According to anthropologist Edison Carneiro, the pure and severe aspects of Brazilian neoclassicism are akin to the formalism that French art historian, René Julian, termed 'rigorous classicism'.
22. The Portuguese *sobrado* was a two-storey dwelling with a basement entrance that was connected to the first floor by a central staircase. See Eduardo Schnoor, 'Das casas de moradia às casas de vivenda', in Mattos de Castro and Schnoor (eds), *Resgate: uma janela para o oitocentos* (Rio de Janeiro: Topbooks, 1995), p. 42. According to Weech, more than two storeys was not common, *Brasiliens*, p. 137.
23. BNRJ, Iconography Division, *Fazendas de café de Alta Mogiana: cadernos de fotografia*. The photos of Gilberto Grecco testify to the deforestation and the allotment of land through large rectangular-shaped plots in the second half of the nineteenth century.
24. Isabel da Rocha, 'Arquitetura rural', *Revista Gávea*, no. 2 (1982) p. 63.
25. CPORB, Postmortem Inventory: Bernardo José de Moraes, 1860. Moraes's fortune at his death was equivalent to US$119,794.
26. Cartório Público do Primeiro Ofício de Rio Bonito (hereafter CPORB), Postmortem Inventories: 1845–90.
27. John Lukacs, [miscellaneous publication] Architectural Design Institute, Philadelphia.
28. Roberto da Matta, *A casa e a rua* (Rio de Janeiro: Editora Guanabara, 1987), pp. 31–71; *Carnavais, malandros e heróis* (Rio de Janeiro: Zahar, 1978), pp. 74–8.
29. Emília Viotti da Costa, *The Brazilian Empire: Myths and Histories* (Chicago: University of Chicago Press, 1985), Ch. 6.
30. Susan Besse, *Restructuring Patriarchy: The Modernization of Gender Inequality in Brazil, 1914–1940* (Chapel Hill: University of North Carolina Press, 1996), Ch. 1, fn. 1, p. 207. See also Dain Borges, *The Family in Bahia, Brazil: 1870–1945* (Stanford: Stanford University Press, 1994), p. 47.
31. Borges, *The Family*, p. 47.
32. Shirley Ardener, *Women and Space: Ground Rules and Social Maps* (New York: St Martin's Press, 1981), pp. 212–13. See also Elizabeth Fox-Genovese, *Within the Plantation Household: Black and White Women of the Old South* (Chapel Hill: University of North Carolina Press, 1988).
33. Adèle Toussaint-Samson, *A Parisian in Brazil* (Boston: James H. Earle, 1891), p. 119.
34. Agassiz, *A Journey*, p. 481.
35. Kátia de Queirós Mattoso, *Ser escravo no Brasil* (São Paulo: Brasiliense, 1988), pp. 231–2.
36. Mary C. Karasch, *Slave Life in Rio de Janeiro, 1808–1850*, p. 208.
37. Manuel Querino, *O africano como colonisador* (Salvador: Livraria Progresso, 1954), p. 39. See his collected works, published posthumously in 1938, *Costumes africanos no Brasil*, 2nd edn (Recife: Fundação Joaquim Nabuco, 1988).
38. In his novel, *Senhora*, José Alencar tells of a *fazendeiro* widower whose changes to his daily lifestyle included ordering his female slaves to dress when his visiting daughter-in-law and granddaughter, Aurelia, were present.
39. AN Corte de Apelação, Juízo Municipal de Rio Bonito, 1866. Libelo. Réu: Eufrasina (escrava). Autor: João Antunes Correia Benjamim. No. 673, Cx. 562, Gal. C.

40. *Ibid.*, p. 13. An elegant description of Eufrasina's plight offered to the court by her public defender deserves a mention:

> Tolling the hour of disgrace for the defendant, her honour was sacrificed to the person who presented himself as her benefactor. Being a woman, she yielded, unable to visualize the grim horizon before her. Yet, she believed herself to be free and was comforted by this idea.

41. *Ibid.*, p. 8.
42. *Ibid.*
43. *Ibid.*
44. See Deborah White, *Ar'n't I a Woman?* (New York: Norton, 1985), Ch. 1.
45. AN, Corte de Apelação, Rio Bonito, 1870. Réu: Hermenegildo Lopes Estrela. Autor: Antonio Fernandes da Motta. No. 1506, Cx. 93 (11–4–73), Gal. C. Hermenegildo was a planter from Rio Bonito; Antonio Fernandes was a trader from the port town of Porto das Caixas. See White, *Ar'n't I a Woman?*, p. 101, for a similar case.
46. Erico Veríssimo, 'A educação nacional' (1894), in Robert E. Conrad, *Children of God's Fire* (Princeton: Princeton University Press, 1983), pp. 222–3.
47. *Ibid.*, p. 222; White, *Ar'n't I a Woman?*, pp. 29–61.
48. On degeneration, see Dain Borges, 'Puffy, ugly, slothful and inert': degeneration in Brazilian social thought, 1880–1940', *Journal of Latin American Studies*, vol. 25, (1993), pp. 235–56.
49. Gilberto Freyre, *The Masters and the Slaves* (New York: Alfred A. Knopf, 1946). James Walvin has made a similar observation concerning domestic slaves in the British Caribbean. See *Black Ivory: A History of British Slavery* (London: Fontana Press, 1993), pp. 109–10.
50. AN, Corte de Apelação, Rio Bonito, Eufrasina.
51. Ida Pfeiffer, *A Woman's Journey around the World* (London: Office of the National Illustrated Library, 1850), pp. 43–4.
52. Agassiz, *A Journey*, p. 55.
53. Adèle Toussaint-Samson mentions the travelling salesman as an example of a visitor who, although not socially of a class with the planter and his family, was still housed for a night in the great house. *Une Parisienne au Brésil* (Paris: Paul Ollendorff, 1883), p. 172. English version, *A Parisian*, p. 120.
54. Maria Eugênia Torres Ribeiro de Castro (1862–1916), *Reminiscências* ([np]: Editora Catedra, n.d.). The estate was the Fazenda Cachoeira in Campos, Rio de Janeiro.
55. Ardener, *Women and Space*, p. 21. Locations of guest quarters varied widely depending on the great house layout. On the Middleton Place plantation in Charleston, South Carolina, the location of the guest quarters in a free-standing flanker on the second floor over the laundry room was the most telling spatial association I have come across involving the proximities of personal and impersonal service.
56. Toussaint-Samson, *Une Parisienne*, p. 142.
57. Manuel Moreno Fraginals (ed.), *Africa in America* (New York: Holmes and Meier 1984), p. 12.
58. Stanley J. Stein, *Vassouras: A Brazilian Coffee County, 1850–1900* (Princeton: Princeton University Press, [1957] 1985), fn. 11, p. 134.
59. Flávio dos Santos Gomes, *Histórias de quilombolas: mocambos e comunidades de senzalas no Rio de Janeiro – século XIX* (Rio de Janeiro: Arquivo Nacional, 1993), p. 201. The insurrection, or Manuel Congo slave movement, will be dealt with later.
60. AN, Corte de Apelação, Juízo Municipal de Rio Bonito, 1886. Apelante: Ladislau. No. 1652, Cx. 154, Gal. C. APERJ Estatística dos Setenciados da Penitênciária do Estado do Rio de Janeiro, 1885.
61. Roberto da Matta, *Carnivals, Rogues and the Heroes: An Interpretation of the Brazilian Dilemma* (Notre Dame: University of Notre Dame Press, 1991), p. 65.
62. Toussaint-Samson, *Une Parisienne*, pp. 102–3.
63. Another example of how the French and mulatto planters' commemoration of a saint's day contrasted with the celebrations held in the forest by those slaves responsible for the Saint Domingue massacre is colourfully described in Alejo Carpentier, *The Kingdom of this World*

(New York: Noonday Press, 1994). On slave musicians, see Schnoor, 'Das casas de morada', p. 55; Agassiz, *A Journey*, p. 121.

64. Elizabeth Agassiz described music that was played by a brass band composed of slaves from the estate of Senhor Breves, the prominent planter who held vast estates and thousands of slaves in the highlands near Barra do Piraí in the province of Rio de Janeiro. Agassiz, *A Journey*, p. 121.

65. Toussaint-Samson, *Une Parisienne*, pp. 130–1.

66. George Gardner, *Travels in the Interior of Brazil, Principally through the Northern Provinces and the Gold and Diamond Districts during the Years 1836–1841* (London: Reeve, Benham and Reeve, 1849), p. 36.

67. Higman, *Jamaica Surveyed*. See Nancy Priscilla S. Naro, 'Gender and space on plantations of Brazil, the Caribbean, and the United States South', a paper presented at the Society of Caribbean Studies, Oxford, 1994. A revision of the paper was presented at the Eastern Historical and Geographical Association, Codrington College, Barbados, 1994.

68. Instituto Histórico Geográfico Brasileiro (hereafter IHGB). Censuses taken in 1798 and 1799 of the Portuguese forts in Nova Redondo, Muxima, Encoge and Caconda list the numbers of European and African inhabitants of each fort and the *sobas* and African tribes who farmed and traded within the fort's walls.

69. C.C. Andrews, *Brazil: Its Conditions and Prospects* (New York: Appleton, 1887) p. 164.

70. Lacerda Werneck, *Memória*, p. 58. Weech, *Brasiliens*, stated that all living conditions had to meet with the planter's approval, p. 133.

71. Toussaint-Samson, *Une Parisienne*, p. 81. Weech stated that slaves used wattle and daub for the frame and palm fronds for the roofs of their quarters (*Brasiliens*, p. 138).

72. Thomas Ewbank, *Life in Brazil* (New York: Harper, 1856), p. 365.

73. Hamilton Lindsey-Bucknell, *Um jovem irlandês no Brasil em 1874* (Rio de Janeiro: Hachette, 1976), Ch. 45, p. 93.

74. Ribeyrolles, *Brasil pitoresco*, vols 1 and 2, with photographs by Victor Frond.

75. Andrews, *Brazil*, p. 152.

76. See Toussaint-Samson, *Une Parisienne*, p. 81, on the materials and appearances of the huts.

77. AN, Corte de Apelação. Sumário Crime, 1866. Recorrente: O Juízo. Recorrido: Bento Carlos Ferreira. Maço 228, No. 2954. Gal. C. See also 1862. Recorrente: O Juízo. Recorrido: Bento Carlos Ferreira. Maço 115. No. 988; 1866. Recorrente: O Juízo. Recorrido: Bento Carlos Ferreira. Maço 228, No. 2940. Gal. C.

78. Johann Jakob von Tschudi, *Viagem às provincías do Rio de Janeiro e São Paulo* (São Paulo: Editora Martins [1866], 1976), p. 57; Toussaint-Samson, *Une Parisienne*, p. 104.

79. Stein, *Vassouras*, p. 38, fn. 20.

80. Pfeiffer, *A Woman's Journey*, p. 44; J.B. von Spix and C.F.P. von Martius, *Reise in Brasilien auf Befehl Sr Majestät Maximilian Joseph I* (Rio de Janeiro: Imprensa Nacional [1823], 1938), p. 140; Stein, *Vassouras*, pp. 37–8.

81. Andrews, *Brazil*, p. 165.

82. Toussaint-Samson, *A Parisian*, p. 107; Weech, *Brasiliens*, p. 140.

83. Pfeiffer, *A Woman's Journey*, p. 44.

84. *Ibid.*; Stein, *Vassouras*, p. 37; Von Spix and von Martius, *Reise*, p. 140.

85. Coffee bags were stacked on flat-bottomed coffee boats and transported to the Paraíba River ports. Agassiz, *A Journey*, p. 121.

86. Jean Baptiste Debret, *Viagem pitoresca e histórica ao Brasil, 1816–1831* (São Paulo: Edições Melhoramentos, 1971), p. 64; Karasch, *Slave Life*, p. 263.

87. Weech, *Brasiliens*, p. 14; Pfeiffer, *A Woman's Journey*, p. 45. I will deal in more detail with the diets and eating habits of slaves during the process of transition in Chapter 5.

88. The sacred space or centre where the Afro-Brazilian cult of *umbanda* is conducted is also known by the name *terreiro*.

89. Moreno Fraginals, *Africa in America*, p. 6.

90. African words and expressions continue to inform Brazilian Portuguese. See the lengthy compilation of African borrowings in John T. Schneider, *Dictionary of African Borrowings in Brazilian Portuguese* (Hamburg: Helmut Buske, 1991); Robert W. Slenes, '"Malungu, ngoma

vem!'": Africa encoberta e descoberta no Brasil', *Revista USP*, no. 12 (1991–2), reprinted in *Cadernos Museu Escravatura* (Luanda: Ministério da Cultura, 1995). Moreno Fraginals has also highlighted the secret messages and encoded languages of *abakuá* that was predominant in Cuba. See *Africa in America*, p. 19.

91. Karasch, *Slave Life*, on figures of saints; Slenes, 'Na senzala uma flor'.

92. Toussaint-Samson, *Une Parisienne*, p. 119.

93. Ribeyrolles, *Brasil pitoresco*, p. 51; Karasch, *Slave Life*, p. 243.

94. Stein, *Vassouras*, pp. 206–7.

95. Maria de Lourdes Borges Ribeiro, *O Jongo* (Rio de Janeiro: Instituto Nacional do Folklore, 1984), pp. 18, 20.

96. Meaning: Cane whisky (or money) is on its way. From Aparecida, São Paulo. *Ibid.*, p. 37.

97. Meaning: There is more to this than meets the eye. From Piraí, Rio de Janeiro. *Ibid.*, p. 39.

98. Meaning: The water symbolizes cane whisky; a watered flower grows; happiness develops from cane whisky. From Paratí, Rio de Janeiro. *Ibid.*, p. 40.

99. Stein, *Vassouras*, p. 209.

100. Schneider, *Dictionary of African Borrowings*, p. 114.

101. See Helena Theodoro, 'Religiões negras no Brasil', *Cativeiro e Liberdade*, seminário do Instituto de Filosofia e Ciências Humanas, Universidade do Estado do Rio de Janeiro, 1989, pp. 239–40.

102. AN, Corte de Apelação, Juízo Municipal de Vassouras, 1868. Subdelegacia de Paty do Alferes. Réu: Rodrigo, escravo de Antonio de Azevedo Silva. Autor: A justiça. Cx. 3668, Proc. 6207, Gal. C.

103. See Karasch, *Slave Life*, p. 232, on *caxambú*.

104. Robert E. Conrad, *The Destruction of Brazilian Slavery, 1850–1888* (Berkeley: University of California Press, 1972), Appendices, Table 8, 'Slaves imported into Rio de Janeiro through inter-provincial Trade, 1852–1862', p. 289.

105. *Ibid.*, Table 2, 'Free and slave populations of Brazil, 1874', p. 284.

106. Esther Boserup, *Women's Roles in Economic Development* (Aldershot: Gower with LSE, 1986), pp. 361, 363; Carolyn E. Sachs, *Gendered Fields: Rural Women, Agriculture and Environment* (Boulder: Westview, 1996), p. 6, for general approaches to women's roles.

107. Weech, *Brasiliens*, p. 134; Viotti da Costa, *The Brazilian Empire*, Ch. 6.

108. Stein, *Vassouras*, pp. 163–4.

109. Karasch, *Slave Life*, p. 34.

110. *Ibid.*, pp. 32–4.

111. *Ibid.*, Table 2.4, p. 34.

112. Martin A. Klein, 'Women in the Atlantic slave trade', in Claire C. Robertson and Martin A. Klein (eds), *Women and Slavery in Africa* (Madison: University of Wisconsin Press, 1983), p. 35.

113. In the *município* of Paraíba do Sul, the sex ratio in 1840 among slaves was 232:100 in a total population (free and slave) in which the ratio was 161:100. In 1872, the increase of slave and free women in the town population was reflected in the adjusted sex ratios. The sex ratio of the slave population was 134:100 in a total population with a sex ratio of 107:100. João Luís Ribeiro Fragoso, 'Sistemas agrárias em Paraíba do Sul (1850–1920)', unpublished MA dissertation, Departamento de História, Universidade Federal do Rio de Janeiro, 1983, Table N.4, p. 44.

114. Stein, *Vassouras*, Figure 2, p. 77.

115. *Ibid.*, p. 78, and Figure 3, p. 79.

116. Nancy Priscilla S. Naro, 'From slavery to migrant labour in rural Brazil', *Slavery and Abolition*, vol. 15, no. 2 (August 1994), Table 1, p. 187.

117. Klein, 'Women in the Atlantic slave trade', p. 34.

118. The phrase, 'worlds of government, disorder and labour' was employed by literary critic and writer Antonio Cândido in 'Dialética da malandragem', *Revista do Instituto de Estudos Brasileiros*, no. 8 (1970). Cândido's 'worlds' later formed the contextual basis for historical evaluations of Brazilian nineteenth-century society. The planter class included elite planters, government and military officials, liberal professionals and high-ranking clergy.

119. See Naro, 'Revision and persistence: recent historiography on the transition from slave to free labour in rural Brazil', *Slavery and Abolition*, vol. 13, no. 2 (1992), p. 74.

120. Matthias R. de Assunção, 'Popular culture and regional society in nineteenth-century Maranhão, Brazil', *Bulletin of Latin American Research*, vol. 14, no. 3 (1992), pp. 265–86.

121. CPORB, Manutenção de posse, 1896. Autor: Joaquim Vieira Rangel. Maço 122. I am referring here only to the *situações* and *sítios* of poor farmers. Payment of debt, inheritance, sale, rent and exchange of lands was frequent among prominent planters who owned a small farm within the landed complex of another planter.

122. Von Spix and von Martius, *Reise*, p. 150.

123. Andrews, *Brazil*, p. 135.

124. For a detailed description of free poor farmers and their property and lifestyles, see Hebe Maria Mattos de Castro, *Ao sul da história* (São Paulo: Brasiliense, 1986); Naro, 'Customary rightholders and legal claimants to land in Rio de Janeiro, Brazil, 1870–1890', *The Americas*, vol. 48, no. 4, 1992.

125. Jacob Gorender, *O escravismo colonial* (São Paulo: Ática, 1985), p. 289 *et passim*. Coffee and sugar estate appraisals in postmortem inventories from all of the Vassouras parishes, and from at least ten *fluminense municípios* currently under study, contain listings of families of farmers who lived on and farmed small-scale *sítios* or *situações* with fruit trees, coffee, manioc and cornfields. References and citations in Naro, 'Revision and persistence', pp. 68–85; Stuart B. Schwartz, *Slaves, Peasants and Rebels* (Champagne: University of Illinois Press, 1992).

126. Mattos de Castro, *Ao sul*.

127. Gorender, *O escravismo colonial*, p. 289 *et passim*. On country women, see Andrews, *Brazil*, p. 256.

128. Mawe, *Viagens*, p. 87.

129. Maria Graham, *Journal of a Voyage to Brazil and Residence There. During Part of the Years 1821, 1822, 1823* (London: n.p.,1824), p. 228; Weech, *Brasiliens*, pp. 135, 140–1.

130. Lacerda Werneck, *Memória*, p. 63.

131. See Ciro F.S. Cardoso on peasant breaches in 'O modo de produção escravista colonial na América', in Théo Santiago (ed.), *America Colonial* (Rio de Janeiro: Palas, 1975), p. 121; Ciro F.S. Cardoso, *Agricultura, escravidão e capitalismo* (Petrópolis: Vozes, 1979), pp. 133–54; Ciro F.S. Cardoso, *A Afro-América – a escravidão no Novo Mundo* (São Paulo: Brasiliense, 1982); Ciro F.S. Cardoso and Héctor Pérez Brignoli, *História econômica da América Latina* (Rio de Janeiro: Graal, 1983); Ciro F.S. Cardoso, *Escravo ou camponês? O protocampesinato negro nas Américas* (São Paulo: Brasiliense, 1987), pp. 91–114. For later arguments, see Eduardo Silva and João José Réis, *Negociação e conflito: a resistência negra no Brasil escravista* (São Paulo: Companhia das Letras, 1989), Ch. 2, pp. 22–31.

132. *Instrução para a Comissão Permanente nomeada pelos fazendeiros do Município de Vassouras*, in Eduardo da Silva, 'A função ideológica da "Brecha Camponesa"', *Revista da Sociedade Brasileira de Pesquisa Histórica*, Anais da IV Reunião, 1985, p. 194.

133. Cited in Douglas Libby, *Trabalho escravo e capital estrangeiro: o caso e Morro Velho* (Belo Horizonte: Itatiaia, 1984), pp. 125–6.

134. Stein, *Vassouras*, p. 170.

135. Accounts of trial records in Vassouras and Rio Bonito contain references to a slave accused of robbing money who was seen by witnesses buying drinks for slave friends; slaves who killed masters to rob from them; and slaves who robbed objects from their masters' houses.

136. CPORB, Postmortem Inventory. This tavern keeper's records list the amounts owed by local slaves for matches, soap, kerosene and some food items.

137. *Ibid.*, Luiz Labriola, 1877.

138. *Ibid.*

139. Maria Helena Pereira Toledo Machado, *Crime e escravidão. Trabalho, luta e resistência nas lavouras paulistas 1830–1888* (São Paulo: Brasiliense, 1987), p. 101.

4

Masters and Slaves: Authority and Control

The case of Emerenciana's children: a legal bridge to freedom

The town herbalist in Rio Bonito testified that Emerenciana and her children were slaves because they served and 'were subdued like slaves': 'They collected medicines at the shop, conveyed messages, and lived in submission in the Lemos household.'[1] The herbalist highlighted service and submission as the distinguishing feature of slaves, proof that Emerenciana's children were not free. In attendance to Miguel Luiz de Lemos and his wife, Paula Maria, before her death in 1842, the herbalist's association with the Lemos household where Emerenciana and her children resided was unquestioned, as was his confirmation that she was a domestic slave and the mother of three of the household slaves.

The status of Emerenciana's children lay at the heart of a convoluted inheritance case, which they challenged in the high court of appeals, the Tribunal de Relação in 1856. The legitimate Lemos heirs had refused their mother's inheritance when she died, leaving their father to handle her estate. But after the death of the elder Lemos, the youngest heir, José Luiz, who was in need of cash, sold his share of his mother's inheritance in 1853, only to be informed that it included Emerenciana (by then deceased) and her children. The matter was further complicated, since the three slaves possessed a letter of manumission, written in 1848 by José Luiz's father, the elder Lemos. Addressed to a local businessman who doubled as an inspector and made up military recruitment lists in 1852, the letter explained that although the three children had been slaves, he had freed them.

Emerenciana was a *parda* slave, held in service to the family since 1809 and eventually identified as the slave daughter of the elder Lemos. Details of the relationship between the elder Lemos and Emerenciana's mother are not known, nor is there any information concerning her slave mother. Emerenciana was not sold, but remained in the household as a favoured slave, who gave birth to at least five children and raised three of them, the *pardos* Basílio, Fernando and Maria. The total number of Emerenciana's children and the identity of their father or fathers are not known, but her five children clearly demonstrate that procreation was unimpeded and probably even encouraged by masters like Senhor Lemos. His position as the family patriarch was unquestioned by his wife, his legitimate children, by Emerenciana, or by Basílio, Maria, or Fernando who remained in the Lemos household and to whom he granted letters of freedom. He asked a neighbour and friend to be Fernando's godfather when he was baptized, extending the link of patriarchy to a social equal through godparenthood. But Lemos did not treat all of his slave grandchildren this way. He sold one of Emerenciana's daughters and gave another to his daughter, Isabel; thirty years later, she was still serving as a domestic slave, a status that her three freed siblings never questioned.

The elder Lemos never freed Emerenciana. *Parda* slaves, even those in domestic service, were no different from other slaves in this regard, and they had no autonomous recourse to kin. As stated by Moreno Fraginals, 'family ties could be dissolved by the unilateral or unappealable decision of the master to sell, give up, transfer, or move one or more slaves in a group'.[2]

Under the terms of the mother's 1842 will, Emerenciana and three of her children were left to José Luiz, making the father's later letter of freedom invalid. Antonio da Silva Lemos, an older brother of José Luiz, testified that 'the slaves were held to be freed even before they had received their letters of freedom'.[3] According to witnesses, free status was assumed when Basílio began to ride horseback. It was said that the elder Lemos lent Basílio a horse until he was able to buy one for himself. By the 1850s Basílio had appended Olegário de Lemos to his name and was a recognized local trader and horse-trainer, who also managed one of the family mule-trains, collected bills for the elder Lemos and slaughtered cattle for market. In other words, he lived from his income. His sister, Maria, who appended Luiza da Conceição to her name, was a seamstress. Both carried on their businesses independently without permission, interference from or accountability to anyone. They acted and were treated as freed people.

The lifestyles of the slave children in the Lemos household were also akin to those of free people. Like Emerenciana, they were never assigned to field labour and only handled light domestic chores. A local Portuguese merchant recalled that Maria Caetana Lemos, José Luiz's elder sister, apologized to visitors as she moved them from the dinner table to make room for the slaves, a gesture that attested to their treatment as members of the family. Contesting the herbalist's association of submission with slavery, Maria Caetana claimed that Emerenciana's children were obedient, but that their obedience was out of respect for the person who raised them, as a child shows respect to a parent.

Initially, the three freed defendants were held to be *pessoas miseráveis* (miserable wretches) and the case was thrown out of court in 1853. In 1855, the man who had paid José Luiz for his inheritance appealed against the decision and a local judge upheld the legitimacy of his purchase, ruling that the defendants were to serve their new owner as his slaves.[4] That decision was overruled a year later by the Tribunal de Relação in Rio de Janeiro, where it was argued that 'this could not have been the intention of the person who sold his inheritance rights, contrary to the principles of sane reason and natural law. The case is overturned and the defendants are restored to their full freedom.' The costs of the proceedings fell to the plaintiff.[5]

Table 4.1 Slave values as percentage of total property values in postmortem inventories, Rio Bonito and Vassouras, 1850–85

Year	Slaves as percentage of total assets	
	Rio Bonito	Vassouras
1850	30	n.d.
1855	64	n.d.
1860	52	n.d.
1865	56	n.d.
1870	58	58
1875	58	46
1879–80	57	53
1885	51	30

The total number of inventories registered in the notary public for Rio Bonito (1850–85) and Vassouras (1870–85) are as follows: 1850, two cases; 1855, twelve cases; 1860, eight cases; 1865, six cases; 1870, five cases; 1875, six cases; 1879, three cases; and 1880 only one case out of eight in which the holdings of slaves represented 18 per cent. In 1885, out of a total of twelve cases, seven properties held 51 per cent of their value in slaves, whereas the other five cases held no slaves. There is no indication of how the sampling was done for Vassouras, since neither sampling techniques nor the total number of cases per year are given for Vassouras.

Sources: Stein, *Vassouras*, Figure 5, p. 226; CPORB, Postmortem Inventories, 1850–85.

This case is significant for a number of reasons. First, taking the period into account, it illustrates the ambiguities surrounding property in slaves, the definition of slave families, inheritance involving slaves and the treatment of legitimate and slave children in a society that only six years earlier had suspended the transatlantic slave trade. Slaves were valuable assets and continued to be for at least two or three more decades, accounting for between 30 and 64 per cent of the appraised value of estates in postmortem inventories (Table 4.1).[6]

The Lemos estate would not have qualified for inclusion among those of the prominent and prosperous planter elite of the Rio de Janeiro hinterlands, and that makes it interesting for a second reason. Upon her death in 1842, Senhora Lemos left her husband and five children her property in slaves, who accounted for 50 per cent of the value of the estate and furniture, tools, clothes, buildings, animals and crops that were collectively appraised at the equivalent of US $700. With its modest holdings, the Lemos estate is representative of the sizeable population of small and medium-sized land and slave-owners whose numbers were greater but whose social standing was inferior to the elites in Brazilian plantation society.

The case, therefore, offers an unusual glimpse into the social dynamics at work between masters and slaves and between illegitimate and legitimate children who co-existed under the same roof. The three *pardo* children, the children of other domestic slaves who were raised in the household as *crias da casa*, and Paula Maria and Miguel Luiz's five legitimate children lived under the same roof and shared household tasks. The five legitimate heirs were unanimous in their approval and encouragement of Basílio and his trade. His business dealings extended beyond Braçaná, the highland parish of the family estate, to local markets, where landowners, traders and scribes not only knew him but testified that he was held in esteem and circulated as a free person. Even the plaintiff, who stood to profit enormously from his purchase of the rights to possession of the three children, was one of Basílio's customers for fresh pork, beef and fish. The town herbalist's testimony that Emerenciana and her children were slaves was strongly contested by ten witnesses and family members. However, a decade earlier nobody would have denied their inclusion as property that, like furniture and possessions, could be passed on to a half-brother as his inheritance. At her death, Senhora Lemos had distinguished between legitimate household members and slave property, bequeathing her slave property to her heirs, a decision that was in accord with the times but would cloud the issues of freedom and inheritance as the century advanced.

Although Senhor Lemos followed his wife's example and and did not change Emerenciana's slave status,[7] what he did do makes the case illustrative for a third reason. Miguel Luiz de Lemos furnished Basílio and Maria with skills that were marketable and would provide them with a livelihood as free people in Brazilian society whether they remained in Braçaná or moved away. He enabled them to make the transition from being the property of others to possessing skills of their own. In freedom, his grandchildren were thus identified with a marketable occupation that made them useful earners in a free labour market.

Basílio and Maria's lives were in marked contrast to the lives led by most of Brazil's slaves. They were raised as part of the household headed by their grandfather and engaged in useful activities both there and in the production unit. They lived with the legitimate Lemos children and were testimony to the survival of three generations of slaves in service to the Lemos family. It is not known if Basílio and Maria had families of their own, but their circumstances were indicative of a social milieu that, in select instances, was accommodating ex-slaves in rural Brazil.

Basílio, Maria and Fernando probably applauded the decision of the Tribunal de Relação to favour José Luiz's claim to them. Technically, the decision recognized José Luiz as the master, whose unintentional act impinged on his right as a master and owner of his half-siblings. The matter of the manumission granted by the elder Lemos in 1848 was a separate issue and not dealt with in this case. The plaintiff had less cause to celebrate, since the three ex-slaves accounted for the lion's share of José Luiz's inheritance. Their skills had increased their value to a high 3 contos when the plaintiff bought his right to them in 1853.

Slave family units

Until the suspension of the transatlantic slave trade, childbirth was not encouraged by planters, although the heavy proportion of male slaves, meagre diet and harsh working conditions were effective deterrents to the formation of slave families. While the low number of female slaves also affected birth rates, slave women knew of a variety of means to abort unborn children or to shorten their survival in captivity. The simplest means, following the advice of slave *curandeiras*, was to insert objects into the womb, rub ointments on the abdomen or to induce uterine contractions by drinking infusions of plants such as rue (*ruta*, or *arruda* in Portuguese), the bitter herb that in the medical manual of the American colonial doctor, Thomas Palmer, 'brought down menstruation'.[8] Foetuses who were carried to full term were in constant danger from the childhood diseases, parasites, deformation, accidents and malnutrition that had accompanied the negative rates of growth of the slave population since the onset of the slave trade.[9]

There was a standard treatment for post-partum cases. Slaves were fed chicken bouillon and rice for a week after giving birth and were sent to do light work after three days. Slaves in field labour carried their babies with them in West African style, bound to their backs by lengths of cloth fastened over the midriff and swung under the arm.[10] Babies who were left behind were handled by elderly slaves or slave children, who fed them a thin gruel of cornstarch.

Mary Karasch's work on slave families in the city of Rio de Janeiro in the early part of the nineteenth century, along with the analyses of postmortem inventories for the city and in the rural Rio de Janeiro highland town of Paraíba do Sul conducted by João Luís Fragoso, Manolo Garcia Florentino and José Roberto Góes confirm that irrespective of a slave-owner's intentions, slave families began to appear in the early part of the nineteenth century. The research in Paraíba do Sul focused on the rural estates of prominent *fazenda* owners both prior to and after the abolition of the transatlantic slave trade.[11] Few families were complete – most lacked a father, a mother, a grandparent or siblings – but slave kin groups were identified on large and small estates throughout the Rio de Janeiro hinterland *municípios*, representing in some cases a span of three to four generations.

In Vassouras, most of the large family units were African-derived. Up to the middle of the century, Slenes calculated that 59 per cent of the slaves of the province, 45 per cent of the *pretos* and *pardos* (free and slave) and 32 per cent of the total population were of African origin, leading him to term the period one of African slavery.[12] Flávio dos Santos Gomes found that Vassouras slaves originated from ports in the Congo, Angola, Benguela, Moçambique and Cabinda, and accounted for 74 per cent of the 1404 slaves he researched in the postmortem inventories for the years 1837 to 1840. His findings support John Thornton's argument that most ships drew cargo from one or two African ports.[13] Stein's larger sample, from 1820 to 1860, identified some 50 per cent from Angola and Moçambique and some 30 per cent from Cabundá, Cassange, Ganguella, Inhambane, Moena, Mossambe and Libolo. Few from Mina or Calabar were listed.[14]

Data on the origins of African slaves are imprecise for Vassouras and for Rio Bonito after 1860, since many slave-owners stopped naming specific ports and instead listed from 'Africa' or '*da nação*' as the place of origin. Given the fact that the inter-provincial slave trade was bringing slaves to the southeast who had lived for a period in Brazil, the port of their embarkation from Africa may not have been known. However, in Rio Bonito, where 55 per cent of the listings do contain information on African ports, the Angolan ports of Benguela and Libolo figure prominently. The evidence from both *municípios* support Karasch's and Philip

Table 4.2 Slave population of Vassouras and Rio Bonito, by colour, 1850 and 1872

| | 1850 | | | | 1872 | | | |
| | Pardo | | Preto | | Pardo | | Preto | |
	No.	%	No.	%	No.	%	No.	%
Vassouras	731	3.8	18,479	96.1	2534	14.5	14,959	85.5
Rio Bonito	1758	14.9	10,012	85.1	2299	32.4	4802	67.6

Total slaves: 1850: Vassouras, 19,210; Rio Bonito, 11,770. 1872: Vassouras, 17,493; Rio Bonito, 7101.

Sources: BNRJ, *Recenseamento da população da Província do Rio de Janeiro, Quadro A, 1850*. Directoria Geral da Estatística, *Recenseamento da população da Província do Rio de Janeiro, Quadro A, 1872*. Recompiled by CEDEPLAR.

Morgan's findings that in Southeast Brazil eight in ten slaves came from West Central Africa, although Morgan identified that between one-fifth and one-quarter could be traced to East Africa, in particular Moçambique.[15]

As we have seen, the slave population in Brazil declined steadily after 1850, but in 1872 the proportion of African slaves in the combined slave populations of the court and the province of Rio de Janeiro was still 19.7 per cent of the total registered slave population of 341,576, the highest percentage in the country.[16] The African presence was also prominent in Rio Bonito and Vassouras. Rio Bonito had about half the number of slaves of Vassouras in 1850 and about one-third of the highland *município* in 1872, but in both cases the data reflect a preference on the part of slave-owners for *pretos* (African or first-generation Brazilian children of Africans) over *pardo* slaves. Only in Vassouras, however, was there evidence of planter preference for male over female *pretos* (Tables 4.2 and 4.3).

Preto slaves outnumbered *pardo* slaves among both sexes, confirming a stronger pattern of African-related descent than one of racial mixture. Despite the precarious conditions of survival imposed by slavery and the negative rate of reproduction in the slave population as a whole, Africans and their descendants in both *municípios* were a significant presence two decades after the suspension of the transatlantic slave trade (Table 4.3).

In rural Brazil, large clans and extended families evolved with plantation society, but, generally speaking, historians only began looking for parallels among slave families following the new directions in slave family studies taken by Herbert Gutman in the United States that influenced Brazilian and slave historiography during the 1980s.[17] Data on the number of African slaves who were sold from the slave market of Valongo and the port of Rio de Janeiro between 1822 and 1833 show that 94 of the total of 393 slaves (24 per cent) were female. Of this total, 24.5 per cent were under the age of fourteen; 74.5 per cent were between the ages of fifteen and forty-nine; and 1.1 per cent were over fifty.[18] Despite negative rates of reproduction among the slave population as a whole, domestic slaves like Emerenciana's mother, who raised at least one child, and slave families that have come to light in the studies of prominent estates in the Paraíba

Table 4.3 Slave population of Vassouras and Rio Bonito, by sex and colour, 1872

	Total number of slaves	Male					Female				
		Pardo		*Preto*		% of total slaves	*Pardo*		*Preto*		% of total slaves
		No.	%	No.	%		No.	%	No.	%	
Vassouras	18,475	1267	21	8269	79	57	1267	16	6690	84	43
Rio Bonito	7107	1219	34	2354	66	50	1080	31	2448	69	50

Source: Directoria Geral da Estatística, *Recenseamento da população da Província do Rio de Janeiro, Quadro A, 1872.* Recompiled by CEDEPLAR.

Valley towns prior to 1850 suggest that slave families were forming and developing a kinship structure.

In the aftermath of the suspension of the African trade in 1850, planters encouraged the formation of family units, and the numbers of *crioulo* children (children of African slaves) increased in Rio de Janeiro and São Paulo. Some planters offered freedom as an enticement for a slave who had more than seven children.[19] My sampling of 85 postmortem inventories from the Cartório de Primeiro Ofício in Vassouras, selected at five-year intervals between 1865 and 1888 included evaluating all holdings of slaves instead of restricting the sample to prominent wealthy landowners as was done in Paraíba do Sul. Among the 1346 slaves in the sample, slave families were pervasive. In 80 per cent of the records, slaves *da nação* were listed with their children and in some cases, their grandchildren. The high numbers of *crioulo* and *preto* children confirm that the partners of African slaves were other Africans, a pattern followed by their children, who created families with Africans or with other *crioulos*. The Vassouras postmortem inventory of the prominent Baron of Guanabara, who died in 1875, listed 377 slaves on an estate with an assessed value the equivalent of US$332,000. Nineteen per cent of the slaves were African, ranging in age from thirty-nine to sixty-nine and 48 per cent were listed as *crioulos*. In all, 67 per cent were linked by kinship ties to other slaves in the holding.[20] Herbert Klein and Francisco Vidal Luna have drawn a correlation between the size of holding and marriage rates, concluding that 'slaves generally married within their own units and the larger the size of the slave holdings of their masters, the more likely they were to find marriage partners on the same estate'.[21]

Slave occupations

Manuel Querino stated that African slaves directed their children and grandchildren to an occupation, and my findings confirm this.[22] Planters listed kin groups of children with their parents or, in the event of death, sale, manumission or escape of the parent, listed only the parent's name after the child. The slave *matrículas* (registers) show that slaves in long-standing service with families were also the main holders of skills and occupations on large estates, as were their children. My findings from the Baron of Guanabara's estate link such slaves to occupations and tasks that lay outside of intensive field work and to positions of authority. Three of the four foremen were African. The wife of one handled manioc and maize farming in the *roça* (small area for the cultivation of manioc, maize and beans, often for slave's own use). Africans in long-standing service and their children also held the skilled positions of mule-train driver, barber, artisans of different sorts and chief cook in the great house.[23] In addition, the *crioulos* were engaged in positions of authority or in positions requiring skill in the *roça* and in the great house, but not in the *lavoura* (cultivated fields). The blacksmith (*ferreiro*) was a 49-year-old *crioulo*; the engineer was the son of a resident African slave. A *crioulo* carpenter and his wife had a family of four *crioulo* children. The carpenter's three brothers also lived on the *fazenda*. Another *crioulo* carpenter lived with his midwife wife and their three children. A *crioulo* male was father to four *crioulo* children.

In the great house, the major-domo (*copeiro*) shared domestic duties with his three *crioulo* sisters; another was a *mucama* with six young children; another *crioula* *mucama* worked with her two daughters, who were raising five smaller children. Another headed a family of three daughters and two granddaughters and shared household duties with a woman and her two *crioula* daughters. The household page and his three brothers were also the sons of a *crioula*. This pattern featured in large holdings in the postmortem inventories of both towns, although there were more cases of this type in Vassouras.

A postmortem inventory from the estate of Ezequiel Padilha, who died in 1880, lists 35 per cent of the 164 slaves on his Fazenda Santa Eufrazia as African, who with their children and grandchildren held most of the skilled positions. The aged Mariana and Alipio were the only cooks and the only Africans in household service, although their daughters and those of deceased African slaves were predominant among the sixteen household slaves.[24] The overseer, gardener, stonemasons, carpenter, coachman, two laundresses, two *mucamas* and a seamstress were all children of African slaves. Most of the slaves identified as *roceiros* were Africans or children of African slaves in long-standing service.[25] Custodio, a 46-year-old African; Macharios, 56; Rosa, 52; Elías, 40; Luiz Benguella, 49; and Faustino and his wife Eva were African *roceiros*. Brígida, 28, and Emiliana, 25, were *roceiras*, daughters of José and Josepha Benguella. Candida, 20, Benedicta, 18, and Pedro, 26, were also *roceiros*, children of resident African slaves.

Roça is used interchangeably with the word *lavoura* in some postmortem inventories to indicate the place of assignment of field work, but when the term is employed next to the names of slaves it can also denote the special status of a slave who is employed in food production for themselves or a third party.[26] In the *matrículas* of the estate of José da Rosa Brum, who died in 1885, nine of the 24 slaves were African and three worked with their *crioulo* daughters. The *roça* was listed as the occupation of eight of the Africans and one of the *crias de casa*; the cook was African and her daughter, the *mucama*, was a *cria de casa*. The remaining slaves were assigned to the *lavoura*.[27] Food-crop cultivation would be preferred by most slaves, especially the aged and pregnant, since they were allowed to perform the tasks at their own pace, which was considerably less arduous than that imposed by the driver and his whip under the intensive regime of hoeing, weeding and berry-picking. The harvesting and sale of produce were also a means of accumulating capital to purchase items of daily consumption, farm animals and the purchase price of their freedom.

Authority and fertility in the *senzala*

Manolo Garcia Florentino and José Roberto Góes have taken the issue of slave families a step further, arguing, on the basis of the stable years of the African trade (1790–1807), that aged slaves controlled fertility in the slave quarters. Florentino and Góes's data suggest that elder African males chose fertile young female companions to ensure large families that enhanced their own authority. Elderly African women took young male partners who may have been outsiders with no kinship or other links to slaves in the slave quarters.[28] Their findings suggest that traditional forms of power and control over fertility, a feature of Joseph Miller's evaluation of data on harems in Angola for an earlier period, carried over to the slave experience in the Rio de Janeiro hinterland. According to Miller, in regions touched by the Atlantic trade, children, and especially male children, from enslaved alien women were sold to cover the master's debts. Constantly renewed harems of wives, formed from the ranks of helpless female immigrants, reproduced at rates able to cover their master's obligations to overlords for trade goods and enabled 'lineage elders, patrons, obscure new-comers, and royal appointees to remake themselves as masters of enslaved human capital in unprecedented numbers'.[29] Herbert Klein has argued that in Brazil Africans were, as a group, much older than the native-born slaves and would have commanded greater authority in accord with traditional African custom.[30] Florentino and Góes maintain that the control exerted by elder slaves over fertility remained unaltered in the post-1850 period and confirm power maintenance in African-derived families. In the 1875 postmortem inventory of the Baron of Guanabara, the pattern of births of 70 unmarried African women and 184 *crioulas*, whose partners are not identified, provides evidence in support of the Florentino and Góes findings. Sixteen per cent of the women had given birth at two- or three-year intervals, beginning in the early 1850s and lasting to 1875, when most would have been in their late thirties or early forties.[31] Although a few slave mothers who were born after 1850 began child-bearing as young as twelve, the majority of the women were in their mid-twenties at first recorded birth.[32] They were unmarried and there was no reference to a partner. More significant is the lack of an occupation next to their names. All but five of the 151 children listed were born in or after the suspension of the transatlantic slave trade in 1850, and contributed to the labour force on the *fazenda* as they grew up. Except for five *parda* women and their total of twelve children, the women were all African or *crioulos*. All of the children were listed as *crioulo* apart from ten who were listed as *pardo*. Hebe Maria Mattos de Castro has pointed out that by the 1870s, *pardo* was a social classification and could indicate a free status for descendants of African slaves, constructed on the basis of personal and community relationships.[33] In the Baron of Guanabara's slave holdings, the small number of *pardo* children born in or after 1850 neither confirms nor refutes master–slave involvements. However, since *pardo* and household slaves had a better chance of gaining their freedom than the other slaves, the term might, in fact, have been a social designation of an agreement reached as a result of negotiations between elder slaves and the master over the free status of a slave child.

More detailed samples, together with the names, ages and origins of fathers of the *crioulo* children, from a broad sample of estates would be needed to identify elder African males on the estate and confirm their control over fertility. The practices may have been traditional, originating from some areas of Africa, but in nineteenth-century Brazil it seems more plausible that strategies of power were in play rather than the predominance of tradition.

Masters and slaves

Richard Graham's study of the imperial Fazenda de Santa Cruz in colonial Brazil found that over 65 per cent of the slaves were married or widowed.[34] Florestan Fernandes and Emília Viotti da Costa also confirmed the existence of slave families in wide-ranging circumstances that varied greatly in time and place. In the Baron of Guanabara's *matrículas* only thirteen of the Africans were listed as married couples: six husbands had the same ages as their spouses; one male was older than his spouse; and six of the females were anything from five to twenty years older than their husbands.[35] A married status, or the togetherness of a couple and their children, was a special circumstance and one that suggested a privileged standing that the master awarded to certain slaves. For those so favoured, familiarity with the wiles and whims of their masters was useful in devising strategies of negotiation that, at times, challenged or disobeyed the authority of masters and overseers. Long-standing service familiarized slaves with plantation life and enabled them to mediate with masters concerning the conditions of service, the assignment of tasks and duties and the organization of the labour force assigned to carry them out. Favoured slaves and their families exercised authority over children and were expected to transmit linguistic, religious and work skills that ordered production. Lastly, it fell to them to regiment and socialize new slaves and others with no immediate kinship ties to the norms of the slave quarters and the workforce.

Long-standing service, kinship ties and the exercise of authority over newly arrived slaves enabled African slaves and their families to enjoy greater autonomy, mobility and power over the slave quarters. It is not surprising, then, that in the *matrículas* of the Baron's slaves, he still owned African male and female slaves, with ages ranging from thirty to sixty-nine, who were *doente* (ill), *quebrado* (broken), *aleijados* (crippled) or *cego* (blind). One suspects that they would exert a stabilizing influence over the large numbers of slaves who were born before the 1871 passage of the Free Womb Law (discussed later in this chapter). In the Baron's slave registers, only 42 slave children under four years of age would have been born free under this law. Their 105 less fortunate siblings, born between

1850 and 1871, represented 86 per cent of the total (122) number of slaves in that age range, or one-third of the slave population on the *fazenda*.

Were planters investing in stability through strengthened family ties and imposing their designs and authority over slaves to guarantee a future labour force that they expected to hold in bondage? The widow, Dona Alexandrina de Araujo Padilha, who inherited a successful, diversified and mechanized production unit, which included 121 slaves on an estate worth about US$70,000 in 1880, was able to pay off her husband's debts and remain on the estate. After her husband's death in Vassouras in 1880, she also held on to all of the aged and a half-dozen Africans who were ill, blind or had other physical defects. The slaves that fell to her part of the inheritance were those whom Senhora Padilha, her deceased husband and planters of her generation knew and whose children and grandchildren had been raised with their own. Her decision to keep the elderly slaves may have been charitable, but it also reflects common sense rather than rational market considerations. Just as the elder Padilha carried on a family tradition of land and slave-holding in Vassouras, his elderly African male and female slaves provided stability through the traditional authority that they, like him, assumed with age.[36]

The Baron and Senhora Padilha were not alone. Elder Africans represented 15 per cent of any given slave-holding although in the postmortem inventories of the 1870s and 1880s many were listed as *doente* or *quebrado*. Whereas age, the resulting low market prices and poor levels of productivity would be impediments to an intensive and arduous production routine in which producers were concerned with quotas, Kátia Mattoso has shown that the number of freed elderly slaves never exceeded 10 per cent of the total.[37] The decision to keep aged and infirm slaves was also influenced by financial considerations. The decision of one particular heiress of an indebted estate suggests that when slave-holders were faced with unmanageable expenses, they refused to keep elderly slaves. D. Apolinária, heiress to the estate of her widowed aunt, Aurelia Maria de Paiva, who died in 1885, inherited five slaves – a 59-year-old African field slave named Mariana and a 48-year-old *crioula* domestic slave, Luzia, and her three children, aged five, eight and thirteen – with a value of 500$000 réis, or one-third the total value of the estate.[38] Although she died as the abolition movement was reaching its peak, Aurelia's legacy provided her niece with two slave women and growing children, whose continued service would assure that her family's needs were attended to. Faced with debts that exceeded the value of the estate, however, D. Apolinária informed the district judge that she would pay off her aunt's debts but would refuse the bequest of the elder slave, Mariana.[39] It is not known what happened to Mariana.

Planters were generally ignorant of the great moments of African history, culture and traditions, yet most prominent planters were pragmatic and market conscious. The sizeable African-derived kinship groups brought stability to the slave quarters. Stable and relatively peaceful production units reflected slave authority over language and kinship that proved just as, if not more, effective than the master's patriarchal norms in upholding a precarious balance of authority. On the Baron of Guanabara's estate, family, authority and privileged forms of labour fell to the African *feitor* and his wife, who was the only woman with a sizeable family and the only slave woman assigned to the *roça*. She had six children aged between five and twenty-four years of age: the first was born in 1852 when she was twenty-three, followed by others in 1859, 1864, 1866, 1869 and her last recorded birth in 1870 when she was thirty-nine, one year short of the Free Womb Law that would have seen her last child born into freedom.

If the 1875 slave listings of the Baron of Guanabara's estate are typical of the prominent large estates, they suggest that planters not only encouraged high-status slaves to form slave families but were also inclined to keep the kinship units together. Many slave families may have formed in the slave quarters, but only a select few negotiated a wide range of privileges, including living together and the self-purchase of freedom for themselves or other eligible family members. In fact, Mattos de Castro's suggestion that *pardo* in some cases referred to slaves who were designated for emancipation would suggest a trade-off that fits into this arrangement. In general, however, slave families were not the norm in Brazilian slavery, and any evaluation of them does not contradict the more general findings of Ciro F.S. Cardoso, Robert Conrad, Jacob Gorender and others, whose analyses of census and other documentation have led them to refute the pervasiveness of slave families.[40] Yet, given the dynamism of slave markets from 1850 to the 1870s, and the high rates of return on investments in slaves in that period, it would not be unusual for planters to encourage some formation of large slave families and the training of children for specific skills as a safeguard for their and their own family's future in the rural milieu.[41]

Women and families: the changing nature of the rural population

Women figured prominently in the rural milieu during the halcyon period of coffee cultivation, representing 44 per cent (242,914) of the total provincial population of 556,080 in 1850, a figure that was divided almost evenly between free and slave.[42] Free women were subdivided into categories of white, *pardo*, *preto* and *caboclo*. There were twice as many free whites as *pardos*, small numbers of free *preto* women and a few *caboclos*. Slave women were subdivided into categories of *pardo* and *preto*, in which slaves in the latter category predominated (Table 4.4).

Two decades later, women still represented almost half of the total *fluminense* population. At the local level, in Vassouras, the female population increased from 10,690 in 1850 to 15,996, representing 45 per cent of the *município* population, in 1872. In Rio Bonito, the increase was more dramatic. The female population of 11,154 in 1850 increased to 13,177, accounting for 51 per cent of the total *município* population, in 1872.

A closer examination of the data from the two local censuses reveals changes in the composition of the slave population. In 1850, male slaves in Vassouras out-numbered female slaves by 2 to 1. In 1872, the slave population was slightly higher, but the ratio was approximately three male slaves to every two females. Female slaves increased from 35 to 43 per cent of the *município*'s slave population. In Rio Bonito, over half of the slave population was male in 1850, but by 1872 the slave population as a whole had dropped and the ratio of male to female was

Table 4.4 Female population of the province of Rio de Janeiro, by colour, free and slave status, 1850

Colour	Free female			Slave female		
	No.	%	% provincial population	No.	%	% provincial population
White	76,179	60	14	0	0	0
Pardo	39,345	31	7	9,761	8	2
Preto	10,293	7	2	106,865	92	19
Caboclo	2481	2	0.4	n.d.	n.d.	n.d.
Total	128,298	100	23.4	116,616	100	21

Total population of the province of Rio de Janeiro: 556,080.
Source: BNRJ, *Recenseamento da população da Província do Rio de Janeiro, Quadro A, 1850*.

Table 4.5 Slave population of Vassouras and Rio Bonito, by sex, 1850 and 1872

	1850					1872[a]				
	Male		Female			Male		Female		
	No.	%	No.	%	Total	No.	%	No.	%	Total
Vassouras	12,540	65.2	6670	34.7	19,210	11,479	56.9	8689	43	20,168
Rio Bonito	6262	53.2	5508	46.8	11,770	3573	50.3	3528	49.6	7101

[a]The 1872 data include the addition from 1871 of the Vassouras parish of Mendes to the parishes of Nossa Senhora da Conceição, Paty do Alferes, Sacra Família do Tinguá and Ferreiros. The parishes of Rio Bonito remained the same.
Sources: BNRJ, *Recenseamento da população da Província do Rio de Janeiro, Quadro A, 1850*. Directoria Geral da Estatística, *Recenseamento da população da Província do Rio de Janeiro, Quadro A, 1872*. Recompiled by CEDEPLAR.

about equal. In Rio Bonito's total slave population, the proportion of females increased from 47 to 50 per cent (Table 4.5).

The relationship between free and slave females also changed in both *municípios*. In Vassouras, the female slave population, which represented 62 per cent of the total female population in 1850, was about equal to the free population in 1872. In Rio Bonito, the proportions of slave to free women, roughly equal in 1850, shifted radically in favour of free women, who accounted for 73 per cent of the local population in 1872. The formation of the free labour market was clearly well advanced in the *município* by the 1870s (Table 4.6).

In 1872, changes in the white, *pardo* and *preto* populations in the two *municípios* can also be identified. In Table 4.7, the white male population was greater than the white female population of Vassouras, but the reverse was true in Rio Bonito. The *preto* males and females outnumbered their respective *pardo* counterparts by about 2 to 1 in Vassouras. In Rio Bonito, numbers were almost equal. On the

Table 4.6 Female population of Vassouras and Rio Bonito, 1850 and 1872

	1850					1872				
	Free		Slave			Free		Slave		
	No.	%	No.	%	Total	No.	%	No.	%	Total
Vassouras	4020	38	6670	62	10,690	8038	50	7957	50	15,995
Rio Bonito	5646	51	5508	49	11,154	9649	73	3528	27	13,177

Total population: Rio Bonito: 1850, 22,750; 1872, 25,872
Vassouras: 1850, 28,538; 1872, 35,913

Sources: BNRJ, *Recenseamento da população da Província do Rio de Janeiro, Quadro A, 1850*; Directoria Geral da Estatística, *Recenseamento da população da Província do Rio de Janeiro, Quadro A, 1872*. Recompiled by CEDEPLAR.

Table 4.7 White and non-white population (slave and free) of Vassouras, Rio Bonito and the court city and province of Rio de Janeiro, 1872

	Male			Female			Non-white as % of total population
	White	Non-white		White	Non-white		
		Pardo	*Preto*		*Pardo*	*Preto*	
Vassouras	5357	5810	10,496	4537	4340	8486	74.6
Rio Bonito	5749	3584	3327	6094	3607	3439	62.5
Rio de Janeiro (court city and province)							56.1

Court city and province of Rio de Janeiro, combined male and female: 254,994 *pardos* and 338,853 *pretos*.
Sources: Directoria Geral da Estatística, *Recenseamento da população da Província do Rio de Janeiro, Quadro A, 1872*. Recompiled by CEDEPLAR; Felipe de Alencastro (ed.), *História da vida privada no Brasil*, vol. 2 (São Paulo: Companhia das Letras, 1997), Table 5, 'Porcentagem de negros "pardos" e "pretos" na população total', p. 474.

basis of the sum of the entire non-white (free and slave, *pardo* and *preto*) populations in each town, both places were predominantly non-white, with a heavy concentration of *preto* males in Vassouras. In both *municípios*, there was a greater degree of creolization of the population than was true of the court and province of Rio de Janeiro combined (Table 4.7).

Census data does not correlate colour with social standing or occupation. Vassouras was a town with a sizeable non-white population but was administered by white descendants of Portuguese Crown land grantees, who presided over the socio-economic pyramid. Although the marriage rate in the *município* was low – 72 per cent of free women and 90 per cent of slave women were unmarried – a small inter-married elite of prominent local leaders owned the most prominent estates and clung tenaciously to family name and nobility titles as exclusive definers of political power and influence, backed up by claims to extensive holdings of land, slave property, investments and servants.[43]

Planters in Vassouras resisted alternatives to slave labour and, in addition to substituting women for ageing male labour in the fields, after 1850, encouraged the formation of slave families to safeguard the future and to offset the drift in the market of robust male slaves to the dynamic coffee areas in the Eastern Paraíba Valley. In Rio Bonito, where the transition from slave to free labour was more accelerated, the non-white population was also predominant but for different reasons. The tendency in Rio Bonito was for holders of small numbers of slaves (under twenty) to sell robust male and female slaves to the highland markets, possibly for breeding, leaving slave-holdings that were characterized by a greater number of aged and young female slaves. A case in point is the slave-holding of Maria Joaquina do Nascimento, who died in Rio Bonito in 1860, leaving an estate valued at 7:173$286 of which her two female African slaves, aged fifty and seventy, an African male slave aged thirty-eight, a *crioulo* slave aged fifty-six and two *crioulo* children aged two and five represented one-third of the total value.[44]

In this *município*, where smallholdings of cross-cropped coffee with food production were the norm, slave cultivators, ex-slaves and free farming folk were incorporated into local society. Relationships among slaves, freed slaves and free people were more open than in Vassouras, but the social prestige and capital attached to the ownership of a handful of slaves was still important. When the seven children of the deceased Joana Maria da Conceição informed the court that their father had left the *sítio* and 7000 coffee trees ready for harvest, taking with him the thirty-year-old African slave Marianna and her two *pardo* children aged seven and two and a half, they found themselves bereft of the status associated with the possession of a slave, her child-bearing capacity, the labour of her children and the combined value of the three slaves, which was equivalent to that of the coffee harvest.[45] The widower was the father of Marianna's children and deserted his legitimate family, moving to Araruama, where he established a family production unit with Marianna and her growing children.

Informal family ties that bound female slaves to the master class were a mixed blessing. Slave relationships with the master class were strengthened by children who were born of those unions. There was, however, no guarantee that those bonds would be recognized, and they could be broken by sale or separation of the slave and slave children from the master and his household. Marcia Wright's findings from recent research conducted in East Africa suggest that females of child-bearing age were disposable at a premium as labourers and as multipliers of the population.[46] Her findings bear historical resonance for Brazil.

In the Padilha household in Vassouras, Senhora Padilha held on to the *parda* domestic slaves and their children, who were raised as *crias de casa*. Firmiana was a 52-year-old *parda* domestic slave who, with her daughter, Maria, and Maria's five-year-old daughter, Triphania, remained in the great house. Like all *ingênuos* after 1871, Triphania was listed under the category of 'services'. The status of Luiza, a *parda* seamstress with a baby of six months and a child of three, both listed under 'services', confirmed that although *ingênuo* children were legally born free under the 1871 Rio Branco Law (discussed later in this chapter), they were held in service until the age of eight, when their owners could either free them and receive low-interest shares worth 600 mil-réis from the state, or hold them until they were twenty-one. A Padilha spinster daughter, Carlota, also resided in the great house and inherited Constantina, a *parda* seamstress with two *ingênuo* children, part of the land on the estate and the 32-year-old *parda* slave Luiza and her four children, aged one and a half months to seventeen years of age. A married sister, Francisca, who had already received part of her inheritance in the form of a dowry, inherited a *parda* seamstress, Dionisia, and her two *ingênuos* plus a female field slave, along with some land on the estate.[47]

Warren Dean argued that slave-owners were prone to part with mulatto slaves and their children, since they were regarded as ambitious, desirous of social mobility and impertinent.[48] I would argue on the basis of the Padilha data that household slaves, mainly *parda*, fulfilled reproductive roles and that they and their female children were kept in service for this purpose, at the beck and call of the master class. The *parda* slaves in the Padilha household were trained in a skill that was enhanced by their child-bearing capacity and by the potential of their children, who were probably also destined to learn a skill. Senhora Padilha held on to her household slaves as security for her and her family's future and counted on ties with her family to hold the *parda* household slaves in service.

In contrast, African slaves, especially those in favoured positions, regulated family ties through relations with other Africans or *crioulos*. Marcia Wright argues that slave men who were separated from kin groups became reattached to communities as clients or through definition in an occupation, such as trade.[49] Her findings are also relevant to Brazilian slave outsiders who were inherited, exchanged or purchased and became attached to a slave-holding. Attachment to the household or to a dominant African-derived kin group brought slave outsiders into a fictive kin or collective arrangement. For Florentino and Góes, male attachment was achieved through bonds to elder female slaves who were beyond child-bearing age. No alternative kin groups would emerge from these unions to challenge traditional authority, but the relationship would contribute to the stability of the holdings.

Land and inheritance: the ideals and illusions of freedom

When he freed Emerenciana's children in 1848, the elder Lemos was complying with the law that stipulated that freedom through manumission or self-purchase involved a letter of liberty (*carta de alforria*) transferring the property ownership of the slave from the owner to the slave. When registered and publicly stamped with a notarial seal, the deed was entered in a register, the *livro de notas*, and a copy issued as an official document to the freed person.[50] There was a variety of terms used in the manumission process, but in general there were two principal types of letter: a letter that granted unconditional freedom was called a contract (*título gratuito*); restrictions on freedom, or conditional freedom, were outlined in a contract (*título oneroso*). Unconditional freedom was linked to the market value of a slave, which in turn was associated with robustness, skill, lightness of skin and adaptation to culture, although additional important factors included blood ties to the master and his family and the personal dependence of masters on their slaves.[51] According to Mary Karasch, female domestic slaves benefited over others. Her study of 1319 manumission letters issued in the city of Rio de Janeiro between 1807 and 1831 reveals that their owners, middle-status males in urban occupations, generally freed female slaves under a variety of arrangements that included continued personal service, payment in cash or exchange of freedom for one of the slave's own slaves.[52]

Prior to 1871, self-purchase was a customary rather than a legal right. Third parties – relatives, acquaintances, charitable institutions, religious brotherhoods and governmental agencies – mediated in manumission or self-purchase negotiations between owner and slave. Yet, only the master, not the slave, bestowed the status of *quartado*, which was an arrangement that stipulated a contractual period of labour of eight to fifteen years, and yearly payments that were fixed, irrespective of current slave prices.[53] Proceedings were formalized in courts.

There was a number of ways for slaves to accumulate the price of freedom. The young Irish traveller, Lindsey-Bucknell, wrote that on some of the *fazendas*, slaves 'held plots of land that they cultivate and are permitted to keep the profit from the produce that they sell which they put towards purchase of their freedom whose value is fixed and determined by a judge'.[54] In other cases, slaves were hired out to hawk goods, work as artisans, domestic servants, prostitutes or wet-nurses (as *negros de ganho*).

Prices varied as did conditions. In some cases, slave-owners negotiated freedom in exchange for tasks or personal favours, such as the settlement of scores through a murder, assault and other acts of vengeance, to be performed by slaves against the owner's or his family's foes. João Pedrozo Barreto de Albuquerque, a Vassouras planter, faced charges of freeing his valet, Vicente, in return for the murder of the fumigator of his *fazenda*. Vicente was only freed after he and his master had moved to the court of Rio de Janeiro a year later.[55] In Martins Pena's frivolous play, *O cigano*, based on fact, the slave character, who remained nameless in the play, was duped by gypsies, who offered him decent clothing, good food, cane whisky and a life of leisure in freedom if he deserted his master and lugged a heavy trunk to Minas Gerais.[56] In fact, when the slave was out of earshot, the price to be exacted was revealed as far more sinister and cruel:

> A real idiot! These Blacks are really stupid; they let themselves
> be duped with incredible ease. A few promises, and they are
> ready for anything. . . . This one here we can sell for 600 to 800
> mil-réis in the highlands . . .[57]

Decent clothing, good food, drink and a life of leisure in freedom were the playwright's projection of slave aspirations for freedom.

In the *alforria* documents of Campinas, São Paulo, Peter Eisenberg found that female slaves represented 62 per cent of the *alforriados* during the period 1875 to 1885, but that during the last years of slavery the percentage dropped to 44.2.[58] More importantly, he found that whereas a majority of *alforrias* issued between 1875 and 1885 were conditional upon continued service rather than payment in cash (trade-offs of slaves for freed slaves were uncommon), between 1886 and 1888, 62 per cent were unconditional.[59] The latter figure contrasts with Warren

Dean's findings for Rio Claro, where hardly any slaves were unconditionally freed during the same period. The largest numbers of freed slaves were the *ingênuos* (after 1871), distantly followed by the conditionally freed slaves.[60] My data from Vassouras and Rio Bonito suggest that self-purchase may have benefited more female slaves but, as illustrated below, wills and testaments freed both men and women for dedicated service to their owners. Francisca Thereza de Jesus asked her husband to issue a letter of freedom to Joaquina, her African slave of long-standing service, and to her other slave, Angelica. Upon his death, Lucas and Manoel Crioulo were to be freed 'in thanks for their excellent service to us during our lifetime'.[61] Maria Clara de Oliveira freed five of her male and seven of her female slaves unconditionally, conditionally freed six males and four female slaves to serve her nephew for his lifetime and requested the sale of three slaves to pay the executor of the will.[62]

Despite legally notarized provisions, the private wishes of masters and mistresses were not always respected. Rebuttals or refusals by heirs to honour private wishes, even when notarized in wills and testaments, brought delays and court actions that often took years to settle. Bulky *inventários* on the shelves of notaries public in Rio Bonito and Vassouras attested to family inheritance disputes over contested property, patrimony, family name and claims to slaves or slave infants. In several instances, dissatisfied heirs claimed that executors neglected to declare valuable property – land, slaves, household objects. One case included two skilled African slaves, a cupboard and a chalice that were not included in the household inventory of a deceased Rio Bonito man. In others, personal reasons were given for requests for changes in bequeathals. The son of Genoveva Vargas de Marins requested the court to include in his inheritance a 36-year-old creole slave with whom he had four children.[63] The son and heir to Anna Joaquina de Nascimento's estate claimed for himself the slave who had nursed him as a child and had been in his keeping for his entire life.[64]

Given the widespread accumulation of debts, which accounted for about 17 per cent of the value of rural estates, heirs sold slaves or forced them to work to pay back creditors, even when deceased owners had stipulated that the slaves were to be freed.[65] Heirs of Maria Justina insisted that the slaves Joventino, Jovino and Tarciso should not be freed as she had intended but would work to pay off her debts. Another slave was hocked to a local landowner in repayment of the debt owed him.[66] Esperança, a child slave, lost her status of conditional freedom when it was argued that she was the mutual property of all of the heirs, who subsequently sold her to honour the claims of creditors.[67] The slave, Severina, offered in payment of a debt, stated in 1868 that she, 'black, single, born in Rio Bonito, engaged in farming and domestic labour, and having no defects or vices', was freed by her mistress in a document that contained her mistress's signature and those of two witnesses. Severina lost her case, however, since the person who wrote the letter claimed to have lost it before it could be registered. The letter was also disclaimed, since without the signature of the mistress's husband it would not have been valid.[68] A twist on events was evident in the case of the slaves David and Tobias, whose elderly widowed owner contested their claims to a letter of freedom on the basis that they could not be free because she had mortgaged them to pay a debt. It was illegal to free mortgaged slaves![69]

As the slave population declined and prices for slaves rose after 1850, owners resisted relinquishing slaves unconditionally. Service or self-purchase became the norm. Payment in money was second to payment in service as the most common form of emancipation, and Eisenberg's data show that the agreed-upon values generally reflected local market prices. Postmortem inventories offer few details of slave *pecúlio* (money reserved) or self purchase in the two towns, or of advances of money by creditors to slaves against guarantees of labour. Wills and testimonies made a slave's freedom conditional on continued service to a surviving spouse or family member, but even in the fulfilment of this provision the heirs had the final say. In one instance, in 1852, a deathbed request made to an heir to free all the slaves who were 'deserving of freedom' was received with delight by the four slaves and their children, as it seemed to assure their imminent liberty. The heirs, who would have lost valuable slave property, saw things differently and claimed that all the slaves were lazy and undeserving of liberty.[70] Ana Francisca de Mendonça stipulated that her slave, Severina, and Severina's daughter were to serve her sister for life. Severina's daughter was to be freed when the sister died but Severina was to pass on and serve her goddaughter. Only upon the death of the latter was Severina to be freed.[71]

After the passage of the Rio Branco Law, slaves gained the right to save money accrued from work, donations, legacies and inheritance. In addition, slaves who could afford their own purchase price were given the right to freedom with or without their master's consent. Under the law, freedom could be brokered between slave and master, or could be handled through a private or court-sanctioned third party. In some cases, third parties paid a slave's owner and held the slave to labour until the prearranged amount was paid off. In other cases, slaves begged or collected donations from sympathetic supporters. Some arrangements provided for slaves to pay a stipulated regular amount into a court account or to an approved person. Once agreed, however, the amount could only be changed if the conditions were not fully met by either party.[72]

Robert Slenes has found that 36.1 per cent of the slaves listed in the 1872 slave *matrículas* for the city of Rio de Janeiro had been freed by the time of the 1886–7 *matrículas*. The comparatively low figures of about 8 per cent in the province of Rio de Janeiro and 11 per cent in São Paulo confirm that, where labour alternatives were comparatively scarce or high-priced, slave-owners were far more unwilling to consider them for prime-age male slaves in agricultural activities. The conditionally free status found most slaves trapped in the daily humdrum of lives in forced labour for years unless they held a contract that stipulated a date for their freedom. As Mary Karasch has pointed out, slaves continued to be punished, were obliged to reside with and serve their masters and were held to obedience by the threat of revocation of the contract.[73] Slaves who were represented by a public defender (*curador*) were generally ill-prepared to meet the demands for documents or notarized affidavits. In addition, slaves faced local government delays in establishing emancipation boards and funding. Legal technicalities and evasions were widespread, as were the exaggerated assessments of slaves, the refusal of heirs to release freed slave mothers and their infants and owners' claims for the renegotiation of agreed prices for slave self-purchase. The Angolan slave, Maria, found that although she had negotiated her freedom through a contract with her master that stipulated she had 90 days in which to gather the sum of 90 mil-réis to purchase her freedom, she was sold for 200 mil-réis when that period expired.[74] Maria's appeal to her owner's godmother to intercede on her behalf for an extension of the time-limit only led to the godmother's request that she hand the contract over. Maria refused, claiming to have lost it. Under the pretext of collecting her clothes when her female purchaser came for her, Maria sought out the municipal judge and, on the basis of her contract, requested a holding order. She lost her appeal at the local level but appealed to the Tribunal de Relação in Rio de Janeiro.[75]

The fact that Maria appealed her case is unusual for the times. More significant is the way in which 'conditional' freedom was interpreted. Her court-appointed defender argued that the contract represented a 'promise of her freedom by her senhor', and was upheld by a precedent from 1773: 'Our legislation protects the philanthropic ideas associated with freedom; freedom is thus seen to be a Natural Right and merits stronger support than does slavery.'[76] Her master's contract represented a promise to free her and 'imposed on her an onus to buy her freedom'. Maria, 'upon acquiring that right to freedom, was no longer a "thing", an object of commerce, and could not be sold'.[77] But the plaintiff held to a different principle: 'Slaves are things and not people; under the widespread political rights endorsed by the empire, the Brazilian citizen is guaranteed the right to property in all of its plenitude'.[78]

Maria's plight was plagued by challenges to the authenticity of her documents, questionable legal procedures, selection of witnesses and ultimately her attempted suicide, which brought to the fore the painful and controversial process involved in the transition to freedom. The outcome of the case, settled out of court, is not known, but it addressed a contentious issue that much of slave-holding society abhorred but was not prepared to let pass unnoticed or uncontested.

The courts were complicit in society's concern over the abuses associated with slavery, but were no less complicit in leaving the issue of freedom ambiguously defined. Slaves had more chance of dying than of being set free. Legal delays, failure to appear at court hearings, the loss of vital documents, claims of forgery, the abduction of slaves, and disappearance of key witnesses were all called into play as masters and slaves increasingly took issue with the convoluted question of freedom.

Conditional freedom bridged the legal divide between the ownership of a slave by another person and the slave's repossession of his or her own self. The arguments presented by Maria's lawyer established that a slave who acquired the right to freedom was no longer the property of another, able to be bought or sold. This argument was endorsed in a later case where, according to a district judge in Vassouras, a slave who was conditionally free possessed the right of freedom (*direito de liberdade*) but could not 'enjoy this right because the freedom was conditional on the non-existence [death] of the owner'. The slave's right of freedom gave her 'a release from bondage and from the ownership and usufruct of her owner but maintained the owner's right to profit from her company and benefit from her personal service'.[79] The conditionally free slave emerged from the status of *coisa*, or property of the master, to somebody who owed service and, according to the judge, could not be sold or restored to the condition of slave unless the conditional status was revoked in a court hearing.[80]

'In possession of one's self but held to serve one's master' was the understanding conveyed by Padre Bernardo Antonio Lima de Velasco, who declared in his will that four *crioulo* and three *pardo* male slaves were to be rented for service and freed only after his debts were paid.[81] The same interpretation of conditional freedom was conveyed by a Vassouras judge. He was personally acquainted with the slave, Florência, who had been rented out for service to him in 1868 by her French mistress.[82] Two years later, Florência appeared at his residence claiming to be free and protesting the illegality of her sale by her French owner. She had already attempted to register a complaint against her mistress with the police chief of Rio de Janeiro, but the officer on duty, accusing her of drunken behaviour, had arrested her, placed her in a cell and had her head shaved, a customary police practice when slaves, especially those suspected of prostitution, were taken into custody.

Florência's claim to free status had been motivated by a free man named Pamplona, who had business dealings in the household where the French woman and Florência lived in Vassouras and was Florência's lover. Pamplona was described as unscrupulous by Vassouras residents, who claimed that he followed the two to Rio de Janeiro and issued Florência's manumission letter, signed with two forged signatures. Nothing, apart from the fact that her French owner made her living from renting Florência for service, is known about her. Despite her attempts to pass as a free woman, Florência was sold on three more occasions. Following the initial sale by her mistress, the second owner sold her to a broker named Luís de Carvalho, whose office was on the prestigious Rua do Ouvidor in downtown Rio. He subsequently sold her to Doutor Constantino who, after service of more than a year, annulled her sale. One of the former owners was responsible for her release from jail, on the pretext that she was free, but expected her to serve him again. Florência fled.

A Vassouras resident described the relationship between Florência, and Pamplona as 'illicit' (*relações ilícitas*), but nobody intervened. Given the prevalence of informal relationships in Brazilian society, attempts to prevent a slave and her free lover from meeting would probably have met with little success.[83] The outcome of the case was left to the police chief of Rio de Janeiro to resolve and is unknown. Florência's actions are testimony to an understanding of the importance of social influence. Twice she appealed to mediators with social status: one was a judge and the other was an ex-owner, whom she so convincingly persuaded of her free status that he had her released from jail.

Passing as free

During the second half of the century, passing as a free person became viable for more and more slaves. The numbers of creole slaves and freedmen of mixed racial origin increased, weakening the association of blackness with slavery. The non-white population was growing faster than the white population, and by 1872, of a total population of 1,048,921, *morenos* or non-whites represented 57 per cent.

Of the 593,847 *morenos*, 252,271 were free and 341,576 were slave, outnumbering whites, who totalled 455,074. In the province of São Paulo, the non-white population rose from 43 per cent in 1800 to 57 per cent in 1872; in the province of Rio de Janeiro, the increase was from 28 per cent in 1840 to 38 per cent in 1872; and in Minas Gerais the proportion increased from 49 per cent in 1814 to 68.5 per cent in 1872. In the northeastern provinces of Pernambuco and Bahia, the proportion of non-whites was 83 per cent in 1872.[84]

For Herbert Klein, freedmen in peripheral regions comprised close to half the coloured population, and he estimated a free coloured minority at between 10 and 30 per cent in the major slave-plantation regions of Maranhão, Bahia, Pernambuco, Minas Gerais, São Paulo and Rio de Janeiro. Klein's analysis of the 1872 census data lists Rio de Janeiro province and the court city third after Minas Gerais and Bahia in the number of *morenos*, and second to Minas Gerais in the number of whites.[85]

Passing as a free person became a viable means of becoming free, or at least of being publicly perceived as such, even when chances of otherwise attaining freedom through self-purchase or manumission were ruled out. Passing describes an individual or group's assimilation of physical attributes, mannerisms, wealth, forms and uses of speech, body movements and dress that were characteristic of a dominant class or group. It involved a person's ability to blend so closely into the dominant group that he or she was perceived as belonging to it. In some cases, the assimilated person or group gained access to new opportunities or social circles. In others, slaves circulated alone, undetected in free society.

Fugitive slaves who passed themselves off as free people relied on connivance, support, refuge and loans of money, clothing and transportation from slaves, freedmen and free people to avoid detection and capture. The first steps in passing were to acquire some footwear, get rid of the rough Minas cotton clothing and find some form of transport. Conditionally freed slaves and freedmen wore shoes, bright-coloured imported cloth and rode horses or mules. Passing also required the cosmetic alterations of obvious signs of Africanness – tribal markings, hairstyle, beads and dress – that might serve as a stigma of slavery. Sidney Chalhoub described the runaway slave Jeronimo, who used money stolen from his girlfriend's master in the countryside to disguise himself with new clothing once he reached Rio de Janeiro.[86]

Vital to passing as a free person were physical disguise and secrecy concerning a fugitive's whereabouts. Fugitives sometimes sought refuge with kin, freedmen and sympathetic acquaintances among local people. Three slave brothers who fled from their new master in Cantagalo returned to the premises of their former master in Rio Bonito, occupying a *rancho* in an empty field adjoining the estate where their brother and the son of one of them were still held in bondage. Local people supplied the fugitives with food, weapons, ammunition and clothing, for which they were subsequently prosecuted after a shoot-out ended in the death of one slave and the arrest of the other two brothers.[87] The house slave, Eufrasina, who cursed her master and fled to avoid field labour, was given refuge by a sympathetic neighbour, who testified that she was conditionally free and had been treated and dressed as a free woman, which was incompatible with the status of a slave.[88]

Light-skinned slaves, and slaves who had the sympathies of a family or kin group, had arguably a better chance of being incorporated into a rural milieu, where, through continued service to the same clan or family, they enjoyed local recognition and physical mobility. Personal relationships and ties developed with their master's family and friends, including associations with the masters and slaves on other estates. Slaves sent unaccompanied on errands to the estates of their master's relatives, to nearby towns and as bearers of messages and cargo to distant destinations enlarged networks of contact with kin or other slaves in service. The field slave, Severino, was frequently sent by his master to the local tavern and was known to the local population, who accepted his version of the events surrounding a brawl between a man and his father-in-law.[89] Social events and business errands also enabled slaves to maintain contact with family members who were sent to neighbouring estates to serve relatives of the owner, moved to urban areas or established on newly acquired family holdings in frontier areas.

Emília Viotti da Costa's study of the physical mobility and widespread informal contacts among slaves in Georgetown, Guyana and similar findings by Karasch for Rio de Janeiro, reveal complex and widespread slave networks that handled trade, spread news and, owing to their ability to move around, were instrumental in the planning of conspiracies.[90] Interrogations of slaves accused of participation in conspiracies, insurrections and other collective movements have unveiled a similar pattern of interface among slaves who had kin and fictive kin ties and those whose mobility facilitated the spread of information. A robbery in Vassouras focused on Antônio Monjollo, a slave accused of stealing a sizeable sum from a tavern. Highlighted in the investigation were his wide-ranging network of contacts among the slave and ex-slave acquaintances whom he befriended in his travels with his master. Local authorities accused Monjollo of flashing his money about and buying a round of drinks for a group of slaves in a tavern. Esmeria, a freedwoman, changed a 200 mil-réis note for Monjollo with a local official and was called before the local police chief to testify when she attempted to change another note with the local tax collector. A freedwoman named Madalena also changed money for Antônio Monjollo. Acquitted, when the source of his gains proved to be a lottery win two months before the robbery occurred, the ruling reminded the court of a social reality – slaves were able to acquire large sums of money in activities that were not related to theft.[91]

In fact, the ruling confirmed the commonality of slave business dealings, including playing and collecting winnings at lottery stakes. The case also confirms the impersonal ties that existed between freed people and local officials. Esmeria changed the first 200 mil-réis note with a local national guard captain and attempted to change the second one with the local tax collector. She not only knew both of them but reckoned that they would probably be able to comply with her request. Their reaction is also noteworthy. Suspicious of the large amount of money in the hands of a freedwoman, they used their official positions to verify the origins of the notes.

Ambiguity and controversy over emancipation

The proximity of slaves and their freed and free counterparts in everyday life was bringing the issue of freedom to the forefront of social relations during the gradual legal transition process to a free labour market. It is not surprising, therefore, that in 1871, the controversial Saraiva Bill that gave way to a law passed on 28 September of the same year was seen as a mixed blessing by planters, proponents of emancipation and slaves. The Rio Branco Law, popularly known as the Law of Free Birth or the Law of the Free Womb, set the terms for the formation of the free labour market by ending the previous custom under which a newborn took the legal status of the mother.[92] The law was aimed at the slave family, the most controversial aspect of slavery at that time, and made clear a distinction between free and slave members of a family unit. Slave mothers were unaffected by the law but henceforth their infants were legally free at birth. The law also provided masters with the option to undertake the tutelage of freeborn slave children until they reached the age of majority. In practice, it extended the hold of masters over the bondage of slaves and the 'temporary bondage' of legally free children until the closing years of the century.[93]

In an irregular progression, the 1847 proof of paternity legislation, the 1850 Land Law and the Rio Branco Law legitimized the role of the state in placing limitations on the ownership of property, land and freedom. Under the terms of the Saraiva Bill, seen by its proponent, the prominent Liberal José Antônio Saraiva, as the 'fairest and most gradual method', the state did not confiscate or otherwise deprive slave-owners of their immediate property. Instead, the law aimed at the future: the humanization of the slave womb and the recruitment of the newborn children of slave women into the ranks of citizens. Although in practice the law ushered in a process that would secure the infant labour force under virtual conditions of slavery, the granting of free status by the state was a measure that would be welcomed by *ingênuos*.[94] Passed under the Conservative administration of Rio Branco and designated as the Rio Branco Law, the measures contributed significantly to the tone of a moralistic campaign. Slaves owned by the state were freed immediately, as were slaves who had been abandoned by their owners or included in unclaimed inheritances. However, they were placed under state supervision for five years and were to be contracted out or work in public establishments. Masters were obliged to free newborn children of slave women and to take care of them until the age of eight. In recompense, owners would either be indemnified with long-term bonds or allowed to use the labour of the children until they reached their twenty-first birthday. The yearly emancipation of slaves in all provinces was to be handled through an emancipation fund set up from the proceeds of taxes on slaves, the transfer of slaves as property, fines, specific lotteries, subscriptions, endowments and legacies. Provisions in the law also enabled slaves to keep savings from gifts, inheritances and earnings. Through local justices, who determined the price of freedom, slaves could make deposits towards the purchase and eventual declaration of their freedom, irregardless of whether their masters agreed or not. Although the law abolished the right of slave-owners to revoke freedom on the basis of 'ingratitude', as occurred in the case of the slave Eufrasina, infractions such as drunkenness, violence towards masters, crimes or attempts at flight would annul self-purchase. And even when in possession of their freedom, there was a similar obligation to work for five years or risk being assigned to labour on the public works as a vagrant. The slave population was also targeted for closer identification. All slaves were to be counted and registered within one year of the passage of the law. Registers would include name, age, colour, sex, parentage and occupation. Non-compliance by owners in registering their slaves could result in freedom for the slaves.[95]

Robert Conrad calculated that the law was aimed at half a million *ingênuos*, a not insignificant labour force. Over 60,000 were registered in the province of Rio de Janeiro between 1872 and 1877, another 1170 entered and 1418 left; of these about 18,000, or close to one-third, died, leaving a balance for those five years alone of about 40,000 potential labourers. On a yearly basis, *ingênuos* numbered roughly 10,000, despite the fact that the total slave population was undergoing steady decline. The highest numbers of *ingênuos* were located in Campos (12 per cent of the provincial total) and in the highland coffee-producing areas of the Paraíba Valley (over 60 per cent), where slave-labour holdings were concentrated. Vassouras, for example, registered 3998 *ingênuos*, second only to Valença (5493). The numbers in Rio Bonito were less than half the tally for Vassouras in the same period. In both places, over a quarter of the *ingênuos* died, a mortality rate that is not unusual (Table 4.8).

Table 4.8 Provincial population of *ingênuos*, by region and *município*, 1872–7

Município coffee towns	Registered	Entered	Left	Died
Western Paraíba Valley				
Rio Claro	447	11	36	145
S.J. Príncipe	1206	19	30	364
Barra Mansa	2168	–	43	6757
Piraí	2358	–	75	727
Resende	1891	70	69	524
Valença	5493	58	27	1721
Vassouras	3998	19	42	1273
Total	17,561	177	322	5429
Eastern Paraíba Valley				
Paraíba do Sul	3839	22	110	1213
Cantagalo	3547	164	51	1219
S.M. Madalena	1804	101	44	548
Sapucaia*	838	86	8	176
S. Fidelis	3503	138	39	860
N. Friburgo	1090	60	57	377
Petrópolis	70	4	6	21
Total	14,691	575	315	4414

Table 4.8 *continued*

Lowlands			
Campos	7108	77	40	1595
Angra dos Réis	758	7	59	249
Mangaratiba	240	1	25	70
Itaguaí	1068	3	33	361
Iguassú	1396	–	24	442
Parati	358	3	16	121
Niterói	1763	111	50	508
Estrela	448	3	13	159
Magé	1280	2	105	452
Itaboraí	1519	2	36	451
Total	8830	133	361	2813
Restinga			
Maricá	1212	8	31	372
Saquarema	1182	14	21	411
Rio Bonito	1778	29	84	555
Capivary	953	22	29	268
Araruama	1807	21	41	517
Cabo Frio	1549	6	28	516
B. São João	743	15	35	232
Macaé	2527	30	39	667
S.J. Barra	980	13	23	207
Total	12,731	150	331	3745
Grand total	53,813	1035	1329	16,101

* No data available for 1872–4.

Source: Directoria Geral da Estatística, *Recenseamento da população da Província do Rio de Janeiro, Quadro A, 1872.* Recompiled by CEDEPLAR.

The legal status of the *ingênuos* was the same as a conditionally free slave. Having legally distinguished newborns from captive mothers, siblings, uncles and grandmothers, the law left the execution of the measures to slave-owners who, for the most part, were unchallenged by state and local authorities as they raised slave children as captive property. Although slave-owners complied with the requirements to register their slaves, manipulation of birth dates to avoid inclusion in the provisions of the Rio Branco Law was one of the 'bypass mechanisms' that were employed. Generations of newborn males and females may have been made aware during childhood that the 1871 law distinguished them from other slaves, but the realization of full freedom was clearly in the hands of the master, as was the treatment of *ingênuos* unless slave parents or local authorities intervened. Although deficient diets, unhealthy living conditions and frequent arbitrary punishments were common to slavery, the death rates of *ingênuos* were not high for the nineteenth century, suggesting that some measures to prolong slave lives may have been undertaken by planters who aimed to maintain a productive labour force.

The employment and training of *ingênuos* was not disparaged by planters. In 1859, the prominent Vassouras planter, the Baron of Rio Bonito, warned a meeting of planters that the freed children could represent an element of disorder unless measures were forthcoming that obliged them to work:

> It is a new class of individuals that constitute an exception and for which there must be special regulations; moreover, as their numbers increase, they may, instead of becoming useful, become an element of disorder unless there is a means of obliging them to work.[96]

The Baron lent his approval to proposals that the state assume the costs of educating slave children for agricultural labour up to twenty-one years of age, at which time they would be prepared to contribute to the rural labour market. It is not known, however, if planters were prepared to invest in the future of *ingênuos* in the knowledge that they would have to relinquish any right to their labour once they reached the age of twenty-one. Pressed for solutions to foreseeable short-ages of field labour, and the implications of this for the structure and organization of the rural wage labour market, delegates to the Agricultural Congress reviewed the alternatives. Population transfers and transoceanic migrations were among the most seriously considered possibilities, as some lauded the tireless energy of Chinese labourers. São Paulo planters, in particular, extolled the benefits of European rural labour, and a general accounting was made of the solutions encountered in the post-slave societies of the Americas. Planters expressed interest in regulating the free semi-nomadic rural Brazilian population, but only grudgingly admitted that there were advantages to be gained from employing the locally available 'national' free and freed farm labourer.[97] In comparison with possible or imagined labour alternatives, the 'national' worker fared little better in the eyes of the planter class of the 1870s than in the earlier accounts of travellers such as J.J. von Tschudi in the 1850s, or Auguste de Saint-Hilaire, de Tollenare and Henry Koster at the beginning of the century.[98]

Constraints on the emancipation process

By 1872, the freed class outnumbered the slave population. According to Herbert Klein,

> of the 5.7 million (or 58 per cent) of the population who were colored, some 4.2 million (or over 70 per cent) were freedmen, and this freedmen group was some 43 per cent of the total population in imperial Brazilian society, while the slaves were only 15 per cent.[99]

For the majority of those slaves, freedom would prove unattainable and the harsh manual labour, together with deficient diet, clothing and shelter, would take countless physical and mental tolls. *Ingênuos* who were legally born free joined this small group of slaves whose privileged status and authority distinguished them from the majority of slaves in the slave-holding. As they matured, they constituted a significant, albeit symbolic, *ingênuo* breach, a beacon of freedom within an institution that was already being eroded by slave challenges.

Yet, even among slaves who were likely to experience freedom, marked constraints were in place that limited socio-economic betterment. Even those freed slaves who had blood ties to their masters stood little chance of inheriting land or production units or otherwise advancing into the rigid social hierarchy that was the preserve of their masters. In the first place, inheritance of property was premised on the official paternal registration of legitimate heirs. In both towns, the marriage levels were so low as to discount it as a viable means of establishing a family. The 1872 census data record that approximately 95 per cent of slave women and 73 per cent of free women were unmarried. In a social milieu where informal relationships took precedence over marriage, it fell to civil not Church institutions to validate marital and blood ties. Under such an arrangement, single mothers and natural children of *amazia* (informal consensual union) co-habitation or concubinage stood to be bypassed in matters of inheritance from partners or a propertied parent if not properly registered as heirs. In *de facto*, albeit informal, relationships between slave women and unmarried or married masters, slave children were brought up as *crias de casa*, 'servants in the household', under the authority of masters who might be their natural fathers and answerable to half-brothers and sisters who were the legitimate children of the planter household. As seen in the case of Emerenciana's children, some *crias de casa* were freed and trained in skills that would serve them in the free labour market. Others endorsed the marriages of their freed daughters to free men, gave sons positions as managers and estate overseers, granted them use of land and permission to market produce and bargained the issue of freedom with other family members. Whereas freed slaves and slaves with marketable skills generally enjoyed broader contacts outside of the master–slave relationship and were able to rely upon witnesses and court-appointed defenders to uphold their claims, issues involving freedom were handled differently from those involving claims by slaves to property or inheritance.

In other words, possibilities existed for slaves and ex-slaves to live from their earnings as free people with marketable skills in a free labour society, but skill and work were ultimately linked to public recognition and the effectiveness of fictive kin or horizontal contacts to create conditions for work. Ex-slaves who moved away from a familiar locale risked marginalization unless previously established contacts or family networks were supportive.

In both Vassouras and Rio Bonito, the formal transmission of inheritance, property and social mobility was governed by the planter class. In a very distinct social context involving daily visiting practices among Muslim women in Tunisia that bypassed otherwise strict codes concerning acceptable behaviour, Pierre Bourdieu defined what he termed the limits of acceptable behaviour.[100] In the case of Emerenciana's children, the limits of acceptable behaviour permitted the enjoyment of freedom in Rio Bonito and the engagement in occupations that were endorsed by the Lemos household and recognized by the local population. Although an occupation would assure them a livelihood, the limits of social acceptance were defined by the restrictions placed on the land and property of the family estate. Exclusion from the acquisition of land and property defined and endorsed the limits of acceptable behaviour towards slaves and their children and precluded their social acceptance on a level with legitimate heirs, unless, of course, none existed.[101] Whereas owners might assign favoured slaves and slave children a plot of land and even provide for a cabin, stipulations generally prohibited the sale of property. Caetano José Pereira left to his freed African slave, Victoria, and her five children, land and the provision for his son to build her a cabin, but the property could not be 'alienated or sold' and could only be passed on to her heirs.[102]

The planter class determined family composition and organization, a norm that Antonio Cândido claims was only extended to the lower classes in the aftermath of the abolition of slavery.[103] Fruits of irregular unions were excluded from the domestic circle and either remained as slaves like their mothers or established humble but regular families.[104] Such was the outcome of a court case in which the freed children of a deceased Vassouras bachelor claimed his estate. In 1844, Felisminda Ignácia de Carvalho and her brother Antonio Pedro de Carvalho, children of the slave Narciza, claimed to be the rightful heirs to the estate of Ignácio Borges de Carvalho, who they insisted was their father.[105] Witnesses in their favour drew the court's attention to the children's physical resemblance to Ignácio, their use of shoes, their freedom at baptism, the freed status that their mother enjoyed at the time of Ignácio's decease and their use of his surname.[106] Since they held that it was not common in Rio de Janeiro to give the family name to slave children, this gesture ratified an association by possession and proved Ignácio's admission of paternity. The son, Antonio Pedro, was well known as a horse-trainer (*arreador*), and was allowed to ride about the premises; he also distributed meat to Ignácio's customers, a duty that was not commonly handled by slaves.[107] The daughter, Felisminda, was married to a free man, a union that was witnessed by her godfather, Ignácio's brother. The local priest who had baptized the children testified that Ignácio, out of respect for his mother, who was present at the baptism and in whose household he lived, did not officially declare his paternity of his slave children at the time and was prevented from doing so in his will by his sudden death.

As reasonable and powerful as the children's claims and their witnesses' endorsement were, they were discarded by Ignácio's brothers, who defended their claims to his estate as the next of kin, given the absence of official documents to attest to Ignácio's paternity. They refuted the importance attached to the children's surname, alleging this to be as common a practice as having close relatives stand in as witnesses and godfathers. Narciza was their main target and, freed or not, they discredited her on moral grounds. First, they pointed out that her dress was no different from that of the other slaves, nor were her tasks any lighter. She ran the household but never sat at the table with Ignácio, eating her meals with the children on a mat spread out on the floor. By referring to this practice, a common custom in African village settings and one that in no way was associated with diminished household status, they intended to emphasize that

Narciza did not have sufficient status in the household to merit a place at Ignácio's table.

Narciza's fidelity was also questioned. She was held to be promiscuous, since it was 'common knowledge' that she had given birth to a 'dark child', wandered unrestricted about the *fazenda* and made Sunday sojourns to attend Mass in town in the company of a male slave. At least one witness had 'heard' of her frequent relations with the muletrain drivers who spent the night on the premises, and drew attention to the whiplash marks on Narciza's back, punishment from Ignácio 'in reprisal for her misconduct'. No attempt was made to verify the imprecise claims or identify their source.

The stakes were high, involving land, slave property and family standing. The Borges de Carvalho brothers were trying to keep as much property as possible, but their actions, whether intentional or not, denied Narciza social recognition as a partner and mother in a stable marital arrangement that would enable her and her children to hold property, maintain a household and enjoy local status as a free person on equal footing with them and other family members. Narciza's freedom, her children's free status at baptism, the marriage of her daughter – seen as evidence of a decent woman as opposed to a concubine – were insufficient to remove the social blemish of a slave past. Bolstered by the absence of documentary proof of Ignácio's paternity, the brothers challenged the children's claim, stereotyping Narciza as immoral and promiscuous, behaviour that they, and perhaps the court jurors, held to be a convenient association with all slave women.

The brothers won the estate. Last-ditch appeals to the Tribunal de Relação were to no avail and Narciza and her children were disinherited and divested of a foothold in propertied society, a claim to social status and association with members of the planter class. Ignácio had provided the means for his children to survive in a society of free people – Pedro had marketable skills and Felismunda enjoyed respectability through her marriage. The limits to their claims to upward mobility were imposed by the brothers, who hastened to preserve a closed social circle through the exclusion of Narciza and those with a background or name that they held to be tainted or undesirable. In so doing, Ignácio's mother and the greater family circle also preserved itself from the social ostracism that acceptance of a former slave as a social equal might have entailed at this time. Even in death the individual was subordinated to the collective interests of the family, who united to preserve the practice of excluding undesirable pretenders. Ignácio's privately expressed wishes to the priest were disputed, distorted or simply disregarded by heirs who, with the acquiescence of the court, maintained collective family interests and the landed property that supported them to the exclusion of unwanted kin.

In the 1840s, the freed population in Vassouras was small, and the rarity of this kind of case suggests that few freed children of slaves and their masters who were raised in the family household attempted to claim family inheritance or dispute that claim with other heirs. The passage in a 2 September 1847 decree, of Article 3 that, based on the French civil code, made an official notarized affadivit – a will or a declaration – the decisive proof of paternity, suggests that the courts were being pressed on this issue. Contrary to France, where a civil registry of births, marriages and deaths already existed, Brazilian registries were held by the Catholic Church, and were officiated over by parish priests. Held as acceptable evidence of paternity prior to the 1847 decree, they henceforth ceased to be considered as public documents, and therefore were no longer legally valid, although the baptismal records were still legal proof of maternity. Under the decree, paternity was relegated to the public forum of the notary public and the official registry of scribes. No longer legally valid were declarations of paternity at private baptismal ceremonies on records that were discretely deposited with a local priest or left in family keeping within the confines of a rural estate.

A twofold precedent was therefore established. Owners of land and other immovable property were forced to consider the legal implications of declaring paternity, since it was linked to rights of inheritance. Second, legitimate claimants would be obliged to honour the inheritance of their father's natural and freed slave children. An appeals case involving three children, each mothered by a different slave and fathered by Antonio Soares de Pinho from Vassouras, confirmed the importance of officially registered paternity as a decisive factor in inheritance cases. João took his two half-sisters to court to claim his share in the US$42,559 estate of his bachelor father. The case lasted a decade and João, who carried proof of paternity on his certificate of baptism, lost the ruling in 1871 in favour of the two daughters. Their names, not his, were listed on the notarized will that confirmed them as legitimate daughters and heirs. Similar to the case of Narciza's children, the two daughters and their husbands challenged João's paternity, claiming that his mother, the slave Maria do Bonfim, was 'easily accessible to all men'. She lived with the overseer, who was João's legal guardian and bore him a son in between the two sons allegedly fathered by Soares de Pinho. The latter's refusal to free Maria or to recognize the children as his own fuelled doubts about his paternity of the children.[108] The daughters claimed that the overseer sought to have the court recognize João as the legitimate child of Maria do Bonfim and Soares de Pinho, so that he, as João's legal guardian, would eventually claim the estate. The daughters and their husbands won the case.

It was rare for masters to leave an inheritance to slave mothers, and the slave mothers of Soares de Pinho's children were no exception. Under Brazilian law, the husbands of the two daughters had legal responsibility for the estate. In this way, Soares de Pinho officially recognized his two daughters and endowed them with social respectability as decent women, although their marriages to free men placed legal powers over the estate in the hands of the husbands. In contrast to the Lemos estate, that of Soares de Pinho was a 96-hectare coffee *fazenda* with 24,500 coffee trees, maize and beans, processing and storage units for coffee, a sugar mill, a *venda*, pig farms, a fowl yard and fourteen oxen, with a holding of 43 slaves who were mostly under forty, and whose appraised value accounted for 68 per cent of the total value of the *fazenda*. Legitimacy, freedom and the bequeathal of property in land and slaves signified a transition to citizenship and married respectability, positions of status in society that were mediated by their husbands and upheld by the court.

As freedom loomed larger on the horizon, slave-owners were faced with growing ambiguity in their relationships with their slaves and their peculiar status. On the one hand, slaves continued to be important status symbols, feared by owners, who justified slavery as a necessary evil, a potential threat to the security of property and the domestic household, and, yet, valuable 'others'. As physical proximity and long-standing co-existence narrowed the divide between slave and free, the emergence of the free labour market brought to the fore the viable ways in which slaves, ex-slaves and masters would embark on a gradual emancipation, in which the strategies of each would emerge in discourse, in labour and land arrangements and in the ways in which the market-place was perceived.

Notes

1. AN, Documentação Judiciária. Corte de Apelação, Juízo Municipal de Rio Bonito, 1856. Apelantes: Basílio, Fernando e Maria representados por seu curador. Apelados: Rita Luiza da Silva Neves e outros, viúva e herdeiros do finado Antonio Ribeiro Neves. Cx. 3695, Ap. 6736.
2. Manuel Moreno Fraginals (ed.), *Africa in America* (New York: Holmes and Meier, 1984), p. 12.
3. 'os escravos eram tidos como libertos mesmo antes de terem ganho as cartas de liberdade'. AN, Corte de Apelação, Juízo Municipal de Rio Bonito, 1856. Apelantes: Basílio, Fernando e Maria representados por seu curador.
4. *Ibid.*: 'prestar serviços de escravos que são do autor a quem devem ser restituidos'.
5. *Ibid.*:

    > não podia ser esta a intenção do vendedor [the heir who sold his inheritance] toda contrária aos princípios da sã razão e de Direito natural. Julgam improcedente a ação, os apelantes no gozo de sua plena liberdade e os apelados as custas do processo.

6. Slenes, Robert W., 'Grandeza ou decadência? O mercado de escravos e a economia cafeeira da província do Rio de Janeiro, 1850–1888', in Iraci del Nero da Costa, *Brasil: história econômica e demográfica* (São Paulo: Instituto de Pesquisas Econômicas, 1986), p. 105; Stanley J. Stein, *Vassouras: A Brazilian Coffee County, 1850–1900* (Princeton: Princeton University Press [1957], 1985), p. 225.
7. Karasch cited Burlamaqui, who stated that a master almost never freed the children whom he had had by his slave woman, but the tale of Emerenciana's children suggests otherwise. Mary C. Karasch, *Slave Life in Rio de Janeiro, 1808–1850* (Princeton: Princeton University Press, 1987) p. 348.
8. Whether the rue was to be taken orally as a liquid, as a douche or rubbed on the body to provoke contractions is not specified. Karasch has observed slaves decorated with rue in pictures by the artist, Jean Baptiste Debret. See *Slave Life*, p. 225.
9. Robert W. Slenes, 'Lares negros, olhares brancos: histórias da família escrava no século XIX', *Revista Brasileira de História*, vol. 18 (1988), pp. 189–203; Robert E. Conrad, *The Destruction of Brazilian Slavery, 1850–1888* (Berkeley: University of California Press, 1972).
10. Adèle Toussaint-Samson, *Une Parisienne au Brésil* (Paris: Paul Ollendorff, 1883), pp. 114–15.
11. João Luís Ribeiro Fragoso and Manolo G. Florentino, 'Filho de Inocência Crioula. Neto de Joana Cabinda: un estudo sobre famílias escravas em Paraíba do Sul (1835–1872)', *Estudos Econômicos*, vol. 17, no. 2 (1987), pp. 151–73; Ana Maria Lugão Rios, 'Família e transição', unpublished MA, Universidade Federal Fluminense; Manolo G. Florentino and Roberto Góes, *A paz das senzalas: famílias escravas e tráfico atlântico, Rio de Janeiro, c. 1790–c. 1850* (Rio de Janeiro: Civilização Brasileira, 1997), Chs 7–8. In postmortem inventories from Vassouras and Rio Bonito, slave grandmothers and mothers are listed with their children as domestic servants. However, the inventories are incomplete sources for studying slave

families as they only list those members who are part of a slave-holding. For additional data on slave families in export and non-export economies, see Nancy Priscilla Naro, 'Free labour in rural Brazil', *Slavery and Abolition*, vol. 13, no. 2 (1992), fn. 30, p. 84.

12. Robert W. Slenes, 'Malungo, ngoma vem! Africa encoberta e descoberta no Brasil', *Cadernos Museu Escravatura* (Luanda: Ministério da Cultura, 1995), pp. 11–12.

13. See Flávio dos Santos Gomes, *Histórias de quilombolas: mocambos e comunidades de senzalas no Rio de Janeiro – Século XIX* (Rio de Janeiro: Arquivo Nacional, 1993), pp. 205–210. Thornton's observation is cited by Philip D. Morgan, 'The cultural implications of the Atlantic slave trade: African regional origins, American destinations, and New World development', In David Eltis and David Richardson, *Routes to Slavery: Direction, Ethnicity and Mortality in the Atlantic Slave Trade* (London: Frank Cass, 1997), p. 123.

14. Stein, *Vassouras*, pp. 76–7. I have relied on Stein's data, along with supplements from my sample of extant postmortem inventories and the findings of Slenes and dos Santos Gomes. Many of the court cases and postmortem inventories from the 1860s onwards that Stein consulted in the Câmara Municipal and in the Forum of Vassouras in the 1950s were stored in an inaccessible location and were no longer obtainable in the 1980s. Most are now rehoused in the local Faculdade Severino Sombra, but have not been included in this study.

15. Morgan, 'Atlantic slave trade', pp. 125 and 130.

16. Luiz Felipe de Alencastro (ed.), *História da vida privada no Brasil*, vol. 2 (São Paulo: Companhia das Letras, 1997), Tabela 15, 'Porcentagem de escravos africanos sôbre total de escravos', p. 484.

17. Herbert Gutman, *The Black Family in Slavery and in Freedom, 1750–1925* (New York: Pantheon, 1976); Fragoso and Florentino, 'Filho de Inocência Crioula', pp. 151–73; Rios, *Família e transição*. For different regions and periods, other studies have revealed varied tendencies towards the natural reproduction of the slave population, both in areas reached by the international slave trade and those that remained untouched. See Horácio Gutiérrez, 'Demografia escrava numa economia não exportadora: Paraná, 1800–1830', *Estudos Econômicos*, vol. 17, no. 2 (1987), (March, 1988), pp. 161–88; José Flávio Motta, 'Corpos escravos, vontades livres: estrutura de posse de cativos e família escrava em un núcleo cafeeiro (Bananal, 1801–1829)', unpublished PhD dissertation, Universidade de São Paulo, 1990; Iraci del Nero da Costa, Robert W. Slenes and Stuart B. Schwartz, 'A família escrava em Lorena', *Estudos Econômicos*, vol. 17, no. 2 (1987), pp. 245–95; Clothilde Paiva, Douglas Libby and Márcia Grimaldi, 'Crescimento da população escrava: uma questão em aberto', *Anais do IV seminário sôbre a economia mineira*, CEDEPLAR/FACE/Universidade Federal de Minas Gerais (August 1988), pp. 11–32; Douglas Libby and Márcia Grimaldi, 'Equilíbrio e estabilidade econômica e comportamento demográfico num regime escravista, Minas Gerais no século XIX', *Papéis Avulsos*, no. 7 (December 1988), pp. 26–43. See also Eni de Mesquita Samara, *As mulheres, o poder e a família: São Paulo, século XIX* (São Paulo: Marco Zero, 1989); Robert W. Slenes, 'Lares negros, olhares brancos', pp. 189–302.

18. Florentino and Góes, *A paz das senzalas*, Appendix 2, p. 233.

19. Ronaldo Marcos dos Santos, *Resistência e superação do escravismo na província de São Paulo (1885–1888)* (São Paulo: Instituto de Pesquisas Econômicas da Fundação Instituto de Pesquisas Econômicas, 1980), Ch. 3.

20. Postmortem Inventory, Barão de Guanabara, 1875. See similar findings in Slenes, 'Lares negros, olhares brancos', pp. 189–203; Eni Mesquita, 'A família negra no Brasil: escravos e libertos', *Anais, VI Encontro Nacional de Estudos Populacionais* (ABEP), vol. 3, (Olinda, 1988), pp. 39–58; Fragoso and Florentino, 'Filho de Inocência Crioula', pp. 151–73.

21. Francisco Vidal Luna and Herbert S. Klein, 'Slaves and masters in early nineteenth-century Brazil: São Paulo', *Journal of Interdisciplinary History*, vol. 21, no. 4 (1991), pp. 549–79. Slave-owners largely opposed marriages between slaves who belonged to different owners.

22. Manuel Querino, *O Africano como colonisador* (Salvador: Livraria Progresso, 1954), p. 39.

23. See also Florentino and Góes, *A paz das senzalas*, Table 5, p. 108, on slaves in positions of authority.

24. Cartório Público do Primeiro Ofício de Vassouras (hereafter CPOV), Postmortem Inventory: Ezequiel de Araujo Padilha, 1880.

25. *Ibid.* Most slaves were employed in field labour and slave-owners often did not complete the item for occupation in these cases. The classification, *roceiro*, refers to one who clears the ground for planting, but I have taken it here to mean one who performs this task but also handles planting decisions and organizes the activities of other slaves.

26. Slenes has cited a case in which slaves were employed on a *roça* where the owner had planted maize, beans and manioc. 'Senhores e subalternos no oeste paulista', in Alencastro, *História da vida privada no Brasil*, p. 239. Maria Helena Pereira Toledo states a *roça* to be a planting of beans, in *Crime e Escravidão* (São Paulo: Brasiliense, 1987), p. 94. Weech defined *roça* as a clearing for planting, in *Brasiliens*, p. 134. Barickman writes in *Bahian Counterpoint* on *roças* in Bahia. For general observations concerning gender differentiation in the workforce in African societies, see Jane I. Guyer, 'Food, cocoa and the division of labor by sex in two West African societies', *Comparative Studies in Society and History*, vol. 22, no. 3 (July 1980), pp. 357–64.

27. CPOV, Postmortem Inventory: José de Rosa Brum, 1885.

28. Florentino and Góes, *A paz das senzalas*, pp. 154–9.

29. Joseph C. Miller, *Way of Death: Merchant Capitalism and the Angolan Slave Trade, 1730–1830* (Madison: University of Wisconsin Press, 1988), p. 135.

30. Herbert S. Klein, 'Demografia do tráfico Atlântico de escravos para o Brasil', *Estudos Econômicos*, vol. 17, no. 2 (1987), pp. 129–50.

31. CPOV Postmortem Inventory: Barão de Guanabara, 1875. I have recorded the ages of each slave's eldest and youngest children and subtracted those from the year of the Baron owner's death in 1875. Although masters often ignored or manipulated the ages of their slaves to avoid taxation or to bypass the Free Womb Law (discussed later in this chapter), the exercise gives some indication of the age of the mother at the outset of family raising.

32. There may have been earlier births that were not recorded or women might have delayed menstruation or provoked abortions until they found a suitable partner.

33. *Das côres do silêncio: os significados da liberdade no sudeste escravista, Brasil, século XIX* (Rio de Janeiro: Arquivo Nacional, 1995).

34. Richard Graham, 'A família escrava no Brasil colonial', in *Escravidão, reforma e imperialismo* (São Paulo: Perspectiva, 1979).

35. CPOV, Postmortem Inventory: Barão de Guanabara, 1875.

36. CPOV, Postmortem Inventory: Ezequiel Padilha, 1880. Elder slaves were entrusted with the authority to negotiate with the master class, but they were also involved in resistance movements, suggesting that in its many forms resistance was linked to a breakdown of negotiations with the master class. See Gomes, *Histórias de quilombolas*. On the respect commanded by elder slaves, see Karasch, *Slave Life*, p. 221; White, *Ar'n't I a Woman?*, pp. 115–18.

37. Kátia Queirós Mattoso, *Ser escravo no Brasil* (São Paulo: Brasiliense, 1988), p. 186.

38. CPORB, Postmortem Inventory: Aurélia Maria de Paiva, 1885.

39. The declaration of the heiress, Apolinaria Pereira da Paiva, the wife of the estate executor stated: 'assumirá o pagamento das dívidas reconhecidas. Desiste (a suplicante) da escrava Mariana.' CPORB, Postmortem Inventory: Aurélia Maria de Paiva, 1885.

40. Jacob Gorender, *A escravidão reabilitada* (São Paulo: Atica, 1990); Conrad, *The Destruction*.

41. On dynamic slave markets and high rates of return on investments in slaves, see Slenes, 'Grandeza ou decadência?', p. 105.

42. BN, *Recenseamento da população da província do Rio de Janeiro, Quadro A, 1850*.

43. See Stein, *Vassouras*, Part 3, 'Plantation Society', for a detailed description of the accumulation of fortunes and political recognition of prominent planters.

44. CPORB, Postmortem Inventory: Maria Joaquina do Nascimento, 1860.

45. *Ibid.*, Joana Maria da Conceição, 1845. The combined value of the three slaves was 850$000; that of the coffee was 840$000.

46. Marcia Wright, *Strategies of Slaves and Women* (London: James Currey, 1993), pp. 24–43.

47. CPOV, Postmortem Inventory: Ezequiel Padilha, 1880.

48. Warren Dean, *Rio Claro: um sistema brasileiro de grande lavoura, 1820–1920* (Rio de Janeiro: Paz e Terra, 1977), pp. 127–8.

49. Wright, *Strategies*, p. 41.
50. Karasch, *Slave Life*, p. 335.
51. Mattoso, *Ser escravo*, pp. 176–98; Stuart B. Schwartz, *Slaves, Peasants and Rebels* (Urbana: University of Illinois Press, 1992), p. 47.
52. Karasch, *Slave Life*, p. 336.
53. Laird Bergad comments on Brazil in *The Cuban Slave Market, 1790–1890* (Cambridge: Cambridge University Press, 1995), p. 134.
54. Hamilton Lindsey-Bucknell, *Um jovem irlandês no Brasil em 1874* (Rio de Janeiro: Hachette, 1976), p. 93. On slaves, he wrote:

    estas são geralmente tratados com humanidade e adequadamente
    alimentados, morando em boas cabanas, e em algumas fazendas têm até
    áreas de terra, que cultivam e cujos produtos vendem, sendo-lhes permitido
    conservar o lucro que empregam na aquisição da liberdade; seu valor é fixado
    e determinado por um magistrado.

    On peasant breaches, see Ciro F.S. Cardoso, *Escravo ou camponês? O protocampesinato negro nas Américas* (São Paulo: Brasiliense, 1987), pp. 91–114.
55. AN, Documentação Judiciária. Corte de Apelação, Juízo Municipal de Vassouras, 1863. Recurso crime. Recorrente: O juízo. Recorrido: João Pedrozo Barreto de Albuquerque e Vicente liberto. No. 272, Maço 46, Gal. C.
56. See Karasch on gypsy involvement in the theft of slaves and contraband slave trading. *Slave Life*, p. 50n, 51, 54.
57.
    Forte tolo! Muito burros são estes negros; vão-se deixando enganar com uma
    facilidade que admira. Meia dúzia de promessas, e ei-los prontos para tudo
    . . . Este podemos vender por seiscentos a oitocentos mil para serra acima . . .

    Luiz Carlos Martins Pena, *O cigano*, in *Comédias* (Rio de Janeiro: Ediouro, n.d.), p. 224.
58. Peter L. Eisenberg, 'Ficando livre. As alforrias em Campinas no século XIX', *Estudos Econômicos*, vol. 17, no. 2 (1987), Table 3, p. 185.
59. *Ibid.*, Table 8, p. 197.
60. Dean, *Rio Claro*, Table 5.1, p. 133.
61. CPORB, Postmortem Inventory: Francisca Thereza de Jesus, 1855.
62. *Ibid.*, Maria Clara de Oliveira, 1865. Ages were not listed for the unconditional freedom granted to Augusto, Basílio, Virgilio, Donato, Belamina, Albina, Priscila and José.
63. *Ibid.*, Genoveva Vargas de Marins, 1845.
64. *Ibid.*, Anna Joaquina de Nascimento, 1875.
65. On indebtedness, see Hebe Maria Mattos de Castro, *Ao sul da história* (São Paulo: Brasiliense, 1986), p. 89.
66. CPORB, Postmortem Inventory: Maria Justina, 1860.
67. AN, Documentação Judiciária. Corte de Apelação, Município de Rio Bonito, 1859. Manutenção de liberdade. No. 1175, Cx. 65.
68. *Ibid.*, Juízo Municipal de Rio Bonito, 1868. Réu: Leandro Joaquim da Silva. Autor: Albino Teixeira e Silva. Gal. C, No. 1700, Cx. 105 (11.521).
69. *Ibid.*, 1876. Libelo de escravidão. Réu: D. Guilhermina Maria do Nascimento, proprietária dos serviços de David e Tobias. Autor: José Antonio Martins Sobrinho. No. 586, Cx.12099 (antigo 558) Gal. C.
70. *Ibid.*, Vassouras, 1852. Réu: Polumena Maria da Conceição e outros. Autor: No. 4108 Cx. 1739, Gal.C.
71. CPORB, Postmortem Inventory: Ana Francisca de Mendonça, 1885.
72. See detailed case-by-case analysis of the intricacies involved in slave self-purchase in Sidney Chalhoub, *Visões da liberdade: uma história das últimas décadas da escravidão na corte* (São Paulo: Companhia das Letras, 1990), Ch. 2.
73. Karasch, *Slave Life*, p. 354.
74. AN, Documentação Judiciária. Corte de Apelação, Rio Bonito, 1854. Apelante: A preta Maria por seu curador. Apelado: D. Catarina Luiza da Conceição. No. 6039, Cx. 3689, p. 69. In this case, although the deadline passed, the issue was whether her right to freedom could

be revoked, thus allowing her to be mortgaged or sold. In *A escravidão no Brasil: ensaio histórico-jurídico-social* (Petrópolis: Editora Vozes, 1976), Agostinho Marques Perdigão Malheiro argued that it could not be.

75. AN, Documentação Judiciária. Corte de Apelação, Rio Bonito, 1854. Apelante: A preta Maria por seu curador.
76. *Ibid.*, p. 69.
77. *Ibid.*, p. 63.
78. *Ibid.*, p. 69.
79. APERJ, Fundo da Secretária de Polícia da Província do Rio de Janeiro. Ref. SPP Co. 166.26. De: Delegado de Vassouras para o Chefe de Polícia, 1870.
80. *Ibid.*
81. CPORB, Postmortem Inventory: Padre Bernardo Antonio Lima de Velasco, 1882.
82. APERJ, Fundo da Secretária de Polícia da Província do Rio de Janeiro, 1870.
83. Other cases of liaisons between slaves and free people include the slave Ladislau and his white girlfriend, and Ladislau's slave mother and her lover, who was a free man. In Vassouras, a resident anthill fumigator on a *fazenda* demanded a letter of freedom for the slave girlfriend he had forcibly abducted. I have already mentioned the relationships between Eufrasina and Correia Benjamin in Rio Bonito, and Narciza and her master, Ignácio de Carvalho, in Vassouras. For a lengthier and more detailed evaluation of informal relationships, see Dain Borges, *The Family in Bahia, Brazil, 1870–1945* (Stanford: Stanford University Press, 1994), pp. 113–15, 121–2.
84. David Brookshaw, *Raça e côr na literatura brasileira* (Porto Alegre: Mercado Aberto, 1983), p. 249; Herbert S. Klein, 'Nineteenth-century Brazil', in David W. Cohen and Jack P. Greene (eds), *Neither Slave nor Free: The Freedom of African Descent in the Slave Societies of the New World* (Baltimore: The Johns Hopkins University Press, 1972), pp. 312 and 315.
85. Klein, 'Nineteenth-century Brazil', pp. 312 and 315.
86. Chalhoub, *Visões da liberdade*, pp. 217–18.
87. AN, Documentação Judiciária, Corte de Apelação, Juízo Municipal de Rio Bonito, 1859. Recurso crime. Recorrente: A justiça. Recorrido: Francisco, escravo dos herdeiros de João Clemente de Sá. Maço 78, No. 79, Gal C. See also, Documentação Judiciária, Corte de Apelação, Juízo Municipal de Rio Bonito, 1858. Recurso crime. Recorrente: O juízo. Recorrido: Antonio Maria do Nascimento. No. 438, Cx. 113, Gal. C.
88. AN, Documentação Judiciária. Corte de Apelação, Juízo Municipal de Rio Bonito, 1866. Libelo. Réu: Eufrasina (escrava). Autor: João Antunes Correia Benjamin. No. 673, Cx. 562, Gal. C.
89. *Ibid.*, 1864. Corte de Apelação. Recurso crime. Recorrente: A justiça por seu promotor Dr Francisco José de Souza Nogueira. Recorrido: Francisco Antonio Alves, filho de Antonio Justo da Costa, 28 anos, lavrador, natural de Sumidouro, termo da Vila do Rio Bonito.
90. Emília Viotti da Costa, *Crowns of Glory. Tears of Blood* (New York: Oxford University Press, 1994), Chs 2–3; Karasch, *Slave Life*, pp. 90–1.
91. AN, Documentação Judiciária. Tribunal de Relação, Juízo Municipal de Vassouras, 1849. Réu: Antonio José Pereira. Autor: Antonio Luis da Silva Braga. Libelo. No. 732, Cx. 42, Gal. C.
92. The principle of *partus sequitur ventrem* stipulated that the legal status of a child derived exclusively from the legal status of the mother. Slave women thereby were reproductive agents of the institution of slavery. Mattoso, *Ser escravo*, p. 176; Eisenberg, 'Ficando livre', p. 183.
93. For debates on the 1871 law, see Martha de Abreu, 'Slave mothers and freed children: emancipation and female space in debates on the "Free Womb" Law, Rio de Janeiro 1871', *Journal of Latin American Studies*, vol. 28, no. 3 (1997), pp. 567–80. The term 'temporary bondage' is taken from Schwartz, *Slaves, Peasants and Rebels*, p. 155.
94. Conrad, *Destruction*, p. 72.
95. *Ibid.*, p. 91; Dean, *Rio Claro*, p. 129.
96.   E uma classe nova de indivíduos, que constitue uma excepção, e para a qual é forçoso haver regulamento especial; até porque augmentada ella em número

crescido, bem longe de tornar-se útil, pode constituir um elemento de desordem, desde que não haja recurso para obrigar-a a trabalhar.

Congresso Agrícola, 1878, p. 238. Peter L. Eisenberg, 'A mentalidade dos fazendeiros no Congresso Agrícola de 1878', *Homens esquecidos: escravos e trabalhadores livres no Brasil, séculos XVIII e XIX* (São Paulo: UNICAMP, 1989), pp. 147–8; Conrad, *Destruction*, Chs 6–7.

97. *Congresso Agrícola*, 1878. Expressions of planter sentiment can be found in the official speeches of politicians analysed by Celia Marinho de Azevedo, *Onda negra, medo branco: o negro no imaginário das elites* (Rio de Janeiro: Paz e Terra, 1987). One might suggest, on the basis of a front-page article in the Brazilian daily, the *Jornal do Comércio* of 28 June 1894, that the reference to 'too many parties' as the reason for the lack of assiduousness on the part of the 'national' labourer reflected little change in planter attitudes.

98. Johann Jakob von Tschudi, *Viagem às províncias do Rio de Janeiro e São Paulo* (São Paulo: Editora Martins [1866], 1976); Louis François de Tollenare, *Notas dominicaes tomadas durante uma residência em Portugal e no Brasil nos annos de 1816, 1817, 1818. Parte relativa ao Pernambuco; traduzido do manuscripto francês inédito por Alfredo de Carvalho* (Recife: Empresa do Jornal do Recife, 1905); Auguste de Saint-Hilaire, *Viagem pelas províncias do Rio de Janeiro e Minas Gerais* (Belo Horizonte: Editora Itatiaia, 1980); Henry Koster, *Travels in Brazil*, (Philadelphia: M. Carey and Son, 1817).

99. Klein, 'Nineteenth-century Brazil', pp. 321–2.

100. Pierre Bourdieu, *Outline of a Theory of Practice* (Cambridge: Cambridge University Press, 1977).

101. I have dealt more fully with the limitations that planter society placed on inheritance by slaves in Chapter 5. On inheritance by slaves, see Slenes, 'Senhores e subalternos', p. 267.

102. AN, Documentação Judiciária. Corte de Apelação, Juízo de Orfãos de Vassouras, 1887. Réu: Caetano José Pereira (falecido), Autor: Curador geral. Exame para tutela. F. 178 No. 5013, Cx. 247, Gal. C.

103. Antonio Cândido, cited in T. Lynn Smith, *Brazil: Portrait of Half a Continent* (New York: Dryden Press, 1951), p. 310.

104. *Ibid.*, p. 302.

105. AN, Documentação Judiciária. Corte de Apelação, Juízo Municipal de Vassouras, 1844. Libelo civil de filiação e petição de herança. Réus: Joaquim José Borges de Carvalho; Vicente Borges de Carvalho e outros. Autores: Antonio Pedro de Carvalho; Antonio Soares da Silva e sua mulher Felisminda Ignácia de Carvalho. No. 709, Cx. 40, Gal. C.

106. The prohibition on slaves wearing shoes was also noticed by Ida Pfeiffer in her travels in south central Brazil in the 1840s: *A Woman's Journey around the World* (London: Office of the National Illustrated Library, 1850); Manuela Carneiro da Cunha, *Negros, estrangeiros: os escravos libertos e sua volta à Africa* (São Paulo: Brasiliense, 1985).

107. AN, Documentação Judiciária. Corte de Apelação, Juízo Municipal de Vassouras, 1844. Libelo civil de filiação e petição de herança Ignácio Borges de Cavalho. No. 709, Cx. 40, Gal. C.

108. AN, Documentação Judiciária. Corte de Apelação, Juízo Municipal de Vassouras, 1861. Duplicate copy. Réus: João e José, filhos do finado Antonio Soares de Pinho, representados por seu tutor. Autores: Francisco Maria de Brito casado com Ursula Soares de Brito, e Antonio Madureira Augusto, casado com Lindolfa Soares de Brito (the two women were daughters of Antonio Soares de Pinho), No. 709, Gal. C.

5

Fashioning Freedom: Private Interests, Public Spheres

Persistent beliefs

The wars and trading negotiations that contributed to the enslavement of Africans and the power exerted by masters over the centuries fostered an uncomfortable familiarity between master and slave that was characterized by mutual suspicion, shared superstitions and the fear of supernatural spirits and the priests and priestesses who were their earthly media. Medieval Portuguese beliefs in the supernatural traversed social class, rational consciousness and the cleansing power of Catholic exorcism; such beliefs were carried to Brazil, where they became part of the colonization project.[1] Long-standing features of the Portuguese folkloric canon, including the headless mule (*mula sem cabeça*) and the werewolf (*lobishomem*), were enriched by an African bogeyman, or *negro velho*, and the *quibungo*, an ancient slave/werewolf who devoured children. Inhabiting the dense forests was the monster-man (*bicho-homem*), derived in popular thought from runaway or fugitive slaves who preyed upon unsuspecting travellers and raided plantations to survive.

Masters believed that their slaves were possessed by spirits who materialized in a variety of living forms and entered the body and mind of the believer. Sorcerers, priestesses, diviners and healers were held in awe by the slaves, who were gripped by the fear of spiritual retribution or judgement by other slaves for unpaid homage or disobedience. Yet, African slaves also bore amulets and carried figures of Saint Anthony, Our Lady of the Rosary and Saint Benedict, Catholic saints who were held to offer protection from, but also intercession with, the masters.[2]

Real and imagined terrors were pervasive in the countryside, as the psychological and physical confrontations among the powerful and the weak linked mortals and immortals in daily combat. A delicate and precarious relationship existed between slaves who held their master's confidence in their curing powers and those who were believed to employ their spiritual powers in the leadership of slave resistance and to intimidate reluctant followers. The Brazilian writer,

Joaquim Manuel de Macedo, was an advocate of emancipation on the grounds that the institution of slavery was accountable for witchcraft. He claimed that witchcraft led household slaves to seduce the master, arouse amorous desires among daughters and poison the mistress and children.[3] In an appellate case involving the death of a slave on a prominent Vassouras estate, witchcraft was given as the official reason why the Portuguese overseer had mercilessly beat Miguel. He claimed that the slave was depleting the workforce on the *fazenda* by causing slaves to fall ill.[4] In the controversial and publicized death penalty trial of the landowner, Manuel Motta Coqueiro, a box of clothing belonging to a tenant and his family was found in the slave quarters of the household slave, Balbina, who other slaves claimed to be an African sorceress from Cabinda.[5]

The difference between healers, who cured others by fighting witchcraft, and sorcerers, was unclear in the minds of Catholics, who did not understand African religious traditions. According to Karasch, *Cariocans* (natives of Rio de Janeiro) believed that illness was caused by non-biological forces such as the evil eye, evil thoughts, evil spirits, witchcraft and sorcery.[6] Masters went to slaves for information about herbal potions, poisons, brews and infusions for curing. Given the shortage of physicians in the countryside, elderly African slave healers treated sick animals, their masters and other slaves, whose afflictions included withdrawal, fevers, poisoning and what masters described as 'erratic' behaviour.[7] The terms *feiticeiro* and *curandeiro* were applied to slave midwives, healers and curers, who also employed chanting, rhythmic body movements and divining. The owner and slave master of the Fazenda São José in Rio de Janeiro and Adèle Toussaint-Samson, a French visitor, watched in awe as an eighty-year-old *feiticeiro* dressed in cloth robes cured an ox of a skin parasite and then healed a slave of a snake-bite.[8]

Sorcery and witchcraft haunted Brazilian slave-owners with chilling reminders of the Saint Domingue uprising of 1791. Many were suspicious of African religions, just as slave-owners in Haiti and Jamaica feared the powers of Vodun and Obeah. The outlawed African religions that flourished in Brazil were believed to motivate slaves to rebel. In the slave societies of the Caribbean, the practice of Vodun and Obeah, or any witchcraft rituals, was strictly punished.[9]

Public restrictions on slaves

The punishment of slaves accused of involvement in the largely Muslim Malés rebellion in 1835 in Salvador, Bahia, attests to the public fear of African rituals and religious ceremonies, especially those where the leaders commanded large followings.[10] Ordinance 6 of provincial decree No. 46 of 13 May 1836 focused on dance gatherings or Afro-Brazilian religious ceremonies that included slaves from outside. Freedmen who allowed such ceremonies were to be jailed for eight days and fined 30 mil-réis. Freed Africans, termed foreign freedmen, were to be punished and had to sign a guarantee that they would leave the municipality. Slaves arrested at such gatherings would receive punishment of between fifty and a hundred lashes.[11] The *batuque* and the *caxambú* were social dances but, like *candomblé*, represented long-standing African-derived customs and beliefs. The public prohibition of the rituals in the 1830s document both public fear of the *batuque* and the pervasiveness of the ceremonies, which continued to be the subject of local ordinances aimed at their repression for the remainder of the century. Yet, the number of prohibitions issued suggests that the persistence of African-derived practices was greater than the ability of authorities to curtail them. In the province of Rio de Janeiro the prohibition in 1859 on slave outsiders from attending *candomblé* sessions reflected earlier prohibitions in the wording, but the punishment was now eight days in prison and a fine of 30 mil-réis.[12]

Slave-owners' fear of the collective impact of such rituals on their slaves was matched by an apprehension about drunkenness and the gatherings of slaves in taverns and public places, especially when *capoeira*, an outlawed form of violent assault that involved opponents in agile body movements, was involved.[13] Public authorities regulated these gatherings by fining those who purchased any goods from a slave who had no written permission from their master. Slave *quitandeiras* who traded foodstuffs on Sundays or saints' days were exempt from the restriction.[14] Other measures decreed that the sale, donation, lending, manufacture, repair or provision of gunpowder or weapons of any sort to slaves was illegal. Article 29 of provincial decree No. 1129 of 8 February 1859 stipulated the suspension of a sales licence, a fine and a 30-day prison sentence for anyone caught selling arms or gunpowder to slaves.[15] In addition, the threat of fines, imprisonment and loss of licences were directed at the owners, administrators or cashiers of stores, coffee-houses, taverns and other public houses where slaves sold or administered goods, and to places where more than three slaves were gathered without proof that they were there to make purchases for their masters.[16] In Rio de Janeiro, the local chamber stipulated that slaves without passports from the justice of the peace who were found on land or sea more than 2 leagues from their master's residence were to be arrested as fugitives and receive a hundred lashes. Their master would be charged for all expenses.[17] Slaves who had to be away from their master's plantation at night, on Sundays and on holy days must carry a note attesting to the nature of the task, signed by a master or other person empowered to accept responsibility for the slave. In the absence of such a note, the slave would receive between 25 and 50 lashes.

Public authorities also regulated the self-employment of slaves, ex-slaves and free pedlars, foreign or Brazilian, with the issue of an obligatory licence.[18] Measures were also introduced to regulate slave behaviour in public places. Slaves who obstructed public roads, bridges and highways, appeared in public in a state of undress, used public fountains and lakes for washing clothes or animals, engaged in boisterous diversions or gathered in numbers of three or more on public streets or in taverns were to be apprehended.[19] Surveillance and the supervision of slave activities united the private and public spheres against Brazil's non-citizens. Yet the ordinances and restrictions suggest that there was little official repression of slave usage of public facilities. Despite repeated council prohibitions, slaves used public spaces for private bathing, washing animals and diversion, suggesting that when the provision of basic needs was not met in the private sphere, public spaces would do.

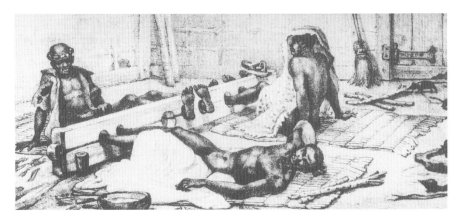

Figure 12 Slaves in the stocks. *Source:* Jean Baptiste Debret, *Viagem Pitoresca e Histórica do Brasil*, 1834. Photos taken between 1816 and 1831.

Slave punishments and resistance

The privately administered torture, whipping, beating, maiming, punitive branding and psychological torment of slaves at the hands of masters, mistresses, overseers, slave-catchers, paid whippers, officials and members of the clergy form a vast and gruesome historiography of human cruelties under slavery.[20] Stanley Stein defined an ideal master as 'an omnipotent, omnipresent, beneficent despot, a father to his "flock" of slaves when they were obedient and resigned, [and one who] became a fierce and vengeful lord when transgressed'.[21] Punishments were deemed a necessary incentive to oblige slaves to work. C. A. Taunay in his *Manual do agricultor brasileiro*, written in 1839, held that slaves resisted labour unless forced by fear, rigid discipline and constant supervision to perform their assigned duties.[22] Whereas the most common form of punishment was whipping, a variety of other cruel methods were used, including branding slaves with a hot iron, mutilation, emptying vats of boiling fat or water on them, confinement in the stocks (*tronco*), the prohibitions or curtailment of leisure activities, starvation, forced use of blocks and chains, neck irons and tin masks, and other forms of physical and emotional torture. Taunay recommended a limit of 50 lashes with a whip of one leather strand, called a *bacalhau*, named after a dish of dried codfish that was popular with Portuguese overseers, whose mark of authority was the whip. He advocated that punishment for repeated runaways, major theft, disobedience, incorrigible drinking and rebellion be handled in the jails of each district. In fact, where public jails existed, whippings of 100 to 400 lashes were often applied for a fee and at the behest of the slave-owner, an arrangement between owner and jail official that signalled the compliance of public authorities with planters in the arbitrary, unregulated brutality directed at slaves. Slave appeals for lesser sentences and reduced punishments were usually delayed or ignored. A runaway slave who had resisted arrest appealed his sentence of 150 lashes and the use of a metal collar for six months. The court doubled his sentence when it reviewed the case.[23]

The pervasiveness of *quilombos*, the haunting memories of the Haitian revolution of 1791 and the uprisings of Malés slaves in Salvador, Bahia, between 1807 and 1835, followed by the Manuel Congo movement in Vassouras in 1838 and a similar movement in the 1840s, fuelled slave-owners' fears of collective slave rebellion.[24] The Manuel Congo episode generated the most apprehension among slave-owners because of its potential to spread to other areas. The Manuel Congo movement in Vassouras involved more than a hundred slaves, mostly African, who supplied themselves with stolen foodstuffs, farm tools, clothes, livestock and weapons from two or three Vassouras *fazendas* to found a *quilombo* in the remote, mountainous confines of the Paraíba Valley. They were eventually defeated and captured by the Marquess of Caxias, local police and national guard forces led by local planters. Manuel Congo, the leader, was hanged in 1839 and seven others accused of insurrection were sentenced to 650 lashes each, administered in doses of 50 per day, and were forced to wear an iron hoop around their necks for three years.[25] The episode was followed by a declaration from a permanent commission of planters set up in Vassouras in 1838 that pronounced the slave to be 'an irreconcilable enemy'.[26]

Given the size of Brazil and the pervasive nature of slavery, widespread collective slave violence was relatively limited. There are several reasons for this. The complex composition of the slave population itself may explain why there were few large-scale revolts or rebellions. Mary Karasch has suggested that the ethnic and social diversity of slaves prevented collective organization around a common aim.[27] Apart from the local measures already mentioned, laws provided for the rapid and severe apprehension of slaves suspected of disorder, including 'evil intentions and thoughts'. The Criminal Code of 1832 (*Código do Processo Criminal de Primeira Instância*) defined an insurrection as 'twenty or more slaves who act freely with force'. Leaders who were free persons would receive the same punishment as slave leaders, and those suspected of aiding, fomenting or encouraging slaves to rebel by furnishing them with arms or other means were likewise subject to punishment under articles 113–15 of the Code. In 1835, Article 1 of the exceptional law No. 4 of 10 June 1835 changed the punishment for slave-inflicted death or grave physical injury to masters and members of their families from imprisonment in the galleys to death:

> Male or female slaves who kill, administer poison, gravely
> wound or commit any other physical offense to their master, his
> wife, relatives who live among them; to the administrator, the
> overseer and their wives who live with them will be punished
> with the death penalty. If the wound or physical assault was
> mild, the penalty would be whipping, to be designated according
> to the seriousness of the particular circumstances.[28]

Public prisons (*casas de correção*) and detention houses existed in major urban centres but were dependent on local public works budgets in the interior.[29] In Rio Bonito, a decree authorized spending public works funds to acquire and convert a privately owned house in the town centre into a town council and courts, although there was still no public jail in the town.[30] Makeshift private quarters on rural estates or in the homes of local slave-catchers and officials were used to confine apprehended slaves, drawing a blurred boundary between public and private authority. Government and society also turned a 'blind eye' to the arbitrary nature of plantation 'justice', where masters served as judge and jury and meted out punishment to their slaves with little interference, except in extreme instances, from the public sphere.[31]

The influence of private authority over the public sphere also assisted government efforts to reassure the population by restricting news of slave violence to local police reports and only occasionally to newspapers or high-level official reports. The 1854 report of the Minister of Justice, José Thomaz Nabuco de Araújo, contained details of six cases of collective slave resistance for the entire country. Five cases dealt with slave conspiracy or revolts and one dealt with 80 slaves in the municipality of São João d'El-Rei in Minas Gerais who fled to the city to request their freedom.[32] In the same year, a police report referred to slaves in a candle factory in Rio de Janeiro who demanded another master and were arrested and jailed until the case was settled.[33] Individual slaves resisted in a variety of ways. The operations of production units were affected by maimed work animals, clogged machines, faulty farm implements and, in extreme cases, burned fields that undermined the daily regime of toil. Absenteeism also affected the labour regime when slaves claimed to be unfit for work due to injury or sickness. Escape was the most common form of individual slave resistance, although suicide by the ingestion of dirt and poison, hanging and infanticide regularly occurred. Flight to isolated fields, deserted stretches of roads, swamps and uninhabited stretches of riverbanks and forests afforded the best chance of avoiding detection by slave-catchers and their dogs who patrolled rural estates and public roads.[34] An escaped slave who leapt from the woods onto an empty stretch of road and conveyed by his gestures his intent to rob and murder Ida Pfeiffer and her companion, before he was apprehended, was described by her as 'desperate'.[35] Deserted stretches of road provided nightly refuge for roving thieves and hired assassins, and it was on such a road at night that the slave, Izidoro, contracted by two household slaves, murdered his master in cold blood near to the *fazenda*, after striking the defenceless wife who, with their child, helplessly witnessed the slaying.[36]

The transfer of slaves, who were sold, exchanged, inherited and given as gifts, in a disturbing practice that negated kinship ties and personal relationships, and often robbed them of the will to survive, accustomed slaves to the physical separation from loved ones and familiar surroundings by reinforcing the concept of *coisificação*.[37] A two-year-old slave girl from Vassouras, given as a wedding present to a couple, continually ran away at age ten to the wife's mother's home. She was exchanged for an African woman purchased in Rio de Janeiro and transferred to the highlands to replace the girl in domestic service.[38] The adult slave and the young girl experienced what thousands like them endured – movement and exchange that were governed by traders who mediated the deals of owners.

Separation from a familiar area was especially traumatic for slaves who had lived in one area for any length of time. Adelaide's malady (mentioned in Chapter 3) was claimed by her seller to be nothing more than temporary emotional stress over separation from her former masters and the place where she had lived for most of her life.[39] A convenient excuse like that served to deflect the attention of potential buyers from the deeper emotional traumas of separation. Change was threatening and, in some cases, slaves turned against other slaves when separation from kin and loved ones was imminent. After his master died in 1857, the slave Lino learned that he was to be sent from Rio Bonito to an heir who lived in the northeastern province of Paraíba. He devised a plan to flee with his slave companion, Paula, but murdered her when she refused.[40] Lino's next moves confirm the greater importance of his kinship bonds over concerns of apprehension or reprisals from Paula's master. Lino walked from the fields where he had murdered Paula to an adjacent farm to bid his sister farewell. He was spotted on the road returning to his master's residence and arrested, charged with Paula's murder and taken under local public custody. Paula's murder eliminated the possibility of transfer to a distant province and a new labour landscape. Local incarceration kept him near his sister and slave companions.[41]

After refusing to sexually 'serve' her master, the slave Justina learned of his imminent move into the interior and his intention to sell her. On the eve of the move, she slipped out of an unbarred window of her master's home, drowned her infant, her *ingênuo* son, and another *ingênuo* she was raising, lay their bodies on the riverbank, slit her throat and implored another slave to shoot her. The separation from her children and from surroundings and people who were familiar prompted her extreme actions. The court's fourteen-year prison sentence prevented her removal from the area.[42]

In both of the above cases the reaction to immediate circumstances governed the slave murders. Yet, the results of their actions removed them from the private sphere of their masters and into the public sphere of the courts and jails. Another course of action was available to the few who had recourse to a patron, godparent or other mediator who might intercede on their behalf, and slaves drew on these contacts to lessen the impact of the full force of public or private 'justice'. In the aftermath of the Manuel Congo episode, a number of escaped slaves voluntarily returned to their masters, accompanied by their godparents or other protectors, who would act as third-party mediators between them and their master.[43]

From the *fazenda* to the courthouse

At mid-century, the lack of public infrastructure in the *municípios* of the province of Rio de Janeiro meant that private houses and *fazendas* were used as makeshift jails. Arbitrary practices went unnoticed or under-reported, and planter recourse to private justice, or plantation 'justice', prevailed over the authority of the public sphere. One prominent landowner declared that even the emperor himself would not enter his property without his consent.[44] In 1855, the murder of a Portuguese overseer on the Fazenda de Santa Anna in the parish of Sacra Família do Tinguá, Vassouras, resulted in a case that highlights the interplay between the public and private spheres.[45] Engracia's anguished cries as she found her husband, the slave Firminio, hanging from a tree echoed through the fields and alerted other slaves who were planting stalks of sugarcane in a newly cleared area near the lagoon on the Fazenda de Santa Anna. Her Brazilian-born son, the *crioulo* Lipoleiro, was the dead man's stepson, and he, along with the slave foreman Antônio and several other field slaves, blamed the Portuguese foreman. Firminio's suicide followed a month's imprisonment in the stocks, to which he was returned after a day of harsh field labour. The Portuguese foreman headed back to the great house to inform one of Rio de Janeiro's largest and most prominent landowners, Pedro Dias Paes Leme, Marquess of São João Marcos, that the slave he had earlier reported missing was dead. The foreman, referred to in the records as Pimenta, never reached his destination, felled in the fields by slaves who exacted the price of his life for the punishment he had meted out to Firminio.[46]

Slave justice varied in intensity and intention, but in this case there was collective retaliation against Fortunato Pimenta de Figueiredo. Lipoleiro related his version of events to local authorities, claiming that he stopped work and pursued Pimenta but that the overseer pulled a gun on him.[47] It misfired. A second pistol shot, directed at the African slave, Félix from Calundá, a field labourer of 30 years' service, grazed his hand. Lipoleiro then claimed that in self-defence he gathered a handful of clay and hurled it at the overseer's head. Other slaves followed suit, and they left Pimenta for dead in the field. A trader who was hunting on horseback nearby testified that he heard a great uproar but assumed it to be caused by dogs that had captured some game. The boy he sent to investigate said he saw a slave, armed with a pistol and a scythe, running away from a body that lay writhing on the ground. A slave cook who was in the fields at the time of the murders testified that Claudino, a *crioulo*, and Félix confessed to the murder to the Marquess and, standing before him on the veranda of the great house, had demanded a chalice to drink the victim's blood.

Other versions were heard. Félix confirmed he was present at Pimenta's death but blamed Lipoleiro and a Brazilian slave named Capitão Leal, who had been imprisoned in the stocks with the dead slave, punished for having an unknown slave on the premises after the gates had been locked. Claudino and the Africans, Clemente from the Congo and Josué from Cabinda, were also accused of plotting to kill the overseer.

Claudino, Clemente and Josué were confined to the stocks. African slaves Lino, from Inhambane in Moçambique, and Martins, from Calundá, whom the *fazenda* owner claimed would know something about the incident, were also placed in the stocks following a brutal beating and whipping. Arrest warrants were issued for the suspects, Capitão Leal, Antônio the slave foreman and a third slave named Luís. They were reported missing.

There was little left of the overseer's skull for medical examiners to analyse. They found that the front of Fortunato Pimenta de Figueiredo's head contained 'only fragments of bone, most of which were scattered with the brains around the cadaver, leaving only a piece of bone at the level of the neck'. The nature of the lesions suggested death by 'blows from spades and clubs that were found on the ground around the body'.

Antônio, who had rushed to the great house brandishing the pistol and spade, claimed that the Portuguese overseer had killed himself, but the Marquess was not convinced. He ordered two workers on the estate to investigate, but as they drew near the body, Claudino, the coachman and field worker who had been born and raised on the *fazenda*, approached them with a sickle and a raised spade, threatening to kill them if they tried to avenge Pimenta's death.[48] As they fled, one of them shouted, 'we are lost as they have just murdered Pimenta'. Borrowing the horse of an approaching trader, he rode to Vassouras to alert the authorities, where he claimed that 'worse things could ensue under the leadership of the slaves'.

The Marquess exercised his authority over his slaves and ordered them to return to the fields to harvest the beans. Questioned by local officials, the Marquess answered for his slaves, blaming the murder of the Portuguese overseer on the hanged slave. As a prominent local figure with court connections and the official voice of the estate, his authority might have been sufficient. However, the presence of the clubs that lay strewn about the overseer's body thwarted his efforts.

The accused leaders were slaves of long-standing service on the *fazenda* and had family ties on the estate. Brazilian-born *fazenda* slaves had grown up in the presence of, and were socialized by, African slaves who had spent the better part of their adult lives in *fazenda* slavery. Whereas kinship ties were a stabilizing feature of slavery, and slaves in long-standing service were familiar with their master's ways and the operations of the *fazenda*, Pimenta was viewed with contempt for his treatment of Firminio. Long-standing service generated grievances and in this case Brazilian and African slaves were united in redressing the slave's suicide. The arrest and confinement of the accused leaders by the public authorities removed the slaves from the private justice of the *fazenda*.[49]

The Marquess's reaction suggests that this was not his first encounter with slave 'justice', nor his first experience with the authorities. By blaming the overseer's murder on the dead slave he expected to have the matter dismissed. As the authorities pressed for details of the incident, he had slave informants whipped, confined to the stocks and hunted down. The arrest and removal by officials of six suspected slaves to the public jail in Vassouras frustrated the Marquess's intentions of restoring order on his estate. Public authorities and the courts were not insensitive to slave-provoked murders, or to the arbitrary nature of plantation justice and the authority of the Marquess over his slaves. The matter was ultimately settled in the public courthouse.

Under Article 1 of an exceptional law of 10 June 1835 that followed the last of the Malês revolts in Bahia, Brazilian-born slaves Claudino, Lepoleiro and Capitão Leal and Africans Félix de Calundá, Martins and Lino were formally charged with the murder of the administrator and imprisoned. Lino died in jail of disease. At the trial, the others gave conflicting individual and collective accounts of the event, accusing each other of the murders.[50]

Not enough evidence existed to condemn any one of the slaves, and the lack of eyewitnesses to the crime left the court with a dilemma: to sentence all of the accused to death or absolve them all of the murder. Six slaves of long-standing service represented no great loss to the labour force of the most influential slave-owner in the area, but the decision of the court to absolve all of the suspects and return them to the *fazenda* left the slaves with their lives spared, although they were subject to plantation justice. In the long run, the private sphere of the Marquess recovered and he presumably came to terms with or sold his valuable slave property. The private sphere and plantation 'justice' had the final word in this case. A slave was dead, as was an unpopular overseer, whose death was celebrated by his slave counterpart and the slaves themselves. Their demand for a chalice from which to drink the overseer's blood suggested a spiritual bond that was probably shared by many of the African and Brazilian slaves on the *fazenda*.

This case is another illustration of what the Brazilian anthropologist Roberto da Matta has defined as the hierarchical-complementarity axis, which involves multiple ethnic behaviour codes that complement each other and maintain the integrity of the social universe. In da Matta's study of the folkloric figure Pedro Malasartes, the hierarchical-complementarity axis was mediated by wealth and power. Malasartes, a son of poor farming parents, outwitted and brought about the downfall of a rich and unscrupulous landowner by executing to the letter the demands the landowner made on him. Yet, the defeat of the landlord did not better Malasartes's social standing or overturn the rigid social hierarchy.[51] Neither did the murder of the overseer alter the status of the slaves who murdered him. Although their collective agency did bring the private sphere of master–slave relations under closer scrutiny by the public authorities, ultimately the private sphere prevailed and the slaves were restored to their master, to be dealt with by him.

Moral authority

Brazil's response to European and American developments concerning the ending of slavery was gradual. The measures taken by the former colonial power, Portugal, approved the emancipation of newborn slave children in the home country in 1856 and two years later passed a decree to abolish slavery in all Portuguese territories over a twenty-year span. Great Britain had abolished the transatlantic slave trade in 1807 and ushered in the abolition of slavery in British colonies in 1834, an act that was followed by France in 1848. A diplomatic agreement between Great Britain and Brazil in 1831 provided for the suspension of the transatlantic trade in Africans and the freedom of slaves taken from captured slave ships. Yet, two more decades elapsed before the effective suspension of the transatlantic slave trade took place.

Legislative gestures regarding slavery initially aimed to clarify the status of the slaves who were taken from captured slavers. A decree in December 1853 stipulated that an African who was 'liberated' by the Rio mixed commission could demand complete freedom by 1859. In September 1864, *emancipados* who had served the 14-year apprenticeships that were stipulated by the mixed commission were officially freed, although most remained in bondage.[52]

The decade of the 1860s marked a watershed between the 1850s and the abolitionist pressures that spread in the 1870s from urban bases, publicizing the injustices of slavery to a receptive public, court system and lawmakers. As had also been true in the American Civil War (1861–5), the War of the Triple Alliance (1864–70) that engaged Argentina, Brazil and Uruguay on the battlefront against Paraguay freed slaves for enlisting in defence of the patria. Some 6000 Brazilian slaves were freed by slave-owners to join the forces of the Triple Alliance, yet the transition of slaves to citizens and from citizens to soldiers for service in Brazil's armed forces proved a symbolic but not widely endorsed gesture in the direction of emancipation.[53]

In the 1860s, public denunciations of the cruel punishments and treatment meted out to slaves forced the authorities to investigate cases of excessive cruelty. In Paraíba do Sul, the son of a local *fazendeiro* and those who carried out a punishment that was so severe that the slave died were arrested and sentenced.[54] Slave-owners were opposed to public intervention and claimed responsibility for the moralization of their slaves. At 8 o'clock one morning, a Rio Bonito landowner was held incommunicado in his house while police searched his premises for a slave who was reported to have been beaten to death and buried. Slaves on the estate confirmed the punishment and led inspectors to the victim, who was found working in the manioc patch of the slave-owner's son-in-law who lived next door. The physician and the pharmacist who examined him described him as severely beaten but not at risk of dying.[55] The landowner registered an official complaint, claiming that the interrogation of his slaves and the police search of his premises violated his right to teach morality (*moralizar*) to his 60 slaves. The police inspector's justification for his actions in the search illustrated a different viewpoint on morality. According to his report, after hearing rumours from the neighbourhood inspector that Bernardino Ignácio da Costa had excessively punished and killed José, *crioulo*, the police inspector had sought confirmation. Having searched the manioc farm and found the slave alive and recovering, he departed, stating that he had 'responded to the rigorous need to maintain the moral force of slave-owners'.[56]

Specific issues, such as the punishment of slaves, were discussed at the highest levels. In 1861, the inhumane and excessive punishment by whipping was addressed by the Minister of Justice in a communiqué to the President of the province of Rio de Janeiro. He urged judges to graduate the punishment of whipping in consideration of the age and strength of the delinquent:

> because it is recognized, as physicians claim, that each time the
> number of lashes exceeds two hundred this is always followed by
> disastrous results; and that the application of punishment
> should be suspended as soon as the person, in the doctor's
> opinion, cannot endure it without danger.[57]

The effectiveness of this measure proved largely symbolic. A public prosecutor's indictment of an overseer who had cruelly whipped and imprisoned in the stocks an ailing slave in Vassouras in 1878 stated that 'those articles [of the criminal code] which speak of superior arms cannot be understood to apply to the abuse of an instrument permitted to slave-owners and their representatives for the punishment and discipline of the slaves'.[58]

The issue of moral authority over slaves also embroiled the police commissioner of the court and capital city of Rio de Janeiro in disputes with slave-owners accused by their slaves of personal abuse. Cases involving unmarried mulatto slave women between twelve and twenty-eight years of age, whose charges of prostitution against their owners led to their gratuitous emancipation, highlighted the issue of public regulation over private property. According to historian, Sandra Lauderdale Graham, the unsuccessful attempts of Rio de Janeiro police commissioner and judge, Miguel José Tavares, to launch regulatory laws governing prostitution in the city were at the heart of the matter.[59] The campaign was 'criticized for high-handed use of authority that transgressed the rights of property' at a time when debates over the 1871 Rio Branco Law invoked fears that the state's regulation of daily life would erode the exercise of private authority over slavery.[60]

Transition at a gradual pace

Brazil's imperial head of state, Dom Pedro II, favoured emancipation, but only in his May 1867 address from the throne did he touch on the matter of slavery's end. He underscored the need to respect property rights and agriculture, while observing carefully and 'at an opportune time' the issue of slave emancipation.[61] Two years later, a cautionary step that has been identified as the first effective direct state intervention in the master–slave relationship was taken – law No. 1695 of September 1869. Under Article 2, the sale of slaves at public auction was banned and the separation of a husband and wife, or child under fifteen from his mother, was disallowed.

The widespread conviction among slave-owners that slaves with families were productive, stabilizing and less likely to escape or rebel may have been the motivating force behind the regulation of the institution of the slave family. Whatever the reasons, the most contentious debates over slavery that resulted in the Rio Branco Law enlisted the involvement of the state in the issue of slave families, and heralded in a vital stage of the transition process. Hardly pursuant of humanitarian or enlightenment ideals, the 1871 law targeted specific aspects of emancipation – slave newborns and self-purchase – subjecting each to detailed bureaucratic stages. Only in the 1880s did an imperial measure commute death sentences to a lifetime of galley labour for personal crimes committed by slaves, leading to confinement in public facilities and a supervised public work regime as an alternative to the *fazenda*. Two more laws in 1885 stipulated the conditions of freedom for slaves over sixty years of age and prohibited public whipping.

Taken chronologically, the measures confirmed an evolving transition process initiated from above, yet the time lag between each law is indicative of a political dilemma. On the one hand, the state upheld its moral authority to intervene in the private master–slave relationship. On the other, proponents of private rights challenged state interference in all matters involving private property, especially those related to slavery.

Regional divisions attested to disunity in the approaches of Brazilian planters to the emancipation process and may explain why the polarization of planter interests that led to the American Civil War had no equivalent in Brazil. Regional interests rather than political issues prevailed in northeastern Brazil among sugar planters whose holdings of slaves spanned generations. Planters substituted slaves who had been sold to the coffee areas of the south with locally available free labourers, who were marginalized from semi-subsistence production by the cyclical regional droughts. The tendency to employ free labour weakened the support for slavery, and abolition in Ceará in 1883 and in Amazonas a year later signalled a growing regional reluctance collectively to defend slavery. In the Western Paraíba Valley towns like Vassouras, where most planters had invested their capital in slaves, Robert B. Toplin identified hard-core planters who were being marginalized by their refusal to consider alternatives to slave labour. Social prestige, political power and economic dependency informed their appeals to the state for compensation for emancipated slaves. In contrast, for progressive planters in the sugar-producing areas of Campos and Recife and in the dynamic coffee areas in the northwest of São Paulo, where economic motives also lay behind planter commitments, immigrant and family-based labour from Europe proved a viable solution and was crucial to sealing the fate of slavery in 1888.[62]

Brazilian captives

Slaves were not immune to the pressures of urban abolition movements and the journals and newspapers that served as fora for such intellectuals and politicians as Joaquim Nabuco, José do Patrocínio, André Rebouças and Luiz Gama and their attempts to rally public support behind the abolition cause in the 1870s and 1880s. Brazilian-born slaves, who by the 1870s outnumbered African slaves, formed an *onda negra* (black wave) that was spreading in the country and causing concern for slave-owners.[63] São Paulo planters from Rio Claro and Campinas expressed their unease through petitions to the provincial president in 1871. They distinguished 'brutalized and mostly dim-witted Africans' who were 'easy to dominate' from Brazilian slaves who 'were born, raised and participated in the ways and customs of the dominant culture, possessing a broader intellectual range than their ancestors and aspirations compatible with their stage of development'. By 'stage of development', the implication was that they had surpassed the passive subservience of their predecessors. To press home their point, the petitions held Brazilian-born slaves to be behind the decay of the moral order through the murders of overseers and the exodus of slaves from rural estates.[64]

Brazilian-born slaves were conversant in Portuguese, raised in a rigid social hierarchy, albeit one that allowed for physical mobility, and were familiar with patriarchal controls and the ways in which power could be manipulated. The generations of slaves who were born after 1850 were Brazilian and, despite the African presence and influence in the slave quarters, grew up in a creolized society with Brazilians, 55 per cent of whom were non-white in 1872 and increasingly free. Free *pretos* and *pardos* accounted for 4.2 million, whites for 3.8 million and slaves for 1.5 million in that year. The composition of the local populations in Vassouras and Rio Bonito was typical of the transition that, excepting São Paulo, was quietly replacing the association of non-whites and slavery with a new identity that linked non-whites to the free labour market (Table 5.1).

The 1871 law also impacted on the ways in which, in the shifting demographic landscape, slaves viewed slavery and pressed for its abolition. In 1873, heirs to an estate in Sumidouro in northeastern Rio de Janeiro promised the slaves that things would continue as they had been under the former master, including the allotment

Table 5.1 Free non-white population of the parishes of Vassouras and Rio Bonito, 1850 and 1872

		Vassouras				
		1850			1872	
Parish	Total	Free non-white		Total	Free non-white	
		No.	%		No.	%
N.S. da Conceição	10,086	1238	12	10,664	3421	32
Ferreiros	–	–	–	4555	874	19
Paty do Alferes	11,489	1648	14	14,440	3053	21
Mendes	–	–	–	3340	943	28
Sacra Família do Tinguá	7063	1178	17	6143	2139	35
Total	28,638	4064		39,142	10,430	

		Rio Bonito				
		1850			1872	
	Total	Free non-white*		Total	Free non-white	
		No.	%		No.	%
Rio Bonito	16,500	3591	22	18,120	3928	22.0
N.S. da Boa Esperança	7150	1527	21	7752	3000	39.0
Total	23,650	5118		25,872	6928	

* Includes mulattos (*pardos*) but not Indians.
Sources: BNRJ, *Relatório do Presidente da Província, do Rio de Janeiro*, 1850. Directoria Geral da Estatística, *Recenseamento da população da Província do Rio de Janeiro, Quadro A*, 1872. Census columns were not accurately added at the time and account for discrepancies in the final tallies.

of provision grounds. Alleging that they were free Brazilians under the 1871 law, the slaves refused to serve their new owners.[65] Four years later, planters in the same area sent a petition with 500 signatures to the emperor, calling for measures to deal with growing slave criminality and insubordination: 'The situation of rural establishments is profoundly shaken and altered, the ties of discipline ruptured and the prestige and moral force of slave-owners entirely broken.'[66]

Lavradores and *jornaleiros*

Changes in official occupation categories also signified official recognition of the advance of the free labour market. Referring to the 1872 census, Mattos de Castro argues that the legal identifier, 'slave', was substituted with the social identifier, 'occupation', reflecting a revision of the terminology in accord with the changing labour landscape. The occupational category 'domestic labour' listed 129,816 women and 45,561 men, but the category was not further subdivided by slave and free categories. Farming was subdivided into two specific categories: *lavrador* and *jornaleiro*, terms that had been in use since colonial times. *Lavrador* was a free farm worker who tilled the soil with slaves and sometimes owned the land. For Mattos de Castro, the terms *lavrador* and *jornaleiro* (a servant and labourer paid by the day) reveal how the legal identifier of 'slave' was being replaced by the social identifier of 'occupation'.[67] Although the category *lavrador* was an occupational identifier for 503,744 men and 304,657 women, *jornaleiro* figures for men and women were much lower and roughly the same: 49,195 men to 45,293 women. The shift in the meaning of the terms is not clearly explained in the census and does not correlate with the use of *lavrador* as a slave occupation in the slave *matrículas*. The finding although suggestive of changing attitudes as the free labour market formed, is not conclusive.[68]

Manumission and the obstacles to freedom in Rio Bonito and Vassouras

Manumission proceedings were a reflection of the ability of slaves to finance their freedom and that of family members. The annual averages of manumission in Campinas, São Paulo, increased from 7.1 between 1849 and 1858 to 329 in the 1869–78 period, and to 161.9 in the final decade of slavery, 1879–88.[69] Peter Eisenberg and Jacob Gorender confirmed that the majority of manumitted slaves were urban *pardo* females in domestic service, although female slaves were a minority in the slave population as a whole.[70] In 1874 in Campinas, less than one-third of the female slave population worked in domestic service, yet two-thirds of the freed slaves were engaged in this activity.[71] Explanations point to the preference for male slaves and the higher prices they commanded in a market that demanded heavy physical labour in the field. Cheaper female slaves could more easily come up with the lower prices for their freedom.[72] Through plying technical skills, trading, wet-nursing and prostitution, or through affective ties to the planter class, slave women could elicit collaboration in their passage to freedom from men whose patriarchal standing would suffer little change as a result. Eisenberg's data for Campinas confirm that between 1851 and 1885, the numbers of female *alforrias* exceeded those of males, reaching a peak in the latter decade of 62 per cent of all *alforrias*; yet it must be said that a significant number of children under ten and women over fifty years of age figured in the tallies.[73]

On the basis of a sample of 1206 slaves whose manumission cases were appealed to the Appellate Court in Rio de Janeiro, males slightly outnumbered females: 52.6 per cent to 46.4 per cent.[74] In terms of the most common legal path to freedom, letters of *alforria* prevailed over other forms of freedom in the period between 1851 and 1870.[75]

Increases in manumission numbers attested to the general appeal of emancipation, but complications and legal intricacies continued to hamper slave attempts to be free. In 1881, the Appellate Court heard a case involving six slaves, whose master offered them as collateral for a debt despite their claim to freedom.

The case had been disputed for a decade after José Antonio de Carvalho, listed in the *Almanak Laemmert* as a *lavrador*, won a suit against Francisco da Silva Chavão for a debt of 3:610$886 plus interest of 1 per cent for unpaid and overdue letters of credit. In light of the elapse in time and the inability of the defendant to repay the loan, the plaintiff claimed six field slaves, ranging in age from fourteen to fifty-three, whom the defendant had offered as collateral, 'free of any onus or legal complication'.[76] The six slaves petitioned the municipal judge to review the case, given that their letter of freedom, dated 26 August 1872 and passed by their owner in exchange for lifetime service to him, made it illegal for them to be offered as collateral in April 1873. A subsequent letter of 10 November 1877 removed the conditional clause and granted full freedom to the defendants who, according to local witnesses with whom they took refuge, lived and were treated as free. The slaves won a decision of the local court that declared null and void their sale to repay the loan. When appealed, the case was reversed by the Tribunal da Relação of Rio de Janeiro on the basis of the testimony of a scribe, who declared under oath that the dates on the letter of freedom had been altered from 1877 to 1872. The public defender appointed to represent the slaves made an impassioned plea to the judge:

> Senhor! The appellants are poor disgraced souls who deserve the protection of the most august and exalted Court under your Honour's jurisdiction. The freedom that was granted by their owner is disputed by the avariciousness of money and cannot triumph where the law, reason and the justice of venerable judicial authorities reigns. My wards will suffer a tremendous injustice with a revision of the previous sentence that confirmed their liberty. I hope that the review of this matter will be subject to the customary justice that reigns in the revered High Court.[77]

The outcome of the case is unknown.

An indebted widow also defended her ownership of the services of three male slaves who were claimed by creditors but who stated that they had enjoyed conditional freedom for a decade. Failing to produce the letters of freedom, their appeals were quashed.[78] Eloy, a slave whose mistress left him to the executor of her estate upon fulfilment of the terms of her will, claimed his freedom in 1887 on the basis that the terms of the will were not honoured in full.[79] Nor did an ex-slave's status as a free man alter the court's ruling on his murder when his former master resorted to 'plantation justice'. Slaves described the beating and murder of the ex-slave by his former master as he entered the great house in search of warmth. When the local court learned that there were no eyewitnesses and that the only informants were household slaves who by law were forbidden to testify in court, especially in a case that involved their master, the prime suspect was absolved. Yet one wonders if any member of the court gave any thought to the fact that the prostrate body that officials found dumped in the courtyard belonged to a non-citizen who by nature of his manumission had become a citizen.[80]

Table 5.2 Brazilian sugar and coffee exports, 1856–85

Years	Sugar as percentage of total export value	Coffee		
		Annual tons	Average value in pounds (£)*	Percentage of total export value
1856–60	21.2	164,160	5,635,000	48.7
1861–5	14.0	153,300	6,863,400	49.3
1866–70	10.7	192,840	6,737,400	42.5
1871–5	11.8	216,120	10,487,800	52.0
1876–80	11.8	219,900	12,103,000	60.7
1881–5	13.7	311,760	11,359,000	58.8

* Nominal value unadjusted for inflation.
Source: Adapted from Peter L. Eisenberg, *The Sugar Industry of Pernambuco, 1840–1910* (Berkeley: University of California Press, 1974), Table 2.

Changing landscapes: redoubled resistance

Tensions among masters and slaves in the 1870s and 1880s were heightened by fluctuations in Brazil's coffee export market. Coffee's total export value exceeded that of sugar by three or four times in the 1860s, and by five or six times in the 1870s. Yet, planters also faced a decline in the buying power of the mil-réis due to the disadvantageous mil-réis/pound sterling exchange rate in the 1860s. International coffee prices recovered in the first half of the 1870s, peaked in 1874, gradually fell again, recovered slightly in 1879 and plummeted during the years 1880 to 1883. The average pound sterling value of coffee was £6,737,400 for the 1866–70 period; this jumped to £10,487,800 in 1871–5 and reached £12,103,000 in the 1876–80 period. At the end of the 1870s coffee accounted for 60.7 per cent of total export value.[81] The mil-réis/pound sterling exchange rate dipped in the early 1870s but rose from the middle of the decade well into the 1880s (Table 5.2).

According to Flávio Versiani, the export price of coffee per bag declined from £95 in the beginning of the 1860s to approximately £60 per bag in 1870.[82] Unfavourable exchange rates also affected planters' ability to meet pound sterling equivalent payments of imported goods and luxury items. From the 1860s, planters pushed for increased quotas of coffee to offset these factors, and adopted a two-pronged strategy to increase working hours and workloads. The increase in the murders of overseers and, in some cases, masters that intensified planter concerns about slave rebellions in the 1860s and 1870s was related to the impact on slaves of the vicissitudes of the export market, longer hours, heavier workloads and, possibly, news of the Civil War in the United States.

The escape of the three African brothers, Calixto, Francisco and Baltazar from a coffee *fazenda* in the eastern highlands of Cantagalo, where they had been sold, is suggestive of the resistance of slaves to heavy work regimes in a strange environment and to the strength of their kin ties. They returned to the familiar surroundings of their former master's estate, where they set up a *rancho* and did odd jobs until the local authorities came to arrest them. Confronted with certain return to the coffee fields of Cantagalo, they resisted and ambushed their pursuers.[83]

To curtail slave protests, planters mobilized free farmers to increase surveillance of slaves, report sources of unrest on rural estates and capture runaways. They also appealed for national guard battalions to back up the police authorities and facilitate the apprehension of fugitive slaves. Increasing reliance on public authorities in the face of potential slave unrest loosened the resolve of local planters to shun the involvement of local authorities or the judicial system in private plantation justice.

The demonstrations of force did not, however, stem the tide of the *onda negra*. Private patrols and public policing did not deter slaves from violent attacks on authority figures on the *fazendas*. In fact, slaves in long-standing service were held to be a motivating force behind many of the episodes. Police also suspected that slaves who were separated from familiar surroundings and kin in the northeast by their transfer in the inter-provincial slave trade had little to lose from resistance, revolt or escape. Mieko Nishida has also argued that after 1851, formal institutions for mutual aid among slaves were being replaced by greater reliance on personal networks. Taken together with the change from ethnicity based on African nationality to ethnicity denoting colour, slaves from northeastern areas may have been individually motivated to undertake the risks of resistance to achieve their freedom.[84] Rio de Janeiro's provincial president reported that slaves from these areas were of 'poor character and incorrigible conduct', yet such reports did not quell the demand or the inter-provincial slave trade from other provinces.[85]

Fazenda configurations

The expansion of coffee production altered the physical landscape, as coffee fields invaded forested areas. Previously inaccessible caves and inhospitable mountainous areas that had provided refuge for runaway slaves were exposed as cultivation drew production units closer to the wilderness. Deforestation also affected navigable tributaries and riverbeds, eroding some and drying up others that had previously offered a means of escape. As distances shortened between the slave quarters and the semi-wild and wilderness areas of the forests, the seclusion and secrecy of forested retreats for dances, chants, sacrifices and ritual celebrations were also exposed.

Drawing on police and newspaper accounts from Rio de Janeiro and São Paulo, Celia Azevedo Marinho, correlated the changing *fazenda* layout with shifts in slave resistance. Despite a greater degree of absenteeism among masters, slave violence was still aimed at authority figures and was followed by confession and the surrender of slaves to the public authorities, where they were confined in public jails and sent to trial.[86] In the provincial president's annual reports to the legislature, instances throughout the province of assassinations of overseers and masters by their slaves figured prominently in the 1860s and 1870s. Four cases in Campos involved slaves who had murdered the overseer, master or mistress.[87] In two instances in Vassouras, overseers were murdered by slaves, one by shooting and the other by a knifing.[88] Under this form of resistance, slaves were taken from the *fazenda* to a public prison and a probable future on a hard-labour gang that was supervised and answerable to public authority. The transfer from the private sphere of the *fazenda* to public imprisonment in a *depósito* or makeshift prison in the case of slaves accused of the murder of the Portuguese overseer in Vassouras in 1856 resulted in the restoration of the slaves to the private justice of the *fazenda*. By the 1870s, the public clamour for the courts to be involved led to trial in a public forum that was unlikely to blindly restore slaves to the private justice of their masters. Still, the issue of flogging remained contentious; public opposition was not vociferous enough to change this punishment, which remained paramount until 1886.

Quilombos: fuelling freedom from the *fazenda*

Within *fazendas*, the changing dynamics of slave resistance that were compromising the stability of the labour force were also accompanied by challenges to traditional authority. It will be remembered that in 1872, most of Brazil's one and a half million slaves were Brazilian born, outnumbering African slaves, who represented only 9 percent of the total slave population. In the southeastern provinces, however, African-born slaves represented 23 per cent of the slave population of the court, and 19 per cent of the slave population of the province of Rio de Janeiro.

The influence and traditional authority of African male elders over language, traditions, customs and religion in family groupings that also kept new slaves in check was subsiding as aged Africans succumbed to illness and death, outnumbered by younger Brazilian-born slaves, *ingênuos*, fugitives and freedmen. Whereas Africans of long-standing service aged with their masters over the years and were influential figures in negotiations over the welfare of slave families, work regimes, leisure time and provisioning, younger slaves were prone to fight rather than flight to attain their freedom.

New alignments in the formal and the informal, the legal and the illegal, the worlds of order and those of disorder, were aimed at redesigning relations of labour to land. At the heart of tensions were customary rights to improvements made to land, an issue that was highlighted by police reports of slaves establishing *quilombos* within the confines of rural estates. In his analysis of police reports on the *quilombos* of Rio de Janeiro, dos Santos Gomes encountered a complaint submitted by Manuel Cruz Sena, an owner of two estates in the eastern coastal area of Macaé. In 1876, Cruz Sena demanded police intervention against his slaves who had set up a *quilombo* on his land. Police investigations revealed that most of the nine African slaves and the 25 *crioulos* were related. Among the fourteen women and twenty males, there were also ties of godparenthood. The Rio Bonito origins of two *crioulo* slaves confirm that Manuel Cruz Sena, a notorious and devious trader from Rio Bonito who figures in two criminal investigations uncovered in that town, had moved with his slaves to Capivary and then to Macabú, a peripheral coastal area of Macaé in eastern Rio de Janeiro known for contraband slave dealings. Police reports recorded that 'the local *quilombolas* assaulted and killed travellers, *fazenda* owners and farmers from the surrounding areas, provoking a reign of terror in the *município*'.[89] Cruz Sena informed local police that slaves from both *fazendas*, including his private valet, had armed themselves in *ranchos* in the interior of his estate and were robbing and pillaging his estate. They were undeterred by his attempts to destroy the *quilombo*. One would have expected that Sena's appeal for public intervention to restore his authority over his slaves might have elicited a prompt response from local forces. The outcome was very different. The local police chief, a prominent *fazendeiro*, informed the slaves that he would mediate (*apadrinhar*) their demand to be sold to another owner. In this case, then, slaves rejected the authority of their master and organized an alternative system of production to sustain them until their demands for a new owner were met. The case is significant, since it reveals that slaves were renouncing the moral authority of an unjust master, not the institution of slavery.

Claims to improvements based on customary rights to work the land had a long-standing precedent in rural Brazil. John Luccock reported on the customary incorporation of *de facto* farmers on private estates, where an agreed exchange of services took place with the *de jure* owner. Provision grounds had provided slaves with a customary access to land that offered an alternative to purchase or inheritance, from which they were by law excluded. One might therefore conclude that the establishment of armed *quilombos* on Cruz Sena's *fazenda* demonstrated a collective slave alternative that bypassed officially endorsed channels of exclusion. The slaves erected *quilombos* to safeguard the customary rights to production and trade that the owner was threatening to undermine. Their actions could be classified as spontaneous, in Eric Hobsbawm's term, as those of primitive rebels, since they repudiated the authority of an unjust master, appropriated for themselves the fruits of their labour, guaranteed their food production, but did not demand a change in their slave status. Although Cruz Sena played upon police fears of widespread social disturbance in the expectation of galvanizing official repression and ensuring the removal of the slaves to public jails, the police response was very different. The public sphere in this case stood between the slaves and their owner, presenting a direct challenge to the moral authority of the slave-owner. Even if police authorities had reacted as Cruz Sena incorrectly predicted they would, the slaves still had a good chance of being arrested and facing a lifetime of galley labour rather than continued enslavement to an unjust master.[90]

Official explanations for the informal and illegal appropriation of *fazenda* property are not forthcoming. The tactics of Cruz Sena's slaves intensified the general unease among planters over slave agency, the legal grounds that permitted slaves to receive and save money. A settlement of fugitives in the midst of their fields alerted planters to the risks of involving slaves in confrontations over land and labour that might result in the burning of crops, loss of property and physical injury. From the point of view of dissatisfied slaves, the appropriation of privately owned property challenged the bases for long-standing *de jure* claims to land and redefined the legal and the informal arrangements of authority. On a practical level, rebellious slaves faced little chance of survival in clandestine refuges outside of the *fazendas*, where they would be dealt with as runaways. In the Cruz Sena case, slaves appropriated the master's estate as the safest haven and the most viable option. Slave provision grounds and food supplies were maintained, kinship networks and local affinities between resident slaves and fugitives were secured and fugitive slaves enjoyed a semi-autonomous status unbound by the strictures of slavery.

In this respect, the escape of the three African brothers, Calixto, Francisco and Baltazar from Cantagalo and their return to Rio Bonito takes on additional importance as a strategy for survival.[91] Their mini *quilombo* became a focal point for the reaffirmation of traditional and often conflicting ties that linked the worlds of order, disorder and labour. When the owner of the estate and the police authorities came to arrest them and return them to their new owner in the highlands, the slaves set up barricades. The slave brother and a son of Francisco who had remained on the estate were called by the owner to retrieve injured policemen from the fugitives' hideaway. Once the policemen were safely out of fire, however, the negotiations ceased and in the ensuing shoot-out, only Francisco survived. He was sentenced to 300 lashes and fitted with an iron collar for one year.[92]

The transition process that moved rapidly ahead in the 1870s and 1880s was strengthened by the sizeable non-white Portuguese-speaking free population, by *ingênuos*, freed slaves and the association of occupations with the free labour market that blurred distinctions between slaves and non-slaves. The proximity between slaves and free farmers in work and in leisure on rural estates during the gradual implementation of the free labour market brought ever-more-attainable visions of freedom – release from arduous forced labour and from the hoe in the coffee rows, and, instead, the prospect of a garden plot, a cabin, a few domestic animals and a future in Brazil.[93]

The numbers of slaves continued to decline rapidly. Between 1884 and 1887, the Brazilian slave population fell by 42 per cent, from 1,240,806 in 1884 to 723,419 in the year prior to emancipation. These figures contrasted sharply with the 28 per cent decline that occurred over the previous two decades, from a high of 1,715,000 in 1864.[94] Of the slaves in bondage in the 1880s, 67 per cent were concentrated in the southeast of Brazil, in Minas Gerais, Espírito Santo, Rio de Janeiro and São Paulo, suggesting a correlation between dynamic coffee and foodstuffs production and planter resistance to labour alternatives. Mass movements of slaves who abandoned the *fazendas* in 1886 and 1887 hastened the official declaration of emancipation on 13 May 1888. With the exception of mechanized production units and the effective replacement of slaves in São Paulo by immigrant labour, the emancipation decree irreversibly altered the labour scenario of the commercial plantation system as it had been traditionally operated.[95]

Privately owned land constituted a bounded territory distinct from the public body of the monarch or imperial state. After emancipation, that bounded territory and the attachment to the land became the contested forum for nationhood. In response to the refusal of the state to compensate slave-owners for the loss of their slaves, the interests of those who came to see their wealth, status and political identity as vested not in royal favour but in the ownership of land were turned against the monarch in the name of national interests.[96]

Notes

1. Laura de Mello e Souza, *O diabo na terra de Santa Cruz* (São Paulo: Brasiliense 1987).
2. Robert W. Slenes, 'Malungu, ngoma vem! Africa encoberta e descoberta no Brasil', *Cadernos Museu Escravatura* (Luanda: Ministério da Cultura, 1995); Mary C. Karasch, *Slave Life in Rio de Janeiro, 1808–1850* (Princeton: Princeton University Press, 1987), Ch. 9.
3. Joaquim Manuel de Macedo, *As vítimas algozes: quadros da escravidão* (São Paulo: Editora Scipione [1869], 1991).
4. AN, Documentação Judiciária, Corte de Apelação, Juízo Municipal de Vassouras, 1864. Recorrente: Raimundo dos Santos Queiroz. Recorrido: A justiça. No. 38, Maço 58, Gal. C.
5. See Nancy Priscilla Naro, 'Fact, fantasy or folklore? A novel case of retribution in nineteenth-century Brazil', *Luso-Brazilian Review*, vol. 33, no. 1 (summer 1996).
6. Karasch, *Slave Life*, p. 264.
7. Slave knowledge of plants and herbal cures is pervasive in literature concerning descriptions of slave medicine in the American South. Deborah Gray White has been among those historians who have explored this issue: *Ar'n't I a Woman?* (New York: W.W. Norton and Co., 1985), pp. 85, 115–16.
8. Adèle Toussaint-Samson, *Une Parisienne au Brésil* (Paris: Paul Ollendorff, 1883), p. 133.
9. Philadelphia, The Library Company. One such proceeding in 1823 was a trial over an anti-witchcraft ritual in Berbice. At the plantation Buses Lust the slave Willem, alias Sara, alias Cuffey was convicted as an Obeah man (Confou man) for the murder and subsequent burial of the negress Madalon, in which he was aided by four other slaves. Willem called himself Abdie Toboko – 'God's almighty child' – and he and his wife were seen in the negro houses of the plantation Op Hoop van Beter, where he administered cures to slaves. On Sunday, he danced the 'vigilant' and administered a drink to the other negroes. After that, they beat Madalon with a broom, calabash sticks and brush from the coconut tree. Willem knocked Madalon down with a shovel and then rubbed pepper in her private parts. He was heard telling Madalon that they were not killing her but driving the bad story out of her head. Another driver tied her hands and ran up and down the path with her so that the bad things would come out of her head. Ashes were strewn across the road to hide the signs of the punishment from the overseer. On the second night, Willem tied Madalon to the mango tree, where she was beaten with fire sticks and other weapons. Towards morning she was found dead. Willem was accused and tried for Madalon's murder and sentenced

> to be conveyed from prison to the plantation Op Beter where he would be delivered into the hands of the public executioner, and in the presence of this Court to be hung by the neck on the Mangoe tree under which the negress Madelon was suspended during her aforesaid punishment, until he be dead, after which his head to be severed from body and stuck in a pole, to be placed on said estate, there to remain until destroyed by the elements or birds of prey and the body to be interred under the aforesaid Mangoe tree.

The slave accomplices were sentenced to 300 lashes at the tree on which Willem was condemned; brand-marked, degraded as drivers and afterwards set to work in chains on the Op Beter plantation for one year.

   See Proceedings of the Court of Criminal Justice of the colony, Berbice, on the trial of the Negro Willem, alias Sara, alias Cuffey, for murder of the negress Madalon; and also the trials of the negroes Primo, Mey, Kus and Corydon, for aiding and abetting in said murder. Colonial Office, 14 May 1823, R.J. Wilmot Hoton.

10. João José Réis, *Rebelião escrava no Brasil: a história do levante dos malês* (São Paulo: Brasiliense, 1986); Eduardo Silva and João José Réis, *Negociação e conflito: a resistência negra no Brasil escravista* (São Paulo: Companhia das Letras, 1989), pp. 62–78, 99–122.
11. Cited in Robert E. Conrad, *Children of God's Fire* (Princeton: Princeton University Press, 1983), pp. 257–9.
12. Article 32, *Coleção de leis, decretos e regulamentos da província do Rio de Janeiro de 1859* (Rio de Janeiro: Typographia do Correio Mercantil).
13. Carlos Eugênio Líbano Soares, *A negregada instituição: os capoeiras do Rio de Janeiro* (Rio de Janeiro: Prefeitura da Cidade do Rio de Janeiro, Secretária Municipal de Cultura, Departamento Geral de Documentação e Informação Cultural, Divisão de Editoração, 1994), Part I.
14. Article 57, *Coleção de leis*.
15. *Ibid.*, Article 29.
16. *Ibid.*, Article 71.
17. Arquivo Geral da Cidade do Rio de Janeiro, Códice 6-1-28, *Escravos: posturas, 1838–1840*, 1–3, Article 9.
18. Conrad, *Children*, pp. 157–9.
19. *Ibid.*
20. For Brazil, see Robert Brent Toplin, *The Abolition of Slavery in Brazil* (Kingsport: Kingsport Press, 1972); Robert E. Conrad, *The Destruction of Brazilian Slavery, 1850–1888* (Berkeley: University of California Press, 1972); Karasch, *Slave Life*, Ch. 10; Lana Lage da Gama Lima, *Rebeldia negra e abolicionismo* (Rio de Janeiro: Achiamé, 1981), Ch. 1; Silvia Lara, *Campos de violência* (Rio de Janeiro: Paz e Terra, 1986), Chs 2 and 3; Sidney Chalhoub, *Visões da liberdade: uma história das últimas décadas da escravidão na corte* (São Paulo: Companhia das Letras, 1990); Soares, *A negregada instituição*, Part 2.
21. Stanley J. Stein, *Vassouras: A Brazilian Coffee County, 1850–1900* (Princeton: Princeton University Press [1957], 1985), p. 134.
22. C.A. Taunay, *Manual do agricultor brasileiro* (Rio de Janeiro: Tipographia Imperial, 2nd edn, 1839). See also Weech, *Brasiliens*, on the need for force and tasks to occupy slaves' time (pp. 134–5, 138, 140).
23. AN, Rio Bonito, 1858. Recorrente: O juízo. Recorrido: Antonio Maria de Nascimento. No. 438, Cx. 113, Gal. C.
24. Réis e Silva, *Negociação e conflito*, pp. 99–122; Kátia de Queirós Mattoso, *Ser escravo no Brasil* (São Paulo: Brasiliense, 1988), Ch. 6; Stein, *Vassouras*, Ch. 6; Gama Lima, *Rebeldia Negra*, Ch. 2; João José Réis and Flávio dos Santos Gomes (eds), *Liberdade por um fio: história dos quilombos no Brasil* (São Paulo: Companhia das Letras, 1996), pp. 263–90; Flávio dos Santos Gomes, *Histórias de quilombolas: mocambos e comunidades de senzalas no Rio de Janeiro – século XIX* (Rio de Janeiro: Arquivo Nacional, 1993); Alaor Eduardo Scisinio, *Escravidão e a saga de Manoel Congo* (São Paulo: Achiamé, 1988).
25. Gomes, *Histórias de quilombolas*, pp. 179–81; 202.
26. See 'Instruções para a comissão permanente nomeada pelos fazendeiros do município de Vassouras', Rio de Janeiro, 1854. Apprehension and arrest were commonly followed by death or the infliction of painful public physical punishment – hanging, flogging, the stocks, forced labour – combined with isolation, deprivation of food and often sale, with the intention of setting an example to the other slaves. Karasch, *Slave Life*, Ch. 10; Lara, *Campos de violência*; Chalhoub, *Visões da liberdade*; Warren Dean, *Rio Claro: um sistema brasileiro de grande lavoura, 1820–1920* (São Paulo: Paz e Terra, 1977), Ch. 3; Stein, *Vassouras*, Ch. 6.
27. Karasch, *Slave Life*, p. 326.
28. *Coleção das leis do Império do Brasil*, 1835; Karasch, *Slave Life*, p. 328.
29. Líbano Soares, *A negregada instituição*, Part 2.
30. Decree No. 1558 of 16 December 1871, *Coleção de leis, decretos e regulamentos da província do Rio de Janeiro de 1871* (Typografia do Diário do Rio de Janeiro, 1871), p. 194.
31. Gomes, *Histórias de quilombolas*. Report from Bahia on 29 January 1835 of police chief, Francisco Gonçalves Martins, to the president of province, in Conrad, *Children*, p. 411.
32. *Relatório da repartição dos negócios da justiça apresentado na segunda sessão da nona legislatura pelo*

respectivo Ministro e Secretário de Estado José Thomaz Nabuco de Araújo (Rio de Janeiro, 1854), pp. 1–6, cited in Conrad, *Children*, pp. 411–13.

33. Santos, *Histórias de quilombolas*, p. 347. See also the case of slaves who demanded to choose their own master, in Maria Helena Pereira Toledo Machado, *Crime e escravidão: trabalho, luta e resistência nas lavouras paulistas, 1830–1888* (São Paulo: Brasiliense, 1987), pp. 115–16.

34. The most detailed account of a slave's life in hiding is by the Cuban slave, Estéban Montejo. See Miguel Barnet, *Episode in the Life of a Runaway Slave* (Willimantic: Curbstone, 1994); Karasch, *Slave Life*, on resistance and runaways, Ch. 10.

35. Ida Pfeiffer, *A Woman's Journey around the World* (London: Office of the National Illustrated Library, 1850).

36. AN, Documentação Judiciária, Corte de Apelação, Campos. Réu: Izidoro. Acusação: assassinato de José Coelho dos Santos. No. 1397, Cx. 3699, Gal. C.

37. *Coisificação* means a piece of property: slaves were considered as objects to be used and misused like property.

38. AN, Documentação Judiciária, Corte de Apelação. Juízo Municipal de Vassouras, 1852. Réu: Antonio Luis Pereira. Autor: José Teixeira de Magalhães. Libelo. No. 294, Cx. 542, Gal. C.

39. *Ibid.*, Rio Bonito 1870. Réu: Hermenegildo Lopes Estrela. Autor: Antonio Fernandes da Motta. No. 1506, Cx. 93 (11–4–73), Gal. C.

40. *Ibid.*, Tribunal do Jury, 1857. Réu: Lino, escravo de José Joaquim de Araujo. Autor: A justiça por promotor. Cx. 3700, Ap. 2. The slave Raimundo informed the authorities that Lino had said that due to his imminent separation from Paula, 'poderiam capá-lo e que ninguém se utilizaria dela', p. 38 verso.

41. *Ibid.*

42. AN, Documentação Judiciária, Corte de Apelação, Campos, 1878. Processo crime. A justiça por seu promotor contra Justina, escrava de Antonio Paes da Silva. No. 41, Cx. 9, Gal. C. For a detailed description of this case, see Hebe Maria Mattos de Castro, 'Laços de família e direitos no final da escravidão', in Luiz Felipe de Alencastro (ed.), *História da vida privada no Brasil*, vol. 2 (São Paulo: Companhia das Letras, 1997), pp. 346–50.

43. Santos, *Histórias das quilombolas*, p. 201.

44. Margarida Souza Neves, Edmilson Rodrigues Martins and Francisco Calazans Falcon, *A Guarda Nacional no Rio de Janeiro* (Rio de Janeiro: Pontifícia Universidade Católica do Rio de Janeiro, 1971).

45. AN, Documentação Judiciária, Corte de Apelação, Vassouras, 1855. Recurso crime. Recorrente: O juízo. Recorrido: Claudino, Felix, e outros, escravos do Marquês de São João Marcos. No. 616, Maço 52, Gal. C.

46. Emília Viotti da Costa's findings confirm that among the principal causes of slave reprisals and revolts were the punishments that slaves or family members received: *Da senzala à colônia* (São Paulo: Difusão Européia do Livro, 1966), p. 310.

47. *Ibid.*, p. 309, for slave assassinations of masters and overseers, followed by surrender to the authorities.

48. See note 45.

49. Sidney Chalhoub cites a case where a slave confessed to a crime, preferring prison in a public jail to slavery: *Visões da liberdade*, p. 224. Slave violence towards overseers increased in the 1860s. Cases, such as the shooting of an overseer in Paraíba do Sul in 1860 and others, were reported in *Relatório do presidente da província do Rio de Janeiro*, 1860; 1861–80. See also Daniel McCann, 'The whip and the watch: overseers of the Paraíba Valley, Brazil', *Slavery and Abolition*, vol. 18, no. 2 (1997), pp. 30–47.

50. An appeal was turned down by the Tribunal da Relação under Article 80 of the 3 December 1841 law. Expenses and court costs were charged to the municipality of Vassouras. Toledo Machado cites a 1876 case from Campinas of slaves who agreed to collectively take the blame for a murder and to jointly blame anyone who did otherwise. See *Crime*, p. 95.

51. Roberto da Matta, *Carnivals, Rogues and Heroes: An Interpretation of the Brazilian Dilemma* (Notre Dame: University of Notre Dame Press, 1991), Ch. 5, pp. 198–230.

52. Leslie Bethell, *The Abolition of the Brazilian Slave Trade* (Cambridge: Cambridge University Press, 1970), p. 383.

53. Hendrik Kraay, 'Slavery, citizenship and military service in Brazil's mobilization for the Paraguayan war', *Slavery and Abolition*, vol. 18, no. 3 (1997). For a detailed account of a black regiment from Bahia and the repercussions of service in the Paraguayan war, see Eduardo da Silva, *Prince of the People* (London: Verso, 1992).

54. The sentence was not specified. IHGB, *Relatório do Presidente da Província do Rio de Janeiro*, 1860.

55. AN, Documentação Judiciária, Corte de Apelação, Rio Bonito, 1867. Processo crime. Recorrente: O juízo – Bernardino Ignácio da Costa. Recorrido: Capitão Gabriel Moreira Damasco, Police Chief of Rio Bonito.

56. *Ibid.*

57. Coleção das decisões do governo de 1861, Ministry of Justice, 10 June 1861, p. 289, cited in Conrad, *Children*, pp. 314–15.

58. McCann, 'The whip and the watch', p. 35.

59. Sandra Lauderdale Graham, 'Slavery's impasse: slave prostitutes, small-time mistresses and the Brazilian Law of 1871', *Comparative Studies of Society and History*, vol. 33 (1991), pp. 680–1. See also Lenine Naquete, *O escravo na jurisprudência brasileira: magistratura e ideologia no segundo reinado* (Pôrto Alegre: n. p., 1988), Ch. 9 and p. 88, cited in Hebe Maria Mattos de Castro, *Das cores do silêncio: os significados da liberdade no sudeste escravista, Brasil, século XIX* (Rio de Janeiro: Arquivo Nacional, 1995), p. 206.

60. Graham, 'Slavery's impasse', p. 685.

61. *Fala do Throno*, 22 May 1867, in Bethell, *Abolition*, pp. 386–7.

62. Toplin, *Abolition of Slavery*, pp. 9–19.

63. Celia Azevedo de Marinho, *Onda negra, medo branco: o negro no imaginário das elites* (Rio de Janeiro: Paz e Terra, 1987); Gomes, *Histórias de quilombolas*, p. 333.

64. Warren Dean, *Rio Claro*, pp. 125–6.

65. Gomes, *Histórias de quilombolas*, pp. 349–50.

66. APERJ, petition of 22 December 1877, cited in Gomes, *Histórias de quilombolas*, p. 333.

67. See Hebe Maria Mattos de Castro, 'Beyond masters and slaves: subsistence agriculture as survival strategy in Brazil during the second half of the nineteenth century', *Hispanic American Historical Review*, vol. 68, no. 3 (1988).

68. Conrad, *The Destruction*, Appendices, Table 19, 'Slave occupations, 1872', p. 299. The close male and female numbers suggest that food producers formed a strong component of this category.

69. Peter L. Eisenberg, 'Ficando livre: as alforrias em campinas no século XIX', *Estudos Econômicos*, vol. 17, no. 2, (1987), Table 2, p. 181.

70. Jacob Gorender, *O escravismo colonial* (São Paulo: Atica, 1985), pp. 354–5; Eisenberg, 'Ficando livre', pp. 175–216.

71. Eisenberg, 'Ficando livre', p. 194.

72. *Ibid.*, p. 184.

73. *Ibid.*, Table 3, p. 185.

74. Mattos de Castro, *Das cores do silêncio*, Figure 25, p. 212.

75. *Ibid.*, Table 18, p. 209.

76. AN, Documentação Judiciária, Corte de Apelação, Rio Bonito, 1881. Processo civil. Apelante: José Antonio de Carvalho. Apeladas: Iria, Lidia e outros. No. 335, Cx. 560, Gal. C.

77. *Ibid.*: 'Sendo, notória a injustiça que sofrerão os meus curatelados com a reforma do Acordão que confirmou sua liberdade, espero a concessão da Revista, fazendo assim este reverendo Supremo Tribunal a costumada justiça.'

78. *Ibid.*, 1876, Libelo de escravidão. Réu: Dona Guilhermina Maria do Nascimento. Autor: José Antonio Martins Sobrinho. No. 586, Cx. 12099 (antigo 558), Gal. C. The case was reopened in 1880 by the public defender of one of the slaves named Emiliano, who had been granted conditional freedom in 1860 that would revert to full freedom after service for 35 years. The service was non-transferable and since Emiliano's mistress had rented him out to a third party and then abandoned him in a public deposit for four years, the defender held that Emiliano was technically free. He won the case but the decision was appealed by the widow in 1880. The final outcome of the case is unknown.

79. *Ibid.*, AN. Corte de Apelação. Juízo Municipal de Vassouras, 1887. Réu: Américo Brasileiro

da Costa Moreira. Autor: Eloy por seu curador. Natureza do Processo: Liberdade. No. 4226, Maço 1745, Gal. C.

80. *Ibid.*, Rio Bonito, 1866. Recorrente: A justiça. Recorrido: Bento Carlos Ferreira.

81. Peter L. Eisenberg, *The Sugar Industry of Pernambuco, 1840–1910* (Berkeley: University of California Press, 1974).

82. Flávio Rabelo Versiani, 'Industrial investment in an "Export" economy: the Brazilian experience before 1914', University of London, Institute of Latin American Studies, Working Papers, no. 2, n.d., pp. 11–13.

83. AN, Documentação Judiciária, Corte de Apelação, Juízo Municipal de Rio Bonito, 1859. Recurso crime. Recorrente: A justiça. Recorrido: Francisco, escravo dos herdeiros de João Clemente de Sá. No. 79, Maço 78, Gal. C. See also, *ibid.*, 1858. Recurso crime. Recorrente: O juízo. Recorrido: Antonio Maria do Nascimento. No. 438, Cx. 113, Gal. C. I referred to the brothers in reference to their escape from the coffee-producing highland town of Cantagalo. Offered refuge and provided with gunpowder, bullets and arms from local traders and sympathizers, they set up *ranchos* in vacant fields on two separate occasions in 1857 and 1858 and supplied wood, performed odd jobs and traded in foodstuffs with local tavern keepers for several months before an official party consisting of the municipal judge, police soldiers and planters arrested and returned them to the highlands.

84. Mieko Nishida, 'Gender, Ethnicity and Kinship in the Urban African Diaspora: Salvador, Brazil, 1808–1888', PhD dissertation, The Johns Hopkins University, 1991.

85. *Relatório do Presidente da província do Rio de Janeiro*, 1 August 1850, p. 7.

86. Azevedo de Marinho, *Onda negra*, Ch. 2; Emília Viotti da Costa, *Brazil. Myths and Histories* (Chicago: University of Chicago Press, 1985).

87. IHGB, *Relatório do Presidente da Província do Rio de Janeiro*, 1873. In one of the cases, the slave Antonio was absolved for shooting and killing the overseer who was whipping his partner. In the other cases the master was beaten to death by a few of his slaves.

88. *Ibid.*, 1872–9. In addition to Campos and Vassouras, slaves poisoned their mistress in Macaé in 1876, and in 1878, in the same *município*, a slave knifed a man accused of harbouring runaways whom he forced to work in his fields. In Saquarema in 1877, a slave knifed his master to death.

89. References to Manuel Cruz Sena are cited in dos Santos Gomes, *Histórias de quilombolas*, pp. 326, 333 and 342.

90. *Ibid.*, pp. 326–31.

91. AN, Documentação Judiciária, Corte de Apelação, Rio Bonito, 1859. Recurso crime. Recorrente: A justiça. Recorrido: Francisco, escravo dos herdeiros de João Clemente de Sá. No. 79, Maço 78, Gal. C. See also, *Ibid.*, 1858. Recurso crime, Recorrente: O juízo. Recorrido: Antonio Maria do Nascimento. No. 438, Cx. 113, Gal. C.

92. The *rancho* that the brothers set up on their former owner's empty field reverted to the owner, and local tavern keepers and sympathizers of the fugitive slaves were arrested and prosecuted for aiding and abetting them. AN, Documentação Judiciária, Corte de Apelação, Rio Bonito, 1862. Recurso crime. Recorrente: O juízo. Recorrido: Antonio Maria do Nascimento. No. 438, Cx. 113. Gal. C.

93. See Chalhoub, *Visões da liberdade*; Mattos de Castro, *Das cores do silêncio*, on visions of freedom.

94. Robert E. Conrad, *Os últimos anos da escravatura no Brasil* (Rio de Janeiro: Civilização Brasileira, 1975), p. 6; Conrad, *The Destruction*, Table 3, 'Slave populations, 1864–1887', p. 285.

95. Caio Prado Jr, *A história econômica do Brasil*; Conrad, *Os últimos anos da escravatura*, 'Introdução. As fundações da escravatura brasileira'; Eisenberg, *Modernização sem mudança*; George Reid Andrews, *Blacks and Whites in São Paulo, Brazil, 1888–1988* (Madison: University of Wisconsin Press, 1991), Ch. 2.

96. In the context of rural England, Elisabeth K. Helsinger has explored the links between private interests in property and the attitudes of landowners towards monarchy. See *Rural Scenes and National Representation: Britain, 1815–1850* (Princeton: Princeton University Press, 1997), p. 20.

6

The Transition to Free Labour

In his 1884 study of Brazil, the Frenchman, Louis Couty, predicted the future of three classes of Brazilian coffee planters. The first was the small but wealthy elite who had diversified their investments in slaves, *fazendas*, *engenhos*, government bonds and stocks in the railroad networks that had been inaugurated in Brazil in the 1850s. This group, he stated, would survive the decline in international coffee prices, just one of the crises that were unfolding in that decade. The second class of planters were those who remained solvent despite mismanaged investments in land, railroads, houses and mills. They faced the 1880s with few savings and liquidated estates. The third group were already insolvent – planters who had increased plantings over the previous decade, purchased slaves and installed processing machines. The short-term profits from expansion and mechanization were now outweighed by unpayable debts to coffee brokers, banks and wealthy landowners. Faced with declines in exports, overdrawn credit and relief from the Bank of Brazil and from coffee brokers, and unable to replace unproductive slaves, make improvements to property, repair machines or invest in immigrant *colonos* (tenant farmers) this class was doomed to lose their land and crops.[1]

The publication of the annual report of loans and mortgages by the mortgage division, which was instituted by the Bank of Brazil in 1867, confirms Couty's dire predictions for the province of Rio de Janeiro.[2] In the previous decade, a comparison of the imperial court capital of Rio de Janeiro (*município neutro*), the provincial capital of Niterói and the neighbouring provinces of Minas Gerais, São Paulo and Espírito Santo with the province of Rio de Janeiro reveals that mortgages to the latter represented 50 to 61 per cent of all bank mortgages.[3] Of those, the fact that the bulk went to *fazendeiros* in hinterland highland *municípios*, following a careful assessment of each request, suggests that lending institutions encountered propitious opportunities for the coffee economy and for the planters who sought loans. Valença and Vassouras topped the list, followed by Cantagalo, Paraíba do Sul and Resende (See Table 6.1).

Following an annual report in 1883 that raised concerns over the future of the coffee economy, annual bank reports up to 1891 became more detailed and included the total area in hectares and the type of cultivation on estates in each *município*. Furthermore, the assessed values of slave-holdings were separated from the total value of the rest of the estate. Against the original mortgage, which

Table 6.1 Yearly mortgage loans, Banco do Brasil to five *municípios*, 1871–82

Município	Mortgages[a]	Fazendas[b]	Slaves[c]	Loan	Mortgage value
Valença	38	45	3950	3,366:000	7877:847
Vassouras	37	52	3125	2,962:475	7283:160
Cantagalo	35	37	1682	1,629:559	2417:269
Paraíba do Sul[d]	28	31	1446	1,498:000	3518:274
Resende[e]	27	31	1262	1,187:000	2782:765

[a] Refers to the number of mortgages in each *município*.
[b] Refers to the total number of *fazendas* receiving mortgages in each *município*.
[c] Refers to the total number of slaves on mortgaged *fazendas* in each *município*.
[d] Data missing for 1875, 1878 and 1881–2.
[e] Data missing for 1880.
Source: Banco do Brasil, movimento de hipotecas por ano, repartição de hipotecas, *Relatório apresentado à assembléia geral dos acionistas do Banco do Brasil,* for the years 1871–82.

was not to exceed half the value of rural properties or three-quarters of urban real estate, outstanding balances were recorded for each *município* on a yearly basis.[4] In relation to mortgages of *municípios* in other provinces, in 1883 Vassouras rated second in importance to the São Paulo *município* of Campinas, where 46 mortgages on 49 *fazendas* with totals of 2600 slaves were assessed at a total value of 8,584:592$. There were 37 mortgages on 42 coffee *fazendas* in Vassouras, totalling 2848:380$. These included 2766 slaves, who were valued at a total of 6726:598$. Juiz de Fora in Minas Gerais and the sugar-producing area of Campos in Rio de Janeiro came next. Yet in Rio Bonito, there was but one mortgage of a coffee and sugar producing *fazenda* with 56 slaves. The value of the entire estate was 107 contos and 940 mil-réis and the 35 conto mortgage had been paid off by 1889.[5]

The postmortem inventories of both *municípios* tell a somewhat different story. In Vassouras, 92 postmortem inventories were registered at five-year intervals between 1885 and 1920. The worst years were 1895 and thereafter when debts of 18 were equal or greater than the total value of the estate of the deceased; 26 declared impoverishment; 14 declared total ruin. In Rio Bonito, 2 of 22 postmortem inventories signalled impoverishment; 7 declared total ruin.

Loans from Rio coffee factors, local individuals and merchants made up 31.6 per cent of loans secured by mortgages on coffee plantations. Mortgage banks, of which the Bank of Brazil accounted for 61.3 per cent, made up the rest.[6] Planters were paying off their debts in the 1870s and until 1884, when the Bank of Brazil and other lenders suspended credit to planters, the coffee sector was seen as a profitable sector for investment and credit advances.[7] Yet time was running out. As Robert W. Slenes has suggested, Western Paraíba Valley planters, and those who underwrote the costs and expenses for their estates, erred in their predictions for the long-term duration of the coffee cycle in their areas.[8] For some, the loans made mechanization and expansion possible; for others, they delayed the effect of declines in yields and limitations on forested acreage that began to affect production in the 1860s, was aggravated in the 1870s, became irreversible with emancipation and continued unabated into the 1890s. Planters in the Western Paraíba Valley whose collateral consisted almost solely of land and slaves were the most adversely affected. The separate assessments of slaves from the body of estate property confirmed not only the significant investment in slave labour that, according to Pedro Carvalho de Mello, was a very profitable one, but also the potential loss to slave-owners as the death of slavery approached.[9] For example, a 513-hectare Vassouras *fazenda* in 1884 was valued at 80 contos, but the 78 slaves held on it were worth an additional 62 contos, or 44 per cent of the total property assessment of 142 contos and 825 mil-réis. The average per-head value of the slaves on the estate was 805 mil-réis, as compared with the value per hectare of the land at 156 mil-réis. The bank offered a mortgage of one-third of the assessed value of the estate, or 55 contos.[10]

Assessed values varied widely. In Minas Gerais, the value of slaves in the mortgages in two *municípios*, Mar de Espanha and Carangola, represented 25 per cent and 19 per cent respectively of the collective values of the estates. In Mar de Espanha, the average per-slave value was 861 mil-réis and the per-hectare land value was 95,651 réis, whereas in Carangola slaves were assessed at a higher average of 1:055 but land per hectare was 52,974 réis. In Pirassinunga, São Paulo, by contrast, eleven slaves on a 302-hectare estate accounted for only 20 per cent of the estate value, but the average per-slave value was a high 1:272, as was the per-hectare value of the estate at 235,347 réis. Taking other factors into account, the higher value of the slaves would have suggested a young, robust slave labour force on a well-watered property with expansive forest reserves, making it potentially the most promising of the four cases when it came to repaying the bank debt.[11]

Planter options

Matters did not improve, since coffee exports and the average mil-réis price per sack of exported coffee fluctuated on a downward curve, as did the conto/dollar exchange rate. In addition, annual average nominal slave prices, which were in the high 800s and 900s at the outset of the decade, had fallen to the 300 and 400 level in 1887 and 1888.[12] Vassouras planters responded in a variety of ways to the crushing reality that commercial plantation agriculture as they knew it was on the verge of collapse. Some packed up possessions, capital and slaves and migrated to the expanding coffee frontiers of São Paulo, Minas Gerais and Espírito Santo, where, according to a study of Itapemirim, Espírito Santo, family members from Vassouras and Valença had established themselves.[13] Others rode out the crises by remaining on their property, turning the land to more productive use through rental, sharecropping and tenantry arrangements that included alternatives to slave labour. In 1885, the edition of the *Almanak Laemmert*, the Yellow Pages of the time, carried a solution to the labour crisis in the form of an advertisement that was placed by the prominent Vassouras *fazendeiro*, Dr Manoel Peixoto de Lacerda Werneck:

> On this fazenda, all labour is carried out by free workers who
> compose a colonial nucleus of twenty families, almost all of
> German origin. The sharecropping contract applies to the coffee
> crop but all harvested grains fall to the sharecropper.[14]

The planter Lacerda Werneck, like his father who had written the planters'
manual decades before, stood at the helm of a plantation complex that was
redefining its needs in light of the onset of free-labour market relations. Like
many planters in the expanding coffee fields of northwestern São Paulo, Lacerda
Werneck placed his production units under the care of immigrant families. His
announcement foretold of a foreign alternative to slave and local free labour in
the form of immigrant *colonos* from Germany. The contract included halving the
coffee crop with the *colonos* and provided for their ownership of foodcrops.

The published announcement was in accord with the labour preferences of
prominent planters, who maintained a traditional attitude towards the link of
land ownership to social standing and prestige but maintained a progressive
stand on modernization, mechanization and immigrant labour. Lacerda Werneck
not only publicized a viable alternative to slave labour through recourse to free
family units but also upheld the customary rights of farm workers to use the land
for food production. The introduction of foreign labour also cushioned Lacerda
Werneck against abolitionist calls for land reform to benefit ex-slaves.

Abolitionists linked reform of the land system to the liberation movement.
Subdivision of large properties and the development of small agricultural properties formed one proposal. The abolitionist engineer, André Rebouças, advocated
a plan whereby landowners would sell or rent plots of land large enough to permit
crop rotation. These would include pastures and forests of 20 hectares (nearly 50
acres) sold to freedmen, immigrants and farmers to grow traditional export crops
and sell the harvested products to the former landowner for milling.[15] In December 1880, Rebouças demanded emancipation, land distribution to ex-slaves, a
land tax and laws to encourage the sale and subdivision of the 'enormous
territorial properties of the nefarious landocratic barons of the Empire'.[16] Vis-
count Henrique Beaurepaire Rohan also advocated the division of large
land-holdings into small properties that would produce staples and food crops
such as manioc and maize for a central processing unit run by the original
landowner. Agricultural schools, a church, shops and other provisions near the
processing unit would form the nucleus of the settlement. Under this scheme,
large properties would not be destroyed, since the landowner would still have a *de
jure* claim to the land. He would also charge an annual quitrent and a fee for
processing his produce. The plan would convert ex-slaves into *colonos*, linking
them to property, and would also appeal to subsistence producers, who would
have a lifetime *de facto* use of the land as lessees.[17]

Lacerda Werneck's announcement preceded by three years the formal and
official emancipation of slaves. His solution was neither innovative nor original,
having been unsuccessfully tried in the 1840s in the São Paulo town of Rio Claro
by Senator Nicolau Vergueiro, and reintroduced in São Paulo in the 1880s.[18] But
Lacerda Werneck was a pragmatist. Whereas the abolition of slavery in the
provinces of Ceará in 1883 and in Amazonas a year later fuelled parliamentary

debates over slavery, abolition and plantation production, the diminishing forest reserves, shortage of capital to diversify crops, fluctuations in the exchange rate of the mil-réis and irregular trends in the international prices of coffee were displacing Western Paraíba Valley coffee production as competitive commercial plantation agriculture advanced elsewhere.

By 1888, the situation for barely solvent and insolvent planters was critical. The emancipation process was finalized by decree on May 13, when the *Lei Aurea* (Golden Law) abolished chattel slavery and freed the upwards of 700,000 slave men and women who were still held in bondage. Sixty-seven per cent of slaves were located in the southeast: 27 per cent in Minas Gerais; 22 per cent in the province of Rio de Janeiro; 15 per cent in São Paulo; 2 per cent in Espírito Santo: and 1 per cent in the capital court city.[19] The reprieve from bankruptcy that planters expected in the form of government indemnification for freed slaves was not forthcoming and, according to mortgage data, implied a loss of approximately 40 to 50 per cent or more of their assets. In addition, the market for coffee *fazendas* hit an all-time low. Even if the government had indemnified planters for the value of their slaves, repayment to banks and the treasury at going rates would still be impossible since the value of estates was less than the original mortgage value.

Two months after emancipation *fazendas* were reportedly being abandoned, freedmen were hard to find for hire at any price, and official predictions foretold of a doomed agriculture.[20] 'Unfortunately, the fields [*lavoura*] are lost, dis-organization is total, and discouragement [*desânimo*] is general, everything is turned askew [*revoltado*].'[21] Planter bitterness towards the monarchy for freeing slaves without indemnification was matched by hostility towards the slaves who abandoned them. One disgruntled planter introduced himself in a letter to the Conservative minister, João Mauricio Wanderley, Baron of Cotegipe, as a humane slave-owner. He claimed to have freed his slave wet-nurses after his eight children were grown up, and allowed ex-slaves to raise chickens, pigs and even livestock on his property. In need of labour to harvest his crops, he offered newly freed labourers a daily wage of 10 to 12 mil-réis plus food three times a day, clothes and medical care. His efforts were futile. The ex-slaves abandoned his premises, and he added, 'the great hordes of slaves wandering along the roads were unwilling to labour and would turn into bands of thieves'.[22]

Other Conservative Party stalwarts sent petitions and appeals with hundreds of signatures. They blamed the Congress, the 'violence of the Princess Regent' and the domination of foreign commerce over the fate of the country as respons-ible for their collective misfortunes. Antonio Manuel de Gusmão e Souza, owner of the Fazenda de Amparo, wrote on 17 July 1888:

> I am a monarquist as I have already stated, but I see that every-
> thing is so bad, and that the Republic cannot be worse than what
> befalls our government. Forgive and pardon me the writing of
> my pen.[23]

Another predicted the imminent downfall of the monarchy if the Princess Regent acceded to the throne:

The princess desired freedom for the class that worked the fields; but she did not consider the other class that also requires freedom. To this effect we are also freeing ourselves and have 240 and some republican votes that will tip the scales at the first election.[24]

Post-emancipation rural society

On 15 November 1889, a military *coup d'état* ushered in a Republic. The change brought greater autonomy to the provinces, which under the new regime became states, and to the provincial presidents, now governors at their helm. There was little relief for debtors, impoverished planters or others who expected government safeguards or welfare measures. Export prices of Brazilian coffee fell sharply in the 1890s and reached an all-time low in 1898, the same year in which the bubble of excessive financial speculation known as the *encilhamento* burst.[25]

Looking back over the previous decade in 1905, the owner of the Fazenda Santa Fé in Cantagalo reminisced about the calamity that had engulfed the coffee *municípios* of the Western Paraíba Valley and was rapidly approaching the Eastern Paraíba Valley where he lived. Jeronymo de Castro Abreu Magalhães blamed the war between Russia and Japan for reduced foreign demand for coffee in the 'poverty and disorder-ridden populations of Poland and adjacent areas'.[26] In addition, he held the expanding coffee frontier and abundant harvests in São Paulo accountable for the excess supply of Brazilian coffee on international markets, although the state government in 1902 had prohibited new coffee plantings for five years. Jeronymo claimed that the selling price was lower than his production costs, and he bemoaned the fact that Nature had been kind and generous to the São Paulo coffee producers but plagued Rio de Janeiro planters with droughts, floods, blight and locusts. Jeronymo also charged the government with levying taxes to cover 'extravagant costs for the introduction of foreigners of different breeds in detriment to the Brazilian people of colour'.[27] Most of all, he targeted what he termed 'a new breed of locust', the *politicantes* (Brazilian political predators), who 'voted taxes right and left to fill the public coffers and then depleted them by fraud'. Planters, he claimed, were underwriting the costs of coffee over-supply by paying high rail-freight rates and taxes to cover extensions of interior railways to new coffee frontiers and the ports near to them. In fact, a provincial law of 23 June 1882, passed in response to the complaints of food producers served by the Cantagalo Railway and the Rio Bonito branch, reduced freight rates on foodstuffs but maintained the rates for the rail transport of coffee and sugarcane.[28] For Jeronymo, soaring labour and maintenance costs and the rising costs of living were depleting a purchasing power that was already eroded from the fall in demand and the international market price of coffee. By his own estimates, between 1900 and 1907 low coffee prices had reduced his income by 100,000 contos.

Jeronymo was pragmatic and had set about rectifying the situation in 1905. He reduced expenditure, including salaries, and, above all, diversified his crops.[29] But time was against him and he joined a generation of indebted planters who were not benefited when a monopolistic credit system aimed at shoring up export staples was established by the government price-support programmes under the 1906 Taubaté Agreement.

From slaving to farming

Emancipation dealt a final blow to commercial plantation agriculture as it had been known in Brazil since colonial times. Despite difficulties in the sector, however, coffee production continued to be Brazil's predominant economic mainstay under the First Republic. Bankrupt estates were either bailed out by family members or sold by creditors. Migrant ranchers from Minas Gerais introduced a post-coffee landscape in which livestock grazed on the desolate slopes where green gold had flourished for decades.[30] Scions of prominent coffee families whose professional education bestowed them with the title of *doutor* (university graduate; also social title for person of importance) sought positions in the civil service, politics and liberal professions in upcoming places, the capital or other urban areas.[31] According to one foreign observer:

> Families who enjoyed earlier prerogatives retained pride of
> ancestry, social deference, and many holdings remained in their
> hands and proved a greater source of wealth than ever before.
> Industry and commerce were creating a new aristocracy of
> wealth to displace the old aristocracy of land tenure and lineage
> [as the] old order visibly change[d]. The aristocracy of wealth
> and education [was] being recruited from elements who could
> claim no particular pride of blue blood in veins.'[32]

In post-emancipation Vassouras the increase of 24 per cent in the white population, approximating that for the province/state of Rio de Janeiro during the same period (27 per cent), attested to the fact that neither Vassouras nor the other coffee towns in the Western Paraíba Valley were abandoned. The transfer of the parish of Mendes out of the jurisdiction of Vassouras under redistricting and the exodus of ex-slaves contributed to a decline in population in the 1890 census (Table 6.2).

Labour arrangements

The planter Lacerda Werneck adopted the labour preference of São Paulo planters who had engaged European *colonos* in a post-emancipation arrangement that prioritized the *empreitada* or task system. Although there was no challenge to land ownership under this arrangement, it proved to be an exception to the general post-emancipation labour systems. The majority of ex-slave-owners incorporated local and ex-slave labour to meet production needs through sharecropping, tenantry or renting.[33] On the Rispoli estate in Vassouras, for example, twenty, mainly male ex-slaves and some local farmers, worked to a monthly pay scale that

Table 6.2 Population of Rio Bonito, Vassouras and Rio de Janeiro province, 1850, 1856, 1872, 1890 (in thousands)*

	Rio Bonito				Vassouras			
	1850	1856	1872	1890	1850	1856	1872	1890
Free	10.9	12.9	18.7	27.0	9.4	16.5	19.0	36.4
Slave	11.7	9.2	7.1	–	19.2	18.4	20.1	–
Total	22.6	22.1	25.8	27.0	28.6	35.0	39.1	36.4

	Court**				Province/state of Rio de Janeiro			
	1850	1856	1872	1890	1850	1856	1872	1890
Free	262.5	–	226.0	522.6	185.9	215	490	847
Slave	293.5	–	48.9	–	189.2	176	292	–
Total	556.0	–	274.9	522.6	375.1	391	782	847

* Owing to different methods employed in the 1872 and 1890 censuses, detailed comparisons of the figures can be misleading. I have used the figures to make broad comparisons that are compatible with qualitative sources for the 1890s.
** 1856 data not tallied for court.
Sources: BNRJ, *Relatório apresentado à assembléia Legislativa Provincial do Rio de Janeiro*, 'Quadro demonstrativo da distribuição da população ... 1854'; Directoria Geral da Estatística, *Recenseamento da população da Província do Rio de Janeiro, Quadro A, 1872*. Recompiled by CEDEPLAR; Stanley Stein, *Vassouras*, p. 296; *Recenseamentos 1890*.

was based on the number of days worked in a month. The pay ranged from 1,000 to 1,800 réis. For the twelve months of 1896, the average monthly rate per worker was approximately 1,400 réis and, despite disruption that he linked with emancipation, the owner claimed that the system was working.[34]

Antonio da Costa Bernardes, a prominent Rio Bonito landowner and official in the local national guard, died just before the proclamation of the Golden Law. His family inherited diversified production and processing units for sugar, coffee and manioc, a brick factory, several *vendas* and incomplete plans for a railway on his *fazenda*. Small farms within his *fazendas* and lists of overdue rents confirmed that subdivided land was rented to resident farmers, some of whom were probably ex-slaves. Following his death, his son, José, who held the rank of major in the local national guard, requested permission to deduct from the estate the payment due to coffee harvesters:

> The slaves have been freed. I was obliged to employ workers
> from outside who, with the ex-slaves who remained on the
> *fazenda*, harvested the coffee and performed other services – the
> division of lands for crops, care of animals and processing of
> manioc. For those who refused to work for a fixed salary, I listed
> the payment due them beside each one's name, the number of
> days worked and the amount of coffee harvested.[35]

Fourteen of Costa Bernardes's 39 slaves remained on the *fazenda* and the others were local hired hands. José da Costa Bernardes received no reimbursement for the ex-slaves and was paying for work that had been assumed under the pre-capitalistic labour relations of slavery. In real market terms, the assessed value of each slave was less than 400 mil-réis prior to the death of the elder Costa Bernardes, yet the estate appraisers lowered the values further to between 50 and 300 mil-réis, a reflection of the demise of the slave market a month before emancipation was officially declared.

The ex-slaves who remained on the premises agreed to work for a fixed monthly salary which was approximately half of what the day-workers were earning.[36] The reasons for the slaves' decision are not known but were probably influenced by staying together, unequal competition from landless farmers for jobs, and a lack of the personal relationships that employment in the outside labour market would require. The pay scale for outside help came to 500 mil-réis, a tiny outlay for an estate estimated at 47 contos, but a significant amount to be paying out in cash when credit was in short supply. Workers' refusal to work for anything but a *jornal* or daily wage suggests that short-term seasonal cropping was preferred to contracts that held labourers to an estate for a period of a year or more. In short, the refusal of local day labourers to work under such conditions might suggest why planters such as Lacerda Werneck opted for immigrant labour.

Costa Bernardes bridged the divide between the traditional commercial slave-operated plantation of his father's generation and the onset of the free labour market in which monthly salaries and daily wages were demanded by ex-slaves and local labourers. There were no claims to ownership of the property and the estate remained in his name although former slaves and local supplements contributed to the internal proletarianization of the free labour force.[37]

Emancipation did not signify a clean slate for ex-slaves, as a letter written by Costa Bernardes, dated 5 May 1888 (one week before the decree of the Golden Law), implies. The letter contained a request to a local judge to appraise the value of the labour of one female slave. Costa Bernardes stated that he would pay the slave's remaining manumission costs minus the amount of the judge's appraisal. This request clearly posits the slave's labour as having a free-market salary equivalent. The slave was paying the price of her freedom under the *pecúlio* terms set up in 1871, but Costa Bernardes's offer placed the woman in a situation that would carry forward her debt beyond the end of slavery. In one week, she would pass from a slave to freed woman who, still in arrears for the price of her freedom, would become an indebted servant.[38] If some of the other renters who were in arrears to the estate were ex-slaves, the Major was poised to secure labour for his harvest through the implementation of a debt–credit relationship.

Free-market equivalents for a day's work were also charged by a creditor for the labour of his slaves on another person's estate. Antonio Francisco da Costa charged the daughter of Manoel José da Silveira 180,000 réis (US$99) for 120 days of field labour and weeding; 90,000 réis (US$49.50) for 60 days of work in the cornfields; 31,500 réis (US$17.30) for 21 days of hoeing in the upper coffee field; and 90,000 réis (US$49.50) for 60 days of gathering and cleaning coffee beans. The average per diem charge per slave was 1500 mil-réis or 82 US cents.[39]

Enduring bondage

Emancipation officially liberated slaves from chattel bondage but not from the plantation complex or dependency relationships. Elderly slaves of long-standing service with nowhere to go, and ex-slaves who were held by debt or other obligations to their former masters, remained or drifted back to the estates of their captivity. Brazilian novelist, Paulo Henrique Coelho Neto, claimed that decadence overtook the land and misery confronted ex-slaves, whose places were taken by the immigrant. The *colono* arrived penniless in Brazil, but soon congregated to gamble, drink and to sell his share of the coffee harvest to the Portuguese tavern owner. The ex-slave, Sabino, the protagonist of Coelho Neto's story, *Banzo*, claimed: 'the blacks were dying of starvation on the roads, they had nowhere to live, nobody wanted them, and they were persecuted. Even the land was ungrateful to them, but it was dying, ending. This was its revenge.'[40] In 1895, long-standing ex-slaves on the estate of Eugênio de Avellar Corrêa faced eviction when his widow was informed of the intentions of her husband's creditors to possess the *fazenda*. The cabins of *colonos* had been burned down but ex-slaves were still tending to the 11,000 coffee trees and planting corn and black beans between them. Called to testify, three of the ex-slaves confirmed that the estate was their mistress's dowry, upholding her claim that the *fazenda* could not be alienated from her ownership. The court decision to recognize her right to the land assured them of continuity and of a place to live, stability that would have been undermined had the property been forfeited.[41]

Caetana, a freedwoman in Rio Bonito whose master left her and several other ex-slaves plots of land to farm on his property, stood her ground against the onslaughts of an enraged lover. She successfully appealed for help to her ex-master's brother, a prominent person of local authority and influence. He defended her but would not acknowledge her dependence on him beyond safeguarding her right to cultivate the plot of land. Beyond usufruct, she had no claim to the land.[42] Favoured ex-slaves like Caetana were commonly granted a plot of land to farm during their lifetimes. Yet, for Anna Maria Paes, a freedwoman, her former master's offer of land for her to farm aimed at keeping her in service and near to her son, Clemente, who was still his slave.[43]

In rare instances, ex-slaves purchased land but, as in the following example, purchase was also mediated by the landowner. Benedicto de Moraes, an African ex-slave who had the same surname as his former master, died in Rio Bonito in 1889 aged eighty. He left his two surviving children and their mother two contiguous plots of land totalling seventeen hectares and property worth the equivalent of US$500, located on the periphery of his former master's estate. From one plot that contained a small cornfield, a manioc patch, a thicket of coffee bushes – terms all too familiar in descriptions of small properties, but too inaccurate to permit credible statistical calculations – Benedicto processed maize and manioc with two mortars and a manioc press in a dilapidated building that served as a manufactory. On the other plot he fenced in a grazing area for an old blind horse and a lame mule. A thatched cottage, which served as the run-down living quarters, completed Benedicto's holding. Benedicto exchanged excess cornmeal and manioc flour for kerosene, candles, meat and tobacco, sold on credit at a neighbouring *venda*. Benedicto's estate covered his debts to the *venda*, leaving his heirs to embrace the onset of the Republic in 1889 free of the constraints of abject poverty that forced many small farmers into the ranks of the rural proletariat.[44]

Workers aplenty but nobody to farm

The post-emancipation rural milieu was an arena where ex-slaves, migrant and semi-subsistence farmers, immigrants and small-scale producers vied with each other and with European immigrants for incorporation into the rural labour force. Wealthy states, like São Paulo, underwrote the costs and conditions of immigration to attract European labourers with families to the newly opened coffee fields in the north and northwest of the state. In other states, the selection of the labour force and the negotiation of the working conditions were left to individual landowners.

Elizabeth Helsinger has argued for 'conflicting meanings of the land' and claims that these are 'invoked in a struggle for cultural representation, which is also a struggle for political representation'.[45] A plot of land to landless farmers, including ex-slaves, offered the chance of a livelihood that, although not free from the constraints of dependency on an ex-master or landowner, was a step in that direction. For ex-masters, land was an element of a livelihood that rested on leisure and command over involuntary labour forces. Official pronouncements echoed these concerns and aimed to harness land and labour to benefit modernization programmes that posited a regeneration of intensive coffee cultivation and some agricultural diversification.

It will be remembered that the 1850 Land Law restricted the privatization of public lands to sale. Lands that were temporarily occupied by squatters, slaves and semi-nomadic cultivators were excluded from qualification as legal claims. Under the wording in Article 6:

> Simple plots, deforestated or burned areas in fields and forests, huts or similar types of shelter that are not linked to effective agriculture or [the quality of] dwellings as described in the statutes above, will not qualify for revalidation of *sesmarias* or other government grants, or for the legitimation of occupancy.[46]

Public authority over the delimitation of lands in the public domain, including land occupied by squatters and others who had no deed to the land they farmed, was later passed to the states by the 31 May 1891 Torrens Law.[47] Ex-slaves, squatters and landless farmers were thereby marginalized from any formal and official claims to the land they farmed. Apart from customary ties to land that were mediated by landowners, incorporation into the rural milieu was restricted to kin and personal informal ties to landed or influential local figures. Claims by slaves to the inheritance of fathers who were members of the master class were not likely to succeed, short of official recognition by a notarial act. Generations of illegitimate children – ex-slaves, squatters and poor landless farmers – were

Table 6.3 Death records of Africans, Brazilian ex-slaves and children of slaves, Rio Bonito and Vassouras, 1889

Município	Africans	Brazilian-born ex-slaves	Children of slaves	No information	Registered deaths in município	
					No.	%
Rio Bonito	18	30	23	0	71	14
Vassouras	26	31	6	1	64	27

Total registered deaths in *município* of Rio Bonito = 493; total registered deaths in *município* of Vassouras = 236

Source: Rio Bonito. Registro Civil: Livro de Obitos, 1° distrito [N.S. da Conceição do Rio Bonito] and 2° distrito [Boa Esperança] 1889. Vassouras. Registro Civil: Livro de Obitos, N.S. da Conceição, 1889.

pitted against each other in a free labour market in which individual skills and qualifications were not only fiercely competitive but also favoured those with access to persons of influence.

For Africans, who represented under 5 per cent of the population, the obstacles to freedom that were overcome in 1888 were outweighed by age, illness, poor productivity and diminished authority over kin and family groups. They faced few options for incorporation in the post-emancipation society and, according to death records (*óbitos*) from Vassouras and Rio Bonito during the year following abolition, they were stigmatized by slavery even in death, registered as Africans, ex-slaves or as children of an ex-slave (Table 6.3). *Crioulo* offspring or offspring of *parda* slaves with skills had better chances of incorporation into the rural milieu through recourse to fictive or real kinship, personal contacts and friendship. Most of these were mediated by ex-masters, godparents or those a rung higher on the social ladder. Ex-slave women generally survived precariously in the same domestic trades at the base of the socio-economic pyramid that had engaged them under slavery – as maids, cooks, nursemaids, laundresses, street vendors and prostitutes. According to June Hahner, 80 per cent of those engaged in domestic service in 1920 were women, a figure that accounted for 19.3 per cent of Brazil's total female population.[48]

Migration

Migration to evolving frontiers had always been an option in a country as large as Brazil. In Vassouras, planter reluctance to consider alternatives to slave labour, coupled with restrictions on access to public lands, probably explains why freed non-whites emigrated with their families to areas beyond the mainstream coffee-producing areas of the Paraíba Valley. After 1888, decadent coffee areas of the Western Paraíba Valley experienced an out-migration as those benefited by the *Lei Aurea* moved away in search of land. As I have pointed out elsewhere, the

Table 6.4 Population of Vassouras, Rio Bonito and province/state of Rio de Janeiro, by colour, 1872 and 1890

	White			Non-white		
	1872	1890	% change	1872	1890	% change
Rio Bonito	11,843	9133	−16	13,957	17,701	+26.8
Vassouras	9894	13,026	+24	29,142	22,505	−22.7
Province/state						
Rio de Janeiro	311,197	395,590	+27	471,597	481,254	+2.0

Source: Directoria Geral da Estatística, *Recenseamento da populaçãoda população da Província do Rio de Janeiro, Quadro A, 1872; Recenseamento geral da República dos Estados Unidos do Brasil em 31 de dezembro de 1890.*

decline of the non-white population by 22.7 per cent from 1872 to 1890 in Vassouras was a noteworthy contrast to the rest of the state of Rio de Janeiro, where the non-white population increased by 2 per cent.[49] Marginalized healthy and able ex-slaves and landless farmers abandoned the coffee *fazendas* of the Western Paraíba Valley, seeking salaried employment in the expanding coffee frontiers of western São Paulo and the emerging factory towns of Nova Friburgo and Petrópolis in the Eastern Paraíba Valley[50] (Table 6.4).

Ex-slaves also headed to the peripheries of the coffee areas, to decadent sugar-producing areas and to the lowlands, where land was plentiful for small-scale semi-subsistence production to supply local and growing urban markets. Rio Bonito was one of them; neighbouring Capivary, where manioc production was intensified, was another. In Rio Bonito, the decrease of the white population by 16 per cent from 1872 to 1890 contrasted with the increase in the non-white population by 27 per cent in the same period.[51] In Capivary, the white population declined by 6.4 per cent and the non-white population increased by 50.9 per cent between 1872 and 1890.[52] The transition from slave to free labour in both *municípios* was in line with the rest of Brazil, where the needs were met locally instead of through immigrant labour. As planters sold, rented or divided up their estates, ex-slaves and landless farmers moved into the area. Land rentals and arrangements such as sharecropping, tenantry and small-scale food production were profitable, given the availability of local and regional markets. Public lands that were also available for purchase within *fazendas*, on the municipal peripheries and in the hills incorporated ex-slaves, migrants and their families into a rural milieu in which they controlled their work regimes, produce and land use. This post-emancipation scenario resembled the emergence of a peasantry, composed of diverse family units who were mainly engaged in semi-subsistence agriculture.

Another option for ex-slaves was to join a rural–urban migration to São Paulo, Niterói or the court-turned-federal district of Rio de Janeiro. The extension of the railroad to Vassouras in the 1870s, and to Rio Bonito a decade later, made access to Rio de Janeiro accessible to a labour force who had turned semi-nomadic as a

Table 6.5 Population of the city of Rio de Janeiro, 1890–1920

	Total	Non-white	%	White	%
1890	522,651	194,862	37	327,789	63
1895	598,300	217,977	36	380,323	64
1900	685,738	244,009	36	441,729	64
1905	787,671	273,520	35	514,151	65
1910	895,920	303,345	34	592,575	66
1915	1,016,225	335,423	33	680,802	67
1920	1,155,969	371,530	32	784,439	68

Source: Sam C. Adamo, 'The broken promise: race, health and justice in Rio de Janeiro, 1890–1930', unpublished PhD dissertation, Department of History, University of New Mexico, 1983, Appendix A, Table 75, p. 292. By 1920, the population of the state of Rio de Janeiro was 1,559,371, approximately 400,000 greater than the population of the Federal District.

result of the coffee crisis and the inability to purchase land. Furthermore, the railroad made access to free land possible, even if the land was located at some distance in the Eastern Paraíba Valley or in São Paulo. Eighteen per cent of the urban population of Rio de Janeiro during the First Republic came from the interior. Low-ranking, manual, unskilled part-time jobs existed, as did earnings from vagrancy and begging for seekers of freedom far from the rural milieu. Given the average annual rates of increase of *pardos* and *pretos* in Rio de Janeiro, a figure that hovered around 2 to 2.5 per cent between 1890 and 1920, takers of this option were not insignificant. As shown in Table 6.5, the non-white population never represented less than one-third of the city population, despite the fact that the majority population was white (Table 6.5).[53]

There was also a marked rural migratory drift to the expanding coffee frontiers of neighbouring states or to the final coffee frontier in the northeastern corner. In 1890 railway links were planned between Vassouras and Petrópolis as the eastward flow to newly emerging markets gained momentum.[54] Annual average rates of growth in the Eastern Paraíba Valley *municípios* of Sumidouro, Pádua and Itaperuna were the highest of Rio de Janeiro between 1872 and 1890 (see Appendix 4)[55]. In Itaperuna, the fringe of the expanding coffee economy bordering on the neighbouring state of Espírito Santo, low salaries and poor working conditions were offset by land availability. The influx of non-white migrants into the area attested to opportunities for small-scale agriculture and for salaried jobs on emerging coffee estates. According to Arrigo de Zetirry, a *Jornal do Comércio* reporter, employers had mixed views about hiring ex-slaves that some viewed as outsiders who worked as *jornaleiros* and were a 'fluctuating' but abundant source of labour, originating from the less prosperous or isolated areas of Rio de Janeiro.[56] But supporters held freedmen to be excellent field workers as long as there was constant supervision since 'even the most laborious if left to his own designs would relax to the state of complete indolence'.[57] Freedmen were also criticized for having 'no desire for improvement and no love for saving'.[58] Generalizing from his observations of freedmen on the Usina do Capim, Arrigo de Zetirry summed up the economic plan of the freedman as follows: 'Earn one, spend one, earn ten, spend ten – the sum is always zero'.[59]

There was also a small influx of foreign immigrant workers into the area. In 1882, the *Jornal do Comércio* reported that sharecropping had proven workable for foreign immigrants, who were not commonly attracted to field labour on sugar estates. The Santa Clara *fazenda* in the *município* of São Fidelis was a successful example. The bulk of the local labour force was drawn from freedmen and Brazilian labourers migrating from the declining coffee economies of the Western Paraíba Valley and southern Minas Gerais.[60] On the coffee *fazenda* belonging to state assemblyman João Antonio Alves de Brito, 38 of the 128 families who tended 500,000 coffee trees were Brazilian families; 42 were families of former slaves on the estate; 11 were families of freedmen who had been slaves elsewhere; 28 were families of European *colonos*; and 9 were local hirelings who came to harvest the coffee crop. Although Italian and Portuguese women and children worked in field labour, Brazilian women had, according to Zetirry, 'deserted farm labour'.[61] There were 600 people in the entire colony, including 58 farmhands (*camaradas*) employed to process the coffee. The daily wage was 3$000 réis, not including food. Some families worked on a task or piecework basis (*empreiteira*), hired to cut down and burn the forest in preparation for coffee planting.

Sharecropping was not a popular option with ex-slaves in the emerging coffee regions of Rio de Janeiro. They expressed a lack of *vontade* (will), owing to the absence of any market incentives to increase productivity. Fixed-term contracts, which held labour until after the harvest, and planters' market-oriented aims were incompatible with the real benefits of sharecropping.[62] Those benefits included the security of a place to live and farm and a means to accumulate capital more profitably than the *empreitada* or task labour common in São Paulo. But the lack of opportunities to supplement income with other forms of employment were further aggravated, since good farming lands were said by ex-slaves to always be taken by others.[63]

Food production gradually provided the means to accumulate additional capital. *Jornal do Comércio* reports focused on Campos, where sugar exports declined in the 1890s. There, *colonos* and day labourers reverted to semi-subsistence production. Denying that ex-slaves were leaving small sugar mills because of the decline in sugar exports, the *Jornal* attributed ex-slaves' rejection of work on the sugar estates to unprofitable labour conditions. *Colonos* or cane farmers received a half, sometimes two-thirds, of the harvested cane, but were obliged to give the rest to the owner of the field, who then deducted the costs of planting, tilling and transporting the cane to the central mill, from where it was sold.

Colonos and sharecroppers turned instead to harvesting maize. Joined by owners of small mills who were unable to mechanize their establishments, they devoted their days to food production and local milling, which, in addition to the sale of livestock, found outlets in local markets.[64] One report stated: 'A cart of corn is worth 16$ whereas half a cart of cane is worth 10$000, 11$000 or 12$000.[65] Owners of industrialized sugar *usinas* were quick to capitalize on this trend and during slack hours agreed to allow ex-slaves to cultivate subsistence garden plots. The Usina das Dores in Campos even distinguished between freedmen, who worked exclusively in subsistence agriculture, and 'national' *colonos*, who laboured in the canefields. Each category of worker was paid 2000 réis a day.

Customary rights: non-negotiable claims

Use of a plot of land for food production was by now a generally recognized customary right for workers on rural estates and a viable means of getting by for small landowners, seasonal workers, day-workers, squatters, tenant farmers and sharecroppers. An outstanding, and still unresolved, feature of customary rights was related to ownership of food crops and improvements, an issue that pitted planters against renters, sharecroppers and the seasonal hands on whom they most relied. In 1895, for example, the tenant farmer, José Antônio da Rosa and his wife brought a lawsuit against the *fazenda* owners Miguel Affonso Coimbra and his wife.[66] The source of the contention was improvements that the plaintiffs had made to the *fazenda*. Jose Antônio da Rosa had arranged with the original owner of the Fazenda das Cruzes in Vassouras to improve the property at the owner's cost. The costs included planting coffee and fruit trees, and planting a cane field. The *fazenda* was subsequently sold and the tenants stayed on, but were never reimbursed for the improvements. They then added three thatched-roofed cabins, a pigsty, a silo, a coachhouse and a coffee *terreiro* and increased the number of cane and fruit trees. The *fazenda* was sold for a third time, and under a new arrangement, José Antônio and his wife became sharecroppers. They planted coffee on most of the lands, increased the cane field, planted corn and beans and constructed a processing mill, to the tune of 10 contos. When the new owner claimed the harvested coffee as his, José Antônio sought and was granted a judicial mandate to secure his claim (*manutenção de posse*) to the improvements – untouched until the case was settled.

The court heard that the first owner agreed to pay 170 réis for the coffee bushes after four years and agreed to forego rights to improvements. A new contract with the second owner, which reduced the 170 réis to 150 réis, was agreed with Miguel Afonso, the third owner of the *fazenda*. At the termination of the contract, he entered into a crop-sharing (*meação*) arrangement in 1894 and 1895, but did not pay José Antônio for the coffee trees. José Antônio initially agreed to turn over half of the coffee harvest, but then changed his mind, turning down the sharecropping contract and claiming the coffee and the improvements, crops included, as his property.

The case illustrates the heightened scrutiny of rental, tenantry, sharecropping and squatting arrangements that landowners targeted to rationalize and make land use more profitable for themselves. *De facto* and *de jure* claims to small farms, and the crops and improvements made to them, within the confines of landed estates resulted in the eviction without compensation of squatters. Cultivators who faced eviction turned to the courts to negotiate the sale or reimbursement of their improvements to the land. In some cases they were successful and the court sent appraisers to determine the amount of compensation due to them. In others, their claims were challenged and even denied under new legislation. A court decision against the sale of a *situação* by a claimant drew attention to Regulation 9549, passed in 1885, that forbade the mortgage of any property that was not legally held. Aimed at curtailing the customary practice whereby landless producers freely sold or exchanged *situações* among themselves or mortgaged their contents, the measure subjected these holdings to the dictates of the *de jure* owners of the property.

Citizenship *às avessas*

Slaves had crossed the divide to free labour, but the free labour market was not yet governed by capitalistic features that afforded any choice about employment, the negotiation of working and salary conditions and unrestricted physical mobility. In fact, ex-slaves were continually impeded from social and economic choice by restrictions on land claims and ownership that dated from mid-century. Equally long-standing restrictions governed claims to inheritance. The curtailment of political expression was also sealed by a literacy requirement that became a precondition for voting under the electoral law of 1881. This law established the direct vote, and although not specifically aimed at ex-slaves, they and most of the country's population were impeded by illiteracy from exercising basic electoral rights.[67]

Although the process of transition from slave to free labour was formally finalized in 1888, it hardly affected the rigid vertical social hierarchy or the planter class at its helm. Informal control mechanisms such as debt service relationships and the subjection of semi-nomadic landless farmers to dependency relations kept alive the unequal social relations that were long-standing features of plantation society. Skills learned over the years slaves enabled carpenters, ironworkers, goldsmiths, tailors, barbers, construction supervisors, dentists, musicians, mule-train drivers and traders to form the basis of what Joel Rufino dos Santos has termed a black bourgeoisie.[68] Yet he argues that there was no place to develop the embryo of a black bourgeoisie, especially in urban areas, where preference was given to skilled immigrant labour.[69] For most ex-slaves, the transition to freedom brought a choice that involved the rejection of field labour but, in view of limited alternatives, the options were restricted to unskilled labour. Menial tasks of the lowest order in the civil service, recruitment into the lowest ranks of the military, domestic and farm service, along with odd jobs, gave ex-slaves a monopoly over low-status occupations.[70] In major cities, ex-slaves also served rival political groups, individuals and political and government officials as bodyguards and as street fighters (*capoeiras*), who were ordered by those in political office to stir up crowds at opposition political rallies and settle scores with rivals.[71]

Involuntary labour

In contrast to the post-Civil War American South, no legal restrictions existed on physical movement or migration. The incorporation of ex-slaves and autonomous farmers into the productive cycle through contract labour and assignment to agricultural colonies was one way of regulating the activities of semi-nomadic wanderers and keeping control over the potentially disruptive sectors of the rural milieu. Less overt forms of control involved banning idleness, begging and vagrancy. Infractors were either removed from the streets or channelled into menial jobs in the rural areas. In the interior, members of local councils proposed measures to restrict physical movement through the implementation of a passport system to control the circulation of ex-slaves among the rural estates, enlistment in the army and enforcement of municipal codes against vagrancy, unemployment and begging.[72] Under the Penal Code of 1890, vagrants were defined as 'individuals who had no fixed residence, had no regular profession or work, had no income or other known means of support'. The definition of the homeless clearly highlighted the importance of locale and connections in establishing a person's place in society. The homeless were defined as 'those who have no permanent place anywhere in the Republic or are not waged or otherwise connected to a person or a family'.[73] Prison sentences for begging were also tougher for those regarded as fit to work, as opposed to those who were genuinely ill or unfit. Vagrancy laws not only aimed at controlling crime but also singled out as a criminal those who had no means of support or fixed residence, and engaged in prohibited or morally offensive occupations. Vagrants were obliged to sign a statement that they would find employment within fifteen days of completing their sentence.[74] The objective of the laws was to assign to the responsibility of an employer or a public institution the watchful eye of the state over potential sources of social disquiet and disorder.[75]

Social constraints were also in play for those who drifted too far from familiar places and the 'good word' of an ex-patron, godparent, or ex-slave kin, companion or free labourer. I have mentioned elsewhere that the stigma of slavery hounded ex-slaves in the entries in Rio Bonito's parochial death records, where ex-slaves were identifiable by the entry 'benefited by the Golden Law'.[76] In an attempt to verify this occurrence elsewhere, I compared Rio Bonito's parochial death records with those of Vassouras. There I found no reference to the Golden Law, owing to a lack of information regarding the origins and status of ex-slaves who died impoverished in the care of the Santa Casa de Misericórdia Hospice. Even family members, neighbours or other persons who registered the death of the deceased offered little information concerning occupation or place of origin. In the third sample of death registers, taken in the northeastern corner of the state, the stigma of slavery was obscured by an even greater stigma: the inability of anybody to provide information concerning the origins of most of those who died on that newly settled frontier. In Natividade the population hailed from elsewhere, attested to by the blank entries in the death records that beyond the name and sex of the deceased and a doctor's certificate that identified the cause of death offered no personal details.[77]

Rufino dos Santos has highlighted the paradox that the ex-slave and non-white population was edged out in a refashioned republican order by white European immigrants, who were held to be consistent with an ideal of modernization and progress along Western European lines. He argues that whereas the decadent *fazendas* in low productivity areas in the Western Paraíba Valley incorporated ex-slave part-time workers and paupers, the advancing São Paulo coffee frontier, an area of high productivity, rejected ex-slaves as lazy, unskilled and unfit to meet the demands of capitalistic conditions.[78]

Marginalization from civil, political and social claims to citizenship may also explain why African customs and traditions have persisted in Brazil to this day. Brazil's newly freed citizens edged towards the precipice of official oblivion: citizens in name but not in practice, citizens who were outsiders on the inside and were immersed in a form of citizenship turned round or backward (*às avessas*). The formation of Afro-Brazilian social circles, including the culture of the *festa*, held the celebration of the African past to be one of popular diversions, celebrations, a perpetual 'good time', even though Rufino dos Santos argues that it played conveniently into the ideology of exclusion that sought justification for the obstacles to social progression represented by the legacy of Africa.[79] Through entities and institutions that he has termed 'of blacks for blacks,' those on the outside created the means to survive.[80]

In urban São Paulo, the entities took the form of mutual-aid brotherhoods, organizations, newspapers, godparenthood ties and Afro-Brazilian religious communities. Through the revitalization of cultural traits that linked Afro-Brazilians with their ancestors to a distant African past, urban and rural ex-slaves found the political and cultural bases for solidarity. For Robert Slenes, Africans sought to redesign the frontiers between ethnic groups through keeping alive original identities with contacts, partners, through fictive kinship and horizontal networks.[81] A Jamaican term, 'brethren-friendships', best describes the horizontal ties of solidarity that provided for alternative mechanisms of survival in a society and labour market that was selective, governed and regulated by modernizing elites who sought to erase the stigma of slavery or at least to control those who survived its demise. In the refashioned ethnically diverse plantation complex in São Paulo, ex-slaves were as peripheral to the labour force as they were in the urban milieu of São Paulo city. In the rest of Brazil, however, cultural bonding and brotherhood among Afro-Brazilians of African descent and their descendants cushioned the transition from slaves to citizens and provided channels of economic incorporation through what Kim Butler has termed integrationist, alternative integrationist and separatist patterns.[82] The force of Africa was most celebrated in Bahia through cultural means such as the religious traditions that relied on fictive or real kinship ties to bond ex-slaves with one another through the *caxambú*, the mortal combatants of the *capoeira* dance and celebrants of the festivals led by the priests and priestesses of *candomblé*, where a Brazilian adopted the assumed identity of an African within the spiritual context.[83] Continuity and adherence to the past reproduced an imagined and unifying spiritual ideal of the African past that shored up the lived experience of brotherhood.

The same was less true for the *pardos*, especially those in domestic service. Based on the data from Rio Bonito, I would argue that *pardo* slave women relied less on ties with an African past than on dependent ties with the master class. Whereas a small but favoured African and *crioulo* kinship group solidified family ties with each other as a means of negotiating with the master class during and after slavery, *pardos* remained in domestic service in the rural household of the master, dependent upon personal ties for employment contacts for offspring, health care and white patronage.

Ex-slaves and those who sought in the African cultural past their own curing, rituals and cultural survival expressed their beliefs through spiritual celebrations in undisclosed locales. Spiritual centres were generally located, like *quilombos*, in remote areas of cities or in isolated spots in the countryside due to the surveillance and repression of police and legal authorities. Practices associated with curing and rites of magic were singled out in raids on the homes and spiritual centres of priests and priestesses, folk healers and cartomancers. Six months after abolition, Provincial Law 3020 legislated fines for illegal meetings and stipulated fines for healing that involved dances and *candomblés*.[84] Three statutes in the Criminal Code of 1890 that remained unaltered until 1940 justified the raids and closing of such establishments. Statute 156 criminalized the use of magic and healing, and outlawed curing without a scientific diploma, including the use of medicine, dentistry and pharmacy. Sentences included a prison term of one to six months with a 100 to 500$000 réis fine. Statute 157 made the practice of spiritualism, magic and the use of charms to arouse hate or love and to cure diseases a criminal offence with the same sentence. Article 158 made ministering or prescribing substances for cures as a healer a crime with the same prison terms and fines as Articles 156 and 157.[85] The repression of spiritual centres in the city of Rio de Janeiro and the hinterland, with parallels in Salvador, Bahia, suggests that the popular appeal of African-derived spiritual celebrations was condemned by elites less for their ritual significance than out of fear of the multi-class and multiracial nature of the celebrants, including Brazilian whites and European immigrants who were found to frequent them when arrests were made.[86]

Although the statutes may have warned some followers away from spiritual priests and priestesses and folk healers, Afro-Brazilian spiritual centres survive to this day and have widespread cross-class and cross-racial appeal. Yvonne Maggie has explained that conflicting belief systems and agendas were resolved through negotiation and consensus between dominant and dominated. The interface of different cultural roots and practices, a feature of Brazilian slavery that had no counterpart in the master–slave systems of the American South, made possible the hierarchical complementarity that embodied the co-existence of the unofficial, informal and sometimes illegal with the official, formal and legal. This contributed to the gradual nature of the transition process in Brazil, one that bypassed the conflagrations of Saint Domingue and the American South. One is reminded of Helsinger's argument that

> through contiguity or distance, political status, genealogy, and race, economic, social, and cultural relations of dominance and subordination such as class and gender were organized and reinforced to create degrees of difference on a spectrum from national citizenship to national subjection.[87]

During the Old Republic and after, the descendants of slaves, although legally incorporated members of the nation, remained socially and politically among the most subjected of its citizens.

Notes

1. Louis Couty, *O Brasil em 1884: esboços sociológicos* (Brasília: Senado Federal and Fundação Casa de Rui Barbosa, 1984), pp. 133–4.
2. Articles 1 and 2, Law No. 1340, 12 September 1866, *Leis e regulamentos do Brasil*. Article 2 stipulated that mortgages would henceforth be regulated by the Civil Code and rescinded relevant clauses in the Commercial Code.
3. Banco do Brasil, *Relatório apresentado à assembléia geral dos acionistas do Banco do Brasil na reunião de 31 de julho de 1871* (Rio de Janeiro: Typografia do Apóstolo, 1871). Reports were consulted for 1872–83.
4. Article 13, Clause 5, Law No. 1340.
5. Banco do Brasil, repartição de hipotecas, 'Movimento de hipotecas por província/estado, município, e ano', *Relatório apresentado à assembléia geral dos acionistas do Banco do Brasil*. Yearly reports for the years 1883–91.
6. Joseph E. Sweigart, *Coffee Factorage and the Emergence of a Brazilian Capital Market, 1850–1888* (New York: Garland, 1987), Table 4.1, p. 143; Banco do Brasil, *Relatório apresentado à assembléia geral dos acionistas . . . de 31 de julho de 1871*.
7. Robert W. Slenes, 'Grandeza ou decadência? O mercado de escravos e a economia cafeeira da província do Rio de Janeiro, 1850–1888', in Iraci del Nero da Costa (ed.), *Brasil: história econômica e demográfica* (São Paulo: Instituto de Pesquisas Econômicas 1986), p. 134.
8. *Ibid.*, pp. 141–2.
9. Carvalho de Mello argued that on the basis of the sale and rental prices of slaves in the court and in Vassouras, the average annual rate of return on investments in slaves in the coffee economy was higher than any other capital application. See 'Aspectos econômicos da organização do trabalho na economia cafeeira do Rio de Janeiro, 1850–1888', *Revista Brasileira de Economia*, vol. 32, no. 1 (January/March 1978).
10. Banco do Brasil, repartição de hipotecas, 'Movimento de hipotecas por província/estado, município, e ano', *Relatório apresentado à assembléia geral dos acionistas do Banco do Brasil*. Yearly report for the year 1884.
11. *Ibid.*
12. Sweigart, *Coffee Factorage*, Table E.2, 'Indicators of the Rio coffee economy, 1850–1888', p. 302.
13. Vilma Paraíso Ferreira da Almada, *Escravismo e transição: o Espírito Santo (1850–1888)* (Rio de Janeiro: Graal, 1978), p. 74.
14. *Almanak Laemmert*, Vassouras, 1885, p. 1176: 'Nesta fazenda todo o trabalho é feito por braços livres, compondo-se o nucleo colonial de 20 famílias, quasi todas de origem allemã. O contrato é de parcería na colheita do café, pertencendo ao parceiro todos os cereaes que puder colher.'
15. André Rebouças, *Agricultura nacional*, pp. 1–7, 111–12, 120, 367–32, cited in Robert E. Conrad, *The Destruction of Brazilian Slavery, 1850–1888* (Berkeley: University of California Press, 1972), p. 160.
16. Rebouças articles in *O abolicionista* (1 November 1880); *Diário e notas*, pp. 291–2; *Gazeta da Tarde*, 3–4, 7–11 December, cited in Conrad, *The Destruction*, p. 161.
17. Henrique de Beaurepaire Rohan, *O futuro da grande lavoura e da grande propriedade no Brasil: memória apresentada ao Ministério da Agricultura, comércio e obras públicas* (Rio de Janeiro: Typografia Nacional, 1878), pp. 10–12.
18. Warren Dean, *Rio Claro: um sistema brasileiro de grande lavoura, 1820–1920* (Rio de Janeiro: Paz e Terra, 1977), Ch. 4.
19. Conrad, *The Destruction*, Appendix, Table 3, p. 285. Conrad notes that from 1864 to 1887, the slave population declined from 1,715,000 to less than half that figure.
20. Instituto Histórico Geográfico Brasileiro (hereafter referred to as IHGB). Coleção Cotegipe, letter from Basílio Garcia Terra to Barão de Cotegipe, Freguesia de Monte Verde, 15 July 1888.
21. *Ibid.*, letter from José Caetano Alves d'Oliveira to Barão de Cotegipe, Fazenda de Santa Rita, 3 November 1888.
22. *Ibid.*, letter from Antonio Manuel de Gusmão e Souza to Barão de Cotegipe.
23. *Ibid.*

24. *Ibid.*, letter from Basílio Garcia Terra to Barão de Cotegipe, 15 July 1888.

25. The *encilhamento* was a period of intense speculation that occurred at the onset of the Old Republic in 1889; it was generated by the issuing by private banks of notes that exceeded the revenue available to the federal and state governments. The volume of paper money in circulation doubled, although the foreign exchange value of the Brazilian mil-réis plummeted, bringing the boom to an end in 1891 and ruin to many of its investors.

26. AN, Documentação Judiciária. Coleção Zélia: Jeronymo de Castro Abreu Magalhães, letter of 8 June 1905, Cx. 135.

27. *Ibid.*, letter of 2 July 1909, Cx. 135.

28. *Ibid.*, letter of 29 October 1907. For rates on foodstuffs, see Deliberação Provincial, 23 June 1882, *Coleção de leis, decretos atos e decisões do governo da província do Rio de Janeiro em 1882* (Rio de Janeiro: Typographia Montenegro, 1882).

29. *Ibid.*, Coleção Zélia, letter of 5 April 1905, AP13, Cx. 4.

30. Sílvia Fernandes Padilha, 'Da monocultura a diversificação econômica: um estudo de caso de Vassouras, 1880–1930', unpublished MA dissertation, Universidade Federal Fluminense, 1977. Vassouras continued to produce coffee and only in the 1920s did cattle-rearing make large contributions to the local economy. Stanley J. Stein, *Vassouras: A Brazilian Coffee County, 1850–1900* (Princeton: Princeton University Press [1957], 1985), Epilogue.

31. Sérgio Buarque de Holanda stated that after the crisis of the old agrarian institution, members of the dominant classes easily moved to liberal professions, not needing to labour with instruments that would be a reminder of the servile condition. *Raízes do Brasil*, p. xix.

32. C.C. Andrews, *Brazil: Its Conditions and Prospects* (New York: Appleton, 1887), p. 526.

33. Biblioteca da Câmara Municipal, Vassouras, *O agricultor*, quoted in *Novidades*, 9 February 1888. Stein, *Vassouras*, p. 252; Dean, *Rio Claro*; Sweigart, 'Financing and Marketing'. A study of birth, baptism and death registers in Paraíba do Sul reveals the sharp reduction in the coloured population in the aftermath of emancipation. See Ana Maria Lugão Rios, 'Familia e Transição (familias negras em Paraíba do Sul), 1872–1890', Master's thesis, Universidade Federal Fluminense, 1990.

34. CPOV, Postmortem Inventory: Rafael Rispoli e Maria Rosa da Conceição, 1900.

35. CPORB, Postmortem Inventory: Coronel Antonio da Costa Bernardes, 1888, Maço 61.

36. *Ibid.*

37. As per one of the outcomes dealt with in David Goodman and Michael Redclift, *From Peasant to Proletarian: Capitalist Development and Agrarian Transition* (Oxford: Blackwell, 1981), p. 104 and Ch. 4.

38. CPORB, Postmortem Inventory: Coronel Antonio da Costa Bernardes, 1888.

39. CPOV, Postmortem Inventory: Manoel José da Silveira, 1880. The final settlement of the estate, worth US$11,514 in 1880, took place eight years later.

40. Paulo Henrique Coelho Neto, *Banzo* (Pôrto: Livraria Chardon, 1927), pp. 19–35, 26.

41. CPOV, Postmortem Inventory: Eugênio de Avellar Corrêa, 1895.

42. AN, Documentação Judiciária. Corte de Apelação, Juízo Municipal de Rio Bonito, 1860. Recurso crime. Recorrente: Ignácio Carvalho Ramos. Recorrido: A justiça. Caetana.

43. *Ibid.*, Processo Crime, Escravos, Campos, 1878. No. 41, Cx. 9, Gal. C.

44. CPORB, Postmortem Inventory: Benedicto de Moraes, 1889.

45. Elizabeth K. Helsinger, *Rural Scenes and National Representation: Britain, 1815–1850* (Princeton: Princeton University Press, 1997), p. 15.

46. Law No. 601 and regulation (18 September 1850), *Lei de Terras (disposição sôbre as terras devolutas e as adquiridas por posse ou sesmaria*, cited in Paulo Bonavides and Roberto Amaral (eds), *Textos políticos de história do Brasil* (Brasília: Senado Federal, 1996), vol. 2, pp. 172–6.

47. Hebe Maria Mattos de Castro, *Das cores do silêncio: os significados da liberdade no sudeste escravista, Brasil, século XIX* (Rio de Janeiro: Arquivo Nacional, 1995), p. 391.

48. June Hahner, 'Women and work in Brazil, 1850–1920', in Daurel Alden and Warren Dean (eds), *Essays Concerning the Socio-Economic History of Brazil and Portuguese India* (Gainesville: University of Florida Press, 1977), pp. 87–117.

49. Nancy Priscilla Naro, 'Customary rightholders and legal claimants to land in Rio de Janeiro, Brazil, 1870–1890', *The Americas*, vol. 48, no. 4 (1992), pp. 511–16.

50. Stein, *Vassouras*, Epilogue; Lugão Rios, 'Família e transição'.

51. Naro, 'Customary rightholders', p. 515.

52. The non-white population in Capivary increased by 50 per cent between the two censuses. See Hebe Maria Mattos de Castro, *Ao sul da história* (São Paulo: Brasiliense, 1986), pp. 166–88.

53. In comparison, the non-white population of Salvador, Bahia, in 1890 was 107,250 of around 1,820,000, according to figures cited in Kim D. Butler, *Freedoms Given, Freedoms Won: Afro-Brazilians in Post-abolition São Paulo and Salvador* (New Brunswick: Rutgers University Press, 1998), p. 133.

54. A railroad link between Vassouras and Petrópolis was projected in 1890. BNRJ, *Coleção de léis, decretos, altos decisões do governo da província do Rio de Janeiro*, Decree No. 85, 17 May 1890.

55. One can draw misleading results from comparisons between the 1872 and 1890 censuses. The high annual rates of growth for Sumidouro (9.2 per cent), Pádua (5.7 per cent) and Itaperuna (5.2 per cent) are but a few examples. Between 1890 and the census of 1920, Sumidouro's population declined. This was due less to a halt in migration than to the redistricting of municipal boundaries during this period, especially since Pádua registered an annual rate of growth of 3.1 per cent and Itaperuna increased at an annual rate of 2.9 per cent.

56. *Jornal do Comércio*, 20 June 1894, p. 1, columns 3 and 4. Robert W. Slenes's discovery of the 1890s articles in the *Jornal do Comércio* led to widespread consultation of the articles, although citations and interpretations differed. See Sheila de Castro Faria, 'Terra e trabalho em campos dos Goitacazes: 1850–1920', unpublished MA dissertation, Universidade Federal Fluminense, 1986; Nancy Priscilla Naro, 'Revision and persistence: recent historiography on the transition from slave to free labour in rural Brazil', *Slavery and Abolition*, vol. 13, no. 2 (1992); Mattos de Castro, *Das cores do silêncio*, Chs 16–18.

57. *Ibid.*

58. *Ibid.*, 4 August 1894, p. 1, columns 1 and 2.

59. *Ibid.*, 28 August 1894, p. 1, columns 1 and 2.

60. *Ibid.*, 20 June 1894, p. 1, columns 3 and 4.

61. *Ibid.*, 28 June 1894, p. 1, columns 1 and 2.

62. Naro, 'Revision and persistence', p. 76.

63. *Jornal do Comércio*, 5 July 1894, p. 1, columns 1 and 2. The same situation existed in the post-Civil War American South and is recorded in documents of the Freedmen's Bureau, Freedmen and Southern Society Project, Department of History, University of Maryland. See, for example, A-8611, January 1867, report from the Claiborne Parish, Louisiana, which states the unwillingness of freedmen to contract for even a year, because they wished to work where and when they pleased. See also A-8510, January 1867, from H.H. Osbourn in Iberville, West Baton Rouge, Louisiana. Osbourn attributed the refusal of freedmen to sign contracts to 'some superstitious power or other ignorance' that controlled their actions. Two workers stated that their word was good, but they would not sign a contract.

64. *Jornal do Comércio*, 3 August 1894, p. 1, columns 1 and 2.

65. *Ibid.*, 18 August 1894, p. 1, columns 1 and 2.

66. OAB/CPON, Livro de Manutenção e Posse. José Antônio da Rosa e Mulher, Suplicantes, 1895. Referred to in Naro, 'Customary rightholders', p. 509.

67. José Murilo de Carvalho, *Teatro das sombras: a política imperial* (Rio de Janeiro: IUPERJ/Vértice, 1988), p. 147. 19.14 per cent of men and 10.35 per cent of women were literate according to the 1890 census. See Murilo de Carvalho, *Construção da Ordem* (Rio de Janeiro: Campus, 1980), p. 65.

68. Joel Rufino dos Santos, 'O negro no Rio pós-abolição: marginalização e patrimônio cultural', *Estudos Afro-Asiáticos*, no. 15 (1988), p. 43. See Mary Karasch, *Slave Life in Rio de Janeiro*, p. 70, for references to the pre-1850 period on slaves whose work for merchants, artisans, builders and traders provided knowledge of bookkeeping, retailing, metalworking, craftwork and reading skills that were marketed in freedom.

69. Rufino dos Santos, 'O negro no Rio pós-abolição', p. 44; Reid Andrews also adopts this viewpoint with reference to the marginalization of ex-slaves in São Paulo.

70. Karasch, *Slave Life*, p. 70.

71. Caricatures of *capoeiras* appeared in the popular *Revista Ilustrada* from 1889 to 1904. Also, see Nancy Priscilla Naro and Gizlene Neder, 'A instituição policial na cidade do Rio de

Janeiro e a construção da ordem burguesa no Brasil', in Nancy Priscilla Naro, Gizlene Neder, and José Luís Werneck da Silva, *A polícia na corte e no distrito federal, 1831–1930*, Série Estudos, No. 3 (Rio de Janeiro: Pontifícia Universidade Católica do Rio de Janeiro, 1993), pp. 238–40; Samuel Adamo, 'The broken promise', unpublished PhD dissertation, Department of History, University of New Mexico, 1983, p. 292.

72. *Jornal do Agricultor* (Vassouras: Câmara Municipal, 1884).

73. *Código Penal dos Estados Unidos do Brasil*, 1890, Law No. 261, Article 37; Regulation no. 120, Articles 299 and 300; *Código do Processo Criminal*, Article 409.

74. *Código Penal*, Book III, Ch. 13, Article 399. Dos vadios e capoeiras.

75. Adamo, 'The broken promise', Appendix A, Table 75, p. 292.

76. Nancy Priscilla Naro, 'Os limites de comportamento aceitável e mecanismos de dominação social no meio rural brasileiro, 1850–1890', *Estudos Afro-Asiáticos*, no. 15 (1988), p. 40. The death records for 1888 to 1894 were researched in the Registro Civil of the *município* of Rio Bonito.

77. *Municípios* of Rio Bonito, Vassouras, Natividade. Registro Civil, Livro de Obitos, 1889, 1894, 1899, 1909.

78. Rufino dos Santos, 'O negro no Rio pós-abolição', p. 45.

79. The term is taken from Rufino dos Santos, 'O negro no Rio pós-abolição', p. 47. Despite virtually total neglect during slavery, there was a mild surge in scholarly interest in African backgrounds and heritage at the end of the century. Keen to highlight the contributions of African traditions, customs, rituals and the significance of amulets, rituals and ceremonial foods to Brazilian culture, renowned scholars Silvio Romero, João Ribeiro, Leite de Vasconcellos and Câmara Cascudo combed the meanings of the African legacy. Yet for the prominent Bahian physician, Raymundo Nina Rodrigues (1862–1906), the exercise of familiarizing himself with African physiognomy, religions and cultures was dictated by foregone conclusions. Influenced by Henry Thomas Buckle's climatic determinism, Arthur de Gobineau's racial theories, Louis de Agassiz's link of racial mixture with physical and mental debilitation and Cesare Lombroso's association of criminal behaviour with certain identifiable physical characteristics, he proposed a link between African heritage and the degeneracy and backwardness that hindered the progress of the mass of the population in the closing years of the nineteenth century. Nina Rodrigues published his initial findings in Portuguese in the *Revista Brasileira* and in an ethnographical study in French of contemporary Afro-Brazilian religious communities that was entitled *L'Animisme fétichiste des nègres de Bahia*. See Thomas Skidmore, *Black into White: Race and Nationality in Brazilian Thought* (Durham: Duke University Press, 1993), pp. 28–32; Dain Borges, 'Ugly, lazy, slothful', *Journal of Latin American Studies*, (1993). Also, see Robert Levine, *Vale of Tears* (Durham: Duke University Press, 1990) for post-emancipation views on slavery in Brazil.

80. Rufino dos Santos, 'O negro no Rio pós-abolição', p. 47.

81. Robert W. Slenes, 'Malungu, ngoma vem!': Africa encoberta e descoberta no Brasil', *Cadernos Museu Escravatura* (Luanda: Ministério da Cultura, 1995), p. 13; *The Demography*, p. 188.

82. Butler, *Freedoms Given, Freedoms Won*, pp. 63–4.

83. See the distinction made by Kim Butler between Bahia, where cultural norm dominated, and São Paulo, where occupations and professional associations provided ex-slaves with the means for incorporation into local society. *Ibid.*, Ch. 4 and 6. On assumed ethnicity, see p. 55.

84. Lei no. 3020. 16 de Novembro de 1888, cap. IV, artigos 47,48 and parágrafo único. *Coleção de Leis, Decretos, Atos e Decisões do Governo da Província do Rio de Janeiro* (Rio de Janeiro: Typographia Papelaria Parisiense, 1888).

85. *Código Penal*, Decree of 11 October 1890 (Rio de Janeiro: Imprensa Nacional). For a detailed description of the legislation, see Yvonne Maggie, 'Religiões mediúnicas e a cor de seus participantes', *Estudos Afro-Asiáticos*, no. 15 (1988), p. 49.

86. Maggie, 'Religiões mediúnicas', pp. 51–4. On the licensing and repression of drumming, *capoeira* and *candomblé* in Salvador, Bahia, see Butler, *Freedoms Given, Freedoms Won*, pp. 182–8, 204. Butler has also argued that the *candomblés* incorporated mixed-race protectors and public relations representatives to diminish the attacks and raids on the *terreiros* by municipal officials.

87. Helsinger, *Rural Scenes and National Representation*, p. 10.

=== 7 ===

Epilogue

The process of transition from slave to free labour explored in this study of Vassouras and Rio Bonito has been linked to the broader issue of defining rurality in Brazil.[1] In this book, I have examined how the social and political struggles over customary rights pursued by slaves and free cultivators impacted on their incorporation or exclusion in the rural milieu. In both towns, changing social relations prevailed during the transition process, as free and slave identities increasingly began to merge in everyday lives and practices. Yet, rurality involved different agendas. Vassouras was typical of a social milieu in which planters who rejected alternatives to slave labour tenaciously tightened their grip on slaves and land. Most lost the struggle to restore the rural reality that was swept away in the final decades of the nineteenth century. For ex-slave-owners, rurality was centred on the struggle to maintain the status quo of unequal social relations and dependent ties that were characteristic of the plantation complex, a rigid vertical social hierarchy in which planter elites, *de jure* claimants to land and those who monopolized labour and violence during the era of slavery disputed hegemony over the private sphere and over immigrant or local labour.

For ex-slaves in Vassouras, rurality was centred initially on the struggle for freedom. Freedom brought a new civil identity as a citizen in the patria of Brazil, yet it coincided with the formation of a free labour market that generated another struggle, this time aimed at incorporation and new dependent ties. Kin and family, skills, earnings, a fixed residence and work were the channels to incorporation in the social hierarchy of rural society. Lack of access to land, or claims to inheritance from former masters, left most ex-slaves facing dependency even in new areas where there was land available for occupation.

Vassouras emerged from the transition process with its vertical social hierarchy in disarray but intact. Holders of traditional influence and local power aimed to maintain a selective and exclusive social hierarchy, despite the fact that titles of nobility, one of the social mainstays of traditional authority under the monarchy, were no longer recognized under the First Republic. The occupants of the great houses of the Paraíba Valley still held out as purveyors and conduits of social mobility for favoured former occupants of the slave quarters and the landless population. They carried on the traditional vertical relationship characterized by dependency, an exchange of favours on an unequal basis that promised little ascension to those on the low rung of the social milieu. In this way, the hierarchy of complementarity in the post-emancipation social hierarchy persisted in places like Vassouras, although the traditional authority of masters and Africans over their respective kin groupings, the composition of families and the training of offspring in a skill or occupation was no longer viable.

Rio Bonito was a more open society owing to the influx over more than two decades of a free and freed non-white migrant population. The death records from 1889 attest to a population where whites accounted for 44 per cent of the deceased and non-whites 63 per cent. Ex-slaves or descendants of slaves made up 14 per cent in the death registers, and although a few elderly ex-slaves were buried in their masters' cemeteries, it seems that most died in penury in the local Casa de Caridade.[2]

The influx of a free local labour force made immigrant labour unnecessary and the availability of land for purchase or exchange alongside the railway, on the *município*'s periphery and upwards into the hills and mountain ranges suggests a gradual and less fraught transition process than was true of Vassouras. Based on evidence from the registers of land sales for the immediate post-emancipation years, most properties were small, ranging from 2 to 20 hectares, and most formed part of estates. Centrally located and developed properties in areas of early settlement such as Rio dos Indios, Rio Vermelho, Viçosa, Braçanã and the town centre commanded the highest prices. The majority, selling at between 100 and 600 mil-réis in the 1880s, were small plots in peripheral hilly areas of the *município* such as Subúrbios, Lavras, Serra do Sambê, Basílio and the borders of the neighbouring *município* of Capivary. For example, the sale of 6 hectares of land in the southern area of Subúrbios in November 1890 was illustrative of a trend to sell small plots of land or, in a few cases, to mortgage properties.[3] Landowners were cushioning themselves against future hard times; family farming units were investing in land ownership.

Rio Bonito was not alone. A similar pattern of occupation was also taking place in neighbouring Capivary, judging by the 50 per cent increase in the non-white population between 1872 and 1890.[4] Sharecropping and small-scale family production of manioc and other foodstuffs were supplying railways and markets in the Bay of Guanabara networks.

The Rio Bonito land registers confirm a transition process in the lowlands in which rurality incorporated landless farmers rather than excluded them. Land was available to those already in the locale who could afford to buy it. In addition, dependency relationships served to secure the position of those who were favoured by ex-masters or employers. The African ex-slave Benedicto de Moraes, who crossed the boundary to freedom and ended his days as a landowning farmer and citizen in Rio Bonito, illustrates the conditional nature of incorporation. Benedicto's freedom and his acquisition of a plot of land on the edge of his former owner's estate was accomplished through the acquiescence of his former master. Benedicto was incorporated into the vertical social hierarchy as a citizen and landowner, but this transition was mediated by a social benefactor. His case stands out as an example of a new-found citizen whose attachment to a personal benefactor enabled him to celebrate freedom as an owner of land in the competitive free labour market. Not all were so fortunate.

In both Vassouras and Rio Bonito, rurality was redefined by the refashioned commercial plantation system. Coffee, the symbolic banner of the past, an advancing force of green gold that had devastated pristine forested landscapes, yielded in defeat to grass-covered slopes occupied by droves of cattle. Social tensions involving *de jure* claims to land and *de facto* customary rights to land and improvements made to land continued to embroil rural dwellers in disputes. Land use became a fulcrum for the struggle to establish political identity through fixed residence and employment in a post-emancipation environment that valorized work as a mainstay of order and progress. At the heart of the struggles involving land access were family production units, which emerged as both the defining element of stability in the rural sector and the source of social unrest.

In post-emancipation family farming units, the division of labour between males and females was more flexible in domestic, field and trading activities. Family production units among the poor were defined by those who resided in, or were attached by, informal family ties to the household. In general, women's roles were defined by reproduction, simple food farming through slash-and-burn methods and by domestic tasks that kept them close to home. Farming women continued fetching water, gathering firewood, raising plants, cultivating food and raising livestock for family needs. In settled conditions, men handled the heavy farm tasks such as ploughing and hoeing and the transportation of produce to market.

Family production units were also a vital element of migrant labour although the initial reluctance of ex-slave women to work in plantation labour linked the gendered element to domestic employment or limited seasonal field work during the harvest season. In either case, rural women continued to operate within a context of limited local options that restricted them to domestic, field, garden and market activities. Legal matters were handled by men, but women who developed ties to their homes and environments, even if those ties were mediated by the relationship to land through a birthplace, a place of childhood, of marriage or settlement, possessed the basic elements to form an identity to a place. Through that identity a sense of patria was possible, although access to land was vital.[5]

I have pointed out elsewhere that the modernization process and the refashioned plantation complex continued to provide the Brazil of the First Republic with an economic mainstay centred on the countryside.[6] There was continued reliance on cheap and abundant labour, a semi-nomadic seasonal labour force that could not meet the literacy requirements to vote or invest in training for a skill. The predicament that faced small producers and landless rural workers was whether to migrate to areas of available land or join the rural proletariat in temporary *fazenda* employment.

Order and progress

The fulfilment of a programme of modernization at the onset of the Old Republic in the state of Rio de Janeiro depended upon reforms to the coffee economy and the incorporation of ex-slaves and autonomous freedmen into the production cycle. State governor of Rio de Janeiro, Alberto de Seixas Martins, proposed restricting itinerant rural workers to one place through contracts and the establishment of agricultural colonies. He alerted state legislators of the need to act:

> It is the duty of the state to avoid the disappearance of coffee,
> the source of the social and financial wealth of its inhabitants,
> threatened by the increase of production in other regions of
> Brazil and in other countries.[7]

He proposed immediate measures to rehabilitate coffee in former markets, to expand consumption in new markets and to reduce taxes on European imports of necessary equipment. To do this, he requested cost-cutting measures, the progressive reduction of taxes on coffee exports and the improvement of internal transport networks. Over the long term, he proposed increases in agricultural production in the state, aided by reforestation, division of private land-holdings, supply of capital and credit to farmers and 'investment in a fixed and hardworking rural population'.[8] Finally, he advocated education for small farmers as a means of removing them from the isolation in which they lived. His proposal was to incorporate them into agricultural societies where they would enjoy daily contact with more intelligent and cultured farmers, who would stimulate them to adopt more advanced farming methods.[9]

Altogether, this modernization proposal aimed to channel surplus labour into regulated, supervised and quota-based production units. The governor presided over a state where the legacy of world attention to the coffee *fazendas* of the Paraíba Valley still served to preserve the myth of coffee as the harbinger of a golden era of prosperity. Although the dynamic core of the international coffee export market had moved to neighbouring São Paulo, the governor rested his hopes on the regeneration of the coffee economy and viable ways to incorporate into it potentially disparate elements of the population. His proposals went largely unfulfilled, as coffee producers, faced with bumper crops, appealed to the federal government to bail them out with price supports.

A contemporary of Alberto Seixas was Nilo Peçanha, who rose subsequently to the governorship of Rio de Janeiro and succeeded in implementing major reforms in the rural sector. Peçanha envisioned the modernization of the state's economy through diversified agriculture rather than a single reliance on the regeneration of coffee. His proposals were aimed at small-scale farmers, whom he saw as vital to the success of this plan. His reference to the bleak, decadent coffee areas of the Western Paraíba Valley, including Vassouras, recalled the decay brought by ageing coffee trees, soil depletion, the closure of the natural frontier, crises in international markets and the costs of railroad transportation.[10] Fundamental to his argument, however, was the admission that these formed only part of a larger equation that involved the availability of, and incentives to, labour.

The October 1915 edition of the *Correio de Vassouras* carried a summary of Nilo Peçanha's presidential speech, in which reference was made to the transformation of the oldest coffee areas into cattle ranches. Admitting that the diffusion of cattle-rearing was important to promote colonization in large unpopulated open areas, Peçanha held it to be unsuitable in a state where land was already claimed

Table 7.1 Brazilian exports in *contos de réis* and US dollars,* 1920–1

Product	Contos de réis	Dollar equivalent
Coffee	1,025,993	256,498,000
Indian corn (maize)	949,219	237,305,000
Cotton	485,992	121,448,000
Sugar	417,310	104,328,000
Rice	319,132	79,786,000
Beans	232,556	58,139,000
Maté	156,000	39,000,000
Tobacco	129,950	32,488,000
Manioc	114,461	28,615,000

* Market value established by Department of Agriculture – 4,284,684:189$000 (4 mil-réis to 1 $US) = 1 billion dollars.
Source: James G. Herman, *Brazil after a Century of Independence* (New York: Macmillan, 1925), pp. 293–4.

and inhabited. He linked the decline of the coffee economy to the silent but steady population exodus to the expanding coffee areas in the interior of São Paulo and Minas Gerais that offered wellbeing, wealth and acceptable working conditions. The exodus threatened the very stability of the social foundation of Rio de Janeiro:

> Since São Paulo and Minas Gerais have been offering and
> continue to offer better labour conditions, wealth and wellbeing
> than we do, migrant patterns will drift from the state of Rio de
> Janeiro to those states – as sure as the force of the ancients, the
> 'ubi bene, ibi patria' will, as in all times and in all places be their
> reason for being.[11]

Ten years later, coffee still held pride of place as the country's chief export, 'representing in recent years an export value greater than that of all products put together'.[12] Yet, for Herman G. James, coffee had a silent partner. Indian corn or maize, a product that hardly figured among exports, was 'more than five times as great in weight as is that of coffee, occupies half again as much area as the latter, and is but little behind coffee in the money value of the whole crop'.[13] James cited US Department of Agriculture statistics for 1920–1 to back up his claim (Table 7.1).

James's figures pointed to a reality that was hidden in Brazilian official records but was consistent with the incorporation of rural cultivators into areas of post-emancipation rural society at the margins of large-scale dynamic plantation agriculture for the export economy. At the northeastern tip of Rio de Janeiro state and in the outlying lowlands east and south of the capital, family-based production units and small-scale farming establishments attested to the co-existence of large-scale with medium and small land-holders, *de jure* with *de facto* claimants to land and rural proletariat workers with semi-subsistence producers. Comparisons of population trends between 1872 and 1920 confirm the drift of population to areas where land was available for cross-cropping coffee and food crops. Whereas Western Paraíba Valley towns experienced zero or negative growth rates, towns where land was still available on the fringes of the coffee region, like Rio Claro and Santa Teresa, increased in size, as did the eastern tip of the Eastern Paraíba Valley, where the high rate of population growth is indicative of the labour possibilities associated with the emerging coffee frontier in Pádua, Natividade and Itaperuna (see Appendix 4).

Ownership of land may have been a desirable aim for landless farmers, as inheritance was to slaves born to the master class, but squatting and the effective occupation of land and the improvements made to it provided alternative means for survival. Customary right became one component of the unwritten hierarchical complementarity of the unofficial and official, legal and illegal, *quilombo* and *de jure* claimants to land and power that enabled the officially disenfranchised and dispossessed to silently stake a claim to the countryside. Custom and kinship provided the bases for the disenfranchised and landless to stake a claim to citizenship. Largely bypassed socially and occasionally addressed in official or newspaper reports, one might refer to a citizenship *às avessas*.

The different agendas that faced post-emancipation Brazil invoked multiple visions of community and competing agendas by and for officially recognized and alternative collectivities. Whereas a new form of nation-making consistent with the progressive aims of modernization relied on unravelling the slave-related past, the illusion of a single nation was challenged by heterogeneous agendas of a regional and class nature. Ex-slaves, the long-standing urban and rural poor and recently arrived immigrants stood at the peripheries of the progressive order. For those still linked to Africa in spiritual and cultural ways, the ideals of patria represented a common dream, a shared imagination that was centred on Brazil, not Africa. Yet, another century would elapse before the African contribution to the making of Brazil was recognized and a collective concept of nation began to be identified.

Notes

1. On rurality, see Sarah Whatmore, *Farming Women: Gender, Work and Family Enterprise* (London: Macmillan, 1991).
2. The death records and inventories do not specify labour conditions. CPORB. Forum. Registro Civil. Livros de Obitos, 1888–1894, 1899, 1909.
3. CPORB, Livro de notas, 1870–1920. See No. 6, p. 50, escritura de Compra e Venda. Outorgante vendedor: Joaquim Antonio da Fonseca. Outorgada compradora: Carolina Maria Lima. The registers included Escrituras de Troca, Escritura de Compra e Venda and Escritura de Dívida e Hipoteca.
4. Hebe Maria Mattos de Castro, *Ao sul da história* (São Paulo: Brasiliense, 1986) p. 53.
5. Roderick Barman, *Brazil: The Forging of a Nation, 1798–1852* (Stanford: Stanford University Press, 1988); Helsinger, *Rural Scenes and National Representation* (Princeton: Princeton University Press, 1997), p. 15.
6. Nancy Priscilla Naro, 'Customary rightholders and legal claimants to land in Rio de Janeiro, Brazil, 1870–1890', *The Americas*, vol. 48, no. 4 (1992), pp. 485–517; 'The transition from slavery to migrant labour', *Slavery and Abolition*, vol. 15, no. 2 (1994), pp. 183–96.

7. BN: Presidente do Estado Alberto de Seixas Martins, *Mensagem à Assembléia Legislativa em 15 de setembro de 1898*.

8. *Ibid.*

9. *Ibid.*

10. *O Município*, 8 July 1901, with excerpts from 13 June 1901 and 22 June 1901. By 1900, the impact of past crises reached the Vassourense Railroad, which could no longer be maintained locally at the cost of 4:000$000 réis per year. Recommended solutions included returning to animal-drawn streetcars to lessen the costs of rail transportation.

11. F.J. Oliveira Vianna, 'O caso fluminense', 24 October 1915, in *Correio de Vassouras*, 12 September 1916, p. 1. The original text reads:

    > Desde que o ecumeno paulista e mineiro entre a oferecer, como já está
    > offerecendo, condições de trabalho, riqueza e bem estar, maiores do que o
    > ecumeno fluminense, correntes migratórias se estabelecerão naturalmente da
    > terra fluminense para a terra paulista e mineira – e isto pela força de sua lei, a
    > que 'ubi bene, ibi patria' dos antigos dá, em todos os tempos e sob todas as
    > latitudes, a sua razão de ser.

12. Herman G. James, *Brazil after a Century of Independence* (New York: Macmillan, 1925), p. 293.

13. *Ibid.*, pp. 292–3:

    > Conclusions drawn, as they frequently are, from the export statistics,
    > regarding the economic activities of a country, are, therefore, likely to be very
    > misleading. [Illustrates point with coffee.] Coffee . . . is today the chief article
    > of export of Brazil, representing in recent years an export value greater than
    > that of all products put together. Indian corn, on the other hand, practically
    > does not figure among exports at all.

Appendices

Appendix 1 *Caboclo* population of Rio de Janeiro province, by country and *município*, 1840

County	Município	Indigenous males	Indigenous females	Total for county	Percentage of provincial population*
Resende	Resende	277	280	557	
	São João Príncipe	253	272	525	
	Barra Mansa	321	307	628	
	Total	851	859	1710	0.42
Vassouras	Barra do Piraí	136	110	246	
	Vassouras	190	188	378	
	Valença	41	41	82	
	Paraíba do Sul	23	18	41	
	Total	390	357	747	0.18
Cantagalo	Cantagalo	17	14	31	
	Nova Friburgo	0	2	2	
	Total	17	16	33	0.008
Niterói	Niterói	65	78	143	
	Magé	7	4	11	
	Iguassú	36	28	64	
	Total	108	110	218	0.05
Itaboraí	Itaboraí	15	15	30	
	Santo Antonio de Sá Maricá	15	10	25	
		27	13	40	
	Total	57	38	95	0.02

County	_Município_	Indigenous males	Indigenous females	Total for county	Percentage of provincial population*
Campos	Campos	301	327	628	
	São João da Barra	13	22	35	
	Total	314	349	663	0.16
Cabo Frio	Cabo Frio	421	466	887	
	Macaé	110	97	207	
	Total	531	563	1094	0.27
Angra dos Réis	Angra dos Réis	16	20	36	
	Itaguaí	307	295	602	
	Paratí	60	34	94	
	Mangaratiba	145	168	313	
	Total	528	517	1045	0.25
Grand total		2798	2817	5615	1.38

* Total provincial population: 404,705.

No census data was forthcoming from Nossa Senhora da Conceição do Paquequer in the district of Cantagalo; Jacotiaga, Pilar and Inhomerim in the district of Niterói; Tamby and Santíssima Trindade in the district of Itaboraí; Desterro de Quissamã, Curato do Carapebús and Curato do Barreto in the district of Cabo Frio.

Source: BN, _Quadro estatístico da província de Rio de Janeiro, segundo condições, sexo e côres_, 1840.

Appendix 2   Free population of Rio de Janeiro province, by county, 1840

County	_Município_	White		Pardo		Black		Total
		Male	Female	Male	Female	Male	Female	
Resende	Resende	3553	3348	1059	985	179	139	9263
	São João Príncipe	1696	1472	705	624	136	132	4763
	Barra Mansa	1707	1541	599	536	145	125	4653
	Total	6956	6361	2363	2145	460	396	18,681
Vassouras	Barra do Piraí	2299	1975	711	589	119	87	5780
	Vassouras	1879	1502	1026	894	275	292	5868
	Valença	2071	1300	955	708	121	99	5254
	Paraíba do Sul	1977	1843	1271	1278	415	369	7153
	Total	8226	6620	3963	3469	930	847	24,055

County	Município	White		Pardo		Black		Total
		Male	Female	Male	Female	Male	Female	
Cantagalo	Cantagalo	829	688	455	429	125	90	2616
	Nova Friburgo	1201	1067	278	240	45	43	2874
	Total	2030	1755	733	669	170	133	5490
Niterói	Niterói	3908	3495	1451	1816	607	831	12,108
	Magé	1645	1405	995	1275	436	548	6304
	Iguassú	1318	1224	1077	1196	350	475	5640
	Total	6871	6124	3523	4287	1393	1854	24,052
Itaboraí	Itaboraí	3809	3776	2453	2666	504	587	13,795
	Santo Antonio de Sá	915	856	786	995	187	278	4017
	Maricá	3902	4089	1519	1735	288	344	11,877
	Total	8826	8721	4758	5396	979	1209	29,889
Campos	Campos	8253	8357	2905	3342	873	1076	24,806
	São João da Barra	1019	1041	348	390	73	71	2942
	Total	9272	9398	3253	3732	946	1147	27,748
Cabo Frio	Cabo Frio	4977	5006	2541	3011	433	577	16,545
	Macaé	1385	1104	508	505	71	78	3651
	Total	6362	6110	3049	3516	504	655	20,196
Angra dos Réis	Angra dos Réis	4488	4277	1320	1455	234	290	12,064
	Itaguaí	2279	1857	902	911	317	358	6624
	Paratí	1206	1210	378	482	146	190	3612
	Mangaratiba	1164	1017	427	445	116	140	3309
	Total	9137	8361	3027	3293	813	978	25,609
	Sum total	57,482	53,450	24,669	26,507	6195	7219	175,522*

Sum total			
By category	110,932	51,176	13,414
Percentage	63.20	29.16	7.64

* I have revised the additions in the census and have arrived at a total of 175,522. No census data was forthcoming from Nossa Senhora da Conceição do Paquequer in the district of Cantagalo; Jacotiaga, Pilar, Inhomerim in the district of Niterói; Tamby, Santíssima Trindade in the district of Itaboraí; Desterro de Quissamã, Curato do Carapebús, Curato do Barreto in the district of Cabo Frio.

Appendix 3 Population of slave, free, non-white and white (in percentages) in coffee-export and internal-market *municípios* in Rio de Janeiro province, 1872

Município	Slave	Free	Non-white*	White	Free non-white*
Western and Eastern Paraíba Valley highlands coffee-export *municípios*					
Resende**	33	67	46	54	13
Barra Mansa**	43	57	60	40	17
Vassouras	54	46	73	27	19
Valença	54	46	73	27	19
Paraíba do Sul	48	52	68	32	20
Cantagalo	62.5	37.5	75	25	12.5
S. Maria Madalena**	57	43	70	30	13
Sapucaia	46	54	63	37	17
S. Ant. Pádua	34	66			
Itap./Nativ./Itab.			70	30	
Other highland *municípios*					
Rio Claro**	33	67	55	45	22
Petrópolis‡	6	94	31	69	25
Nova Friburgo	27	73	58	42	31
Brejo, Restinga and Guanabara mixed-crop regional market *municípios*					
Campos	37	63	64	36	27
São Fidelis	38	62	62	38	24
Angra dos Réis**	21	79	49	51	28
Mangaratiba**	22	78	50	50	28
Itaguaí**	35	65	63	37	28
Iguassú	33	67			
Estrela**	61	39	81	19	20
Magé	40	60	67	33	27
Itaboraí	30	70	53	47	23
Paraty**	17	83	45	55	28
São Gonçalo**			51	49	
Rio Bonito**	28	72	54	46	26
Capivary**	23	77	55	45	32
Araruama**	39	61	60	40	21
Cabo Frio	33	67	62	38	29
Barra de S. João**	40	60	65	35	25
Macaé**	37	63	59	42	22
S. João da Barra	31	69	48	52	17
Maricá**	35	65	69	31	34
Saquarema	30	70	58	42	28

* The 1872 census subdivides slaves into *preto* (black) and *pardo* (mulatto). I have

subtracted 'slaves' from total 'non-whites' and expressed the free non-white population in percentages.

** *Municípios* where local boundaries were unchanged from the previous census.

‡ Site of imperial palace.

Source: Directoria Geral da Estatística, *Recenseamento da população da população da Província do Rio de Janeiro, Quadro A, 1872.*

Appendix 4   Population and annual average rates of population growth in *fluminense municípios*, by micro-region, in 1872, 1890 and 1920

Município	1872	1890	Annual average rate of growth, 1872–90 (%)	1920	Annual average rate of growth, 1890–1920 (%)
Western Paraíba Valley					
Rio Claro*	3,462	8,973	5.4	9,787	0.3
Resende*	28,954	29,671	0.1	28,210	−0.2
Barra Mansa*	25,766	21,607	−0.9	26,622	0.7
S. João Marcos	8,708	13,328	2.4	7,404	−1.9
Pirai	18,326	26,760	2.1	14,222	−2.1
Barra do Pirai	10,412			28,324	
Vassouras	34,003	36,483	0.4	51,551	1.2
Valença	31,700	33,623		41,389	
Santa Tereza	4,244	12,973	6.4	14,389	0.3
Eastern Paraíba Valley					
Paraíba do Sul	31,239	27,351	−0.7	52,474	2.2
Petrópolis*	7,219	13,574	3.6	67,574	5.5
Teresópolis				18,628	
Nova Friburgo	16,641	24,753	2.2	28,651	0.5
Sapucaia	14,676	17,584	1.0	19,100	0.3
Sumidouro	1,848	8,915	9.2	8,811	−0.1
Carmo				13,326	
Duas Barras				19,391	
Cantagalo	20,227	26,067	1.4	37,112	1.2
S.Seb.do Alto				12,681	
S.Seb.do Paraíba		5,879			
S.Ma. Madalena*	13,068	21,091	2.7	24,405	0.5
Itaocara	8,362	10,283	1.2	31,088	3.8
Pádua	8,771	23,594	5.7	59,590	3.1
Itaperuna	15,544	38,354	5.2	90,807	2.9
Brejo					
Campos	79,298	74,684	−0.3	175,850	2.9
São Fidelis	18,779	23,309	1.2	41,356	1.9

Município	1872	1890	Annual average rate of growth, 1872–90 (%)	1920	Annual average rate of growth, 1890–1920 (%)
			Guanabara		
Angra dos Réis*	21,813	19,237	−0.7	21,412	0.4
Mangaratiba*	7,468	13,985	3.5	7,763	−1.9
Itaguaí*	13,875	13,569	−0.1	15,771	0.5
Iguassú	21,065	19,709	−0.4	33,394	1.8
Paraty*	12,194	10,765	−0.7	13,544	0.8
Niterói	29,102	34,217	0.9	86,238	3.1
São Gonçalo*	8,176	17,811	4.4	47,090	3.3
Magé	18,737			18,816	
Itaboraí	25,926	23,973	−0.4	33,394	1.8
			Restinga		
Maricá*	16,218	10,373	−2.5	18,037	1.9
Saquarema	14,075	18,926	1.7	24,783	0.9
Rio Bonito*	25,973	27,017	0.2	24,999	−0.3
Capivary*	17,286	21,481	1.2	25,406	0.6
Araruama*	22,109	16,886	−1.5	25,668	1.4
S. Pedro d'Ald.	13,998	9,233	−2.3	19,659	2.6
Cabo Frio	8,128	10,382	1.4	16,475	1.6
Barra de S. João	9,341	11,635	1.2	13,910	0.6
Macaé*	25,149	35,793	2.0	60,280	1.8
S. João Barra	16,832	33,099	3.8	34,030	0.1
Total	721,464	842,666		1,457,777	

*Municípios where local boundaries were not redistricted.
Sources: Recenseamento da população do Império do Brasil a que se procedeu no dia 1 de agosto de 1872. Rio de Janeiro 1873–76. Directoria Geral da Estatística. Ministério de Indústria e Viação e Obras Públicas. Directoria Geral de Estatística. Sinopse do Recenseamento de 31 de dezembro de 1900. R.J. Typografia de Estatística, 1905. Directoria Geral da Estatística. Recenseamento do Brasil Realizado em 1890. Directoria Geral da Estatística. Recenseamento do Brasil Realizado em 1 de setembro de 1920. Vol. 1. 1922.

Bibliography

The bibliography is arranged as follows:

Archives and Libraries
Unpublished Documents
Published Government Documents
Reports of Provincial Presidents, Vice-Presidents and Police Authorities
Almanacs, Newspapers, Journals
Bank Reports
Maps and Photographs
Dictionaries and Encyclopedias
Polemical Literature
Travellers' Accounts
General Works

Frequently cited sources are referred to by the abbreviations which appear in parentheses after full name.

Archives and Libraries

Rio de Janeiro

Arquivo Nacional (AN)
Biblioteca Nacional (BN)
Instituto Histórico e Geográfico Brasileiro (IHGB)

Niterói

Arquivo Público do Estado do Rio de Janeiro (APERJ)

United States

Columbia University Library
The Johns Hopkins University Library
The Library Company, Philadelphia, Pennsylvania. Colonial Office. (LC)
New York Public Library
Princeton University Library
University of Pennsylvania Library
Yale University Library

United Kingdom

University of London
  Institute of Commonwealth Studies
  Institute of Latin American Studies
  King's College
  Senate House Library
The British Library

Unpublished Documents

Arquivo Nacional. Documentação Judiciária. Corte de Apelação.
  Juízo Municipal de Vassouras.
  Juízo Municipal de Rio Bonito.
  Coleção Zélia.
Banco do Brasil, Rio de Janeiro. Repartição de hipotecas.
Biblioteca Nacional.
  Seção de Iconografia.
  Seção de Periódicos.
  Almanak Administrativo, Mercantil e Individual da Corte e Província do Rio de Janeiro
  (Almanak Laemmert), 1845–1885.
Instituto Histórico Geográfico Brasileiro, Rio de Janeiro.
  Coleção Ministro Cotegipe.
Arquivo Público do Estado do Rio de Janeiro, Niterói.
  Livro Paroquial de Registro Terras. Município de Vassouras, 1854–56.
  Livro Paroquial de Registro de Terras. Município de Rio Bonito 1854–56.
  Fundo da Secretária de Polícia da Província do Rio de Janeiro. 1860–1880.
Estatística dos Setenciados da Penitênciária do Estado do Rio de Janeiro.
Forum. Ordem dos Advogados do Brasil, Vassouras, Rio de Janeiro. Inventários
  Post Mortem, All records ending in 0 and 5: 1865–1890.
Forum. Cartório Público do Primeiro Ofício de Notas, Vassouras, Rio de Janeiro.
  (CPONV) Inventários Post Mortem. All records for years ending in 0 and 5:
  1890–1920.
Registro Civil. Vassouras, Rio de Janeiro. Livro de Obitos. All records ending in
  9: 1889–1894.

Cartório Público do Primeiro Ofício de Notas, Rio Bonito, Rio de Janeiro. (CPORB)
Inventários Post Mortem, All records for years ending in 0 and 5: 1845–1920.
Livro de Notas. Escrituras Públicas, 1850–1920.
Registro Civil. Rio Bonito, Rio de Janeiro. Livro de Obitos. All records for years ending in 9: 1889–1894.
Registro Civil. Livro de Obitos. Natividade, Rio de Janeiro. All records for years ending in 9: 1889–1894.
Colonial Office Records. The Philadelphia Company, Philadelphia, Pennsylvania.

Published Government Documents

Coleção das Leis do Império do Brasil of the years 1831, 1835, 1850, 1869, 1871, 1885.
Coleção de Leis, Decretos e Regulamentos da Província do Rio de Janeiro de 1859 (Rio de Janeiro: Typographia do Correio Mercantil, 1959).
Coleção de Leis, Decretos, Atos e Decisões do Governo da Província do Rio de Janeiro em 1888, Vol. 1 (Rio de Janeiro: Typographia Papelaria Parisiense, 1888).
Código Criminal do Império do Brasil. Rio de Janeiro (1831).
Código Penal dos Estados Unidos do Brasil. 1890. Rio de Janeiro: Imprensa Nacional.
Código do Processo Criminal, Article 409.
Directoria Geral da Estatística. *Recenseamento da população do Império do Brasil a que se procedeu no dia 10 de Agosto de 1872*. 21 vols. Rio de Janeiro, 1873–1876. Revised compilation by Centro de Desenvolvimento e Planejamento Regional (CEDEPLAR) of the Universidade Federal de Minas Gerais in Belo Horizonte, Minas Gerais.
Directoria Geral de Estatística. *Sinopse do Recenseamento de 31 de dezembro de 1900*. (R.J. Tipografia de Estatística, 1905).
Recenseamento geral da República dos Estados Unidos do Brasil em 31 de dezembro de 1890. Distrito Federal. Rio de Janeiro, 1895.
Directoria Geral da Estatística. *Recenseamento do Brasil Realizado em 1 de setembro de 1920*. Vol. 1. 1922.
Fallas do Trono, 1857–1862.

Reports of Provincial Presidents, Vice-Presidents, and Police Authorities

Mensagem enviada à Assembléia Legislativa do Estado do Rio de Janeiro pelo presidente Dr Joaquim Maurício de Abreu. Na 1a sessão da 2a Legislatura, em 15 de novembro de 1895.
Mensagem apresentada à Assembléia Legislativa. 1898.
Relatório do Presidente da Província do Rio de Janeiro, 1 March 1840, 'Quadro estatístico da população da província do Rio de Janeiro segundo as condições, sexos e côres, 1840.'

Relatório do Vice-Presidente da Província do Rio de Janeiro, o Comendador João Pereira Danique Faro, 1850.

Relatório do Presidente da Província do Rio de Janeiro, 15 April 1851, 'Recenseamento da população da província do Rio de Janeiro feito em 1850.'

Relatório do Presidente da Província do Rio de Janeiro, 5 May 1851.
'Quadro A: População absoluta dos municípios, freguesias e curatos.'

Relatório apresentado à Assembléia Legislativa Provincial do Rio de Janeiro. 'Quadro demonstrativo da distribuição da população . . . 1854.'

Relatório apresentado à Assembléia Legislativa da Província do Rio de Janeiro. 1857.

Relatório do Presidente da Província do Rio de Janeiro, 1878, 'Quadro demonstrativo da distribuição da população nas differentes freguezias da Província do Rio de Janeiro, com a área de cada uma, número de habitantes por kilômetro quadrado, e respectivos dados da estatística escolar, organisado pela Directoria das Obras Públicas da mesma Província em 1878.'

Relatório do Presidente da Província do Rio de Janeiro. 1860–1885.

Relatório do Chefe de Polícia. IN *Relatório do Presidente da Província do Rio de Janeiro*. 1860–1883.

Relatório da repartição dos negócios da justiça apresentado na segunda sessão da nona legislatura pelo respectivo Ministro e Relátorio do Presidente da Província do Rio de Janeiro. 1850–1880.

Relatório da repartição dos negócios da justiça apresentado na segunda sessão da nona legislatura pelo respectivo Ministro e Secretário de Estado José Thomaz Nabuco de Araújo (Rio de Janeiro, 1854).

Relatório apresentado à Assembléia Legislativa do Estado do Rio de Janeiro. 1898–1920.

Almanacs, Newspapers, Journals

Jornal do Agricultor. Vassouras. Câmara Municipal. 1884.

O Município. Vassouras. 1899–1902.

Jornal do Comércio. Rio de Janeiro.
Series of 27 articles, 'A lavoura no Estado do Rio de Janeiro'. 20 June 1894 to 10 April 1895.

The Port Folio. 1821.

Almanak Administrativo, Mercantil e Industrial da Corte e Província do Rio de Janeiro (*Almanak Laemmert*), 1855–1885.

Bank Reports

Banco do Brasil. Movimento de hipotecas por ano. Repartição de hipotecas. *Relatório apresentado à Assembléia geral dos acionistas do Banco do Brasil*, 1871–1882.

Maps and Photographs

Biblioteca Nacional. Iconografia.
  Rio de Janeiro. *Carta topográfica da Capitania do Rio de Janeiro. Feita por ordem do Côde de Cunha, Capitão General e Vice Rey do Estado do Brazil,* por Manoel Vieyra Leão, Sargento Môr e Governador do Castelo de São Sebastião da Cidade do Rio de Janeiro em o anno de 1767.
  Grecco, Gilberto, *Fazendas de Café de Alta Mogiana. Cadernos de Fotografia.*
London, England. Institute of Historical Research. Cândido Mendes de Almeida, ed. *Atlas do Império do Brasil. Comprehendendo as respectivas divisões administrativas, ecclesiásticas, eleitoraes, e judiciárias dedicado à Sua Magestade o Imperador o Senhor D. Pedro II destinado à Instrução pública no Império com especialidade à dos Alumnos do Imperial Collegio de Pedro II* (Rio de Janeiro: Lithographia do Instituto Philomáthico, 1868).

Dictionaries and Encyclopedias

Cândido de Figueiredo, *Novo Dicionário da Língua Portuguesa,* 4th ed. (Lisbon: Sociedade Editôra Arthur Brandão e Companhia, [1925].
Antonio Moraes Silva. *Diccionario da Lingua Portugueza – recopilado dos vocabulários impressos até gora, e nesta 2a edição novamente emendado e muito acrescentado* (Lisboa: Typographia Lacérdina, 1903).
Instituto Brasileiro de Geografia e Estatística. *Enciclopédia dos municípios brasileiros* (Rio de Janeiro: Serviço Gráfico do IBGE, 1959).

Polemical Literature

'Instruções para a Comissão Permanente Nomeada pelos Fazendeiros do Município de Vassouras,' Rio de Janeiro (1854).
Congresso Agrícola. Ed. fac-similar dos anais do Congresso Agrícola, realizado no Rio de Janeiro em 1878, (Rio de Janeiro: Fundação Casa de Rui Barbosa), 1988.
Beaurepaire Rohan, Henrique de. *O futuro da grande lavoura e da grande propriedade no Brasil; memória apresentada ao Ministério da Agricultura, Commércio e Obras Públicas.* Rio de Janeiro, 1878.

Travellers' Accounts

Agassiz, Mr. and Mrs. Louis, *A Journey in Brazil* (Boston: Ticknor and Fields, 1868).
Burton, Richard, *Explorations of the Highlands of the Brazil.* 2 vols (London: 1869).
——*Viagens aos planaltos do Brasil* (Coleção Brasiliana, n. 375, vol. 2 [1868].
Corrêa, Junior, *Da Corte à Fazenda Santa Fé* (Rio de Janeiro: Typographia Universal de E. e H. Laemmert, 1870).

de Tollenare, Louis François. *Notas dominicais tomadas durante uma residência em Portugal e no Brasil nos anos de 1816, 1817, e 1818: parte relativa a Pernambuco* (Recife: Departamento de Cultura. 1978).

Debret, Jean Baptiste, *Viagem Pitoresca e Histórica ao Brasil*. Translated and edited by Sergio Milliet. 3 vols in 2 tomos (São Paulo: 1954).

——*Viagem pitoresca e Histórica ao Brasil* (São Paulo: Edições Melhoramentos, 1971).

——*Brasil Império* (São Paulo: Difusão Nacional do Livro).

Ewbank, Thomas, *Life in Brazil* (New York: Harper & Brothers, 1856).

Gardner, George, *Travels in the interior of Brazil, principally through the northern provinces, and the gold and diamond districts during the years 1836–1841* (London: Reeve, Benham, and Reeve, 1849).

Graham, Maria, *Journal of a Voyage to Brazil and Residence There. During Part of the Years 1821, 1822, 1823* (London: no publisher listed, 1824).

Henderson, James, *A History of the Brazil; comprising its geography, commerce, colonization, aboriginal inhabitants, etc.* (London: Longman, Hurst, Rees, Orme, and Brown, 1821).

Kidder, Daniel P., *Sketches of Residence and Travels in Brazil*, vol. 1 (Philadelphia: 1845).

——*Reminiscências de viagens e permanência no Brasil (Província do Rio de Janeiro e São Paulo)* (São Paulo: Livraria Martins, [1845], 1972).

Koster, Henry. *Travels in Brazil in the Years from 1809 to 1815*, 2 vols (Philadelphia: M. Carey and Son, 1817).

Lindsey-Bucknell, Hamilton, *Um jovem irlandês no Brasil em 1874* (Rio de Janeiro: Hachette, 1976).

Luccock, John, *Viagens. Notas sôbre o Rio de Janeiro e partes meridionais do Brasil* (São Paulo: 1975).

——'*Notes on Rio de Janeiro and the Southern Parts of Brazil Taken during a Residence of Ten Years in that Country from 1808 to 1818,*' excerpts in *The Port Folio*, vol. XII, July–December 1821.

Mawe, John, *Viagens ao Interior do Brasil* (São Paulo: Editôra Itatiaia e Editôra da Universidade de São Paulo, [1812], 1978).

——*Travels in the Interior of Brazil particularly in the Gold and Diamond Districts of that Country* (Philadelphia: M. Carey, 1816).

Pfeiffer, Ida, *A Woman's Journey around the World* (London: Office of the National Illustrated Library [1850].

Ribeyrolles, Charles de, *Brasil Pitoresco* (São Paulo: Livraria Martins Editôra, 1941).

——*Brasil Pitoresco*, 2 vols (São Paulo: [1859], 1976).

——*Brasil Pitoresco* (1980).

Rugendas, João Maurício [Johann Moritz], *Viagem pitoresca através do Brasil* (São Paulo: 1967).

——*Viagem pitoresca através do Brasil* (São Paulo: Livraria Martins [1940].

Saint-Hilaire, Auguste de, *Segunda viagem do Rio de Janeiro à Minas Gerais e São Paulo* (São Paulo: Companhia Editôra Nacional, [1822], 1938).

——*Viagem pelas províncias do Rio de Janeiro e Minas Gerais* (Belo Horizonte: Editôra Itatiaia, 1980).

Spix, J.B. von and Martius, C.F.P. von, *Reise in Brasilien auf Befehl Sr. Majestät Maximilian Joseph I* (Rio de Janeiro: Imprensa Nacional [1823], 1938).

Toussaint-Samson, Adèle, *A Parisian in Brazil* (Boston: James H. Earle, 1891).

——*Une Parisienne au Brésil* (Paris: Paul Ollendorff, 1883).

Tschudi, Johann Jakob von, *Viagem às províncias do Rio de Janeiro e São Paulo* (São Paulo: Editôra Martins, [1866]. 1976).

Walsh Robert, *Notices of Brazil in 1828 and 1829* 2 vols (London: 1830).

Weech, J. Friedrich von, *Brasiliens Gegenwärtiger Zustand und Colonialsystem Besonders in Bezug auf Landbau und Handel. Zunächst für Auswanderer* (Hamburg: Hoffmann und Campe, 1828).

General Works

Abreu, Martha, 'Slave mothers and freed children: emancipation and female space in debates on the "Free Womb" Law, Rio de Janeiro, 1871', *Journal of Latin American Studies*, vol. 28, no. 3 (1996).

Adamo, Samuel, 'The broken promise: race, health and justice in Rio de Janeiro, 1890–1930', unpublished PhD dissertation Department of History, University of New Mexico, 1983.

Alden, Dauril, *Royal Government in Brazil* (Berkeley: University of California Press, 1968).

Alencar, José Martiniano de, *Senhora*. 2 vols (Rio de Janeiro: Garnier, 1875).

Alencar, *O tronco do Ipê* (Ediouro, n.d.).

Alencar, *Til* (1872).

Alencar, *Iracema* (1865).

Alencar, *O Guaraní*, 4th edn (São Paulo: Atica, 1982).

Alencastro Graça Filho, Afonso de, 'Os convênios da carestia: crises, organização e investimentos do comércio de subsistência da corte (1850–1880)', unpublished MA, dissertation. Departamento de História, Universidade Federal do Rio de Janeiro, 1991.

Alencastro, Luiz Felipe de, 'Vida privada e ordem privada no Império', in Luiz Felipe de Alencastro (ed.), *Imperio: a corte e a modernidade nacional*, vol. 2 of Fernando A. Novais (ed.), *História da vida privada no Brasil*, 4 vols (São Paulo: Companhia das Letras, 1997).

Allemão, Francisco Freire, 'Memória: Quais São as Principaes Plantas que Hoje se-acham aclimatadas no Brasil?', *Revista do Instituto Histórico Geográfico Brasileiro*, vol. 19 (1856).

Almada, Vilma Paraiso Ferreira de, *Escravismo e Transição: O Espírito Santo (1850/1888)* (Rio de Janeiro: Graal, 1984).

Anderson, Robert Nelson, 'The *quilombo* of Palmares a new overview of a Maroon state in seventeenth-century Brazil', *Journal of Latin American Studies*, vol. 28, no. 3 (1996), pp. 545–66.

Andrews, C.C., *Brazil: Its Conditions and Prospects* (New York: Appleton, 1887).

Andrews, George Reid, *Blacks and Whites in São Paulo, Brazil, 1888–1988* (Madison: University of Wisconsin Press, 1991).

Andrews, George Reid, 'Black and white workers: São Paulo, Brazil, 1888–1928', in Rebecca Scott *et al.*, *The Abolition of Slavery and the Aftermath of Emancipation in Brazil* (Durham: Duke University Press, 1988).

Antonil [Andreoni], João Antonio. *Cultura e opulência do Brasil por suas drogas e minas* (São Paulo: Companhia Editôra Nacional [1711], 1967).

Ardener, Shirley, *Women and Space: Ground Rules and Social Maps* (New York: St Martin's Press, 1981).

Assunção, Matthias Röhrig, 'Elite politics and popular rebellion in the construction of the post-colonial order. The case of Maranhão, Brazil (1820–1841)', *Journal of Latin American Studios*, vol. 31 (1999).

Barickman, Bert, *A Bahian Counterpoint: Sugar, Tobacco, Cassava and Slavery in the Recôncavo, 1780–1860* (Stanford: Stanford University Press, 1998).

Barman, Roderick, *Brazil: The Forging of a Nation, 1798–1852* (Stanford: Stanford University Press, 1988).

Barnet, Miguel (ed.), *Biography of a Runaway Slave*. Translated by W. Nick Hill (Willamantic, CT: Curbstone Press, 1994).

Bastide, Roger, *Estudos afro-brasileiros* (São Paulo: Perspectiva, 1973).

Bergad, W. Laird, Iglesias, Fe and Barcia, Maria del Carmen. *The Cuban Slave Market, 1790–1880* (New York: Cambridge University Press, 1995).

Besse, Susan, *Restructuring Patriarchy: The Modernization of Gender Inequality in Brazil, 1914–1940* (Chapel Hill: University of North Carolina Press, 1996).

Bethell, Leslie, *The Abolition of the Brazilian Slave Trade* (Cambridge: Cambridge University Press, 1970).

Bethell, Leslie (ed.), *Brazil: Empire and Republic, 1822–1930* (Cambridge: Cambridge University Press, 1989).

Binzer, Ina von, *Os meus romanos: alegrias e tristezas de uma educadora no Brasil* (Rio de Janeiro: Paz e Terra, 1980 [1881].

Bonavides, Paulo and Amaral, Roberto (eds), *Textos políticos de história do Brasil*, 8 vols (Brasília: Senado Federal, 1996).

Borges, Dain, *The Family in Bahia, Brazil, 1870–1945* (Stanford: Stanford University Press, 1994).

Borges, Dain, 'Puffy, ugly, slothful and inert': degeneration in Brazilian social thought, 1880–1940', *Journal of Latin American Studies*, vol. 25, (1993), 235–56.

Boserup, Esther, *Women's Roles in Economic Development* (Aldershot: Gower with LSE, 1986).

Bourdieu, Pierre, *Outline of a Theory of Practice* (Cambridge: Cambridge University Press, 1977).

Boxer, Charles Ralph, *The Golden Age of Brazil, 1695–1750* (Berkeley: University of California Press, 1962).

Braga, Greenhalgh, *Vassouras de Ontem* (Rio de Janeiro: Companhia Brasiliense de Artes Gráficas, 1975).

Brandão, Berenice Cavalcante, Rohloff de Mattos, Ilmar, Rezende de Carvalho, Maria Alice, *A polícia e a força policial no Rio de Janeiro*, Série de Estudos PUC, no. 4 (Rio de Janeiro: Pontifícia Universidade Católica do Rio de Janeiro, 1981).

Brookshaw, David, *Raça e Cor na Literatura Brasileira*. Translated by Marta Kirst (Pôrto Alegre: Mercado Aberto, 1983).

Brown, Larissa V. 'Internal Commerce in a Colonial Economy: Rio de Janeiro and

Its Hinterland, 1790–1822', unpublished PhD dissertation, University of Virginia, 1986.

Buarque de Holanda, Sérgio (ed.), *História Geral da Civilização Brasileira*, (São Paulo: Difusão Editorial, S.A. n.d.).

Buarque de Holanda, Sérgio, *Raízes do Brasil*, 21st edn (Rio de Janeiro: José Olympio Editôra, 1989.

Butler, Kim. *Freedoms Given: Freedoms Won* (New Brunswick: Rutgers University Press, 1999).

Campos, Marilia and Pitzer, Renato Rocha, 'A possibilidade de uma História Agrária a partir dos Inventários: Uma Abordagem Metodológica,' *Revista Arrabaldes*, vol. 1, no. 2 (1988).

Campos, Pedro Moacyr. *História Geral da Civilização Brasileira*, vol. 2 of *O Brasil Monárquico*, 5 vols (São Paulo: Difusão Editorial do Livro, 1985).

Cândido, Antonio, 'Dialética da malandragem', *Revista do Instituto de Estudos Brasileiros*, vol. 8 (1970).

Cardoso, Ciro Flamarion Santana, *Agricultura, escravidão e capitalismo* (Petrópolis: Vozes, 1979).

Cardoso, Ciro Flamarion Santana, *A Afro-América: a escravidão no Novo Mundo* (São Paulo: Brasiliense, 1982).

Cardoso, Ciro Flamarion Santana, *Escravo ou camponês? O protocampesinato negro nas Américas* (São Paulo: Brasiliense, 1987).

Cardoso, Ciro Flamarion Santana, (ed.), *Escravidão e abolição no Brasil* (Rio de Janeiro: Zahar, 1988).

Cardoso, Ciro Flamarion Santana and Brignoli, Héctor. *História Econômica da América Latina* (Rio de Janeiro: Graal, 1983).

Cardoso, Ciro Flamarion Santana, 'O modo de produção escravista colonial na América', in Theo Santiago (ed.), *América Colonial* (Rio de Janeiro: Editora Palas, 1975).

Carneiro da Cunha, Manuela, *Negros, estrangeiros: os escravos libertos e sua volta à Africa* (São Paulo: Brasiliense, 1985).

Carpentier, Alejo. *The Kingdom of this World*. Translated by Harriet de Onís (New York: Noonday Press, 1994).

Carvalho, José Murilo de, *Teatro das sombras: a política imperial* (Rio de Janeiro: IUPERJ/Vértice, 1988).

Carvalho, José Murilo de, *El desarrollo de la ciudadanía en el Brasil* (Ciudad de Mexico: Fondo de la Cultura, 1993).

Castro, Hebe Maria Mattos de, *Ao sul da história* (São Paulo: Brasiliense, 1986).

Castro, Hebe Maria Mattos de, *Das cores do silêncio: os significados da liberdade no sudeste escravista, Brasil, século XIX* (Rio de Janeiro: Arquivo Nacional, 1995).

Castro, Hebe Maria Mattos de, 'Beyond masters and slaves: subsistence agriculture as survival strategies in Brazil during the second half of the nineteenth century', *Hispanic American Historical Review*, vol. 68, no. 3 (1988).

Castro, Hebe Maria Mattos de and Schnoor, Eduardo (eds), *Resgate: uma janela para o oitocentos* (Rio de Janeiro: Topbooks, 1995).

Castro, Hebe Maria Mattos de, 'Laços de família e direitos no final da escravidão', in A. Novais (ed.), *História da vida privada no Brasil*, vol. 2 (São Paulo: Companhia das Letras, 1997).

Castro, Maria Eugênia Torres Ribeiro de, *Reminiscências* (Editôra Catedra, Rio de Janeiro: 1893, [1979])

Chalhoub, Sidney, *Visões da liberdade: uma história das últimas décadas da escravidão na corte* (São Paulo: Companhia das Letras, 1990).

Coelho Neto, Paulo, *Banzo* (Porto: Livraria Chardon, 1927).

Cohen, David W. and Greene, Jack P. (eds), *Neither Slave nor Free: The Freedom of African Descent in the Slave Societies of the New World* (Baltimore: The Johns Hopkins University Press, 1972).

Conrad, Robert Edgar, *The Destruction of Brazilian Slavery, 1850–1888* (Berkeley: University of California Press, 1972).

Conrad, Robert Edgar, *Os últimos anos de escravatura no Brasil, 1850–1888*. Translated by Fernando de Castro Ferro (Rio de Janeiro: Civilização Brasileira, 1975).

Conrad, Robert Edgar, *Children of God's Fire: A Documentary History of Black Slavery in Brazil* (Princeton: Princeton University Press, 1983).

Conrad, Robert Edgar, *World of Sorrow: The African Slave Trade to Brazil* (Baton Rouge: Louisiana State University Press, 1986).

Conrad, Robert Edgar, *Tumbeiros: O Tráfico de Escravos para o Brasil* (São Paulo: Brasiliense, 1985).

Couty, Louis, *O Brasil em 1884: esboços sociológicos* (Brasília: Senado Federal, 1984).

Curtin, Philip D. *The Rise and Fall of the Plantation Complex: Essays in Atlantic History* (Cambridge: Cambridge University Press, 1990).

Da Matta, Roberto, *Carnavais, malandros e heróis* (Rio de Janeiro: Zahar, 1978).

Da Matta, Roberto, *A casa e a rua* (Rio de Janeiro: Editora Guanabara, 1987).

Da Matta, Roberto, *Carnivals, Rogues and Heroes: An Interpretation of the Brazilian Dilemma* (Notre Dame: University of Notre Dame Press, 1991).

de Tollenare Louis François, *Notas dominicaes tomadas durante uma residência em Portugal e no Brasil nos annos de 1816, 1817, 1818. Parte relativa ao Pernambuco; traduzido do manuscripto francês inédito por Alfredo de Carvalho* (Recife: Empresa do Jornal de Recife, 1905).

Dean, Warren, 'Latifundia and land policy in nineteenth-century Brazil', *Hispanic American Historical Review*, vol. 51 (1971).

Dean, Warren, *Rio Claro: A Brazilian Plantation System, 1820–1920* (Stanford: Stanford University Press, 1976).

Dean, Warren, *Rio Claro: um sistema brasileiro de grande lavoura, 1820–1920* (Rio de Janeiro: Paz e Terra, 1977).

Dean, Warren, 'The Brazilian Economy, 1870–1930', in Leslie Bethell (ed.), *Cambridge History of Latin America*, vol. 4 (Cambridge: Cambridge University Press, 1985).

Dean, Warren, *With Broadax and Firebrand* (Berkeley: University of California Press, 1995).

Dias, Gonçalves, *Os Timbiras* (1857).

Drescher, Seymour, 'Brazilian abolition in comparative perspective', in Rebecca Scott *et al.*, *The Abolition of Slavery and the Aftermath of Emancipation in Brazil* (Durham: Duke University Press, 1988).

Eisenberg, Peter L., *The Sugar Industry of Pernambuco, 1840–1910: Modernization without Change* (Berkeley: University of California Press, 1974).

Eisenberg, Peter L., *Modernização sem mudança* (São Paulo: UNICAMP/Paz e Terra, 1977).

Eisenberg, Peter L., 'Ficando livre as alforrias em campinas no século XIX', *Estudos Econômicos*, vol. 17, no. 2 (1987).

Eisenberg, Peter L., *Homens esquecidos: escravos e trabalhadores livres no Brasil, séculos XVIII e XIX* (São Paulo: UNICAMP, 1989).

Eltis, David and Richardson, David, *Routes to Slavery: Direction, Ethnicity and Mortality in the Atlantic Slave Trade* (London: Frank Cass, 1997).

Faria, Sheila de Castro, 'Terra e Trabalho em Campos dos Goitacazes: 1850–1920', unpublished master's thesis, Universidade Federal Fluminense, 1986.

Fausto, Boris (ed.), *História Geral da Civilização Brasileira*, vol. 3, *O Brasil Republicano*, vol. 2, *Sociedade e instituições (1889–1930)*, 2nd edn (São Paulo: Difusão Editorial do Livro, 1977).

Ferrez, Gilberto, *Pioneiros da cultura do café na era da independência* (Rio de Janeiro: Instituto Histórico Geográfico Brasileiro, 1972).

Florentino, Manolo Garcia, *Em costas negras: uma história do tráfico atlântico de escravos entre a Africa e o Rio de Janeiro (séculos XVIII e XIX)* (Rio de Janeiro: Arquivo Nacional, 1995).

Florentino, Manolo Garcia and Fragoso, João Luís Ribeiro, ' "Filho de Inocência Crioula: Neto de Joana Cabinda": Um estudo sôbre famílias escravas em Paraíba do Sul (1835–1872)', *Estudos Econômicos*, vol. 17, no. 2 (1987).

Florentino, Manolo G. and Goés, José Roberto, *A paz das senzalas: famílias escravas e tráfico atlântico, Rio de Janeiro, c.1790–c.1850* (Rio de Janeiro: Civilização Brasileira, 1997).

Forte, João Mattoso Maia, 'Notícia Histórica e descritiva de Vassouras' in Greenhalgh Braga (ed.), *Vassouras de Ontem* (Rio de Janeiro: Companhia Brasiliense de Artes Gráficas, 1975).

Fox-Genovese, Elizabeth, *Within the Plantation Household: Black and White Women of the Old South* (Chapel Hill: University of North Carolina Press, 1988).

Fraginals, Manuel Moreno (ed.), *Africa in America* (New York: Holmes and Meier, 1984).

Fragoso, João Luís Ribeiro, 'Sistemas agrárias em Paraíba do Sul (1850–1920)', unpublished MA dissertation, Departamento de História, Universidade Federal do Rio de Janeiro, 1983.

Fragoso, João Luís Ribeiro, *Homens de grossa aventura: acumulação e hierarquia na praça mercantil do Rio de Janeiro (1790–1830)* (Rio de Janeiro: Arquivo Nacional, 1992).

Fragoso, João Luís Ribeiro and Florentino, Manolo Garcia, 'Filho de Inocência Crioula: Neto de Joana Cabinda: um estudo sôbre famílias escravas em Paraíba do Sul (1835–1872)', *Estudos Econômicos*, vol. 17, no. 2 (1987).

Fragoso, João Luís Ribeiro and Pitzer, Renato Rocha, 'Barões, homens livres pobres e escravos: notas sôbre uma fonte múltipla-inventários post-mortem' *Revista Arrabaldes*, vol. 1, no. 2 (1988), pp. 29–52.

Franco, Maria Sylvia Carvalho, *Homens livres na ordem escravocrata* (São Paulo: Kairós Livraria Editora Leta, 1983).

Freyre, Gilberto, *The Masters and the Slaves* (New York: Alfred A. Knopf, 1946).

Gomes, Dias, *O Guarani* (1857).

Gomes, Flávio dos Santos, *Histórias de quilombolas: mocambos e comunidades de senzalas no Rio de Janeiro – século XIX* (Rio de Janeiro: Arquivo Nacional, 1993).

Goodman, David and Redclift, Michael, *From Peasant to Proletarian: Capitalist Development and Agrarian Transition* (Oxford: Blackwell, 1981).

Gorender, Jacob, *O escravismo colonial* (São Paulo: Atica, 1985).

Gorender, Jacob, *A escravidão reabilitada* (São Paulo: Editora Atica, 1990).

Graham, Maria. *Journal of a Voyage to Brazil and Residence There During Part of the Years 1821, 1822, 1823* (London: 1824).

Graham, Richard, 'A família escrava no Brasil colonial', in *Escravidão, reforma e imperialismo* (São Paulo: Perspective, 1979).

Graham, Richard, *Patronage and Politics in Nineteenth-Century Brazil* (Stanford: Stanford University Press, 1990).

Graham, Sandra Lauderdale, 'Slavery's impasse: slave prostitutes, small-time mistresses and the Brazilian Law of 1871', *Comparative Studies of Society and History*, vol. 33, (1991), pp. 669–94.

Graner, Maria Paula, 'A estrutura fundiária do município de Araruama: 1850–1920. Um estudo de distribuição de terras: continuidades e trans-formações', unpublished MA dissertation, Departamento de História, Universidade Federal Fluminense, 1985.

Grecco, Gilberto, *Fazendas de café de Alta Mogiana: cadernos de fotografia*

Gutiérrez, Horácio. 'Demografia escrava numa economia não-exportadora: Paraná, 1800–1830', *Estudos Econômicos*, vol. 17, no. 2 (1987).

Gutman, Herbert, *The Black Family in Slavery and in Freedom, 1750–1925* (New York: Pantheon Books, 1976).

Guyer, Jane I., 'Food, cocoa and the division of labor by sex in two West African societies', *Comparative Studies in Society and History*, vol. 22, no. 3 (1980).

Hahner, June, *Emancipating the Female Sex: The Struggle for Women's Rights in Brazil, 1850–1940* (Durham: Duke University Press, 1990).

Helsinger, Elizabeth K., *Rural Scenes and National Representation: Britain, 1815–1850* (Princeton: Princeton University Press, 1997).

Herman, James G., *Brazil after a Century of Independence* (New York: Macmillan, 1925).

Higman, B.W., *Jamaica Surveyed: Plantation Maps and Plans of the Eighteenth and Nineteenth Centuries* (San Francisco: Institute of Jamaica Publications, 1988).

Karasch, Mary C., *Slave Life in Rio de Janeiro, 1808–1850* (Princeton: Princeton University Press, 1987).

Klein, Herbert S., 'Demografia do tráfico atlântico de escravos para o Brasil', *Estudos Econômicos*, vol. 17 (1987).

Klein, Herbert S., 'Nineteenth-Century Brazil', in David W. Cohen and Jack P. Greene (eds), *Neither Slave nor Free: The Freedman of African Descent in the Slave Societies of the New World* (Baltimore: Johns Hopkins University Press, 1972).

Kraay, Hendrik, 'Slavery, citizenship and military service in Brazil's mobilization for the Paraguayan war', *Slavery and Abolition*, vol. 18, no. 3 (1997).

Kuznesof, Elizabeth, *Household Economy and Urban Development: São Paulo, 1765 to 1836* (Boulder, Col.: Westview Press, 1986).

Lago, Luís Aranha Corrêa, 'O surgimento da escravidão e a transição para o trabalho livre no Brasil: um modelo teórico simples e uma visão de longo prazo', *Revista Brasileira de Economia*, vol. 42, no. 4 (1988).

Lamêgo, Alberto Ribeiro, *O homem e a serra* (Rio de Janeiro: Serviço Gráfico do Instituto Brasileiro de Geografia e Estatística, 1930).

Lamêgo, Alberto Ribeiro, *O homem e a Guanabara* (Rio de Janeiro: Serviço Gráfico do IBGE, 1948).

Lara, Silvia, *Campos de violência* (Rio de Janeiro: Paz e Terra, 1986).

Lenharo, Alcir, *As tropas da moderação: o abastecimento da Corte na formação política do Brasil, 1808–1842* (São Paulo: Símbolo, 1979).

Levine, Robert M., *Vale of Tears: Revisiting the Canudos Massacre in Northeastern Brazil, 1893–1897* (Berkeley: University of California Press, 1992).

Libby, Douglas, *Transformação e trabalho em uma economia escravista* (São Paulo: Brasiliense, 1988).

Libby, Douglas and Grimaldi, Márcia, 'Equilíbrio e estabilidade econômica e comportamento demográfico num regime escravista, Minas Gerais no século XIX', *Papéis Avulsos*, no. 7 (December 1988), pp. 26–43.

Lima, Lana Lage da Gama, *Rebeldia negra e abolicionismo* (Rio de Janeiro: Achiamé, 1981).

Linhares, Maria Yedda L. *História do abastecimento: uma problemática em questão (1530/1918)* (Brasília: Binagri, 1979).

Linhares, Maria Yedda L. (ed.), *História Geral do Brasil* (São Paulo: Brasiliense, 1990). 2nd edn (Rio de Janeiro: Editora Campos, 1996).

Linhares, Maria Yedda L. and Teixeira da Silva, Francisco Carlos, *História da Agricultura Brasileira: combates e controvérsias* (São Paulo: Brasiliense, 1981).

Lobo, Eulália L., *História do Rio de Janeiro (do capital comercial ao capitalismo industrial e financeiro)*, 2 vols (Rio de Janeiro: Instituto Brasileiro de Mercado de Capitais, 1978).

Lockhart, James and Schwartz, Stuart. *Early Latin America: A History of Colonial Latin America and Brazil* (Cambridge: Cambridge University Press, 1983).

Loureiro Muniz, Célia Maria, 'Os donos da terra', unpublished MA dissertation, Departamento de História, Universidade Federal Fluminense, 1979.

Lovejoy, Paul E. *Africans in Bondage: Studies in Slavery and the Slave Trade: Essays in Honor of Philip D. Curtin on the Occasion of the Twenty-fifth Anniversary of African Studies at the University of Wisconsin* (Madison: University of Wisconsin Press, 1986).

Lovejoy, Paul E. and Rogers, Nicholas, eds. *Unfree Labour in the Development of the Atlantic World* (Ilford: Frank Cass, 1994).

Luna, Francisco Vidal and Klein, Herbert S., 'Slaves and masters in early nineteenth-century Brazil: São Paulo', *Journal of Interdisciplinary History*, vol. 21, no. 4 (1991).

Macedo, Joaquim Manuel de, *As vítimas algozes: quadros da escravidão* (São Paulo: Editora Scipione [1869], 1991).

Machado, Maria Helena Pereira Toledo, *Crime e escravidão: trabalho, luta e resistência nas lavouras paulistas, 1830–1888* (São Paulo: Brasiliense, 1987).

Maggie, Yvonne, 'Religiões mediúnicas e a cor de seus participantes', *Estudos Afro-Asiáticos*, no. 15 (1988).

Malheiro, Perdigão, *A escravidão no Brasil: ensaio histórico, jurídico, social*, 3rd edn (2nd edn, integral) (Petrópolis: Editora Vozes, 1976).

Marcos dos Santos, Ronaldo, *Resistência e superação na província de São Paulo (1885–1888)* (São Paulo: Instituto de Pesquisas Econômicas da Fundaçâo Instituto de Pesquisas Econômicas, 1980), Ch. 3.

Margarido, Alfredo. *Estudos sôbre literaturas das nações africanas de língua portuguesa* (Lisboa: A Regra do Jogo, 1980).

Marinho, Celia Azevedo de, *Onda Negra, Medo Branco: O negro no imaginário das elites* (Rio de Janeiro: Paz e Terra, 1987).

Marinho, Celia Azevedo de, *On Hell and Paradise: Abolitionism in the United States and Brazil, A Comparative Perspective* (New York: Garland, 1995).

Martins, Edmilson Rodrigues, Falcon, Francisco C. and Neves, Margarida de Souza, *A Guarda Nacional no Rio de Janeiro*, Série PUC, no. 5 (Rio de Janeiro: Pontifícia Universidade Católica do Rio de Janeiro, 1981).

Mattoso, Kátia de Queirós, *Ser escravo no Brasil* (São Paulo: Brasiliense, 1988).

Mattoso, Kátia de Queirós, *Família e sociedade na Bahia do século XIX* (São Paulo: Corrupio, 1988).

McCann, Daniel, 'The whip and the watch: overseers in the Paraíba Valley, Brazil', *Slavery and Abolition*, vol. 18, no. 2 (1997).

McGlynn, Frank and Drescher, Seymour (eds), *The Meaning of Freedom: Economics, Politics and Culture after Slavery* (Pittsburgh: University of Pittsburgh Press, 1992).

Mello, Pedro Carvalho de, 'Aspectos econômicos da organização do trabalho na economia cafeeira do Rio de Janeiro, 1850–1888', *Revista Brasileira de Economia*, vol. 32, no. 1, (1978).

Mello e Souza, Laura de, *O diabo na terra de Santa Cruz* (São Paulo: Brasiliense 1987).

Metcalf, Alida, *Family and Frontier in Colonial Brazil* (Berkeley: University of California Press, 1992).

Miller, Joseph C., *Way of Death: Merchant Capitalism and the Angolan Slave Trade, 1730–1830* (Madison: University of Wisconsin Press, 1988).

Moreira, Nicolau J., MD, *Brazilian Coffee* (New York: 'O Novo Mundo' Printing Office, 1876).

Moseley, Benjamin, MD, *A Treatise Concerning the Properties and Effects of Coffee* (London: J. Sewell, 1792).

Motta, Márcia Menendez, 'Proprietários de terra e arrendatários-escravistas em uma região produtora de gêneros alimentícios (São Gonçalo, 1808–1892)', *Revista Arrabaldes*, vol. 1, no. 2 (1988), pp. 87–100.

Motta, Márcia Menendez, 'Pelas "bandas d'além"/fronteira fechada e arrendatários escravistas em uma região policultura. 1808–1888', unpublished MA dissertation Departamento de História, Universidade Federal Fluminense, 1989.

Nabuco, Joaquim, *O Abolicionismo* (Petrópolis: Vozes, 1988).

Nabuco, Joaquim, *Minha formação* (São Paulo: 1947).

Nabuco, Joaquim, *Abolitionism*. Translated by Robert E. Conrad (Urbana: University of Illinois Press, 1977).

Naro, Nancy Priscilla, 'Limites do comportamento aceitável e mecanismos de dominação social no meio rural brasileiro: 1850–1890', *Estudos Afro-Asiáticos*, no. 15, (1988).

Naro, Nancy Priscilla, 'The transition from slavery to migrant labour in rural Brazil', *Slavery and Abolition*, Special Issue, vol. 15, no. 2, (1994).

Naro, Nancy Priscilla, 'Revision and persistence: recent historiography on the transition from slave to free labour in rural Brazil', *Slavery and Abolition*, vol. 13, no. 2, (1992).

Naro, Nancy Priscilla, 'Customary rightholders and legal claimants to land in Rio de Janeiro, Brazil, 1870–1890', *The Americas*, vol. 48, no. 4 (1992).

Naro, Nancy Priscilla, 'Fact, fantasy, or folklore? a novel case of retribution in nineteenth century Brazil' *Luso-Brazilian Review*, vol. 33, no. 1 (1996).

Naro, Nancy Priscilla, 'Rio studies Rio: ongoing studies of Rio de Janeiro, Brazil', *The Americas*, vol. 43, no. 4 (1987).

Naro, Nancy Priscilla, 'Space and gender-related social arrangements on nineteenth century plantations in the Americas', paper presented to the Society for Caribbean Studies, Oxford University, 5 July 1994.

Naro, Nancy Priscilla, 'Gender and space on nineteenth century plantations: Brazil, the Caribbean, and the United States South', Eastern Historical and Geographical Association, 25th Anniversary Meeting, Codrington College, Barbados, 4 February 1994.

Neder, Gizlene, Naro, Nancy Priscilla, Werneck da Silva, José Luís, *A Polícia na Corte e no Distrito Federal*, Série Estudos, no. 3, (Rio de Janeiro: Pontifícia Universidade Católica do Rio de Janeiro, 1981).

Neves, Margarida Souza, Martins, Edmilson Rodrigues and Falcon, Francisco Calazans, *A Guarda Nacional no Rio de Janeiro* (Rio de Janeiro: Pontifícia Universidade Católica do Rio de Janeiro, 1971).

Nishida, Mieko, 'Gender, Ethnicity and Kinship in the Urban African Diaspora: Salvador, Brazil, 1808–1888', PhD dissertation, Johns Hopkins University, 1991.

Novais, Fernando A. (ed.), *História da vida privada no Brasil*, 4 vols (São Paulo: Companhia das Letras, 1997).

Oliveira, Dezidério Luiz de, Júnior. *Legislação sôbre os municípios, camarcas, e distritos abrangendo o período de 8 de março de 1835 à 31 de dezembro de 1925* (Rio de Janeiro: Typographia do Jornal do Comércio de Rodrigues & Cia., 1926).

Padilha, Sílvia Fernandes, 'Da Monocultura à diversificação econômica: Um estudo de caso de Vassouras, 1880–1930', unpublished Master's thesis, Universidade Federal Fluminense, 1977.

Paiva, Clothilde, Libby, Douglas and Grimaldi, Márci, 'Crescimento da população escrava: uma questão em aberto', *Anais do IV seminário sôbre a ecomomia mineira*, CEDEPLAR/FACE/Universidade Federal de Minas Gerais (August 1988).

Pena, Luiz Carlos Martins, *Comédias* (Rio de Janeiro: Ediouro, n.d.).

Pires, Fernando Tasso Fragoso, *Antigas fazendas de café da província fluminense* (n.p.; n.d.).

Prado, Caio, Jr, *A História Econômica do Brasil* (São Paulo: Brasiliense, 1988).

Prado, Caio, Jr, *Formação do Brasil Contemporâneo: Colônia* (São Paulo: Martins Editora, 1942).

Prado, Caio, Jr, *The Colonial Background of Modern Brazil*. Translated by Suzette Macedo (Berkeley: University of California Press, 1967).

Prado, J.F. de Almeida, *Jean Baptiste Debret* (São Paulo: Editora Nacional, 1973).

Querino, Manuel, *O Africano como colonisador* (Salvador: Livraria Progresso, 1954).

Raposo, Inácio, *História de Vassouras* (Niterói: SEEC, 1978).

Reis, Elisa and Eustáquio Reis, 'Elites agrárias e a abolição no Brasil', *Dados*, vol. 31, no. 3 (1988).

Réis, Jaime, 'From *banquê* to *usina*: social aspects of growth and modernization in the sugar industry of Pernambuco, Brazil, 1850–1920', in K. Duncan and I. Rutledge (eds), *Land and Labour in Latin America: Essays on the Development of Agrarian Capitalism in the Nineteenth and Twentieth Centuries* (Cambridge: Cambridge University Press, 1977).

Réis, João José, *Rebelião escrava no Brasil: A História do Levante dos Malês, 1835* (São Paulo: Brasiliense, 1986).

Réis, João José, *Slave Rebellion in Brazil: The Muslim Uprising of 1835 in Bahia* (Baltimore: The Johns Hopkins University Press, c.1993).

Réis, João José, and Santos Gomes, Flávio (eds), *Liberdade por um fio: História dos quilombos no Brasil* (São Paulo: Companhia das Letras, 1996).

Ribeiro, Maria de Lourdes Borges, *O Jongo* (Rio de Janeiro: Instituto nacional do folklore, 1984).

Rios, Ana Maria Lugão, 'Família e transição (Famílias Negras em Paraíba do Sul, 1872–1920)', unpublished MA dissertation, Departamento de História, Universidade Federal Fluminense, 1990.

Robertson, Claire C. and Klein, Martin A. (eds), *Women and Slavery in Africa* (Madison: University of Wisconsin Press, 1983).

Rocha, Isabel da, 'Arquitetura rural', *Revista Gávea*, no. 2 (1982).

Rodrigues, Antonio Edmilson Martins, Falcon, Francisco C., Neves, Margarida de Souza, *A Guarda Nacional no Rio de Janeiro*, Série PUC, no. 5 (Rio de Janeiro: Pontifícia Universidade Católica do Rio de Janeiro, 1981).

Rodrigues, Raymundo Nina. *Os Africanos no Brasil*, 3rd edn (São Paulo: 1945).

Rufino dos Santos, Joel, 'O negro no Rio pós-abolição: marginalização e patrimônio cultural', *Estudos Afro-Asiáticos*, no. 15 (1988).

Russell-Wood, A.J.R., *The Black Man in Slavery and in Freedom in Colonial Brazil* (New York: Oxford University Press, 1982).

Russell-Wood, A.J.R., *A World on the Move: The Portuguese in Africa, Asia and America 1415–1808* (New York: St. Martin's Press, 1992).

Sachs, Carolyn E., *Gendered Fields: Rural Women, Agriculture and Environment* (Westview: 1996).

Santiago, Theo (ed.), *America Colonial* (Rio de Janeiro: Editora Palas, 1975).

Santos, Ronaldo Marcos dos, *Resistência e superação do escravismo na província de São Paulo (1885–1888)* (São Paulo: Instituto de Pesquisas Econômicas da Fundação Instituto de Pesquisas Econômicas, 1980).

Sauer, Carl. *Land and Life: A Selection from the Writings of Carl Ortwin Sauer*, ed. John Leighly (Berkeley: University of California Press, 1963).

Schneider, John, *Dictionary of African Borrowings in Brazilian Portuguese* (Hamburg: Helmut Buske, 1991).

Schwartz, Stuart B., *Sugar Plantations in the Formation of Brazilian Society: Bahia 1550–1835* (Cambridge: Cambridge University Press, 1985).

Schwartz, Stuart B., *Slaves, Peasants and Rebels* (Urbana: University of Illinois Press, 1992).

Schwartz, Stuart B., and Lockhart, James, *Early Latin America: A History of Colonial Latin America and Brazil* (Cambridge: Cambridge University Press, 1983).

Scisinio, Alaor Eduardo, *Escravidão e a saga de Manoel Congo* (São Paulo: Achiamé, 1988).

Scott, Rebecca, Seymour Drescher, George Reid Andrews, Hebe Maria Mattos Gomes de Castro, Robert M. Levine, *Exploring the Meaning of Freedom in Post-Emancipation Societies: A Comparative Perspective* (Durham: Duke University Press, 1988).

Shields, Rob, *Places on the Margins: Alternative Geographies of Modernity* (London: Routledge, 1991).

Silva, Eduardo, *Barões e escravidão: três gerações de fazendeiros e a crise da estrutura escravista* (Rio de Janeiro: Nova Fronteira, 1984).

Silva, Eduardo, 'A função ideológica da "brecha camponesa"', *Anais da IV Reunião: Sociedade Brasileira de Pesquisa Histórica*, São Paulo (1985).

Silva, Eduardo, *Memória sôbre a fundação de uma fazenda na província do Rio de Janeiro* (Brasília: Senado Federal, 1986).

Silva, Eduardo, *Prince of the People* (London: Verso, 1992).

Silva, Eduardo, and Réis, João José, *Negociação e conflito: a resistência negra no Brasil escravista* (São Paulo: Companhia das Letras, 1989).

Siqueira, Alexandre Joaquim de, *Memória Histórica do Município de Vassouras* (Rio de Janeiro: 1852).

Skidmore, Thomas, *Black into White: Race and Nationality in Brazilian Thought* (Durham: Duke University Press, 1993).

Slenes, Robert Wayne, 'The Demographics of Brazilian Slavery', 2 vols, unpublished PhD dissertation, Stanford University, 1976.

Slenes, Robert Wayne, 'Grandeza ou decadência? O mercado de escravos e a economia cafeeira da província do Rio de Janeiro, 1850–1888', in Iraci del Nero da Costa (ed.), *Brasil: história econômica e demográfica* (São Paulo: Instituto de Pesquisas Econômicas, 1986).

Slenes, Robert Wayne, 'Lares negros, olhares brancos: histórias da família escrava no século XIX', *Revista Brasileira de História*, vol. 18 (1988).

Slenes, Robert Wayne, ' "Malungu, ngoma vem!": Africa encoberta e descoberta no Brasil', *Cadernos Museu Escravatura* (Luanda: Ministério da Cultura, 1995).

Slenes, Robert Wayne, 'Senhores e subalternos no oeste paulista', in A. Novais (ed.), *História da vida privada no Brasil* (São Paulo: Companhia das Letras, 1998).

Smith, T. Lynn, *Brazil: Portrait of Half a Continent* (New York: Dryden Press, 1951).

Soares, Carlos Eugênio Líbano, *A negregada instituição: os capoeiras no Rio de Janeiro* (Rio de Janeiro: Prefeitura da Cidade do Rio de Janeiro, Secretária Municipal de Cultura, Departamento Geral de Documentação e Informação Cultural, Divisão de Editoração, 1994).

Stein, Stanley J, *Vassouras: A Brazilian Coffee County, 1850–1900*, (Princeton: Princeton University Press [1957], 1985).

Sweigart, Joseph Earl, *Coffee Factorage and the Emergence of a Brazilian Capital Market, 1850–1888* (New York: Garland, 1987).

Taunay, Affonso de Escragnolle, *Pequena história do café no Brasil (1727–1937)* (Rio de Janeiro: Departamento Nacional do Café, 1945).

Taunay, Carlos Augusto, *Manual do agricultor brasileiro. Obra indispensável a todo o senhor de engenho, fazendeiro e lavrador, por apresentar huma idéa geral e philosóphica da agricultura applicada ao Brazil, e ao seu especial modo de producção, bem como noções exactas sôbre todos os gêneros de cultura em uso, ou cuja adopção fôr proficua, e também hum resumo de horticultura, seguido de hum epítome dos princípios de botânica e hum tratado das principaes doenças que atacão os pretos* (Rio de Janeiro: Typographia Imperial, 1839).

Teixeira da Silva, Francisco Carlos, 'Morfologia da escassez: crises de subsistência e política econômica no Brasil colonial: Salvador e Rio de Janeiro (1680–1790)', unpublished PhD dissertation, Departamento de História, Universidade Federal Fluminense, 1990.

Theodoro, Helena, 'Religiões negras no Brasil', *Cativeiro e Liberdade*, seminário do Instituto de Filosofia e Ciências Humanas, Universidade do Estado do Rio de Janeiro, 1989.

Thornton, John, *Africa and Africans in the Making of the Atlantic World, 1400–1680* (Cambridge: Cambridge University Press, 1992).

Thurber, Francis B., *Coffee from Plantation to Cup* (American Grocer Publishing Association, 1881).

Toplin, Robert Brent, *The Abolition of Slavery in Brazil* (Kingsport: Kingsport Press, 1972).

Verger, Pierre, *O fumo da Bahia e o tráfico dos escravos do golfo de Benim* (Salvador: 1966).

Verger, Pierre, *Flux et refluxe de la traite des nègres entre le golfe de Bénin et Bahia de todos os santos du dix-septième au dix-neuvième siècle* (Paris: Mouton, 1968).

Versiani, Flávio Rabelo, 'Industrial investment in an "export" economy: the Brazilian experience before 1914', University of London, Institute of Latin American Studies, Working Papers, no. 2, n.d.

Viotti da Costa, Emília, *Da senzala à colônia* (São Paulo: Difusão Européia do Livro, 1966).

Viotti da Costa, Emília, *The Brazilian Empire: Myths and Histories* (Chicago: University of Chicago Press, 1985).

Viotti da Costa, Emília, *Crowns of Glory, Tears of Blood* (New York: Oxford University Press, 1994).

Viotti da Costa, Emília, *The Brazilian Empire: Myths and Histories*, 2nd edn (Chapel Hill: University of North Carolina Press, 2000).

Walvin, James, *Black Ivory: A History of British Slavery* (London: HarperCollins, 1992).

Watts, David. *The West Indies: Patterns of Development, Culture and Environmental Change since 1492* (Cambridge: Cambridge University Press, 1987).

Werneck, Francisco Peixoto de Lacerda, *Memória sôbre a fundação de uma fazenda na província do Rio de Janeiro* (Brasília: Senado Federal/Fundação Casa de Rui Barbosa [1847], 1985).

Whately, Maria Celina, *O café em resende no século XIX* (Rio de Janeiro: José Olympio Editora, 1987).

White, Deborah, *Ar'n't I a Woman?* (New York: W.W. Norton and Co., 1985).

Wood, Betty, *Women's Work, Men's Work. The Informal Slave Economies of the Lowcountry, Georgia* (Athens: University of Georgia Press, 1995).

Wright, Gavin, *Old South, New South* (Baton Rouge, LA: Basic Books, c.1986).

Wright, Marcia, *Strategies of Slaves and Women* (London: James Currey, 1993).

Index

Page numbers in *italics* refer to figures; page numbers in **bold** refer to tables.